ACLS History E-Book Project

Reprint Series

The ACLS History E-Book Project (www.historyebook.org) collaborates with constituent societies of the American Council of Learned Societies, publishers, librarians and historians to create an electronic collection of works of high quality in the field of history. This volume is produced from digital images created for the Project by the Scholarly Publishing Office and the Digital Library Production Service at the University of Michigan, Ann Arbor. The digital reformatting process results in an electronic version of the text that can be both accessed online and used to create new print copies. This book and hundreds of others are available online in the History E-Book Project through subscription.

Many of the works in the History E-Book Project are available in print and can be ordered either directly from their publishers or as part of this series. For information refer to the online Title Record page for each book. Inquiries regarding this series can be directed to info@hebook.org.

ACLS
HISTORY E-BOOK

http://www.historyebook.org

Medieval and Renaissance Pistoia

THE SOCIAL HISTORY OF AN ITALIAN TOWN, 1200–1430

Topographical Map of the Province of Pistoia.
Source: ASF, Piante delle Rr. Rendite, Scaffale N, Palchetto 8, No. 48.

Medieval and Renaissance Pistoia

THE SOCIAL HISTORY
OF AN ITALIAN TOWN, 1200–1430

by David Herlihy

YALE UNIVERSITY PRESS
NEW HAVEN AND LONDON, 1967

Designed by Sally Sullivan,
set in Palatino type,
and printed in the United States of America by
Connecticut Printers, Inc., Hartford, Conn.
Distributed in Canada by McGill University Press.

Library of Congress catalog card number: 67-13437

Preface

In preparing this study, the author has accumulated many debts, the recognition of which is a pleasure as well as an obligation. A fellowship granted by the Guggenheim Foundation enabled him to spend a year of research in the archives of Pistoia and of Florence in 1961–62. The staffs in the State Archives in both cities were cordial and helpful; in particular, Dott. Francesco De Feo of Florence went to considerable trouble to find materials after the author's departure and to have them microfilmed for him. Gratitude must also be expressed to Mr. Giuseppe Maggiori of Florence, who was kind enough to take the author (and his family) on many automobile trips through the Tuscan countryside, and to instruct him with his own, first-hand experience of the region's agriculture.

Professor Robert S. Lopez, of Yale University, read the entire manuscript and made many suggestions for its improvement. The author was first made aware, now more than ten years ago, of the fascination of Italian history through Professor Lopez's teaching and writings, and he has never ceased to learn from him.

Professor Richard Webster, of the University of California at Berkeley, placed at the author's disposal his rich knowledge of Italian literature and history. Father Anthony Via, of Gonzaga University, took time out from a stay in Florence to aid in the search for maps. The author would also like to express his thanks to Mr. Walter E. Langsam of the Yale University Press, for his able guidance and counsel in preparing the manuscript for the printers.

The Madge Miller Research Fund Committee of Bryn Mawr College and the Graduate Research Committee of the University of Wisconsin through grants-in-aid helped substantially in the purchase of microfilms, and librarians at both institutions were helpful and patient in serving the author's numerous requests for interlibrary loans. Thanks are also due to the staff of the Cartography Laboratory of the University of Wisconsin for the preparation of the two maps. Parts of chapters 3, 4 and 6 appeared in slightly different form in the *Economic History Review* in December 1965, and the author is grateful to the *Review*'s editor, Mr. R. M. Hartwell, for permission to republish.

Finally, the author is indebted to his wife, who patiently put together many of the book's tables and offered valuable comment on text and interpretation. Without her unstinting help, this book would have been much later in appearing, if indeed it would have appeared at all.

D. H.

Madison, Wisconsin
May 1966

Contents

List of Tables and Graphs

Graphs

Abbreviations

The following abbreviated references have been used to designate archival deposits and published works which are cited in more than one chapter. For works cited in only one chapter, the full title is given in the first reference, and an abbreviated title is used in all subsequent citations.

AESC	*Annales-Économies-Sociétés-Civilisations.*
Alberti, *Famiglia*	Leon Battista Alberti, *Opere volgari,* I: *I Libri della famiglia, Cena familiaris, Villa.* Ed. Cecil Grayson. Scrittori d'Italia, 218. Bari, 1960.
ASF	Archivio di Stato di Firenze.
ASI	*Archivio Storico Italiano.*
ASLSP	*Atti della Società Ligure di Storia Patria.*
ASP	Archivio di Stato di Pistoia.
Bowsky, "Impact"	William M. Bowsky, "The Impact of the Black Death upon Sienese Government and Society," *Speculum,* 39 (1964), 1–34.
Breve populi	*Breve et ordinamenta populi Pistorii anni mcclxxxiiii.* Ed. L. Zdekauer. Milan, 1891.
BSP	*Bullettino Storico Pistoiese.* Old series, 1899–1958; new series, 1959 ff.

Capitoli	*I Capitoli del comune di Firenze. Inventario e regesto.* Ed. C. Guasti. Florence, 1896.
Carpentier, *Orvieto*	E. Carpentier, *Une Ville devant la peste. Orvieto et la peste noire de 1348.* Paris, 1962.
CEH	*Cambridge Economic History,* II: *Trade and Industry in the Middle Ages;* and III: *Economic Organization and Policies in the Middle Ages.* Cambridge, 1952 and 1963.
Chiappelli, "Disegno"	L. Chiappelli, "Disegno della più antica storia di Pistoia," *BSP,* 29 (1917), 129–60.
Chiappelli, "L'Età longobarda"	L. Chiappelli, "Pistoia nell' età longobarda," *ASI,* 79 (1921), 227–338.
Compagni, *Cronaca*	Dino Compagni, *Cronaca.* Ed. I. Del Lungo. RIS, new ed. 9, pt. 2. Città di Castello, n.d.
Cristiani, *Pisa*	E. Cristiani, *Nobilità e popolo nel comune di Pisa. Dalle origini del podestariato alla signoria dei Donoratico.* Naples, 1962.
Davidsohn, *Forschungen*	R. Davidsohn, *Forschungen zur Geschichte von Florenz.* 4 vols. Berlin, 1896–1908.
Davidsohn, *Geschichte*	R. Davidsohn, *Geschichte von Florenz.* Berlin, 1896–1925.
de Roover, *Medici Bank*	R. de Roover, *The Rise and Decline of the Medici Bank.* Cambridge, Mass., 1963.
EHR	*Economic History Review.*

Estimario	ASP, Provvisioni e Statuti, Tomus 699. Estimario della città (1415).
Fioravanti, *Memorie*	Iacopo Maria Fioravanti, *Memorie storiche della città di Pistoia.* Lucca, 1758.
Fiumi, *San Gimignano*	E. Fiumi, *Storia economica e sociale di San Gimignano.* Florence, 1961.
FSI	Fonti per la Storia d'Italia.
Herlihy, "Direct Taxation"	D. Herlihy, "Direct and Indirect Taxation in Tuscan Urban Finance, ca. 1200–1400," *Finances et comptabilité urbaines du XIIIe au XVIe siècle* (Brussels: Centre "Pro Civitate," 1964), pp. 385–405.
Herlihy, *Pisa*	D. Herlihy, *Pisa in the Early Renaissance. A Study of Urban Growth.* New Haven, 1958.
Herlihy, "Population"	D. Herlihy, "Population, Plague and Social Change in Rural Pistoria," *EHR,* 18 (1965) 225–44.
Hyde, *Padua*	J. K. Hyde, *Padua in the Age of Dante. A Social History of an Italian City State.* Manchester and New York, 1966.
Jaffé, *Regesta*	P. Jaffé, *Regesta pontificum romanorum.* 2nd ed. Leipzig, 1885–88.
Jones, "Lineamenti"	P. J. Jones, "Per la storia agraria italiana nel Medio Evo: lineamenti e problemi," *RSI,* 76 (1964), 287–348.

Karmin, *Legge*	Otto Karmin, *La Legge del Catasto fiorentino del 1427* (*Testo, introduzione e note*). Florence, 1906.
Liber censuum	*Liber censuum comunis Pistorii.* Ed. Q. Santoli. Pistoia, 1915.
Liber focorum	*Liber focorum districtus Pistorii* (*a. 1226*). *Liber finium districtus Pistorii* (*a. 1255*). Ed. Q. Santoli. FSI, 93. Rome, 1956.
Libro croce	*Libro croce.* Ed. Q. Santoli. RCI, 26. Rome, 1939.
Luca Dominici, *Cronache*	*Cronache di ser Luca Dominici,* I: *Cronaca della venuta dei bianchi e della moria, 1399–1401;* and II: *Cronaca seconda.* Ed. G. C. Gigliotti. Rerum pistoriensium scriptores, 1. Pistoia, 1933 and 1937.
Manetti, Chronicon	Giannozzo Manetti, Chronicon pistoriense, *RIS, 19* (Milan, 1731), 989–1026.
Martines, *Social World*	Lauro Martines, *The Social World of the Florentine Humanists, 1390–1460.* Princeton, 1963.
MGH	*Monumenta Germaniae Historica.*
Monaci, *Crestomazia*	E. Monaci, *Crestomazia italiana dei primi secoli.* New ed. by F. Arese. Rome, Naples, Città di Castello, 1955.
Pagnini, *Della decima*	G. F. Pagnini della Ventura, *Della decima e di varie altre gravezze imposte dal comune di Firenze, della moneta e della mercatura de' Fiorentini fino a secolo XVI.* Lisbon and Lucca, 1765.

Paolini, *Pistoia*	Pietro Paolini, *Pistoia e il suo territorio nel corso dei secoli.* Pistoia, 1962.
Piattoli, *Consigli*	R. Piattoli, *Consigli del comune di Prato.* Bologna, 1940.
Pietro de' Crescenzi, *Opus*	Pietro de' Crescenzi, *Opus ruralium commodorum.* Strassburg, 1486.
Pistoia e la sua provincia	Camera di Commercio, Industria e Agricoltura di Pistoia, *Pistoia e la sua provincia.* Florence, 1962.
PL	*Patrologia latina.* Ed. J. P. Migne. 221 vols. Paris, 1844–64.
Pöhlmann, *Wirthschaftspolitik*	Robert von Pöhlmann, *Die Wirthschaftspolitik der florentiner Renaissance und das Prinzip der Verkehrsfreiheit.* Leipzig, 1878.
Potthast, *Regesta*	A. Potthast, *Regesta pontificum romanorum.* Berlin, 1874.
Prosatori latini, ed. Garin	*Prosatori latini del quattrocento.* Ed. E. Garin. Milan, 1951.
RCI	Regesta Chartarum Italiae.
Relazioni	*Documenti delle relazioni tra Carlo I d'Angiò e la Toscana.* Ed. S. Terlizzi. Documenti di storia italiana . . . per la Toscana, 12. Florence, 1950.
Repetti, *Dizionario*	E. Repetti, *Dizionario geografico fisico storico della Toscana.* Florence, 1841.
RIS	*Rerum Italicarum Scriptores.* Ed. L. Muratori. Milan, 1723–51.

RIS, new ed. — Rerum Italicarum Scriptores. Nuova edizione riveduta, ampliata e corretta con la direzione di G. Carducci. Città di Castello, 1900 ff.

Rospigliosi, *Richordi* — *Libro A di richordi d'Antonio di Taddeo Rospiglioxi* (1459–1498). Ed. L. Andreani. Pisa, 1909.

RSI — *Rivista Storica Italiana.*

Russell, "Advances" — J. C. Russell, "Recent Advances in Mediaeval Demography," *Speculum,* 40 (1965), 84–101.

Russell, *Medieval Population* — J. C. Russell, *Late Ancient and Medieval Population.* Transactions of the American Philosophical Society, new series, 48, pt. 3. Philadelphia, 1958.

Sacchetti, *Trecentonovelle* — F. Sacchetti, *Il Trecentonovelle.* Ed. V. Pernicone. Florence, 1946.

Salimbene, *Cronica* — Salimbene de Adam, *Cronica.* Ed. F. Bernini. Scrittori d'Italia, 187. Bari, 1942.

Salutati, *Epistolario* — *Epistolario di Coluccio Salutati.* Ed. F. Novati. 4 vols. in 5. FSI, 15–18. Rome, 1891–1911.

Salvi, *Historie* — M. A. Salvi. *Delle historie di Pistoia e fazioni d'Italia.* 3 vols. Rome, Pistoia and Venice, 1656–62.

Sapori, "Prezzi" — A. Sapori, "Per la storia dei prezzi a Pistoia. Il quaderno dei conti di un capitano di custodia nel

1339," *BSP*, *29* (1926), 95–108; 145–52; and *30* (1928) 132–38; 166–76.

Slicher van Bath, *Agrarian History* — B. H. Slicher van Bath, *The Agrarian History of Western Europe, A.D. 500–1850*. New York, 1963.

Sozomenus, *Chronicon* — *Sozomeni pistoriensis presbyteri Chronicon universale*. Ed. G. Zaccagnini. RIS, new ed. 16, pt. 1. Città di Castello, 1908.

Sozomenus, Specimen — Sozomeni pistoriensis Specimen historiae, *RIS*, *16* (Milan, 1730), 1057–1198.

Statuta (1546) — *Statuta civitatis Pistorii*. Florence, 1546.

Statuti, ed. Berlan — *Statuti di Pistoia del secolo xii reintegrati*. Ed. F. Berlan. Bologna, 1882.

Statutum potestatis — *Statutum potestatis comunis Pistorii anni mcclxxxxvi*. Ed. L. Zdekauer. Milan, 1888.

Storie pistoresi — *Storie pistoresi (1300–1348)*. Ed. S. A. Barbi. RIS, new ed. 11, pt. 5. Città di Castello, 1907–27.

Tedaldi, "Relazione" — Vincenzo Minuti, "Relazione del commissario Gio. Batista Tedaldi sopra la città e il capitanato di Pistoia, nell' anno 1569," *ASI*, ser. 5, *10* (1892), 302–31.

Tholomeus, *Annalen* — *Die Annalen des Tholomeus von Lucca in doppelter Verfassung*. Ed. B. Schmeidler. MGH, Scriptores, new ser. 8. Berlin, 1930.

Tuscia	*Rationes decimarum Italiae. Tuscia*, I: *La Decima degli anni 1274–1280*. Ed. P. Guidi. II: *Le Decime degli anni 1295–1304*. Ed. M. Giusti and P. Guidi. Studi e Testi, 58 and 98. Vatican City, 1932 and 1942.
G. Villani, *Cronica*	*Cronica di Giovanni Villani*. Florence: Magheri, 1823.
M. Villani, *Cronica*	*Cronica di Matteo Villani*. Florence: Magheri, 1825.
VSWG	*Vierteljahrschrift für Sozial- und Wirtschaftsgeschichte*.
Zaccaria, *Anecdota*	F. A. Zaccaria, *Anecdotorum medii aevi maximam partem ex archivis pistoriensibus collectio*. Turin, 1755.

A Note on Citations

The notarial chartularies at present in the Archivio di Stato at Pistoia are as yet uncatalogued. Unless otherwise stated, the chartularies at Pistoia are the work of the notary Antonio di Puccetto Spada. Many chartularies from Pistoia and its district are also preserved in the Archivio di Stato of Florence. In citations from these chartularies, the number given in parentheses refers to the volume, and is stated whenever several volumes are catalogued under the same number. Thus, L 102 (5) means the fifth volume of the several catalogued under the designation L 102. Entries in the chartularies are identified by date and folio number when the chartulary is paginated. If it is not, the entries are identified by date alone.

The dates of all unpublished documents cited have been adjusted to the modern calendar. At Pistoia in the period of this book, the year began on December 25 and at Florence on March 25.

A Note on Weights and Measures

The weights and measures in common use at Pistoia in the Middle Ages were the following.

The unit of weight was the pound or *libbra* of 12 ounces, each of 24 *denarii* and each denarii of 24 *grani.* The pound was equal to about 323.5 grams, or 0.68 pounds avoirdupois.

The unit of length was the *braccio* (pl. *braccia*), four of which made a *canna.* In measuring cloth, the braccio was approximately equivalent to 0.613 meters or about 2.1 feet. In measuring land, a longer braccio was used, equivalent to 0.74 meters or about 2.4 feet.

The unit of surface area was the *stioro, stiore* or *staioro,* four of which constituted a *coltra.* The stioro was equivalent to about 12.65 *are,* or 0.313 acres.

The unit of dry measure was the *emina, omina* or *staio. Emina* or *omina* were the more usual names for this measure until the fifteenth century, when under Florentine influence the measure came to be more commonly called the *staio.* The emina was divided into two *quatrine* and four *quarti.* It was equivalent to about 25.92 liters, or 0.73 bushels.

The unit of liquid measure for wine was the barrel of 20 *fiaschi,* equivalent to 39.13 liters or about 42.2 quarts.

The unit of liquid measure for oil was the *quaderna.* Two quaderne made an *orcio,* and each quaderna consisted of 6 libbre. The quaderna was equal to 14.83 liters or about 16 quarts.

On these equivalents, see *Tavole di ragguaglio dei pesi e delle misure* (Rome, 1877).

Introduction

The words "Italian Renaissance" have for years borne with them a suggestion of splendid cities, flourishing commerce and agriculture, and an affluent and elegant society. Contemporary writers were in large part responsible for imparting to the Renaissance period its venerable reputation for wealth. They repeatedly boasted that their age was reviving not only letters and learning, but also the arts of refined, comfortable and gracious living.

One of the earliest writers who might be considered a representative of the new learning was Ricobaldus of Ferrara, canon of the cathedral of Ravenna, poet and author of an admired universal history which, in the late fifteenth century, Matteo Boiardo was to render into Italian. In his history written not long after 1297, Ricobaldus described with evident disdain the poor life and bad manners of people living only fifty years before.[1] He thereby implied that his own times had achieved unprecedented wealth and refinement.

According to Ricobaldus' description of their "rude customs," Italians at the time of Emperor Frederick II Hohenstaufen (1212–50) shared at table the same dishes and cups and made little use of utensils. Torches, not candles, illuminated their meals. Men wore unlined furs, and women petticoats made of rough linen. Common folk ate fresh meat only three times a week; on those days, a stew of meat and vegetables made up the midday meal, and the leftover meat was eaten cold for supper. Not everyone drank wine in the summer. Even with a little money, these simple people considered themselves rich. The grooming of girls, involving no use of gold and silver, was mean, and dowries were small. Arms and horses monopolized the interests of men, and Italian towns became crowded with their fortified towers.

1. Ricobaldi ferrariensis historia universalis, *RIS*, IX (Milan, 1727), 128. For ideas of progress and decline as expressed especially by historians of Padua, see N. Rubinstein, "Some Ideas on Municipal Progress and Decline in the Italy of the Communes," *Fritz Saxl, 1890–1948*, ed. D. J. Gordon (London, 1957), pp. 165–83.

This belief that society was attaining new levels of affluence and graciousness found frequent expression in writings of the early fourteenth century. Dante himself, visiting with his ancestor Cacciaguida in paradise, learned of the hardy virtues of old Florence, and also of its plain, poor and simple life.[2] King Robert of Naples, an early patron of the new learning, thought that even morals were improving amid the new abundance. In a letter written in 1333 to cheer the Florentine commune after a disastrous flood, he castigated those admirers of times past who failed to recognize the superiority of the present age:

> As for the grumblings [he wrote] of the believers who say that these times are worse than the olden times, and that God has held back the indignation of his wrath until the present, that he has reserved the present days to spread his anger: let readers read or let them listen to the troubles and sweat, thorns and tribulations, flood, ruination, from the time of Adam. . . . Past is that age of our fathers, far removed from our present storms, when the head of a dead ass sold for that much gold; when dove droppings were purchased with not a little silver; when women bargained together to enslave their own children. Now do we not hold these things in horror? We are shocked to hear these things read, yes! Because we have more for which to rejoice, than for which to complain, in our times.[3]

Surprisingly, the multiplying woes of the middle and late fourteenth century—the Black Death itself—did not, in evident measure, discourage writers from dwelling upon the wealth and splendor of their age. About 1344 Galvano de la Flamma, a Dominican of Milan, included in his chronicle Ricobaldus' paragraph "on the rude customs" of the old Italians, with some few additions.[4] The "antiqui" of the thirteenth century did not even have fireplaces. Moreover, the men of the present were given to luxury and extravagance

2. *Paradiso*, XV, 91–148.
3. The letter is given by G. Villani, *Cronica*, XI, cap. 3 (VI, 32).
4. Gualvanei de la Flamma ordinis predicatorum opusculum de rebus gestis ab Azone, Luchino, et Johanne Vicecomitibus ab anno MCCXXVIII usque ad annum MCCCXLII, *RIS*, XII (Milan, 1728), 1033, "De moribus antiquorum."

in clothing, and drank foreign and expensive wines; *magistri coquinae,* skilled chefs, were highly prized.[5]

Another, this time anonymous, chronicler, who wrote not long after 1354, similarly quoted Ricobaldus' popular description of the bad manners of the thirteenth century and added some new, moralizing flourishes. The plain folk of former years, he related, while poor and uncouth, were self-controlled enough to postpone marriage until the age of 30. Even girls of 20 could sleep in the same bed with the sons of neighbors, *sine peccato.*[6]

Still later in the century, Giovanni de' Mussi of Piacenza placed in his chronicle under the year 1388 a lengthy essay on the changing customs of his age.[7] Again he cited with approval Ricobaldus' paragraph on thirteenth-century manners. This age of poverty and simplicity seems to have lasted, in Giovanni's estimation, to about 1320.[8] In the 1380s, on the other hand, the men of Piacenza were living "splendidly, lavishly, brilliantly."[9] To show their expensive standards, Giovanni cited prices: the well-accoutered young woman was paying 25 to 60 florins for a dress, 25 florins for rings, 70 to 100 florins for a coronet, 100 to 125 florins for a pearl necklace, and so forth. Some fashionable styles showed so much *décolletage* that the breasts looked as if "they wanted to leave the bodice."[10] A household with nine members "and two horses" needed a minimum income of 300 florins per year. Homes were much more elegant, with separate rooms, kitchens and fireplaces. Dishes, utensils and tallow candles were commonplace, and, much in contrast with the old days, people could no longer abstain from wine.

Tuscans as well as Lombards appear convinced of the material

5. Ibid. p. 1034.
6. Anonymi Itali breviarium italicae historicae, *RIS,* XVI (Milan, 1730), 259.
7. Johannis de Mussis chronicon placentinum, *RIS,* XVI (Milan, 1730), 579–84, "De moribus civium Placentiae."
8. At least in regard to household furnishings and the houses themselves. Ibid. p. 528, "et utuntur in domibus eorum pulchrioribus et melioribus arnixiis et vasellamentis, quam solebant a septuaginta annis retro, scilicet ab Anno Christi MCCCXX retro, et habent pulchriores habitationes quam tunc habebant. . . ."
9. Loc. cit. "Homines Placentiae ad presens vivunt splendide et ornate et nitide. . . ."
10. Ibid. p. 580. "Quae Ciprianae [a style of dress] habent gulam tam magnam, quod ostendunt mammillas, et videtur, quod dictae mammillae velint exire de sinu earum."

splendor of the times. In 1401, following a murderous epidemic the year before, a chronicler of Pistoia, ser Luca Dominici, still declared that Florence was "triumphant" for the numbers and good manners of its inhabitants. With more than 60,000 mouths, he affirmed (incorrectly, to be sure) that the city had never been larger.[11] The then humanist chancellor of Florence, Coluccio Salutati (d. 1406), also boasted of the city's wealth and linked it with its cultural leadership: "What city is richer . . . ? What city, without a port, imports or exports more goods? Where is commerce greater . . . ? Where are men more illustrious . . . ? Where Dante, where Petrarch, where Boccaccio?"[12] Leonardo Bruni (d. 1444), another famous humanist, who became chancellor of Florence in 1410, described the city as "most flourishing with the number of its population, splendor of its buildings and magnitude of its affairs"; the seeds "of the best arts and of all human learning [*humanitatis*]," which had seemed almost extinct, were again taking root in such propitious soil.[13]

A proud consciousness of present affluence seems to have grown even stronger as the fifteenth century progressed. Flavio Biondo of Forlì (d. 1463) related how, when he sought to write the history of Europe since the fall of the Roman empire, shame and horror almost deterred him from the task. But encouragement finally came from the hope of recounting the rise of Italy's brilliant cities. These, as everyone knew, "had grown to great size, and, through their wealth and the skill of the men gathered within them, both dignity and glory are returning to the Italy deprived of the Roman republic."[14]

One of the most pointed, and certainly one of the most influential expressions of this idea that the Renaissance was an age of unprecedented prosperity is given in the *Storia d'Italia* of Francesco Guicciardini (d. 1540). Never, wrote Guicciardini, since the fall of Rome,

11. *Cronache*, II, 9, "Lo magnifico comune di Firenze nel decto tempo era triunfante di popolo più che mai, che, secondo si teneva dentro, facea più di xv mila huomini d'arme e più di lx mila di bocche, savissimi cittadini e costumati pieno di molte ricchezze. . . ."

12. Invectiva in Antonium Luschum vicentinum, in *Prosatori latini*, ed. Garin, p. 34.

13. Ad Petrum Paulum Histrum dialogus, *Prosatori latini*, p. 44.

14. "Intelligunt omnes in magnam amplitudinem [urbes] auctas esse per quarum opus virorumque qui in illis coaluerunt virtutem et dignitas adest et gloria Italiae romana respublica destitutae," *Historiarum ab inclinatione Romanorum tres decades* (Venice, 1483), Decade 1, Book 3.

had Italy been so prosperous as in the years preceding the French invasions (1494).[15] Even mountainous and sterile places were cultivated, and the land rejoiced in a large population, abundant merchandise and wealth, magnificent rulers and free and splendid cities. And in this milieu of wealth, plenty and refinement, religion, in Guicciardini's estimation, was practiced majestically; outstanding statesmen abounded, and there also flourished men noble in the mastery of all learning and in every glorious and productive art.

Authors from the fourteenth to the sixteenth century thus depicted a prosperous Italy, and implied that this wealth was a foundation of its cultural accomplishments. The humanists, to be sure, characteristically rejected the assumption that material possessions could alone assure nobility of character, learning or good manners. But most agreed that learning and refinement were best pursued amid comfortable circumstances. Leon Battista Alberti, for example, noted that the poor man could not easily afford the "no few expenses involved in the study of letters."[16]

Writers such as Guicciardini, and the many who before him had similarly lauded Italy's prosperity, clearly influenced the later, great historians who fashioned the modern concept of the Renaissance and advanced the first extensive comments on its economic and social background.

In 1756, Voltaire, although he came short of developing a rounded picture of the Renaissance as a distinct period, still eulogized the civilized life of the Italian towns, which for him as for Flavio Biondo were the only lights of dignity and glory still aglow in the medieval Gothic night. "There," he affirmed, "one lived in comfort with opulence; it was only in their bosom that one could enjoy the pleasures of life. There wealth and freedom finally excited genius, as it had inspired courage."[17] In 1855, in the fifth vol-

15. *Storia d'Italia*, ed. C. Panigada (Scrittori d'Italia, 120; Bari, 1929), I, 2.

16. *Famiglia*, p. 136, "spese, quali non poche si convengono agli studii delle lettere." Flavio Biondo considered that the best students of eloquence were likely to be those" qui honesto nati loco ab urbanis educati parentibus et civilibus innutriti sunt officiis." De verbis Romanis locutionis, in *Scritti inediti e rari di Biondo Flavio*, ed. B. Nogara (Studi e Testi, 48; Rome, 1927), p. 123.

17. From the "Essay on the Manners and Spirit of Nations," cited in W. K. Ferguson, *The Renaissance in Historical Thought* (Cambridge, Mass., 1948), p. 91.

ume of his history of France which first brought the term "Renaissance" into wide popular favor, Jules Michelet proclaimed that the basis of this rebirth of enlightenment was the wealth of Italy's cities. "A religion began in the banks of Florence," he commented in slightly blasphemous terms, "having in gold its real presence and in letters of exchange its religion."[18] Jacob Burckhardt, greatest of all these early architects of the Renaissance idea, in his *Civilization of the Renaissance in Italy* (1860), devoted an entire section, the fifth, to "Society and Festivals." With his usual high artistic mastery of the illuminating detail, Burckhardt depicted a social world in which learning and refinement had become the open doors to preferment, and where the good life itself was consciously constructed as a work of art.

Both Renaissance authors and these later historians thus implanted in the historical consciousness the durable assumption that Italy's cities in the Renaissance glowed with affluence, with the aid of which they restored polished manners and rediscovered humane letters. These first designers of the Renaissance theory did not, however, systematically explore the structure or performance of the period's economy, perhaps because they felt they already knew its basic character. Subsequent scholars sought to correct this omission. Inspired by Burckhardt's brilliant formula, that Italy was the birthplace of the modern world, historians were soon searching out in the Renaissance period the institutional and psychological antecedents of modern economic life. A vast literature has grown up concerning these aspects of the Renaissance economy; because it has already been several times reviewed, perhaps we may be excused with mentioning only a few of the leading authors.[19]

In 1878, in a pioneering study which has not lost its interest, Robert von Pöhlmann argued that the Florentine state in the fifteenth century could be considered, by economic as well as political stand-

18. Cited in Ferguson, *Renaissance in Historical Thought*, p. 174.

19. See the bibliographical review article by W. K. Ferguson, "Recent Trends in the Economic Historiography of the Renaissance," *Studies in the Renaissance*, VII (1960), 7–26; R. S. Lopez, "Hard Times and Investment in Culture," *The Renaissance. Six Essays* (New York: Harper Torchbook, 1962), pp. 29–54; R. S. Lopez and H. A. Miskimin, "The Economic Depression of the Renaissance," *EHR*, 14 (1962), 408–27; and most recently, Ernst Pitz, "Die Wirtschaftskrise des Spätmittelalters," *VSWG*, 52 (1965), 347–67.

ards, a birthplace of the modern world, because it espoused the principles of freedom of trade within its boundaries.[20] Pöhlmann's data did not all the time fully support his enthusiastic conclusions, but his argument is not without some validity and his thesis still awaits an adequate reassessment. Alfred Doren, one of the great names in Florentine and Italian economic history, found anticipations of the modern in the very size and sophisticated organization of the Italian, especially Florentine wool industry, which he considered "the first fully developed capitalistic industry," and "a typical representative of a first high point of modern industrial capitalism."[21] His study of Florentine guilds showed continuing corporate restrictions upon the individual, but Doren maintained that there was no "antinomy" between the conclusions of his own research and Burckhardt's characterization of the Renaissance as an age of freedom.[22] Individualism could flourish within the intelligently administered corporations of the Florentine guild system, and perhaps was even aided by them.

The psychological as well as institutional antecedents of modern economic life were simultaneously attracting attention. By the late nineteenth century, the growing popularity of Marxist analysis added a new theoretical rigor and respectability to the venerable assumption that wealthy merchants, the upper bourgeoisie in sum, were the special promoters and patrons of the new humanist learning. Perhaps the culminating expression of this argument is Alfred von Martin's brief essay, *The Sociology of the Renaissance*, published in German in 1932 and available in English translation since

20. Pöhlmann, *Wirtschaftspolitik*. The contribution made by fifteenth-century states, especially the despotisms, to economic expansion, is still the subject of much discussion. Recently, Douglas F. Dowd, "The Economic Expansion of Lombardy, 1300–1500: A Study in Political Stimuli to Economic Change," *Journal of Economic History*, 21 (1961), 143–60, has argued that the policies of the Visconti despots of Milan greatly stimulated economic growth in that region. On the other hand, P. J. Jones, "Communes and Despots: the City State in Late-Medieval Italy," *Transactions of the Royal Historical Society*, 5th series, 15 (1965), 71–96, tends to minimize the economic contributions of the despots.

21. *Italienische Wirtschaftsgeschichte* (Jena, 1934), pp. 499 and 502. See also his *Die Florentiner Wollentuch Industrie von XIV bis zum XVI Jahrhundert* (Studien aus der Florentiner Wirtschaftsgeschichte, 1; Stuttgart, 1901), pp. 15 ff.

22. *Le Arti fiorentine*, transl. G. B. Klein, II (Florence, 1940), p. 297.

1944.[23] Von Martin pushed this idea that Renaissance culture was modern, bourgeois culture to and perhaps beyond the boundaries of the absurd. He maintained, for example, that nudity in art appealed to the bourgeoisie, because they detested clothes by which the clerical and noble orders paraded their hated feudal privileges and exulted in a kind of democratic nakedness.[24]

In the decade of the 1930s, investigations of the Renaissance economy and society began to take new directions and to assume a new tone. Until then, historians had been largely occupied in the quest for modern origins, as if the interest of ages past was exclusively their contributions to the modern economy and culture. Another problem, which had hitherto not attracted much interest, began to claim attention: was the Renaissance really a period of prosperity and affluence? In beginning to doubt this received opinion, historians may have been absorbing the somber and gloomy mood of the depression years, and the ensuing World War and postwar difficulties hardly helped to clear and cheer the scholarly atmosphere.[25] Somber views of the Renaissance have, at any rate, proliferated in recent decades, and among the scholars with the most surprising conclusions to report have been the economic historians.

As early as the 1930s, the distinguished Belgian historian Henri Pirenne was maintaining that the fourteenth and fifteenth centuries in Europe witnessed, in economic terms, not prosperity but a "cessation of all advance."[26] Pirenne's comments, when compared with judgments since expressed, seem today mild if not timorous. In 1952, the *Cambridge Economic History,* in its second volume, devoted to trade and industry in the Middle Ages, presented two lengthy chapters on trade in the north and in the south of Europe,

23. *Soziologie der Renaissance; zur Physiognomik und Rhythmik bürgerlicher Kultur* (Stuttgart, 1932). *Sociology of the Renaissance,* transl. W. L. Luetknes (New York and Oxford, 1944).

24. *Sociology,* p. 26, "Nakedness, like death, is democratic."

25. A point developed by Professor Franklin Pegues, of Ohio State University, in a paper read to the Midwestern Conference of Medievalists, in October 1964.

26. *Economic and Social History of Medieval Europe,* transl. I. E. Clegg (New York, n.d.), p. 193. On the development of this reassessment of the Renaissance economy, see especially the comments of R. S. Lopez, "Hard Times and Investment in Culture," cited above, n. 19.

written by M. M. Postan and R. S. Lopez respectively.[27] Both authors agreed that severe depression gripped the European economy from the early fourteenth century; although laboring in a field poor in statistics, they were able to garner an impressive harvest of data to support their contentions. Their work, to evaluate it exactly, more truly launched a debate than settled an argument.[28] But no knowledgeable historian could today affirm—at least not without heavy qualifications—that new wealth and new learning were the parallel and twin achievements of the Renaissance period.

While the depth and duration of the Renaissance depression is still much disputed, most scholars would today agree that the period's economy had some bad spots and some bad years. Continuing investigation of the factors behind these economic difficulties has served to darken still further the picture of social life in the fourteenth and fifteenth centuries. A current, widely credited view (which we will examine at some length in chapter 5) holds that the disasters of the fourteenth century, even the Black Death, were not fortuitous interventions but troubles engendered by acute overpopulation in the medieval community. The medieval economy could not nourish its own numbers, and these weak and emaciated peoples fell easy victim to comparatively mild infections. The economic and social history of the fourteenth century becomes, in this harsh reconstruction, the chilling account of a classical Malthusian crisis.

The continuing accumulation of more ample and more reliable demographic data has further emphasized both the dimensions and prolongation of the population plunge in the closing Middle Ages, and a historian, noting the disappearance of two out of three or even three out of four Europeans, can only be appalled by the enormity of the losses. One of the most assiduous students of medieval

27. *CEH*, II, 119–256 and 257–354.

28. See, for example, the contrary views expressed by C. M. Cipolla, *EHR*, 16 (1964), 519–29. A. R. Bridbury, *Economic Growth. England in the Later Middle Ages* (London, 1962), argues that the later Middle Ages were a prosperous period for England. E. Pitz in the *VSWG* (see above, n. 19) concludes that, while in these centuries the total output of the medieval economy may have declined, it was simultaneously experiencing a fundamental change in structure and was coming to rest on a much more highly capitalized productive base, especially in agriculture.

Tuscan demography, Enrico Fiumi, has been so impressed, or depressed, by such figures as to propose a fundamentally demographic interpretation of the "flourishing and decline," as he calls it, of the medieval Tuscan commune.[29] For Fiumi, the period after 1348—the age when the classical revival was just gaining momentum—must be considered in economic and social terms an age of decadence: "the principal cause [of this decadence]—the exclusive cause, I would dare to say—lay in the impressive demographic impoverishment of the [Tuscan] cities and countryside."[30]

These recent interpretations, stressing economic depression, demographic glut, then demographic decadence as the social concomitants of the revival of learning, have badly tarnished the received portrait of Renaissance prosperity and magnificence. But they have not entirely discredited it. Contemporary authors, to be sure, reflecting the Renaissance love of splendor, may well have misled later historians with exaggerated descriptions of the wealth of their society. But their unmistakable pride in (or, for some, concern with) the riches and luxuries of their times still required some basis in fact. It is hard for a modern historian, even when armed with statistics, to declare them completely mistaken in their characterization of their own age. Care must be taken lest the theory of a Renaissance depression prove as misleading as the assumption of Renaissance prosperity which formerly held the field. As the late dean of Italian economic historians, Gino Luzzatto, prudently remarked: "it would be wrong to conclude from these adverse circumstances that Renaissance Italy was in a state of unrelieved economic decay."[31]

The construction of a balanced picture of the period's economic and social experience is today clearly a major *desideratum* of Renaissance studies. Much, to be sure, has already been accomplished toward this end, and American scholars can take pride in sharing in the labors and achievements. The studies of Marvin Becker, Gene

29. "Fioritura e decadenza dell' economia fiorentina," *ASI*, 115 (1957), 385–439; 116 (1958), 443–510; 117 (1959), 427–502, and most recently, the same author's *San Gimignano.*

30. *San Gimignano*, p. 224.

31. *An Economic History of Italy from the Fall of the Roman Empire until the Beginning of the Sixteenth Century*, transl. P. Jones (New York, 1961), p. 141.

A. Brucker, William M. Bowsky, and Lauro Martines—to mention only a few of the younger historians—have explored many areas of high interest for economic and social history.[32] But the research still to be done remains enormous. The attraction of and, in real measure, the obstacle to such research is the great wealth of the Italian archives; they are rich enough, even in the humbler towns, to occupy a scholar for years of his productive life.

This present book is a study of one such humbler town of Tuscany: Pistoia, near neighbor of Florence on the flat plain of the middle Arno valley. While restricted in its geographic purview, the book attempts to present a fairly comprehensive survey of demographic, economic, institutional, social and cultural changes which the city and countryside of Pistoia experienced between the thirteenth and fifteenth centuries.

Pistoia merits attention from historians, if only for the excellence of its surviving sources. It possesses, for example, the oldest and most ample series of surveys of the rural population that has survived for any Tuscan or Italian countryside. Its series of statutes, including the oldest preserved for any Tuscan town, is similarly noteworthy. The city's fund of private documents is good even in the early thirteenth century, and spans the period of the fourteenth-century crisis without thinning out, as happens in many, especially rural areas of Tuscany. Numerous enough to make possible the construction of reliable price and rent series, these documents are still manageable in numbers—a fact of no little convenience for an American scholar who, under the best of circumstances, can spend only a restricted time in foreign archives.

A town of moderate size in the Middle Ages, Pistoia attracts for its history as well as for its archives. In the years of its existence as a free commune (to 1351), it aspired to and achieved considerable commercial prominence and played no minor role in the age's political struggles. The feud between the Black and White Guelfs, for

32. Cf. Marvin B. Becker, "An Essay on the 'Novi Cives' and Florentine Politics, 1343–1382," *Mediaeval Studies*, 24 (1962), 35–82, which is only one of the more recent of the same author's many studies on fourteenth-century Florentine history; Gene A. Brucker, *Florentine Politics and Society, 1343–1378* (Princeton Studies in History, 12; Princeton, N.J. 1962); Bowsky, "Impact," and "The Buon Governo of Siena (1287–1355): A Mediaeval Italian Oligarchy," *Speculum*, 37 (1962), 368–81; Martines, *Social World*.

example, originated within its walls, spread to include Florence, and in 1302 led to the permanent exile of Dante Alighieri from his native city. The poet thus had cause to remember Pistoia with choice invective:[33]

> Ah Pistoia, Pistoia, why do you not decree
> To reduce yourself to ashes . . . .

After 1351 Pistoia, unable to resist the power of its great neighbor Florence, gradually became integrated into the Florentine "district," in a process we shall study.[34] This adds considerably to the interest of its history. The city undoubtedly experienced many of the same social and economic changes, even if it never captured the same brilliance, as Florence, its master and neighbor only 21 miles away. To study Pistoia's society is also to gain some insight into contemporary social movements at the cultural capital of the Tuscan and Italian Renaissance.

The argument of this book frequently rests on the construction and analysis of statistical series. From 1201 to 1430 the series are based on a fairly comprehensive survey of existing documents. These terminal dates have not, however, been rigorously respected in other matters, and documents from both earlier and later years have been cited with some frequency, when they help reveal trends. Prudence requires the acknowledgment that statistics from so early a period, based upon a documentation which while ample is still fragmentary, cannot be considered rigorously exact. But there is no reason to doubt the truth of what they reveal concerning the long-term trends in population, prices, rents and profits.

Reliance on statistical series has also dictated the content and arrangement of most of the chapters. With few exceptions, the chapters consider single topics, and explore them for the book's entire chronological range from the thirteenth to the fifteenth centuries. To have arranged the contents in strictly chronological order would have required dividing the statistical tables, doubling or tripling their number, at the risk of obscuring what they reveal concerning long-term trends. While occasionally awkward, this largely topical arrangement permits, it is hoped, economy and clarity.

33. *Inferno*, XXV, 10–11.
34. See below, chapter 8, pp. 214–31.

The principal focus of this book is the nature and degree of changes experienced by Pistoia's society between the thirteenth and fifteenth centuries—changes in the size and character of its population, the economic activities of its people in town and countryside, governmental institutions, distribution of wealth, social divisions and culture in both its religious and secular manifestations. We think that the changes were many enough and profound enough to justify concluding that by the fifteenth century a society much different from that of the free commune of the thirteenth century was emerging. It was not, to be sure, a "modern" society. By several indicators—the distribution of wealth, the strength of the middle class, the role of factional divisions and factional violence—the society of fifteenth-century Pistoia would have to be considered more primitive, more feudal even, than that of the free city which preceded it. The troubles of the late Middle Ages, in other words, to some extent engendered a lapse back into older forms of social organization and older traditions of social behavior. But if archaic in some of its aspects, Pistoia's Renaissance society also helped develop and support new, distinctive and highly influential cultural attitudes.

It is the author's hope that this study of social change in the small city of Pistoia may contribute toward a better understanding of the broad characteristics of Italian Renaissance society, and a more profound appreciation of the age's stunning cultural heritage.

1

The Formation of the Medieval Territory

Question: *Is it known by public knowledge that the castle and men of Lamporecchio are subject to the jurisdiction of the bishop?*
Answer: *Yes, this is so. However, the city is the sovereign* [domina].

—Witness testifying as to the lordship over Lamporecchio, *Liber censuum*, no. 136, p. 115, 13 Sept. 1221

Pistoia's medieval and Renaissance society was profoundly influenced by the location, size and even the shape of its medieval territory, its *comitatus*, "county," or "contado."[1] To consider its territorial growth, to seek to explain the peculiarities of its shape, is also to discern many of the physical and geographic factors which, over the centuries, have influenced the culture as well as the economy of its people.

THE ROMAN *Ager*

Pistoia itself was founded in the northwest corner of the plain of the middle Arno, about one mile from the Ombrone river, upon a slight elevation in the plain which offered some protection from

1. The Statutes of 1107 (*Statuti*, ed. Berlan, cap. I, p. 1) refer to the territory under the commune's jurisdiction as its "district" ("usque ad quatuor miliaria prope civitatem Pistorii, que sunt nostri districtus . . ."). So also does the survey of ca. 1244, the *Liber focorum*, of which more will be said presently. Its full title is the "Liber focorum districtus Pistorii." "Comitatus," on the other hand, properly refers to the territory of the diocese, the full extent of which was never at Pistoia brought under the commune's control. Often, however,

floods.[2] The plain of the middle Arno, which at its southeast extremity also played host to Florence, is geologically and geographically quite distinctive.[3] Once the basin of an inland sea, it bears the shape of an elliptical saucer, a kind of natural amphitheater some twenty-five miles long and six miles across at its widest point. To the north and northwest beyond Pistoia, the saucer's lip is molded by the tall main ridge of the Apennines and by the high spurs—the Monte della Calvana and the Monte Morello—which spring from it. To the west and southwest, a lower but still fairly rugged Apennine spur, the Monte Albano, limits the basin and by convention marks the division between the middle and lower Arno valley.[4] To the south the rim is formed by the low, rounded but still distinctive hills of central Tuscany.

Traces of Etruscan settlements have been found at Pistoia dating from the fifth century before Christ, but they appear to have been neither sizable nor permanent.[5] Like Florence, its sister city of the plain, Pistoia, in origin and name, must be considered a Roman town.[6] The first literary reference to Pistoia's inhabitants is in Plautus' comedy, "The Captives," written not long after 200 B.C.[7] In the course of a protracted pun, Plautus refers to bakers ("pistorienses") and the context makes it certain that he had the inhabitants of a city or region in mind. Since no other known Roman city bore

---

even in official documents, "comitatus," "contado" and "districtus" are used interchangeably, signifying the territory governed by the commune or simply the rural lands surrounding the city. Cf. the title of the Book of Boundaries of 1255, the "Liber finium seu confinium comitatus seu districtus Pistorii," in *Liber focorum*, p. 269. ASP, Provv. Tomus 10, 7v, 27 Sept. 1336, "plures et multi de districtu et comitatu Pistorii. . . ."

2. On Pistoia in antiquity, see L. Banti, "Pistoriae," *Paulys Realencyclopädie der classischen Altertumswissenschaft*, ed. G. Wissowa, 20, pt. 2 (1950), 1832–35, and Paolini, *Pistoia*, pp. 3–13.

3. G. Dainelli, *Il Bacino di Firenze e il suo antico lago* (Florence, 1936), pp. 3 ff.

4. Cf. G. Villani, *Cronica*, I, cap. 43 (I, p. 63). "E poi uscito per corso del nostro piano, passa tra Montelupo e Capraia presso a Empoli per la contrada di Greti e di Valdarno di sotto a piè di Fucecchio. . . ."

5. Paolini, *Pistoia*, p. 3.

6. On Florentine origins and early settlement on the plain of the Arno basin, see most recently Mario Lopes Pegna, *Firenze dalle origini al Medioevo* (Florence, 1962), pp. 42 ff.

7. *T. Macci Plauti Comoediae*, ed. A. Fleckeisen (Leipzig: Teubner, 1881), p. 69, lines 160 ff., "primundum opus Pistoriensibus."

that unusual name, Plautus almost certainly was making fun of the "bakers" of our own Pistoia.

The true etymology of the city's name is uncertain and, since the Middle Ages, numerous imaginative theories have been offered to explain it: that it refers to a *pestis* or plague (an explanation favored by medieval chroniclers anxious to denigrate the town), that it comes from Greek words meaning "boundary of water" (*pistou horion*) in reference to its site near the valley swamps, that it really does mean bakery or bakeries.[8] This last suggestion, corresponding as it does with the clear Latin sense of its name *pistoria,* seems the most likely.

And this etymology, if true, has instructive implications concerning Pistoia's initial distinction as a Roman town. It must have baked bread, and supplied it for an area difficult to supply, the high Apennines to which it was a gateway. According to Livy, Pistoia did indeed serve as a base of supply for the Roman legions in their long struggle against the Apennine Ligurians (239–174 B.C.).[9]

Pistoia from its origins thus seems to have turned toward the mountains. Only one ancient writer gives some hint of the configuration of its territory. This is the historian Sallust, who recorded the dramatic events of the conspiracy of Catiline against the Senate and the Roman Republic.[10] The rebel Catiline, defeated in 62 B.C. by troops loyal to the Senate, sought to lead the remnants of his desperadoes over the Apennines, in hopes of rekindling his flagging revolt in Cis-alpine Gaul. He entered the "ager Pistoriensis," apparently expecting to cross the Collina pass, the area's easiest and quickest route across the mountains to the Po valley. He was, however, intercepted, defeated again, and killed at a place not now certainly identifiable, but perhaps the modern Campotizzoro.

The word *ager* used by Sallust seems to have been a technical

8. Both Brunetto Latini, *Li livres du trésor* (Paris, 1863), p. 35, and Giovanni Villani, *Cronica,* I, cap. 32 (I, p. 46), maintained that Pistoia derived its name from "pistolenza." In 1569 G. B. Tedaldi, "Relazione," p. 313, was already proposing the derivation from the Greek "pistou horion." For more recent opinions, see Paolini, *Pistoia,* pp. 4–5.

9. *Historiae,* XXXIX, 1. See the comments of A. Chiappelli, "Della topografia antica di Pistoia," *BSP,* 32 (1930), 175.

10. *Gai Sallusti Crispi Libri de Catilinae coniuratione et De bello iugurthino,* ed. R. Dietsch (Leipzig: Teubner, 1885), cap. 57, p. 33.

administrative term, and it suggests that Pistoia, itself undoubtedly an *oppidum* or fortified town, had a constituted and defined territory, which, from the sense of the historian's account, was closely associated with the Apennine passes. While the precise boundaries of Pistoia's Roman *ager* will probably never be known, the configuration of the medieval territory and considerations of administrative logic do make some suppositions likely. In the direction of the Apennines, the medieval territory did not stop at what might seem the "natural" frontier, the mountain watershed. Rather it continued for several miles beyond, down the course of the Collina pass in the direction of Bologna. This asymmetrical frontier, pushing beyond the watershed, has puzzled historians, but there does seem a method in its meanderings.[11] If Roman Pistoia, as seems likely, was responsible for the maintenance of this strategic pass, its territory could not be ended at the watershed. The middle of largely deserted mountains is no place to terminate responsibility. Most likely, the prolongation of the medieval contado over the watershed along the principal route to Bologna was a Roman inheritance, and reflected a Roman interest in maintaining good roads in this difficult mountain area.

Probably also, Pistoia was fulfilling another vital function in the strategic system of Roman communications. The Monte Albano, the Apennine spur which, as we have mentioned, juts out from the main ridge to separate the Florentine plain from the lower Arno valley, was another, if less challenging, obstacle for travellers. Over this, the great Roman highway, the Via Cassia, had to pass. This important road ran from Rome to Florence, down the Arno valley along the base of the Apennines, past Pistoia, across the Monte Albano to Lucca, and then up the coast to Lunigiana, Liguria and the

11. F. Schneider, *Die Reichsverwaltung in Toscana von der Gründung des Langobardenreichs bis zum Ausgang der Staufer (568–1268)*, Bibliothek des kgl. historischen Instituts in Rome, 11 (Rome, 1914), pp. 65–67, maintained that the mountain frontier of Pistoia's medieval contado—particularly its puzzling prolongation past the watershed toward Bologna—was a Lombard arrangement meant to protect the passes from a possible Byzantine counteroffensive, which might come from the direction of Ravenna and the Exarchate. But this part of the Apennines was never a disputed frontier (the Lombards, after all, controlled Bologna too). Pistoia's mountain boundary seems more likely the work of men seeking not to prohibit passage over the mountains but to facilitate it, and these were probably the Romans.

north. This road thus linked Rome with Liguria, with the upper Po valley and with Gaul beyond them. Pistoia was an important station along this Via Cassia, and is so depicted in the "Peutinger Table," that great map of Roman roads made apparently at Constantinople in the fourth century of the Christian era.[12]

Pistoia as a military station also needed close communications with the Roman maritime base at Pisa, but here the direct route was obstructed not only by the Monte Albano but by the great swamp of Fucecchio immediately beyond it. Again, administrative logic demanded that responsibility for routes across mountains or through swamps be not broken in the middle of largely deserted territory but kept unified along the entire length of a difficult course. An ancient association with and responsibility for the routes over the Monte Albano toward Lucca and Pisa may therefore also explain another peculiarity of the medieval territory: the inclusion within it not only of the entire length and both slopes of the Monte Albano but also of the land on the farther shore of the Fucecchio swamp.

This then seems to have been the birthmark given by the Romans to their Tuscan bakery, which the medieval territory never lost: a basic orientation toward the mountains, a close association with the passes over and through both the Apennines and the Monte Albano, a consequent deep penetration of its territory into these mountains and even down the opposite slopes along the course of principal roads. Pistoia was born a strategic city, and this would bring it wealth, renown and enemies.

THE EPISCOPAL DIOCESE IN THE EARLY MIDDLE AGES

A bishop of Pistoia is first mentioned in a papal letter of 496, although the diocese probably owed its origins to the great upsurge in Christian conversions in the fourth century.[13] Concerning the

12. *Weltkarte des Castorius genannt die Peutinger'sche Tafel,* ed. K. Miller (Ravensburg, 1888), segmentum 4, 1. The stations between Florence and Lucca are given as Helana (probably the modern Agliana) and Pistoris.

13. Pope Gelasius I to Helpidius, bishop of Volterra, *PL,* LIX, 145 A (Jaffé, *Regesta,* no. 735), mentioning but not naming "pontifices Pistoriensis, Lucensis et Fesulanus." The history of the church of Pistoia is conveniently summarized by G. Cappelletti, *Le Chiese d'Italia dalla loro origine sino ai nostri giorni,* XVII (Venice, 1862), pp. 73 ff.

church of Pistoia in the early Middle Ages, little information has survived besides the names of bishops, and even these only sporadically. But the names alone suggest that a continuing episcopal administration was forging a link between the ancient territory and the medieval contado. More even than the passing secular regimes of the Goths, Byzantines and Lombards (the last of whom much favored the city for its strategic location), the episcopal government seems to have carried the Roman imprint and firmly impressed it upon the configuration of the medieval territory.[14]

Not until 998, however, does a document convey fairly precise information concerning the diocesan boundaries. In that year Emperor Otto III granted a charter of immunity to the bishop of Pistoia and listed his "possessions and properties."[15] The emperor made no distinction between the bishop's temporal possessions and his spiritual jurisdictions; the Investiture Controversy had yet to make such refinements important. In spite of much vague language, concerning geography as well as jurisdictions, the approximate boundaries of the diocese still emerge. Later a whole series of papal charters, granted to the bishop, to the canons of Pistoia or to individual churches, give an ever more precise indication of the shape of the crystallizing diocese.[16]

These and other sources also illuminate a factor of major importance for medieval administrators and for historians of their work: the roads leading out from the city, through which the bishop brought his spiritual services to his scattered flock. Specifically, Pistoia in the early Middle Ages had become the hub of six major highways, and the influence of them upon the eventual configuration of the diocese is fundamental. These roads were the three

14. Chiappelli, "L'Età longobarda," rather stressed the importance of Lombard administration on the formation of the later contado. However, the Lombard "iudicaria" seems to have been much larger than the diocese and later contado. It included, for example, Fucecchio and Pescia, which never became parts either of the diocese or of the county.

15. *MGH, Die Urkunden der deutschen Könige und Kaiser*, II, 1: *Die Urkunden Otto des III* (Hanover, 1888), no. 284, p. 709.

16. See *PL*, CLI, 317–18 (Jaffé, *Regesta*, no. 5427), 10 Jan. 1090, to the canons of Pistoia. *PL*, CLXIII, 176–77 (Jaffé, *Regesta*, no. 6052), 14 Oct. 1105, to the bishop. *PL*, CLXXIX, 192 (Jaffé, *Regesta*, no. 7639), 21 Dec. 1133, to the bishop. Zaccaria, *Anecdota*, pp. 242–43 (Potthast, *Regesta*, no. 5862), 7 July 1218, also to the bishop.

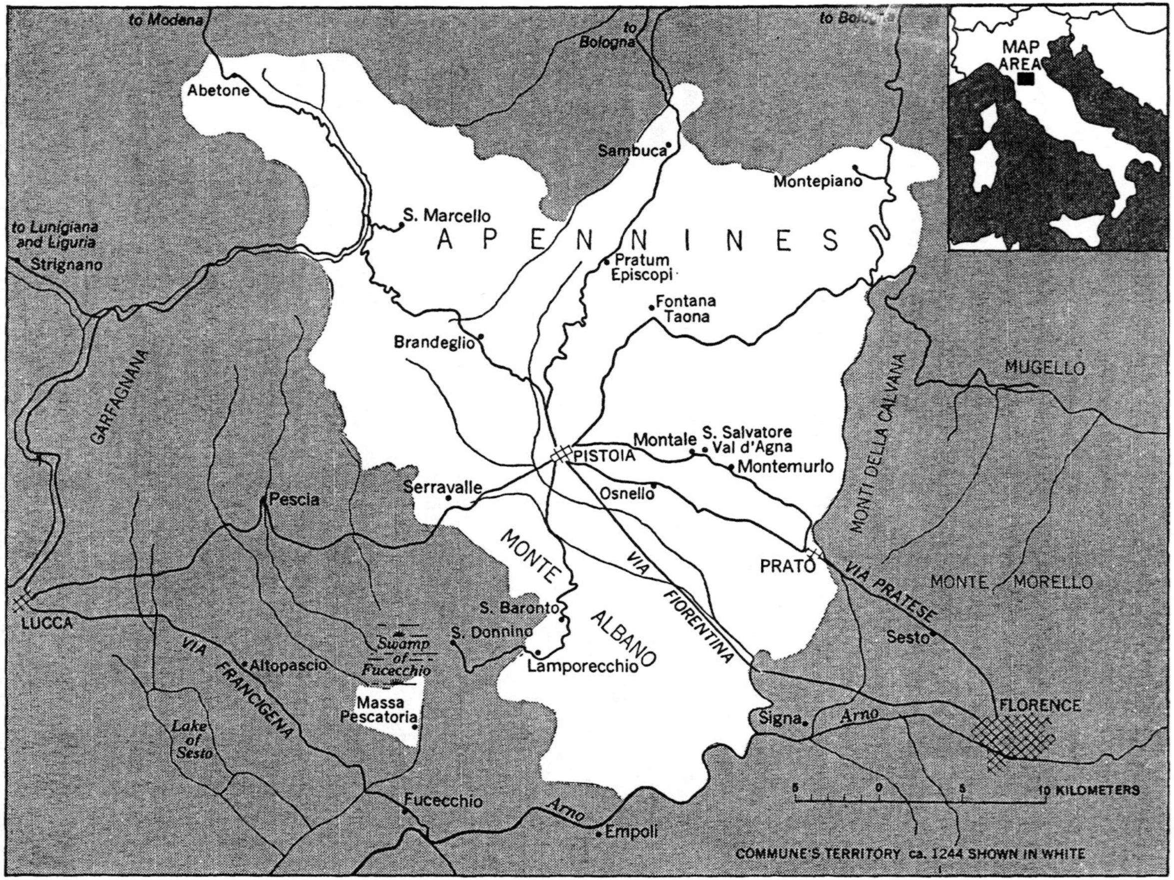

Principal Roads of Pistoia's Countryside

passes across the high main ridge of the Apennines to Lombardy, two passes across the Monte Albano to the lower Valdarno, and the low road across the middle Arno plain to Florence.[17]

Of the three Apennine passes, one led from Pistoia to the Lombard town of Modena. Leaving the city at the northwest gate, the Porta Sant'Andrea or Porta al Borgo, it followed the course of the Brandeglio torrent into the mountains to the castles of Popiglio, Mammiano and San Marcello, the last of which was the real capital of the Pistoiese Apennines. The traveller wishing to cross the mountains then moved up the course of the Lima river, over the main ridge near Abetone, and descended to Modena on the flat Po plain.

Over approximately this route in 217 B.C. the conquering Hannibal had brought his men and his elephants to the plain of the middle Arno, only to watch his great beasts sicken and die in the unhealthy atmosphere produced by the river's then extensive swamps.[18] The route seems active even in Lombard times; one of Pistoia's oldest rural monasteries, San Salvatore at Fanano, had been built along its course before 750.[19] Over this pass, in the twelfth century, the great Lombard monastery of Nonantola brought rents from its Tuscan properties, and by the thirteenth century merchants were following.[20]

But this historic route of soldiers, monks and merchants was also one of the higher mountain passes and, beyond San Marcello, led the traveller through a long and rugged stretch of thinly settled mountain land. By the late thirteenth century it seems important not as a route to Lombardy but principally as an entrance to the mountain valleys of the Lima and the Serchio. This latter region, in the territory of Lucca, was known as the Garfagnana and was famed for its many sheep and abundant supplies of wool. In Pistoia's

17. These six principal roads are all mentioned in the *Statutum potestatis* (1296), V, cap. 12, p. 275, "De stratis custodiendis." The three Apennine passes are there called the "strata de hospitali crucis Brandeline unde veniunt Carfagnini," the "strata de Sambuca" and the "strata de Fonte Taonis." The two roads across the Monte Albano are the "strata de Serravalle" and the "strata de San Barunto." The road to Florence is the "strata hospitalis de Hosnello."

18. According to the account of Livy, *Historiae*, XXI, 58 and XXII, 1–3. Cf. the use made of this story by G. Villani, *Cronica*, I, cap. 43 (I, p. 64).

19. A. Chiappelli, "L'Età longobarda," p. 254.

20. G. Tiraboschi, *Storia dell' augusta badia di S. Silvestro di Nonantola* (Modena, 1784), I, 387 ff.

Statutes of 1296 this road is called the route "whence come the Garfagnini."[21] Significantly, according to these same Statutes, the "merchants of French merchandise" had no responsibility for its maintenance, as they had for another Apennine pass, the "strata Sambuce."[22] From the Garfagnana it was also easy to follow the Serchio down to Lucca—a longer route, but higher and healthier than the more direct way over the Monte Albano which had to rim the swamps of Fucecchio.

By the thirteenth century the most important Apennine pass leading out of Pistoia was the "via de Collina" to Bologna—the "hill road," euphemistically named for a highway which mounted to a height of over 2000 feet. By 1105 the castle of Sambuca had been built to guard it, still in the mountains but on the farther slopes toward Bologna.[23] This road was therefore also called, in recognition of the fort which held it for Pistoia, the "strata Sambuce." Over it flowed the bulk of Pistoia's trade not only with Lombardy but with France as well.

A third, more tortuous way across the mountains was the "strata de Fonte Taonis." After leaving Pistoia from the northeast gate, the Porta Guidi, it swung to the east, over the high Monte La Croce, then came down into the upper valley of the Bisenzio, the river which in its lower course flows past Prato. By moving up the Bisenzio, the traveller could turn northward into the mountains, across the main ridge at the pass of Montepiano, the "flat mountain," and then descend to Bologna. This route was perhaps less important as a way to Bologna than as a link with mountain valleys, with the upper Bisenzio and beyond that, with the Florentine Mugello, as the fertile upper valley of the Sieve river is called. Not only did these routes provide Pistoia ready contact with Lombardy, but they also assured the city close ties with a vast area of the interior mountains.

Of the two passes over the Monte Albano to the lower Valdarno, the shortest crossed that ridge at Serravalle, following the approximate course of the Roman Via Cassia and taking the traveller to

21. See above, n. 17.

22. *Statutum potestatis*, p. 280.

23. The castle of Sambuca is mentioned in the papal privilege of 1105, *PL*, CLXIII, 177.

Pescia and Lucca. The second road, which served as Pistoia's principal link with the great port city of Pisa, moved south from the city along the base of the Monte Albano, then climbed over the ridge at San Baronto to take the traveller past the castle of Lamporecchio to San Donnino on the shores of the swamp of Fucecchio. There boats awaited him, to take him by water over the swamp and down the Arno to Pisa. This important route attracted much attention from the commune in the thirteenth century, which tried to assure that the canals would be clear and the ports open to assure easy passage to Pisa.[24] To the east, the road to Prato and Florence also repeated the course of the Roman Via Cassia, although to avoid the swampy plain it seems to have initially kept more closely than the Roman road to the base of the well-drained mountains.[25] By the late thirteenth century new and more direct routes to Prato and Florence had been constructed, which moved straight across the plain and give proof of better conditions of drainage upon it.[26]

It would be hard to exaggerate the influence of these six great highways on the formation of the diocese, or perhaps better, on the continuing association of certain rural areas with the city. Communications are the soul of any administrative system, and their importance was recognized even in the early Middle Ages. These routes, for example, all but dictated the location of the largest rural monasteries and hospitals, which in turn helped keep them open and passable even in a tumultuous age.[27]

Thus, the mountain road to San Marcello and Modena was main-

24. In 1273 the commune undertook extensive improvements on the "ports" of Cerbaia and San Donnino, on the shores of the swamp of Fucecchio beyond the Monte Albano. See *Breve populi*, p. 83.

25. The Statutes of ca. 1200 (*Statuti*, ed. Berlan, cap. 166, p. 11) mention a "passagium, quod tollitur apud Montemurlum." The fact that this toll—the only one described in the Statutes—was collected at Montemurlo suggests that the road to Prato and Florence then followed the base of the mountains and did not, as the Via Cassia, move directly across the plain through Agliana (see above, n. 12).

26. See below, p. 51, nn. 70 and 71. This successful road building on the plain constitutes a principal part of what J. Plesner called a "road revolution." See his study of Florentine roads in "Una Rivoluzione stradale nel dugento," *Acta Jutlandica*, I (1938).

27. On the contribution made by Pistoia's rural hospitals to "viability" during the early Middle Ages, see L. Chiappelli, "Per la storia della viabilità nell' alto medioevo," *BSP*, 28 (1926), pp. 88 ff.

tained by the hospital of Crux Brandelliana, which also gave its name to the route, and still higher in the mountains, by San Salvatore at Fanano, founded as early as 750.[28] Also high in the mountains, along the direct road to Bologna, stood the hospital of Pratum Episcopi, the "Bishop's Meadow," first mentioned in 1090.[29] The monastery of Sanctus Salvator de Fonte Taonis, founded not long before the year 1000, protected and gave its name to the third important mountain pass leading to the valley of the upper Bisenzio.[30] Farther along this route to Bologna, another monastery, Sancta Maria, stood near the pass of Montepiano leading over the mountains to the Lombard plain.[31]

Along the road to Pisa, several hospitals and monasteries aided the traveller, giving testimony to the antiquity and importance of this link with the sea: at Quarrata at the base of the Monte Albano; at San Baronto high atop the ridge (built 610); and at Cerbaia on the opposite slopes where travellers embarked by *navicelle,* small boats or barges, across the swamp of Fucecchio.[32]

The oldest road to Prato was also supported by the monastery of San Salvatore all'Agna and the later, more direct route by the "Little Hospital," the Spedalino at Osnello, which also gave its name to the road.[33]

28. The hospital of Crux Brandelliana is mentioned in the bull of Urban II in 1090, *PL,* CLI, 317–18. On Fanano, see above, n. 19.

29. Also first mentioned in the bull of Urban II cited in the preceding note. On the history of this hospital, see Q. Santoli, "Pratum Episcopi," *BSP, 18* (1916), 1–33, who incorrectly dates the bull 1089.

30. The monastery had been richly endowed by the Margrave Boniface of Tuscany, and its possessions were confirmed by Emperor Henry II in 1014, *MGH, Die Urkunden der deutschen Könige und Kaiser,* III (Hanover, 1900–03), no. 296, p. 362.

31. The charters of this monastery have been published in *Le Carte del monastero di S. Maria di Montepiano (1000–1200),* ed. R. Piattoli, RCI, 30 (Rome, 1942).

32. The hospital of "Sanctus Ambrosius de Quarrata" is mentioned in the papal privilege of 1090, *PL,* CLI, 317. San Baronto, one of the oldest of Pistoia's rural monasteries, apparently dating from the early seventh century (Salvi, *Historie,* I, 27), was under the patronage and protection of the commune according to the Statutes of ca. 1200 (*Statuti,* ed. Berlan, cap. 19, p. 26, "de possessionibus . . . s. Barunti"). The commune purchased the rights of patronage over the hospital of San Donnino at Cerbaia in 1235, *Liber censuum,* no. 299, p. 205, 28 May 1235.

33. The monastery of San Salvatore is mentioned by 1098, *Libro croce,* no.

The six roads, maintained by these many hospitals and monasteries, provided the skeleton about which the early medieval diocese acquired its fixed and permanent form. As the imperial grant of 998 reveals, the core of the diocese was the city of Pistoia, its surrounding plain, and the mountains that rimmed it.[34] Within the plain, the bishop's territory extended in the direction of Florence to include Prato on the lower Bisenzio. This grant of 998 in fact contains the first documentary references to settlement at Prato, and the inclusion within his diocese of this strategic castle along the Florentine road gave Pistoia's bishop jurisdiction over more than half of the Florentine plain.[35]

In the direction of Lucca, the bishop of Pistoia in 998 owned a court at Pescia, although the court disappears from later charters and Pescia itself eventually came to be included within the diocese of Lucca.

A more remarkable instance of the prolongation of the diocese along the course of principal routes leading out from the city involves the mountain frontier with Bologna. In 998 Pistoia's bishop owned the "villa" of Pavana, located well beyond the Apennine watershed along the principal road to Bologna. This area remained permanently a part of Pistoia's territory, in spite of repeated wars fought by the bishop and commune of Bologna to gain its possession.

Another, perhaps even more striking indication of the influence of principal roads on the shape of the diocese concerns the route to Pisa, which crossed the Monte Albano at San Baronto and took the

---

128, p. 328, Sept. 1098, "terra Sancti Salvatoris sito Angna." The hospital of Osnello stood on the border between the plain communes of Montale and Agliana. See *Liber focorum*, p. 335, for mention of it in 1259.

34. See above, n. 15.

35. The pieve "de Burgo" mentioned in the grant of 998 is apparently the later pieve of Sanctus Stefanus de Prato (*Tuscia*, I, no. 1212), called "de Burgo Cornio." Sanctus Paulus in the charter seems to have been the pieve of Sanctus Paulus de Petriccio (ibid. I, no. 1229) near Prato. Sanctus Ipolitus que vocatur Uisia is certainly the Pratese pieve of S. Ippolito "de Visia," (S. Ypoliti in Piaçanese, ibid. no. 1271). Sanctus Iustus in the charter seems to be the pieve of Sanctus Iustus in Piazanesi (ibid. I, no. 1234) on the plain of Prato. For Prato in the Middle Ages, especially the thirteenth century, see R. Caggese, *Un Comune libero alle porte di Firenze nel secolo XIII, Prato in Toscana. Studi e richerche* (Florence, 1905).

traveller to the shores of Fucecchio. If natural obstacles effectively determined the boundaries of the diocese, the ridge of the Monte Albano, or the wide swamp of Fucecchio, would have been for Pistoia an obvious frontier. But in 998 Pistoia included within its diocese not only the eastern edge of the swamp, but a *pieve* or baptismal church on its western side too, Massa Pescatoria or Massarella.[36] The pieve was separated from its episcopal church by distance, swamp and mountain. But it also lay along the principal route from Pistoia to Pisa, and this would seem to explain its association with the former city. Later in the Middle Ages, the bishop of Lucca was able to acquire the temporal sovereignty and then the spiritual jurisdiction over Fucecchio and its marshes.[37] Massarella remained part of Pistoia's diocese, but was then entirely cut off from its main body by Lucchese lands. Still, the fact that this remote pieve was traditionally tied to Pistoia shows the ancient importance of this route to Pisa, and Pistoia's own ancient responsibility for it.

The episcopal government of the early Middle Ages, the road system it helped support, thus preserved Pistoia's strong links with the high Apennines and the Monte Albano. The bishops also bequeathed to the new, free commune a functioning communications system, which greatly facilitated the extension of its jurisdiction in the countryside. The shape and size of the medieval contado, and even the speed with which it was built, owed much to the effort of Pistoia's earlier rulers, the medieval bishops and perhaps also the Romans before them, to maintain for the city good communications within and through the difficult areas which surrounded it.

THE TERRITORY OF THE FREE COMMUNE, 1105–1351

Consuls at the head of a free commune are mentioned for the first time at Pistoia in 1105, although the commune itself had probably been formed sometime during the last decades of the eleventh century (the earliest known communes, those of Lucca and Pisa, appear

36. Called "de Massa" in the charter of 998, it was still a pieve in 1276–77, *Tuscia*, I, no. 1341, plebes S. Marie de Massa Piscatoria.

37. The lands of Fucecchio passed under the control of the bishop of Lucca with the extinction of the Cadolinghi in 1113. See R. Davidsohn, "Die Kadolinger-Erbschaft," *Forschungen*, I, 83–91.

in 1081).[38] In the Statutes of 1107 Pistoia's consuls are described as ruling a "district" consisting of the city and the land around it to the distance of four miles.[39]

Beyond this original nucleus of territory, the new free commune confronted in the countryside a maze of multifarious and competitive jurisdictions. The *comitatus* or county, first mentioned in 877, had been established by the Carolingian rulers, who had given it the same boundaries as the diocese.[40] But Carolingian rule was short-lived, and the unity of administration, if it had ever been achieved, disintegrated in the chaos of the tenth century.

Of the lords in the countryside facing the free commune, the most important by far was the bishop. His temporalities included a score of courts and villages, and it can be estimated that about 30 per cent of the rural population were at one time his *fideles* or serfs.[41] Three great families of lay counts—the Guidi, Alberti and Cadolinghi—also owned extensive lands in the countryside, but their holdings appear to have been concentrated in the thinly settled areas of the low Fucecchio marshes and the high mountains.[42] Probably not more than 10 per cent of the rural population were ever the serfs of these great noble houses.[43]

38. The earliest document mentioning consuls at Pistoia is in the *Libro croce*, no. 11, p. 350, August 1105, "presentia . . . Bonecti et Placiti et Detisalvi et Gerardi consulum. . . ." On the development of communes in Italy, see most recently H. van Werveke, "The Rise of the Towns," *CEH*, III, especially pp. 24 ff.

39. *Statuti*, ed. Berlan, cap. I, p. 1.

40. The first mention of a "comitatus pistoriensis" is in a bull of Pope John VIII in 877, conceding to the bishop of Arezzo the property of the monastery of St. Thomas the Apostle, Jaffé, *Regesta*, no. 3110, 13 Aug. 877. Cf. Paolini, *Pistoia*, p. 10.

41. The imperial charter of 998 lists as the bishop's property the principal market place of Pistoia, two villas, 19 courts, one mountain and 19 pievi. *MGH, Urkunden Otto des III*, no. 284, p. 709. In the *Liber focorum* of ca. 1244, presently to be discussed, the non-noble families settled on what were once indisputably episcopal lands totaled 2085 households, or about 29 per cent of the non-noble population.

42. The Cadolinghi became extinct in 1113. On their lands see Davidsohn, "Die Kadolinger-Erbschaft," *Forschungen*, I, 83–91. The Conti Guidi first became established in central Italy at the time of Emperor Otto I (d. 955), and the Alberti owed their extensive possessions in the Apennines to the favor of Countess Matilda of Tuscany.

43. Lands certainly the property of the Conti Guidi were Cecina (63 households in the *Liber focorum*), Larciano (199 households), and Montale (113

At the birth of the commune, the larger part of the county's lands seem to have fallen under the jurisdiction of petty nobles, variously called *valvassores, cattani, castellani* or *lambardi.*[44] They seem to have been a numerous group and probably a growing one; it is not too much to say that this tumultuous class of petty lords gives to Italian feudal society its most distinctive stamp.

From about the year 1000 there appear among these petty nobles numerous associations, which functioned as corporate lords or collective seigneuries, owning lands and exercising jurisdiction over the people living upon them. Many were consorteries or family associations, but there were also societies of "Lombards" which were clearly based upon agreement rather than upon blood and inheritance.[45] The free commune in the city, which was also a kind of collective seigneury, bears many resemblances to these rural associations, though the urban commune was from its origins socially and constitutionally a much more complex institution.

From about 1100 to 1250 the free commune of Pistoia succeeded in imposing its superior jurisdiction over all these motley rural powers, and was able to push the limits of its authority almost, though not entirely, to the frontiers of the diocese. This process can be studied with some precision at Pistoia, which possesses the oldest communal statutes in Tuscany as well as a rich collection of acts involving the commune, preserved in its *Liber censuum.*

---

households). The Alberti held Castellione vallis Bisentii (34 households), Montecastellione et Codelupo (35), Usella (11), and Capraria (5). This makes a total of 460 families, or about 6.5 per cent of the contado's population in ca. 1244. However, these great families undoubtedly owned other lands in Pistoia's territory of which we have no record.

44. On the petty nobility in the Tuscan countryside, see especially G. Volpe, "Lambardi e Romani nelle campagne e nelle città. Per la storia delle classi sociali della nazione e del Rinascimento italiano," *Studi Storici*, ed. A. Crivellucci, 13 (1904), 53–81; 167–82; 242–315; and 369–416. According to Volpe, the term "lambardus" or "lombardus" had by the eleventh century lost all racial connotations and designated members of the petty rural aristocracy. In spite of the contrary opinion of Chiappelli, "L'Età longobarda," p. 288, his arguments remain convincing.

45. See Chiappelli, "L'Età longobarda," pp. 259–66, for a list of such consorteries appearing at Pistoia and throughout Tuscany. The earliest at Pistoia is mentioned in 995 ("terra bonifatinga"; see Chiappelli, "Disegno," p. 152). On the nature of these consorteries, see especially F. Niccolai, *I Consorzi nobiliari* (Bologna, 1940).

These documents leave no doubt that the commune's line of advance in the countryside was determined by the great highways we have described, and that the commune itself was following a conscious "road policy" as it extended its power through surrounding rural areas.

Our earliest indication of the commune's enlargement of its territory comes from a provision in the statutes, dating from the late twelfth century. This provision defines the district as including not only the city and the four miles of land surrounding it, but the three hospitals of Fons Taonis, Crux Brandelliana and Sanctus Baruntus, and their properties as well.[46] As we have previously noted, two of these hospitals commanded and maintained two chief passes into and over the Apennines, and the third, San Baronto, guarded the pass over the Monte Albano to the lower Arno valley, to Fucecchio and Pisa. In declaring the possessions of these hospitals part of its district, in extending its patronage over them, the commune was also assuming responsibility for supervising the roads they protected. Like Roman Pistoia and the episcopal government before it, the free commune from its origins was following the roads and turning to the mountains. In another, still later addition to the statutes, probably to be dated at about 1200, the commune added to this list of dependent religious foundations the hospital of Pratum Episcopi, guarding the easiest route to Bologna.[47] In 1235, still pursuing lines of advance marked out by roads and hospitals, the commune purchased from the Conti Guidi the rights of patronage over San Don-

46. *Statuti*, ed. Berlan, cap. 19, p. 26, "Idem statuimus de possessionibus ecclesie de Fonte Taonis et s. Barunti et hospitalis Crucis Brandiliane, que sunt infra nostrum districtum." This redaction of the statutes, while undated, is probably not earlier than 1177, and the published version contains many later additions. See Chiappelli, "Disegno," p. 150. They are therefore usually here cited as the "Statutes of ca. 1200." Capitulum 19 quoted above, however, comes from their initial and certainly older portion. Moreover, the use of the plural "statuimus" shows that the chapter dates from the period when five consuls, rather than a single podestà, were the usual governors of the commune, probably before 1187.

47. *Statuti*, ed. Berlan, cap. 86, pp. 69–70, "habebo in protectione . . . Hoc idem faciam de ecclesia Sancti Salvatoris de Fonte Taonis et Prati Episcopi et Crucis Brandiliane et Sancti Barunti." The use of the singular "faciam" shows that this chapter was added at a time when a single podestà rather than the several consuls had become the usual head of the commune, after 1187 and probably about 1200.

nino, the hospital which, on the shores of the Fucecchio swamp, aided travellers sailing to or returning from Pisa and the sea.[48]

With control of the roads, the city commune could exert a mounting pressure upon the lords, Lombard associations and communes of the countryside. According to a passage in the statutes, again probably dating from about 1200, the consul or *podestà* was authorized to require from any rural noble he saw fit an oath to take up residence in the city and in effect to submit to its jurisdiction.[49] The commune did not seek to abolish the older authorities in the countryside so much as to establish its own superior jurisdiction over them. By the early thirteenth century the commune was successfully demanding taxes, soldiers and services (the last significantly required for the maintenance of roads) from rural communes in apparent disregard of the wishes of the lord whose serfs these rural peoples might have happened to be.[50]

The lords in the countryside offered only sporadic resistance to the commune's growing pretensions. In 1203 the commune dislodged by force count Guido Guerra, of the Conti Guidi, from the strategic castle of Montemurlo, but in 1204 Guido and his Florentine allies retook the castle.[51] In 1208 Pistoia was forced to make peace with Guido, who later sold Montemurlo to the Florentines. This effectively blocked the commune's advance down the road to Prato and Florence. In 1226 the commune purchased the castle of Larciano from the Conti Guidi and in 1240 an extensive area of the upper Bisenzio valley from the Conti Alberti.[52]

The greatest lord in the countryside, the bishop himself, offered somewhat more determined opposition. In 1138, in one of the earliest instances of a dispute between a bishop and a free com-

48. *Liber censuum,* no. 299, p. 205, 28 May 1235.

49. *Statuti,* ed. Berlan, cap. 123, p. 88, "Nobiles homines Pistorii districtus qui videbuntur mihi convenientes et idonei, faciam iurare habiturium civitatis Pistorii sine fraude."

50. In 1221, in a dispute between the bishop and the commune concerning the jurisdiction over the castles of Batoni and Lamporecchio, a witness for the bishop admitted that the communal officials had been demanding all these things "for the past sixty years," but he claimed that it was done by force and "contra ius episcopi." *Liber censuum,* no. 133, p. 106, May to Sept. 1221.

51. Davidsohn, *Geschichte,* I, 646.

52. *Liber censuum,* no. 269, pp. 190–91, 23 Nov. 1226. Ibid. no. 323, p. 217, 16 Sept. 1240.

mune, Atto, the Spanish bishop of Pistoia later honored as a saint, excommunicated the city consuls for despoiling the church of its treasures.[53] This probably indicates an early communal effort to tax ecclesiastical property. In 1226 the bishop of Pistoia, angered by a riot of his own fideles against him at Lamporecchio, which he felt had been condoned if not instigated by the city, excommunicated the podestà and demanded satisfaction.[54] An extensive inquest was held, the instructive record of which has survived, to determine who indeed was lord of the troubled castle of Lamporecchio, the bishop or the city. Most witnesses agreed that the bishop exercised seigneurial rights, *iura,* in the area, but the city commune, as long as memory served, had been collecting taxes, recruiting soldiers and demanding services. As one witness summed it up, the bishop had jurisdiction, but the city was the *domina,* the sovereign.[55] The commune's claim to possess a higher sovereignty over the land was impressing even peasants.

The commune thus extended its power in the countryside by exerting a close supervision over principal roads and by imposing a higher jurisdiction over rural lords, whom it did not otherwise deprive of their prerogatives. The first clear reference to the effective extent of the city's authority in the countryside is contained in a provision in the statutes which probably dates from the early thirteenth century.[56] Into the mountains the city's territory extended as far as Sambuca; to the west toward Lucca the Nievole river served as the boundary. To the south the territory included the pievi of Seiano and San Martino in Campo, which meant that the entire length of the Monte Albano belonged to Pistoia. To the east toward Florence, Montemurlo marked the frontier with Prato.

Sometime about 1244, the commune of Pistoia undertook to count

53. See the "Sancti Attonis episcopi pistoriensis excommunicatio in consules pistorienses," in Zaccaria, *Anecdota,* pp. 211–12, and the letter of Pope Innocent II to the commune in support of Atto, "Super iniuria," *PL,* CLXXIX, 376 (Jaffé, *Regesta,* no. 7917).

54. *Liber censuum,* no. 133, p. 106, May to Sept. 1221.

55. Loc. cit., cited in this chapter's heading.

56. *Statuti,* ed. Berlan, cap. 143, p. 98, "Nullum permittam ducatum prestare alicui foretano, nisi illis, quibus Consules vel Potestas inposuerint pro Communi, a civitate Pistoria ad castrum Sambucam et ad plebem de Seiano et usque ad plebem de Lamporechio et usque ad flumen Nebuli et usque Montemurlum et usque ad ecclesiam s. Martini de Campo."

for tax purposes all the rural hearths of its territory. This *Liber focorum* or Book of Hearths, as the survey was called, has survived to serve as an impressive monument to the success of the commune's expansion and domination of its own territory.[57] The survey is uniform and nearly comprehensive; no respect is taken, in listing the taxpayers, as to who might be the lord over them or their lands.[58] Nor is there any distinction made between freemen and serfs. All commoners were equal, for they were all equally taxpayers. The survey did count and record the names of nobles separately from those of commoners, and presumably some tax concessions were conceded them. But the city retained the right to determine who should be considered nobles, who they were and how many. This already was a challenge to noble privilege; real exemption is assured only for those whose names never appear on a tax role.

At the time of the redaction of the Book of Hearths, Pistoia's boundary within the Florentine plain followed the Agna river to the Calice, along the Calice to the Ombrone, and down the Ombrone to the Arno. It then followed the Arno downstream through the gap of Capraia as far as Castellina, where it swung north along the base of the Monte Albano. It passed and included the castles of Lamporecchio, Larciano and Cecina, but left to Lucca the hilltop fortresses of Montecatini, Monsummano and Montevettolini. Within the mountains, Pistoia's territory extended over a still wider area, from Monte Verruca and Monte Battifolle in the west to the upper Bisenzio valley in the east, penetrating into the mountains as far as the watershed and, at Sambuca, even beyond.

In two directions, however, the commune of Pistoia had failed to attain the limits of the diocese, and both areas were on the plain. Toward Florence, in 1204 the Conti Guidi and the Florentine commune had stopped Pistoia's advance at Montemurlo, and that stra-

57. On the date and nature of the *Liber focorum*, see below, pp. 58–61.

58. The one significant omission from the survey was the commune of Sambuca. According to Salvi, *Historie*, I, 309, Pistoia purchased Sambuca from Filippo Vergiolesi only in 1311, and this probably explains its omission in the earlier survey. It should be noted, however, that both the podestà and the bishop of Pistoia received oaths of loyalty from the men of Sambuca in 1212 and 1256 respectively (see below, p. 57, n. 5), but it would appear that the prerogative to tax the castle was left in the hands of the Vergiolesi.

tegic castle does not appear in the survey of ca. 1244. Pistoia, in other words, never extended its temporal jurisdiction over the *terra Prati*, the "land of Prato," though the area remained part of its diocese. To the west toward Lucca, Massarella on the farther shore of the Fucecchio swamp, while also part of the diocese, never came under the commune's temporal control.

While never attaining the full extent of the diocese, Pistoia's district still included half the mountainous rim encircling the Florentine plain, and this gave Pistoia a large measure of control over passage in and out of this important area. Three cities—Lucca, Bologna and Florence—were vitally interested in these entries and exits, and against all three Pistoia had to fight recurrent and exhausting wars.

Remarkably, the small city was able pretty well to preserve the integrity of its territory until the early fourteenth century. Then in 1329, following a desperate struggle with Castruccio Castracane, lord of Lucca, which had almost cost them their freedom, the Florentines forced Pistoia to yield to them the southern third of the Monte Albano.[59] These were the lands which in 1244 made up the communes of Carmignano, Artimino, Castellina, Vitolini, Baccareto and Capraia.

In 1351 Pistoia fell permanently under Florentine hegemony, and we shall leave to a later chapter a consideration of the methods by which Florence ruled its now dependent city.[60] Our interest here is the shaping of the city's territory. Paradoxically, Florentine power helped protect Pistoia and preserve its frontiers. After 1329 Pistoia suffered no further major losses of its territory, although it had its own loss of freedom to thank for this.

Over long centuries stretching back to Roman times, Pistoia, guardian of roads and passes, thus acquired and retained its largely mountainous inheritance. It remains to consider the wealth and the liabilities which accompanied this rugged legacy.

59. Cf. *Capitoli*, I. 3, p. 5, peace of 24 May 1329. In 1336 the inhabitants of these lands were declared citizens of the Florentine contado, ASF, Provv. Tomus 27, 80r, 5 June 1336.

60. See below, chapter 8, pp. 214–31.

2

The Land and Its Resources

Involano i suoi Monti il pregio a' Colli,
E i suoi Colli a le Valli, e le sue Valli
De' Campi Elisi son più ameni e molli.
E' fiumi son più chiari di cristalli.
Ovunque l'occhio a lei d'intorno estolli,
Vedi far sponda a' suoi fioriti calli,
Bacco e Pomona, ed i suoi Campi tutti
Render selvosi ogni hor piante di frutti.

Her mountains rob the prize from the hills,
And her hills from the valleys, and her valleys
Are more pleasant and delicate than the Elysian Fields.
And her streams are clearer than crystals.
Wherever you raise your eye around her,
You see Bacchus and Pomona
Making a rim for her flowered paths, and all her fields
Render every hour plants of sylvan fruit.

—Scipion Francucci, describing Pistoia, 1624

Among the towns and territories of medieval Tuscany, Pistoia and its contado have this distinction: no other Tuscan city possessed, in so compact an area, such contrasting terrain, ranging from high and rugged mountains to flat and fertile plain. And probably no other Tuscan contado reveals, in so compact an area, such varieties in the economic activities and in the social and cultural traditions of its people.

Pistoia's medieval territory at its maximum extent measured about 900 square kilometers (about 347 square miles). Of these 900 square kilometers, about 460, or more than half, consisted of high hills and mountains, lands over 500 meters in height. Some 270 square kilometers, or about 30 per cent of the territory, comprised what we shall call the middle hills, largely between 200 and 500 meters in elevation. The area of the plain and low hills (roughly between 50 and 200 meters high) constituted about 170 square kilometers, or less than 20 per cent of the total.[1]

These three regions differed considerably in the natural resources they possessed, and they also reveal, even in the Middle Ages, great contrasts in the phasing and rhythm of their economic development. To understand that phasing and rhythm is first to consider the factors which, in each of these three regions, facilitated or obstructed the exploitation of its wealth. And some note must also be taken of the contributions which geographic location made, and the obstacles it presented, to the development of commerce and industry within the city.

THE MOUNTAINS

The mountains of Pistoia, which constituted more than half its medieval territory, include some of the highest and most forbidding stretches of the Apennines. Life within this rugged terrain impressed even the men of the Middle Ages as hard, crude and unrewarding. According to Pietro de' Crescenzi, a Bolognese author who wrote on agriculture not long after 1300, mountain conditions helped convey health and a long life, but mountain people were also restless, unruly, resentful of authority and given to violence.[2] Later in the fourteenth century, the Florentine author Franco Sacchetti noted how even a few possessions could make a man appear wealthy among the characteristically poor mountain residents.[3] In one of his poetic celebrations of the beauties of the Tuscan countryside, Lorenzo de' Medici the Magnificent traced the course of the

1. See below, Appendix I, for a classification of Pistoia's rural communes according to these three regions. For a recent review of Pistoia's economic resources, see C. Ciano, "Note sull'economia pistoiese antica e recente," *Pistoia e la sua provincia*, pp. 49–78, with bibliography.

2. *Opus*, I, 5. "In locis habitalibus altis morantes sunt sani et fortes, multum patientes et vivunt diu." They were also "multum vigilantes et sunt malorum morum inobedientes. . . ."

3. *Trecentonovelle*, no. 173, p. 424, in regard to residents of a mountain commune in the Bolognese Apennines, who were "secondo uomeni d'Alpi . . . assai agiati."

Ombrone river in the mountains above Pistoia. He too mentioned the "poor wealth" of highland families—precarious wealth too, which rivers like the Ombrone were apt to sweep away in their turbulent currents.[4]

The mountain societies have long retained among historians a reputation for isolation, poverty and primitiveness. L. Chiappelli, a dedicated and informed student of Pistoia's history, felt he could discern in the small, dark highlanders the purity of Roman stock, while the men of the plain bore witness in their fair complexions to the Gothic and Lombard inundations of their home.[5]

The mountains were also quite thinly settled in the early Middle Ages. Of the nineteen baptismal churches (*pievi*) listed in the charter of 998, only one, Lizzano, seems to have been located in the high mountains.[6] Even ca. 1244, the high mountains were supporting only 21 per cent of the rural families, although they included more than one-half the territory.[7]

The mountains, in other words, were late in experiencing a vigorous economic development and the growth of relatively large communities within them—the latest in fact of any region of Pistoia's medieval territory. To explain this slow and tardy development is to review the difficulties of exploiting the principal mountain resources.

In regard to agricultural commodities, the mountains were poor but not entirely unproductive. In 1427, as shown by their tax declarations, nearly all the mountain communes raised some wheat, though the rugged land and brief growing season severely limited the quantities which could be grown.[8] Under harsh conditions the raising of cereals required, to be sure, ingenious methods. Pietro de' Crescenzi, who travelled widely throughout Italy observing systems of agriculture, describes a routine of mountain cultivation which he

4. "Ambra, poemetto," stanza 21. *Opere*, ed. A. Simioni (Bari, 1913), I, 296, in which Lorenzo describes a mountain family watching their "poor wealth" swept away in the mountain torrent.

5. "L'Età longobarda," p. 254, n. 3.

6. See above, Chapter 1, n. 15.

7. See below, Table 1, p. 70.

8. The mountain communes are surveyed in ASF, Catasto 265, Montagna di Pistoia.

had probably himself seen practiced in the Apennines.[9] In mountain woods, the limbs of trees would be cut, dried and burned, and the ash broken with a mattock and scattered on the ground. Rye, which could mature quickly in the brief growing season, was then sown, and "it comes forth excellently that year." The grass of mountain meadows could be similarly burned, turned under and rye planted in the charred earth. After the harvest, such fields would be abandoned for seven or more years, to allow the natural vegetation to be replenished. Then the routine could be repeated.

Cereals could be raised in the mountains, though only with difficulty and never in large amounts. In place of wheat, perhaps the most important food in the highlands was the fruit of forests: chestnuts, which along with nuts (*noci*) and acorns (*ghiande*) could be gathered in substantial quantities and were essential to the mountain diet. A widow in 1427, for example, consumed each year six staia of wheat and six of chestnuts. She was clearly a lady of fairly comfortable means, and poorer people undoubtedly ate less of the expensive wheat.[10] So important were chestnuts that a failure of the harvest, which several times occurred in the fourteenth century, brought black hunger to the mountain communes.[11] In 1569 G. B. Tedaldi estimated the harvest of white, dried chestnuts at 100,000 staia.[12] A century later, another estimate set the volume of chestnuts gathered and ground into flour at 300,000 staia per year, not including those eaten fresh.[13] This amount could have fed for a year over 25,000 inhabitants of the mountains, and probably did support nearly that number, as chestnuts did not acquire much commercial importance and were not exported in substantial quantities.

9. *Opus*, Liber III, capo 22, "De siligine." Cf. Jones, "Lineamenti," p. 317.

10. ASF, 265, 659r, declaration of mona Buona che fu di Ghuasparre of the commune of Calamecca. Buona's total assessment was 30 florins, fairly high for a mountain community. In the Catasto, the price for an omina or staio of green chestnuts was only 4 solidi, while a like amount of wheat was worth 15. White and dried chestnuts went for more—8 solidi—but there is little evidence of commercial interest in them.

11. ASP, Provv. Tomus 8, 31v, 16 Jan. 1333, the mountain communes of Popiglio and Crespoli were granted tax immunity "propter temporis asperitatem et defectum castanearum." Ibid. Tomus 19, 35v, 3 March 1346, the "communia vallis Furforis districtus Pistorii, videlicet Cresporis, Serre, Calamecche et Lanciolis" granted immunity for the same reason.

12. "Relazione," p. 318.

13. Salvi, *Historie*, Appendice, p. 69.

Able to supply its people with meal of some sort, the highlands were less able to provide those other staples of the Tuscan diet, oil and wine. To judge from the tax declarations of 1427, the commune of Popiglio, at 523 meters altitude, was already too high for olives.[14] Between 600 and 700 meters, grapes too could no longer withstand the rigorous climate. In 1427, vineyards were still found at Lanciole (601 meters), Crespoli (671 meters) and even Calamecca (693 meters), but not at San Marcello (623 meters) or Cutigliano (670 meters).

The mountaineers sorely missed adequate supplies of grapes and wine, so much so that they frequently descended to lower altitudes, to rob the vineyards of their more favored neighbors. The well-informed Pietro de' Crescenzi mentions a grape much cultivated by Pistoia's vintners for its bitter taste, which discouraged theft by the mountain people.[15] In 1428 the bishop of Pistoia sought to deduct from his tax assessment the costs of guarding a vineyard against forays by mountaineers.[16] As late as 1546, the city Statutes, "noting that in the higher mountains of the city of Pistoia they do not harvest grapes," ordered "that mountaineers do not enter any vineyard of any citizen."[17]

This then would seem to be the most distinctive feature of mountain agriculture, which helps make understandable the region's tardy growth. Agriculture in the highlands could not readily or adequately supply the staples of the Tuscan diet. Mountain communities could not therefore be easily self-sufficient, unless their people were willing to subsist on chestnut meal, with little wheat, oil or wine. But in the early Middle Ages, with poor and unreliable means of transport, a degree of self-sufficiency was essential for a community's survival. To grow, mountain settlements had to wait

14. ASF, Catasto 265, 434r and ff.

15. *Opus*, Liber IV, capo 4, "Item est uva que vocatur affricogna que non est delectabilis ad edendum. . . . Et ideo precipue competit in locis ubi homines uvas invadunt et he due species apud Pistorium pre ceteris diliguntur."

16. ASF, Catasto 189, Beni ecclesiastici, 65r. The vineyard, which was "in luogho molto foresto et insu la strada de' montanini" had to be guarded from the middle of August to the grape harvest in late September.

17. *Statuta* (1546), p. 142, "Quod montanini non intrent aliquam vineam alicuius civis." The preamble reads "Advertentes quod in montanea superiori civitatis Pistorii non recolliguntur uvae, et propterea montanini maxima damna inferunt in vineis comitatus Pistorii. . . ."

upon the prior development of the lowlands, and the establishment of an active exchange with them.

Contact with the lowlands, trade with them, were prerequisite for the development of the richest mountain resources: meadows, lumber, water power and metallurgy.

Potentially the greatest source of wealth in the mountains were the large flocks of animals which might be grazed on extensive upland meadows. In spite of a brief growing season, rain in the mountains, more plentiful than on the plain, enabled grass to grow quickly and abundantly. As the Catasto of 1427 shows, many of these meadows were productive and valuable enough to be enclosed and regularly harvested by mountain families.[18] It is not unusual to find mountain meadows valued, for their productivity, at 20 florins and more. Besides these private meadows, many mountain communes also owned extensive public pastures, upon which, for a fee, men could graze their animals.[19] In 1569 G. B. Tedaldi estimated the number of sheep and goats—"bestie minute da figliare" he called them—in Pistoia's contado at 26,000, and these were principally in the mountains.[20]

In supporting the small animals, these mountain meadows were best exploited through systems of transhumance, that is, through summer grazing in the uplands and winter feeding on the plain. Many such systems were possible at Pistoia. Small flocks, several hundred head in size, need be taken no farther than Pistoia's own lowland areas.[21] But large flocks, which might number 4000 head or more, could not be kept too easily near the intensively cultivated fields surrounding the city.[22] A longer route, avoiding areas of in-

18. ASF, Catasto 265, 2v (commune of Cutigliano), a "prato" which yearly returned 30 some of hay was assessed at 21 florins 8 sol. 9 den. Ibid. 25v, another "prato" returned yearly 40 some, and was assessed at 28 florins 11 sol. 9 den.

19. Ibid. 149r, the "beni del popolo di San Michele a Coricella," included a "quantità di boschi atti a pastura." Ibid. 523r, the "università e commune di Pupiglio" received each year 13 florins as "entrata di pastura."

20. "Relazione," pp. 318–19.

21. ASF, Not. I 85, 29 July 1358, the "pastura Serravallis," feeding 400 sheep from 1 Oct. to middle May, was sold for 20 florins. Z 80, 9 Nov. 1411, 200 "bestie" were to be pastured on the public lands of Santomato, from November to March, for 8 florins.

22. ASP, 18 April 1361, gabella paid to the commune for 4000 "bestias minutas."

tensive agriculture, led down from the mountains along the Lima and the Serchio rivers to the Tyrrhenian shore near Lucca. Still longer, and ultimately more important, was the route which led down from Pistoia's mountains, across the Arno at Fucecchio, through the Sienese contado, finally bringing the flocks to winter pasture along the marshy and thinly settled Sienese Maremma.[23]

This large-scale transhumance obviously could not be organized within the confines of single, isolated, self-sufficient communities. It required complicated negotiations with the many communes through the territories of which the sheep were taken. In 1427, for example, two brothers were simultaneously in debt to the commune of Cutigliano in the Apennines and to the city of Siena "per paschi."[24] Large-scale transhumance further required substantial advances in money, to equip the shepherds with horses and implements, to pay them their not inconsiderable salaries, to buy rights of pasture and often to purchase young animals.[25] The intensive exploitation of these rich mountain meadows required, in other words, the cooperation of lowland communes, often the aid of lowland capital and ultimately the promise of lowland markets.

Larger animals, cattle and horses, could be maintained for the entire year in the mountain valleys, supported by their abundant fodder. Herds of 70 or 80 head are not unusual in the tax declarations of 1427.[26] In Tedaldi's estimate of 1569, the countryside was feeding more than 2000 "bestie grosse" as well as 1110 pairs of oxen for plowing.[27] Many of these animals were kept in the mountains. An aphorism, which a seventeenth-century description has preserved, had it that "as many barrels of wine the plain of Pistoia

23. ASF, Not. B 2811 (6), 11 March 1417, sale of wool "de pecudibus quas dictus Paulus habet in marittima Senarum." The *Statutum potestatis* (1296), p. 173, already refers to "bestias euntes et redeuntes de Maremma."

24. ASF, Catasto 265, 73v, declaration of Pace e Pagholo di Simone.

25. ASF, Catasto 265, 66r, the salary of one shepherd guarding 225 sheep for one year was 12 florins. See also ibid. 414r, a "chavalla la quale tengho insulla dette pechore," worth 7 florins, needed to guard 200 sheep. Ibid. 419v, "sei chavelle da boscho per portare le masserize delle dette pechore e per chavalchare. . . ." Ibid. 416r, a sheep owner, Vanio di Vanocio, owed salaries to eight shepherds for guarding his flocks.

26. ASF, Catasto 264, 419v (commune of Gavinana), herd of 73 vacche or cows, worth 334 florins. Ibid. 9v (Cutigliano), 80 "bestie chavaline tra pichole e grandi," worth 56 florins.

27. "Relazione," p. 318.

produces, that many barrels its mountains produce in milk."[28] But such specialized enterprise again required the support of lowland capital and the incentive of lowland markets.

The mountains were similarly well endowed with industrial raw materials. Stone and lumber, basic to the medieval building trades, were early exploited, though again under apparent incentive from the city. As early as 1107 the Statutes imposed wage limits on stone masons (*magistri petrarum*) and carpenters (*magistri legaminis*), and this concern with prices clearly shows that urban residents were important customers for these specialized artisans.[29] Whether these masters were themselves city dwellers cannot certainly be established. A *marmorarius* is mentioned in a document of 1115, apparently a rural resident, and another *marmoraio* appears among the residents of the mountain commune of Piteglio in the survey of ca. 1244.[30]

But perhaps the best illustration of this principle—that the intensive development of the richest mountain resources demanded close commercial contact with the lowlands and with the city—is Pistoia's iron industry.

By the late Middle Ages, Pistoia was widely renowned for the volume and excellence of its iron production. In the fifteenth century Giannozzo Manetti, the humanist historian of the city, felt compelled to reject as legend the common belief that Pistoia had once been named the "city of iron" because of its "gigantic" number of iron workers and "great abundance" of iron shops.[31] *Fabri* or iron workers appear in Pistoia's documents from at least 1096.[32] Wage ceilings were imposed upon them too in the Statutes of 1107, and in

28. Salvi, *Historie*, Appendice, p. 68, "onde fu ricevuto per antico dettato, che quanti barili di vino il piano di Pistoia rende, altri tanti ne fa di latte la sua Montagna, rispetto al bestiame, che essa mantiene."

29. *Statuti*, ed. Berlan, cap. XXI, p. 11, and cap. XXII, p. 12. The maximum wages to be paid to both sorts of artisans was 5 den. a day from 1 Nov. to 1 April, and 7 den. from 1 April to 1 Nov.

30. *Libro croce*, no. 26, p. 370, July 1115, Guilliccionis marmorarii. *Liber focorum*, p. 185, no. 57.

31. Manetti, Chronicon, p. 1000: "ob ingentem quamdam ferrariorum fabrorum copiam, magnamque hujusmodi, ut ita dixerim, fabricarum et officinarum abundantiam Ferri urbem aliquando cognominatam fuisse tradiderunt."

32. *Libro croce*, no. 3, p. 25, 21 June 1096. See also ibid. no. 63, p. 132, 26 Jan. 1099; no. 76, p. 153, 18 Jan. 1090 (?); no. 128, p. 238, Sept. 1098.

the survey of ca. 1244, they are second only to millers as the most important artisan group in the countryside.[33] Later, of course, the city's iron masters were to make the name of Pistoia known throughout the world through that most famous creation of their craft, the small gun named after their town, the pistol.

To support a large iron industry, Pistoia's mountains offered several resources. Most important were the extensive forests in the highlands which, in a Tuscany poorly supplied with wood, provided charcoal in abundance for smelting. Water power too, at least by the late Middle Ages, had become nearly indispensable for large-scale iron production. It was needed, for example, to help cut the lumber to be baked into charcoal; water-driven saw mills are commonly encountered in the tax declarations of 1427.[34] Water-powered iron works, *fabriche* as they were called, were also numerous in the mountains by 1427.[35] The water seems to have driven the bellows for heating the furnaces and to have powered the trip hammers for working the metal. We might add that power mills of all sorts were then functioning along the mountain streams: to grind cereals, of course, but also to grind chestnuts, crush olives and even to full cloth.[36] How long established such specialized milling had been in the mountains our sources do not reveal; their very silence suggests that wide use of water power, for purposes other than grinding grain or perhaps fulling cloth, was primarily an achievement of the fifteenth century.

The iron industry, well-supplied with fuel and power in Pistoia's mountains, still lacked a raw material which might have appeared essential to it: iron ore. This had to be taken (and was taken, in large volume) chiefly from the island of Elba off the Tyrrhenian

33. *Statuti*, ed. Berlan, cap. XXIII, p. 12, regulating prices ferrarii could charge for horseshoes and nails. For fabri in the *Liber focorum*, see pp. 37, 46, 59, 100, 104, 160, 176, 181, 185, 194, 222 and 252.

34. Cf. ASF, Catasto 265, 357r (commune of San Marcello), "un edificio d'una segha da acqua." Ibid. 345r, a "ficio di segha," 365r, "uno deficio di segha a acqua."

35. Ibid. 367v, a "fabricha d'acqua."

36. ASF, Catasto 261, 485r, "molino overo fattoio [oil press]." Ibid. 265, 669v, a "mulino da macinare chastagne posto nella Piscia" in the mountain commune of Calamecca. Ibid. 2v and 22v, "gualchiere da panni" at Cutigliano, 670 meters high. Ibid. 267v, another "mulino con una gualchiere" in the mountains near Lizzano.

shore, carried the difficult way into the mountains, then brought back as raw iron to the cities for the making of arms and tools.

The prosperity of the iron industry in the mountains required not only ore from distant areas, but capital too (among the more famous investors in the industry was, in the fifteenth century, Lorenzo de' Medici, the Magnificent).[37] Its growth further required strong markets outside the limits of Pistoia's own, relatively thinly populated territory.

The working of iron was a complex industry, and ultimately one of the most successful of those pursued in the mountains. But this industry too could only flourish with the aid of close communications with regions outside the mountains themselves, which provided it essential raw materials, capital and markets.

Without an agriculture that could readily supply its needs, with resources which, while great, could not be exploited in a milieu of isolation and self-sufficiency, the mountain economy shows a phasing or rhythm of development much different from that of the lowlands. Thinly settled in the early Middle Ages, mountain communities participated late in the great economic upsurge after the year 1000. But the mountain economy, if it was tardy in the development of its chief resources, also enjoyed a degree of immunity from the great dislocations of the fourteenth century. Over the years 1244 to 1427, in spite of numerous wars and social disturbances localized in the highlands, the population of the mountains gained relatively in importance, and the sources give the firm impression, which we shall later attempt to illustrate, that animal husbandry and iron making were enjoying considerable vigor in the fifteenth century.[38] The crisis of the fourteenth century, which brought disaster to the saturated economy of the lower hills, did not strike with similar force against the still comparatively underdeveloped economy of the mountains.

THE MIDDLE HILLS

Nearly the reverse of the mountains in the types of resources it offered was the region of the middle hills, land largely between 200

37. Cf. De Roover, *Medici Bank*, pp. 165–66.
38. See below, pp. 176 ff. and pp. 174 ff.

and 500 meters in altitude. Ca. 1244, this region included the entire Monte Albano (the *montanea inferioris* of the sources) and the middle levels of the valleys formed by the many streams—Ombrone, Brandeglio, Bura and other "children of the Apennines"—which poured down from the mountains, "seeking the way," as Lorenzo the Magnificent put it, "to their ancient father."[39] Ca. 1244 the middle hills made up about 30 per cent of Pistoia's territory, though it then contained over 40 per cent of its rural population.

For the middle hills offered several advantages which made them a region of early and soon of remarkably dense settlement.

Perhaps most important, health conditions were excellent within them. Peasants settled on the hills escaped both the harsh climate of the mountains and the "bad air," the *mala aria* or malaria of the poorly drained lowlands. Moreover, all the principal staples of the Tuscan diet—cereals, wine and oil—could be raised upon them, without the need of hard work and substantial investments in draining the land or in working it.

The soils of the middle hills were, to be sure, thin and dry, and were best worked extensively. Pietro de' Crescenzi describes a routine of hillside cultivation which was probably followed by many Pistoiesi from the earliest days of their settlement on the slopes.[40] The great risk of farming in the hills was erosion. To minimize it, some hill peasants, according to Pietro, did not even plow the slopes they were cultivating. They placed the seed upon the unbroken earth and then with a plow or mattock threw some dirt upon it.[41] They thus avoided cutting the soil deeply or even breaking up the large glebes with a mattock. This protected the field from violent rains, which might otherwise sweep down the slopes seed and earth, and "that which was sown would perish." This sort of extensive cultivation could have returned very little, but as long as the population remained small, little was required; it helped preserve the soil

39. The phrases are from Lorenzo's poem "Ambra," stanza 16, "sollecitan la via al padre antico"; and stanza 24, "nell' onde fredde d'Ombron, d'Apennino figlio." See also above, n. 4.

40. *Opus*, Liber II, capo 18, "De cultu agri montuosi et valliculosi."

41. Loc. cit. "Quidam autem subtiliori ingenio humum hanc serunt non exaratam sed duram et postquam seminata est humus evertunt eam super semina aut aratro aut ligone aut alio fossorio et non arant eam nisi semel nec conminuunt in ea magnas glebas. . . ."

and could be pursued with little investment in capital and effort. Even oxen were not needed for its practice.

For oil and wine the terrain of the hills was particularly well suited. As Pietro de' Crescenzi explained it, the high, hot and dry atmosphere of the hills added pungency and flavor to fruit of all sorts.[42] At Pistoia, olives did especially well on the western slopes of the Monte Albano facing Lucca, in the territory of the communes of Larciano and Lamporecchio. In 1569, according to Tedaldi, Pistoia's entire district was producing yearly 12,000 barrels of oil.[43] This was enough to satisfy local needs, though apparently not enough to make Pistoiese oil an export of major commercial importance.

The middle hills were even more productive in wine, which early acquired considerable commercial importance. In 1285 for example, in an effort to monopolize the wine trade, the city imposed delivery quotas on those rural communes which sold wine commercially.[44] Seven communes were ordered to deliver to the city 950 *cogna* of wine (about 7600 barrels). Four of the seven communes were in the middle hills, and they provided three fourths of the wine demanded. In 1569, still according to Tedaldi, Pistoia's territory was producing 215,000 barrels every year, and again the middle hills probably produced the larger part of it.[45] Of this volume, 65,000 barrels were exported to Prato and Florence, to the great profit, says Tedaldi, of Pistoia's vintners.

Wine from the hills was not only abundant; it was also good. In the Catasto of 1427 hill wine was valued at 26 solidi per barrel, almost twice the worth (14 solidi) of wine from the plain. In later centuries, the contrast in value between plain and hill wines seems to have grown even greater.[46]

42. Loc. cit. "Ex his ergo animadvertendum est quod quecumque plante aromaticos et calidos et siccos habent fructus has magis congruit in montibus plantari. . . ."

43. "Relazione," pp. 318–19.

44. See the "Consilium de ordinamentis canevarum et vini vendendi rubrica," Nov. 1285, in the *Breve populi*, Appendix I. The imposts in cogna of wine were: Serravalle, 200; Carmignano, 300; Montale, 150; Marliana, 50; Artimino, 100; Casore, 50; and Baccareto, 100.

45. "Relazione," p. 318.

46. Cf. R. G. Rosati, "Notizie sopra la città di Pistoia nel 1759 raccolte dal Colonello O'Kelley," *BSP*, 15 (1914), 97–105. In 1759, "vino di piano" sold

Salubrious health conditions, variety of products assuring a large measure of self-sufficiency for the hill communities, easy cultivation on the well-drained slopes, made the middle hills the region of most precocious and for long of densest settlement in the medieval countryside.[47] But these same conditions which favored the extensive systems of cultivation characteristic of the early Middle Ages obstructed the more intensive methods, which the support of a much larger population was coming to require. Agricultural production in the hills, easily begun, could not be easily expanded.

The difficulties confronting intensive cultivation in the hills, especially of cereals, are again best explained by the contemporary writer Pietro de' Crescenzi. Intensive cultivation of cereals on the slopes, he says, was possible, but it was difficult, expensive and risky.[48] The soil of the hills was, to begin with, naturally less fertile than that of the lowlands, "for the higher places," he explains, "are deprived of fertility by the flow [of water]." More fertilizer had therefore to be placed on the higher ground than on the lower to balance the loss.[49] Bolognese peasants according to Pietro used fully twice as much fertilizer on the upper as on the lower slopes, though the Tuscans somewhat less. The procuring of these large quantities of fertilizer was a difficult problem for hill farmers. Night soil might be purchased in the city and carted up the hills, or fertilizer provided by cattle in sufficient number supported on the farm. But both these recourses required outlays of capital which few hill peasants were likely to possess.

Moreover, Tuscan routines of intensive cultivation typically included comminuation of the soil with a plow, hoe or mattock. This

---

for lire 1.81 per barrel, "vino di costa" for lire 2.79, and "vino di poggio" for lire 5.04.

47. In 998, 11 of the 19 rural pievi making up the diocese seem to have been located in the hills, although not all these churches can be certainly identified.

48. *Opus*, Liber II, capo 18, "De cultu agri montuosi et valliculosi."

49. Loc. cit. "Agri autem in convexitatibus montium siti frequenter patiunt siccitatem et macredinem, quoniam pingue quod est in ipsis defluit ad valles. . . . Nec letamen equaliter spargitur in montibus per totum sed altius plus letaminis ponitur ubi plus de humore abluitur et secundum quod declinat convexitas de letamine ponitur minus et minus."

deep working of the land aerated it and through capillary action brought fertilizing minerals to the surface for the benefit of growing plants. When pursued on the hillsides, however, these methods greatly increased the risk of erosion. To counter the danger, Pietro sensibly recommended that plowing on the slopes be done "traversely," that is, along the contours, so that "the fertility may stay retained in the furrows, which will flow down if the furrows descend directly."[50] So also, retaining walls (*retinacula per macerias*) could be erected on the lower border of sloping fields following the contour, to prevent erosion and retain the good soil in the fields.

Intensive cultivation of cereals was possible on the slopes, but it required considerable effort, substantial capital outlays, and remained subject to grave risks of drought and erosion. To provide such capital and bear such risks with their own resources was hardly possible for most peasant families, and the prevailing system of tenurial relations, as we shall further see, gave the peasant little capital with which to work while forcing him to assume the greater share of the risk.[51] Still in the thirteenth century, the intensive cultivation of the slopes was encountering formidable obstacles, not only physical and technical but institutional and social as well.

Moreover, even under the best of circumstances, Pietro seems to have retained some doubts about the value of planting wheat on the hills. Only the poorer seed, he recommends, should be used on the hills; the better seed should be saved for the more rewarding soil of the plain.[52]

Differing from the mountains in the resources they possessed, the middle hills also show a different phasing in their medieval economic development. No other region of Pistoia joined so precociously in the great demographic and economic expansion of the high Middle Ages, and no other region experienced so early and so deeply the crisis of their closing.

50. Loc. cit. "Propter quod etiam talia loca [montium] precipiuntur ab agricolis transversum sulcari ut in sulcis stet retenta pinguedo, que decurret in preceps si ex directo sulcus descendet."

51. See below, pp. 133–34.

52. *Opus*, Liber II, capo 18, "Semen igitur in tali agro tenue et non bonum esse tum propter cultus defectum tum propter impossibilitatem retinendi pinguedinem et humorem quibus semina convalescunt."

THE PLAIN AND LOW HILLS

Potentially the richest of Pistoia's agricultural areas, but also the smallest, was the region of the plain and low hills, lands most of which were between 50 and 200 meters high and which comprised less than 20 per cent of the medieval territory. The heart of this area was Pistoia's portion of the Florentine plain, the good alluvial soil of which had been built up over the millennia by a prehistoric sea and, in historical times, by numerous mountain streams pouring down upon it. This water too was a major resource of the plain, as it was available in abundance for drinking, for industry and for agriculture. By the late thirteenth century numerous irrigation projects are mentioned in the sources.[53]

Crops of all sorts grew well in the good, well-watered soil, but the region was especially suited for cereals. Even the relatively inefficient technology of the Middle Ages could achieve a usual return of six to one on the seed, and returns of ten to one were not impossible.[54] In 1569 G. B. Tedaldi placed the total cereal harvest at 350,000 staia of wheat and 180,000 of feed grains. The wheat harvest represented an average return of seven to one on the seed. Of this volume, 112,000 staia of wheat were exported to Prato and Florence and, says Tedaldi, "was turned entirely into gold."[55] Wheat, then, seems to have been the province's most important single export and one of the few products able to earn hard cash for the local economy.

The concentration of agricultural wealth on the plain perhaps can be further illustrated by the fact that according to a recent census—that of 1951—the region of the modern province comparable to the plain and low hills was supporting fully 63 per cent of the agricultural population, as against only 31 per cent ca. 1244.[56]

The men of medieval Pistoia were slow in utilizing the resources of this their richest agricultural area. The great obstacle to its ex-

53. Regulations concerning the use of streams for irrigation purposes are already contained in the *Statutum potestatis* (1296), pp. 140, 179, 187.

54. See below, chapter 6, n. 26.

55. "Relazione," p. 318, "si converte tutto in oro."

56. Calculated on the basis of the numbers of people engaged in agriculture, hunting and fishing in the *Istituto Centrale di Statistica. IX Censimento Generale della Popolazione*, I, fasc. 48, *Provincia di Pistoia* (Rome, 1954).

ploitation was the poor drainage of the land. According to a Tuscan tradition related by Giovanni Villani, a great stone, called the Pietra Golfolina, had once blocked the flow of the Arno through the gap between Signa and Montelupo and caused the Arno, Ombrone and Bisenzio to back up in their channels, creating swamps from Signa to Prato and "nearly to the foot of the mountains."[57] The great stone Golfolina may be considered legendary, but the many medieval swamps on the plain of Florence and Pistoia cannot. Even the toponyms of Pistoia and its surrounding plain preserve the memory of a once water-logged terrain: Pantano (bog), Piscina (pond), Padule (marsh), Acqualunga (long water).[58] One of Pistoia's gates, the Porta Guidi, was also known as the Porta del Pantano, "Bog Gate," as if to warn the traveller of the kind of terrain that he faced in leaving the city.[59] In the late twelfth century the principal road to Prato and Florence, as we have seen, did not strike directly across the plain but kept to the dry base of the mountains.[60] Even the legends of medieval Pistoia refer to rampaging waterways. St. Zeno, bishop of Verona, in 590 supposedly saved Pistoia from a flood; in gratitude, he was made the patron saint of the city.[61]

The swamps and bogs not only hampered communications and cultivation but they also created poor health conditions, supplying only stagnant water for drinking and threatening inhabitants with malarial infections. Pietro de' Crescenzi warned that people living in low areas dwelled in much "vaporosity," breathed bad air and were debilitated by it.[62] With the exception of the city itself and suburban communes, the plain did not play host to large settlements in the early Middle Ages.

The intensive exploitation of the plain's rich lands demanded effective control of the waterways, and this in turn required large public and private investments. Through statutes, we know more of the former than of the latter, though the work of private landlords,

57. G. Villani, *Cronica*, I, cap. 43 (I, p. 64). The great stone was eventually broken up, according to Villani, "per maestri con picconi e scarpelli."

58. Cf. the comments of Repetti, *Dizionario*, IV, 402.

59. According to Salvi, *Historie*, I, 31.

60. See above, p. 23.

61. Salvi, *Historie*, I, 26.

62. *Opus*, Liber I, capo 5, De situ loci habitabilis.

seeking to improve their lands through systems of ditches, certainly had importance.

Already in the Statutes of ca. 1200, the podestà was supposed to keep the streets of the city and suburbs free of pools of water.[63] In the Statutes of 1296, three entire chapters are concerned with controlling the Stella river, a small but troublesome tributary of the Ombrone.[64] The Brana too, another small stream which formed the moat for the city walls and apparently threatened to wash them away, also attracted much attention.[65] By the early fourteenth century, the city impressed visitors with the "gran fossi d'acqua" which had been dug around it, which helped protect the land from floods and incidentally served to delay the approach of hostile armies.[66] Water policy even figured in the relations and disputes between communes; in 1335 a flood on the Agna river provoked a minor diplomatic crisis with Florence.[67] And of course the Ombrone, largest of the rivers near Pistoia, demanded frequent attention; once, after a destructive flood in 1386, the commune undertook the expensive task of dredging its channel.[68] Provisions concerning water control constitute an important part of all later editions of Pistoia's statutes.[69]

While difficult to measure precisely, the success achieved through these and other efforts seems substantial. The road system itself gives evidence of this. Up to about 1200, the road to Prato and Florence had avoided, as we have seen, the lowlands. But by the late thirteenth century, one of Pistoia's principal roads, in fact the mod-

63. *Statuti*, ed. Berlan, cap. 109, p. 81, "Nullum aquarium super vias publicas in civitate Pistoria nec in suis burgis haberi permittam, me sciente."

64. *Statutum potestatis*, p. 272, "De consilio tenendo pro facto Stelle," "De reactando flumine Stelle si ruperuerit," and p. 278, "De providendo super flumine Stelle."

65. Ibid. p. 278, "De aptando flumine Braine, ita quod dampnum non det muro civitatis."

66. Compagni, *Cronica*, III, cap. 13, p. 194, "La città era nel piano, picciioletta, e ben murata e merlata, con forteze e con porti da guerra, e con gran fossi d'acqua. . . ."

67. See the protesting letter sent from the Florentine government to Pistoia, in Zaccaria, *Anecdota*, p. 265, 28 Nov. 1335.

68. ASP, Provv. Tomus 36, 35r, 19 Aug. 1388.

69. Cf. *Statuta* (1546), VI, 54, p. 151, "Cum civitas Pistorii eiusque comitatus et districtus abundet aquis, ipseque propter incuriam hominum eis utentibus veniant in declinationem. . . ."

ern Via Pratese, was running directly across the plain.[70] Probably somewhat later, and certainly by the early fifteenth century, an even more direct route to Florence, the modern Via Fiorentina, was built through the heart of the plain, through lands which in the early Middle Ages had been swampy and thinly settled.[71]

An even better indication of the success of this policy is the relative distribution of Pistoia's rural population.[72] In ca. 1244, as we have said, residents of the plain and low hills constituted about 31 per cent of the entire rural population; a hundred years later, in 1344, they were 40 per cent; by 1427, they made up nearly 50 per cent. The success of the plain in attracting settlers, even under conditions of a greatly declining population, measures also the success achieved in making the land healthier and more productive.

The plain and low hills thus reveal their own characteristic phasing of economic development in the Middle Ages. Marshes and bogs, obstructing agriculture and threatening health, left the plain thinly settled and poorly exploited until well into the thirteenth century. But because the area was tardy and slow in developing, it did not encounter the terrible problem of depleted resources and a saturated economy—at least not to the same measure as did the older center of Pistoiese settlement, the middle hills. For this reason, the communities of the plain, much as those of the mountains, did not have to bear the full ferocity of the fourteenth-century crisis.

THE CITY

Geographic factors also were important in the growth and transformations of Pistoia's commerce and industry.

In regard to commerce, the great advantage which geography

70. See the list of principal roads in the Consilium vini vendendi of 1285, published as Appendix I in the *Breve populi*. The road described as passing "from Chiazzano and so on towards Prato" is certainly the modern Via Pratese. By 1285, in other words, it seems to have replaced the road along the base of the mountains through Montemurlo as the most important link between the two cities. It is worth noting that in this list of principal roads, the modern Via Fiorentina is not mentioned.

71. The Via Fiorentina is mentioned in the Statutes of 1435, ASP, Provv. Tomus 56, 181r, "Quod omnes vie et strate debeant inghiari," contained also in the published *Statuta* (1546), VI, cap. 73, p. 160.

72. For the population figures, see below, table 1, p. 70.

conferred upon Pistoia was proximity to some of the great highways of medieval Italy. Pistoia itself was set upon the road leading to Bologna through the Collina pass. This was one of the busiest of the Apennine passes, and Pistoia was therefore the first Tuscan town to greet many travellers coming from the north. The importance of the road was enhanced by the importance of the great university city of Bologna which attracted scholars from all over the Christian world. As much as commerce itself, services to this international community—the exchange of money, transference of funds and even the carrying of the scholars' valuable books to school—seem to have been the means through which many of Pistoia's great mercantile families accumulated their considerable fortunes.[73] Ready access to Lombardy meant in turn access to France, and Pistoia's merchants were among the first inland Tuscans to explore the great markets beyond the Alps.

Pistoia was also near the important pilgrim highway linking Rome, Lombardy and France: the Via Francigena. Within Tuscany this road followed the coast down from the north, turned inland at Lucca as far as Altopascio, then shifted south once more, to cross the Arno at Fucecchio and move up the Elsa valley, in the direction of Siena and Rome. Between Altopascio and Fucecchio the road skirted, though it did not penetrate, Pistoia's frontiers. But its proximity still allowed the city good contact with Rome and offered its merchants another excellent route to Lombardy and France.

In regard to another great international highway, the sea itself, Pistoia was not conveniently situated, and this must be reckoned a major factor in its failure to fulfill its early commercial promise. Both the Monte Albano and the swamp of Fucecchio hampered communications with the port city of Pisa, and no navigable rivers aided in the conveyance of bulky commodities. As long as mercantile goods remained small and light, such disadvantages were not major, but it was hard and expensive to cart grain, salt or iron ore to the landlocked city.

In 1569 Tedaldi in his description of Pistoia made this discerning remark: "Had the sea been near or at least a navigable stream, one could affirm without hesitation that such a city had the advantage

73. See below, pp. 165–67.

of being placed in the loveliest, most convenient and best site which exists in all Italy."[74]

From the late thirteenth century, Tuscan highways (and waterways too) were being improved in what J. Plesner has called the "road revolution."[75] This steady improvement in communications, continuing even after the Black Death, had a paradoxical impact on Pistoia's commerce. It strengthened its ties with its immediate neighbors—Florence, Prato, Lucca—all less than a day's journey away. It greatly increased the pace of regional exchange. But it also helped undermine Pistoia's international stature as a commercial city. Good roads, regular and intensified exchange, forced the smaller towns to face an ever more damaging competition from their larger and more resourceful neighbors. Good roads brought Pistoia's merchants in particular into full competition with the Florentines. With Florentine banks and markets so easily accessible, attracting the capital and commodities even of its own citizens, Pistoia largely abandoned the conduct of international trade and banking and fell back to the status of a provincial town. Its economy lost much romantic flavor, although it maintained, from an active if humdrum regional trade, no little prosperity.[76]

Important commercially, Pistoia, even at the height of its medieval prosperity, did not achieve comparable stature as an industrial city. It had, to be sure, within its own territory ready access to industrial raw materials, especially raw wool and skins from its large mountain flocks. But it was hampered in developing these resources, partially by its own chronic political and social instability. In this, the very face of its land played a role. Over half its territory consisted of high hills and mountains, and mountain communities were notoriously difficult to govern. Mountain refuges were a constant invitation to civil and social warfare and rebellion, not only for the highlanders but for city factions too.[77] Defeated on the plain, they could still escape to the mountains, in hopes of a quick revanche. In

74. "Relazione," p. 314, "talchè se vi fusse il Mare vicino o pure un fiume navigabile, si potrebbe indubitamente affermare, che tal Città portasse il vanto di essere stata posta nel più bello, più commodo e miglior sito che sia in tutta Italia."

75. "Una Rivoluzione stradale nel dugento," *Acta Jutlandica*, I (1938).

76. See below, pp. 155 ff.

77. See below, pp. 198 ff.

the long history of factional feuds at Pistoia, there were few final victories.

But perhaps the more fundamental reason for the city's failure to develop large local industries was its lack of men, markets and money. Pistoia's population, while it may, as we shall see, appear large in absolute numbers, was small in comparison with that of other Tuscan communes. The rugged contado could support only thin settlement over most of its area and could supply comparatively few men for urban employment. Pistoia, serving the mountains as their gateway, was, to this extent at least, ill-served by them. Small size meant a small industrial labor force and a comparatively weak local market. A weak local market, coupled with the continuing loss of international commercial exchange to Florence, also helped foment at Pistoia an endemic shortage of cash and capital.

The lure of the Florentine market, offering cash payments not easily available at home, inevitably affected the character of the local economy, which turned to the production of commodities the Florentines would buy. They would buy agricultural products readily, iron, wool, raw silk, but few industrial goods. As a subsequent chapter will further illustrate, Pistoia's economy in the late Middle Ages passed under the shadow of the Florentine market, and was remade according to its dictates.[78]

For Pistoia, as for all Tuscan cities, the closing Middle Ages brought profound changes on all levels of life. One remarkable change, which in turn exerted a powerful and pervasive influence upon the medieval and Renaissance town, was in size of population.

78. See below, chapter 7, pp. 148–79.

3

Population, Growth and Decline

No one should therefore wonder if the men of Pistoia, oppressed for so long by the calamities of so many and so protracted domestic seditions and external wars and finally deadly plagues, should appear robbed and deprived of numbers of their fellow citizens. For if we should even casually note all their troubles of every sort, and their separate adversities, we would affirm, not unjustly in our opinion, that they have been warring first with domestic and internal enemies, then with external and foreign enemies, and finally with God Himself, the conqueror of all hosts.

—Giannozzo Manetti,
Chronicon pistoriense, 1447

Alone among the cities of Tuscany and of Italy, Pistoia possesses a source antedating 1250 which systematically surveys a rural population, illuminating not only its numbers but also the geographic distribution of its settlement. That source is the *Liber focorum*, or Book of Hearths, which lists by name 7312 household heads from 124 rural communes. The value of this rich survey is the greater as there have also survived several other both older and more recent demographic sources which, while not so detailed as the Book of Hearths, still preserve accurate information on the size of individual communes or the entire rural population. These documents, together with the Book of Hearths, constitute the oldest and possibly the richest series of population records which exists for any Italian countryside.

In most Italian and European areas, population movements in the cities are better documented and more easily studied than changes in the countryside. At Pistoia, the reverse is true: the earliest complete survey of the urban population dates only from 1415.[1] Nonetheless, much indirect evidence has survived to permit rough estimates of the number of urban residents from the early thirteenth century. It is possible, in other words, to assess the size of Pistoia's population, both urban and rural, even before 1250, and to determine the direction and dimensions of the changes which, in the later Middle Ages, were occurring within it.

THE COUNTRYSIDE

From at least the year 1000, and possibly even before, the rural population of Pistoia was expanding at a rapid pace. Our best indication of this is the multiplication of rural hospitals, monasteries and churches. Almost all the great rural monasteries and hospitals mentioned in the first chapter were founded in the late tenth and eleventh centuries, and their establishment and support certainly required a growing area and density of settlement.[2] Still firmer evidence comes from the increase in the number of pievi or baptismal churches in the countryside. In the imperial charter of 998 the diocese included only 19; by 1218 their number had grown to 32.[3]

This considerable population expansion in the eleventh and twelfth centuries is a fundamental and recognized fact of medieval economic and social history, although it is not certain when precisely it began or even when it ended.[4] Upon this latter question Pistoia's excellent demographic sources can cast some light. They show that some rural communes continued to expand well into the thirteenth century. In 1212, for example, the men of the mountain castle of Sambuca who took an oath of fidelity to the podestà numbered 74; in 1256, in taking a similar solemn oath of loyalty, this

1. ASP, Provv. Tomus 699, Estimario della Città, lists 1090 households for the city's four quarters and 27 parishes.

2. In the countryside only the monasteries of San Baronto (founded about 610) and of San Salvatore at Fanano (founded by 750) date from an earlier period.

3. For the charter, see above, chapter 1, n. 15. For the number of pievi in 1218, see the privilege of Pope Honorius III, "Quoniam omnium solus," Zaccaria, *Anecdota*, pp. 242–43 (Potthast, *Regesta*, no. 5862), 5 July 1218.

4. Cf. C. Cipolla, J. Dhondt, M. M. Postan and P. Wolff, in *IXe Congrès International des Sciences Historiques*, I, *Rapports* (Paris, 1950), pp. 56–80.

time to the bishop, they were 130.[5] In neither oath can the number of absentees be estimated, but the increase in conjurors at a comparably solemn occasion does suggest that this mountain castle had grown substantially, perhaps by as much as 70 per cent. The commune of Larciano in the middle hills counted 199 hearths in ca. 1244, and by 1250 had grown to 215—a fairly considerable increase of 16 hearths in the brief period of eleven years.[6] On the other hand, there is evidence that as early as the beginning of the thirteenth century, some communes were growing hardly at all or were even declining. At Carmignano, 343 men took an oath of loyalty in 1219, suggesting a population of about 1200 persons.[7] In the Book of Hearths of ca. 1244, Carmignano counted 280 families, or about 1300 persons—a gain of no more than 100 persons in 30 years.[8] At Artimino in 1219, 139 persons took a similar oath of loyalty, and the commune probably counted about 490 residents.[9] In ca. 1244 the castle had only 43 hearths; unless the commune's boundaries had been radically altered, the population had fallen drastically to only about 200 persons.[10]

Our evidence of population movements thus points in opposite directions. The safest conclusion to be drawn from it seems to be this: while the medieval population expansion was continuing in some rural communes, it was beginning to lose strength and consistency in the countryside as a whole by the opening decades of the thirteenth century. Overall growth in numbers, if it occurred at all, could only have been small. Evidence from the establishment of churches suggests as much. The number of rural pievi, which had increased from 19 to 32 between 998 and 1218, was still only 34 in 1276–77.[11] The eleventh and twelfth, rather than the thirteenth, centuries were the age of most vigorous demographic expansion.

5. The oaths are published in the *Liber censuum*, no. 24, p. 18, 30 July 1212, and in Zaccaria, *Anecdota*, p. 82, 13 Nov. 1256.

6. The figure for ca. 1244 is from the *Liber focorum*, pp. 121–27. That for 1250 is from ASF, Dipl. Potesterie di Pistoia, 17 May 1250.

7. *Liber censuum*, no. 58, 8 May 1219. The estimate is based on the use of a multiplier of 3.5. For its application in regard to such oaths, see below, chapter 3, n. 57.

8. *Liber focorum*, pp. 74–82. The estimate is based on the use of a multiplier of 4.65. See below, p. 61, for discussion of the figure.

9. *Liber censuum*, no. 60, 11 May 1219.

10. *Liber focorum*, pp. 82–83.

11. *Tuscia*, I, pp. 51–62.

Upon the size and movements of the rural population in the thirteenth century, a flood of light is cast by Pistoia's Book of Hearths. But to utilize this remarkable document most effectively requires a discussion of several problems connected with its text and contents.

The Book of Hearths, as its name implies, is a survey which enumerates the hearths or families, and records the name of the "major person" within each home, for 124 rural communes of Pistoia.[12] Only one commune, that of the castle of Sambuca, seems to have been omitted from it, but because of its relatively modest size the loss may be considered negligible and no effort has been made to compensate for it here.[13]

The 124 communes are arranged according to the four quarters or gates of the city: the Porta Caldatica (21 communes), the Porta Lucchese (38 communes), the Porta Sant'Andrea (23 communes), and the Porta Guidi (42 communes). Within each commune, the noble hearths are counted separately from those of commoners; there are, in all, 263 hearths of nobles, 7049 of commoners, together making a total of 7312 rural households. The notary sometimes added a comment after the names of the householders, mentioning their profession, singling out paupers or those condemned for debt, or noting the absence of taxpayers from the village.[14]

In 1956 Quinto Santoli edited the Book of Hearths in the series "Fonti per la Storia d'Italia." His edition has, unfortunately, several flaws. While the text itself is accurately presented, the statistical tables published with it and meant to summarize its results were either hastily composed or carelessly checked. There are at least 16 errors or inconsistencies between the tables and figures in the text, and Santoli's summaries must therefore be used with caution.[15]

Moreover, Santoli did not resolve satisfactorily a textual problem

12. The communes with the number of hearths they contain are listed in Appendix I (1). See below, pp. 271–73.

13. On the omission of Sambuca, see above, chapter 1, n. 58.

14. Even *jongleurs* and crusaders appear among the rural families. Cf. "Burensis, iugulator," and "Iacobus Ricobaldi, iugulator," *Liber focorum*, p. 228, nos. 19 and 33 respectively. "Ficus Franceschi, crucesignatus," ibid. p. 180, no. 89. "Guidotus Tralignati, cruce signatus," ibid. p. 202, no. 11.

15. In his master table (Prospetto III, *Liber focorum*, pp. 25–33), Santoli transcribed the notary's own total for the quarter of the Porta Caldatica as 1669 instead of the correct 1668, and the hearth figures for the following communes differ in the table from the figures given in the text: Montemagno (313

of major importance connected with the use of the Book: its date. An exact dating is clearly essential for an adequate reconstruction of Pistoia's population history in the thirteenth century. Because of the uniqueness of the Book as the oldest complete survey of an Italian countryside, its dating is also likely to influence our impression of population movements for a much wider area of medieval Italy.

The Book itself contains no date. It is, however, bound together in a single manuscript with another survey, the *Liber finium* or Book of Boundaries, which bears the date 1255. Lodovico Zdekauer, the first scholar to make extensive use of these sources, assumed that both surveys had been redacted at the same time, and he therefore assigned the year 1255 to the Book of Hearths as well.[16] This dating has since passed into the standard surveys of Italian and European population.[17]

Santoli, however, quite rightly criticized this dating.[18] The Book of Hearths lists 124 rural communes, the Book of Boundaries only 108.[19] Would both surveys have been taken the same year with two different administrative divisions prevailing in the countryside? Instead of 1255 for the redaction of the Book of Hearths, Santoli proposed the year 1226. He argued that the redaction of so detailed a document required peaceful conditions in the countryside, and that 1226 was a peaceful year. But this date too must be rejected. A com-

---

popular hearths should be 314; 116 noble hearths should be 117); Casale (322 should be 325); Petruolo (9 should be 18); Lanciole (177 should be 183); Popiglio (192 should be 194); Piteglio (83 should be 84); Sammomme (58 should be 59); Prombialla (16 should be 18); Piazza (15 should be 49); Alfiano (13 should be 16); San Simone (14 should be 15); Casore (36 should be 37); Santomato (93 should be 94); San Quirico (130 should be 129).

16. *Breve populi*, pp. lxx-lxxiii.

17. J. Beloch, *Bevölkerungsgeschichte Italiens* (3 vols. Berlin and Leipzig, 1937–61), II, 186. R. Mols, *Introduction à la démographie historique des villes d'Europe du XIVe au XVIIIe siècle* (3 vols. Louvain, 1954–56), I, 15, n. 7. Russell, *Medieval Population*, p. 110, table 113, mentions 7307 hearths in rural Pistoia in 1284. The source must be the Book of Hearths, but the dating is not explained.

18. *Liber focorum*, pp. 13–15.

19. Santoli first counts 100 communes in the Book of Boundaries (see *Liber focorum*, p. 14) and later 108 (ibid. p. 266). There is some ambiguity as to what communes are actually surveyed and what are mentioned only as boundaries to other communes. I count 108; see below, Appendix I (2), pp. 274–75.

parison of persons named in the Book of Hearths with people appearing in parchments dated 1226 shows only a slight correspondence, although many persons mentioned in the Book appear to be the sons of householders alive in 1226.[20] Moreover, the commune of Montecastiglione, included in the Book, was not acquired by Pistoia until 1240.[21] Comparison of householders mentioned in the Book with those appearing in dated parchments offers a means of dating the Book with some reliability, and such comparisons would place its redaction between late 1243 and early 1245, or probably in 1244.[22] It is hard, of course, to be exact about such dating. As we shall see, the notary was not above padding his lists with the names of former residents who had since disappeared from the villages. The Book, in other words, does not exactly reflect the population for any single year. But the error in our estimated dating, if one exists, could not be a large one.

Another surviving tax survey, a dated *estimo* for the large rural commune of Piuvica, offers further assurance that the Book of Hearths was drawn up about 1244.[23] This estimo was redacted on August 20, 1243, and gives the names and assessments of 238 persons. Of these 238 residents of Piuvica, 170, or about 71 per cent, may certainly be identified with persons appearing in the Book of

20. A partial tax survey of the commune of Piteccio has survived from 1226, ASF, Dipl. Comune di Pistoia, 13 March 1226. Only one of the ten householders whose names are decipherable can be found in the Book of Hearths; on the other hand, as suggested by patronymics, the fathers of three of the householders appearing in the Book of Hearths are mentioned in the survey of 1226 (Sera condam Cipriani in 1226, Salvus Sere in the Book of Hearths; Augustinus filius Malescorti in 1226, Salerno Agustini in the Book; Guidus filius Nepti in 1226, heredes Guidi in the Book; see the *Liber focorum*, pp. 192–94, nos. 102 and 136–40).

21. *Liber censuum*, no. 323, pp. 217–18, act dated 16 Sept. 1240, purchase of the commune of Montecastiglione by Pistoia.

22. A widow, domina Brasta of the commune of Sant'Angelo in Piazza, appeared as a principal in a parchment, ASF, Dipl. Città di Pistoia, 10 Oct. 1243. In the Book of Hearths, she had apparently been replaced as head of her household by her son, *Liber focorum*, p. 209, no. 32. Either she had died or her son had attained his majority, and so the Book should be dated after 20 Oct. 1243. On the other hand, a Henrigus Bianchi, mentioned in the Book of Hearths (*ibid.* p. 230, no. 239) was dead by 28 May 1245 (*Liber censuum*, p. 230, no. 329, 28 May 1245, "heredibus Henrigi Bianchi"). The date 28 May 1245 is thus a *terminus ante quem* for the Book.

23. ASF, Dipl. Comune di Pistoia, 20 Aug. 1243.

Hearths—a remarkably high correspondence, particularly since the two surveys were drawn up by different authorities, the one by the city and the other by the local commune. Not much time could have separated the redaction of this estimo of 1243 from that of the Book of Hearths. Moreover, comparison of the two documents suggests that the Book is the later survey, i.e. that it was redacted after August 1243. In it the notary added after the names of thirteen householders that they had emigrated to the city.[24] These same thirteen, however, appear as rural taxpayers in the estimo of 1243, and this could not have happened if it had been drawn up later than the Book, when the thirteen were supposedly urban residents not taxable in the countryside. The Book of Hearths thus seems to have been redacted not long after August 1243.

Like many fiscal documents, the Book of Hearths seems to have been drawn up in response to the commune's pressing financial need. As a traditionally Ghibelline city, Pistoia was deeply committed to the support of Emperor Frederick II Hohenstaufen in his struggle with the papacy and with the Guelf communes. The city government was having evident financial difficulties in the early 1240s, as it was forced to contract numerous loans from its wealthier citizens.[25] Against this background of an acute need of money, Pistoia seems to have undertaken this thorough survey of its countryside, most likely in 1244.

The Book of Hearths numbers only families, and gives no direct information concerning their size. To estimate the total population on the basis of hearths, a multiplier of 4.65 will be used. The figure represents the actual ratio between persons and hearths, or average household size, prevailing in rural Pistoia according to the Catasto of 1427, and it seemed preferable to use this rather than a figure which would be entirely arbitrary. The implication is that Pistoia's rural households were quite small in the middle thirteenth century, and we have some reason to believe that this was true.[26]

24. *Liber focorum*, p. 44, nos. 21, 71, 160, 161, 162, 191, 193, 195, 196, 199, 200, 239 and 240, for the thirteen residents of Piuvica who are said to be "cives," i.e. residents of the city and who would not therefore have appeared in a later rural survey.

25. ASF, Dipl. Comune di Pistoia, 10 May 1245 and many following, for loans given to the commune by many of its wealthier citizens.

26. See below, pp. 117–18.

The multiplier itself, of course, must be recognized as only approximate, and estimates of population size based upon it should probably be considered conservative.

Ca. 1244, Pistoia's countryside contained 7312 households, or a population of about 34,000 persons—truly a remarkable figure for a region well over half of which was high and thinly settled mountains. The Book of Hearths thus makes manifest the dimensions of the medieval demographic expansion, a true population explosion when considered against the background of the meager economic resources of the age. The Book also gives a partial response to a second demographic problem of considerable interest: by the middle thirteenth century, was the population as a whole continuing to increase?

Light on this question comes from certain peculiarities in the redaction of the survey. The notary seems to have had considerable difficulty locating all the taxpayers. For each commune he not only names the head of each non-noble household, but he also gives a figure supposedly indicating their total number. But for 36 communes his totals do not agree with the number of householders actually named. In 32 of the 36 communes he gives sums higher than the numbers of names actually listed. For the entire countryside, his totals, when correctly added, give a figure of 7118 non-noble householders, although he supplies the names for only 7049. There are, in other words, 69 missing hearths, included by the notary in his count but not otherwise named or identified.

This frequent failure to name as many householders as he assigns to the various communes seems to involve something more than a consistent inability to count. Far the more natural error in counting long lists of items is to skip, and to end with a sum less than the true. Our notary, in 32 out of 36 communes, does the reverse, counting more entries than are there. A more likely explanation for these apparent errors is suggested by the Statutes of 1296.[27] In surveying the countryside in the preparation of a Book of Hearths, the notary was, of course, to count all the hearths he could find, but, direct the Statutes, "for each commune the total of hearths is not to be lowered."

27. *Statutum potestatis*, p. 212.

It is not unlikely that a similar stipulation was in force when our surviving Book of Hearths was redacted, and this would explain why the totals for the communes are so often higher than the hearths they actually contained. The false totals seem to have been quotas based on a previous Book which the notary was intent on fulfilling, not all the time successfully. The notary himself several times states that when the village consul or priest failed to report a traditional number of hearths, he simply added names from the previous survey, whether or not they were still residents of the village.[28] Some men thus appeared as taxpayers who were altogether unknown in the area.[29] But in spite of his best efforts, including the dutiful inclusion on the rolls of absent or unknown persons, the notary failed by 69 hearths to reach his apparent quota.

These missing hearths, and the evident difficulty encountered by the notary in finding live and present taxpayers, shows that the previous survey, the "old Book" frequently mentioned in the surviving *Liber focorum,* had proposed totals and quotas which could not be attained ca. 1244. This in turn implies that the medieval demographic expansion had certainly lost strength and consistency in rural Pistoia by the 1240s, and that the size of the population itself by then may even have passed its medieval peak.

A little more than ten years later, in 1255, another survey, the *Liber finium* or Book of Boundaries, gives additional evidence of a declining population. The Book of Boundaries lists only communes and unfortunately does not number their hearths. But it does record a considerable fall in the number of communes, from 124 in the Book of Hearths to 108 in 1255.[30] This does not, to be sure, strictly indicate the disappearance of sixteen villages. The lost communes were probably simply being included in larger administrative units. Nevertheless, the falling number of rural communes still strongly implies a shrinking population in the countryside.

The Book of Boundaries was drawn up immediately following a

28. *Liber focorum,* p. 121, "Presbiter de Casale venit et pauciores iii quam erant in Libro renunciavit, et sic stetimus illis de Libro." Ibid. p. 219, "Presbiter de isto loco venit et pauciores pronu[n]ciabat quam erant in Libro, et ideo eos de Libro scripsimus."

29. Ibid. p. 207, no. 17, "Acursus Cavitarini. Est in libro veteri, sed presbiter eum non noscit."

30. See below, Appendix I (2), pp. 274–75.

war with Florence (1251–54), and this probably explains the decline.[31] We cannot exclude the possibility that the population which suffered from it later may have made good its losses. The rural population in the middle thirteenth century certainly remained high and suffered no truly catastrophic decline, but what evidence we have suggests that the age of vigorous demographic expansion was already over.

Between 1255 and 1344, no complete surveys of Pistoia's countryside have survived. Lodovico Zdekauer did publish the results of a partial survey, called the *Liber hominum et personarum* or Book of Men and Persons, dated 1293–94.[32] By comparing the Book of Men with the earlier Book of Hearths, Zdekauer concluded that the rural population had declined drastically in the late thirteenth century. Unfortunately, the text of the Book of Men was apparently destroyed in World War II, and the exact nature of the survey cannot now be easily investigated.[33] But the figures of the Book of Men are so out of line with both the Book of Hearths of ca. 1244 and with the later survey of 1344 as to show that it could not have included all rural residents. The commune of Piuvica, for example, had 240 hearths, or about 1100 residents, according to the Book of Hearths, but only 92 persons in the Book of Men; in 1344, its population was a more believable 981 mouths. The Book of Men of 1293–94 is thus certainly not complete; perhaps it was a list of delinquent taxpayers. While it may therefore show widespread tax oppression in the countryside, it cannot be safely used for demographic purposes.

The evidence we have of population movements between ca. 1244 and 1344 is partial, indirect and not entirely consistent. The survey of 1344 shows, as we shall see, a loss in population of nearly 23 per cent from what it had been a century before, but it is extremely difficult to determine when precisely this loss occurred. Much of it is probably directly attributable to the great plague and famine which struck Pistoia only four years earlier, in 1340. Between 1244 and 1340, the population seems to have moved in no consistent direc-

31. Cf. Q. Santoli, "La Guerra con Firenze dal 1251 al 1254," *BSP*, 5 (1903), 51–72.

32. *Breve populi*, p. lxix.

33. I was so informed in 1962 by the clerk of the State Archives of Pistoia.

tion, declining in some periods and growing in others, and registering no large and lasting gains or losses.

The late thirteenth and early fourteenth centuries were politically troubled years for Pistoia. By 1293 many rural communes, crushed by taxes and forced to borrow, were said to be destroyed "because of the voracity and depravity of usurers."[34] In its effort to stay free, Pistoia was also forced to wage an unequal struggle against its larger neighbors, Lucca and Florence, which combined to besiege the city in 1305–06 and for four years, until 1310, ruled its district with an iron hand. By then taxes were so burdensome that "for this reason many people were constrained to leave Pistoia, which remained largely stripped of persons and wealth."[35] Pistoia also suffered from the destructive campaigns waged by Castruccio Castracane, tyrant of Lucca, from 1320 to 1328, against the Florentine commune.

But even in this disturbed period, the picture was not consistently dark and population losses not continuous. The men of Carmignano, for example, who participated in the oath of 1219 to the number of 343, took another oath in 1307, and were counted at 382.[36] The decade of the 1330s, by which time Pistoia was virtually a Florentine dependency, seems to have brought an economic and demographic revival—the culmination really of the city's medieval economic expansion and the calm before the terrible storms of the middle fourteenth century. In 1336, the preamble to another survey, the full text of which has unfortunately not survived, mentioned that "with the aid of divine grace the number of people of the city and contado of Pistoia has increased by no small amount after the [last] said taxation."[37] This may only be a conventional, empty formula, but even the use of such words would show that the city fathers were not yet accustomed, as they were later to become, to think in terms of a contracting population.

The combined famine and plague of 1340, more even than the

34. Document cited in *Breve populi*, p. lxv, "propter voracitatem et pravitatem usurariorum . . . plura de dictis comunibus sint destructa."

35. *Storie pistoresi*, p. 42, "per la qual cosa molta gente fue costretta per necessità a partirsi di Pistoia, si che rimase molto ignuda di persone e d'avere."

36. ASF, Not. I 29, 15 May 1307.

37. ASP, Provv. Tomus 8, 34r, 11 Jan. 1336, "divina gratia favente numerus personarum civitatis et comitatus Pistoriensis sit post dictam taxationem auctus non modicum. . . ."

Black Death of 1348, deserves to be considered the great watershed in Pistoia's medieval demographic and economic history. The sources speak at once of "a lack of trading, crafts and labor," and mention that many residents both of the countryside and city were deserting Pistoia.[38] Generous tax concessions had to be offered to attract immigrants to replace them. The great depopulations of the late Middle Ages were about to gain momentum.

In 1344, four years in advance of the plague, a full survey of the rural population was prepared, and this has survived. It is the first of five similar surviving surveys, dated 1344, 1383, 1392, 1401 and 1404, which were technically *Taxe boccarum* or lists of the fiscal "mouths" of the rural communes of Pistoia.[39] Upon the basis of these mouths, salt quotas were imposed upon the rural communes by the city, and hence only the number of salt consumers is recorded in these lists. A salt consumer was in turn considered to be a person four years in age or older.[40]

To estimate the total population on the basis of these lists of mouths, we must know what part of the population the salt consumers, persons four years or older in age, represented. In 1427, the Florentine Catasto listed not only all the inhabitants of Pistoia's countryside, but also gave the ages of most of them. The ratio of the entire population to those responsible for the salt tax was 1.22.[41] In estimating the size of the entire population on the basis of these lists of mouths, we shall use throughout this multiplier 1.22.

Still later than these lists of mouths, and the final survey we shall include in our series, is the portion of the Florentine Catasto of 1427 which deals with Pistoia.[42] The Catasto, which included all the population, urban and rural, of the entire Florentine district, was to provide the basis for a combined property tax and head tax and thus recorded both the possessions and the numbers of the population.[43]

38. Ibid. Tomus 11, 32r, 26 Aug. 1340. "Cum multi cives et districtuales Pistorii artifices et laboratores propter defectum mercantiarum artium et laborerii discesserint et discedant de civitate et districtu predictis ad alia loca transferentes. . . ."

39. See Appendix I (3–7), below, pp. 276–80.

40. ASP, Provv. Tomus 35, 21v, 17 Feb. 1385.

41. Specifically, 11,456 to 9356.

42. See Appendix I (8), below, pp. 281–82.

43. The laws creating the Catasto Commission of Ten and directing them as to their procedures are edited in Karmin, *Legge*, and Pagnini, *Della decima*,

As a kind of census, the Catasto listed by name all lay men, women and children in the city and countryside. It even gave their ages, and it is therefore one of the earliest surveys in all Europe which permits an accurate reconstruction of the age profile of a population.[44]

The results of the survey were first written down in rough drafts, called *portate*, many of which have survived but which are difficult to read because of the many changes and corrections made in them.[45] A clean copy was then made of the survey and entered into great volumes called *campioni*. The survey of Pistoia, city and countryside, is preserved in six such volumes, and two other smaller volumes provide a summary of the results by naming only the head of the family and his assessment.[46] The 1247 households of the city are described in two of these great volumes; three include the rural households of the suburbs and the contado, and one the mountains.

Through mishandling over the centuries, these volumes have suffered slight damage, specifically in the loss of some few initial and final pages, but on the whole they are in an excellent state of preservation. Moreover, it is possible to discern how many of the tax declarations were lost through comparing the great volumes with the complete summaries. The summaries show that 2536 rural households were originally included in the survey, and of these the final declarations of 2507 have survived. The loss of 29 households, one per cent of the total, is thus almost negligible. Still, to compensate for it, we can estimate that these 29 households contained about 135 persons (29 x 4.65), and we shall add this number to the total of persons actually named.

I, 214–31. For recent comment upon the Catasto, see E. Fiumi, "Stato di popolazione e distribuzione della ricchezza in Prato secondo il catasto del 1428–29," *ASI, 123* (1965), 277–303; Bruno Casini, *Il Catasto di Pisa del 1428–29*, Pubblicazione della Società Storica Pisana, Collana storica, 2 (Pisa, 1964); de Roover, *Medici Bank*, pp. 21–31; and Martines, *Social World*, pp. 99–105.

44. Some incomplete surveys recording ages have survived from the earlier Middle Ages, and from other sources some indirect information concerning age distribution can be gathered, but the Catasto is unequalled by any earlier survey by measure of the comprehensiveness and precision of the data it supplies. See Russell, *Medieval Population*, pp. 47–52.

45. The *portate* are contained in ASF, Catasto, 223–26 for the city of Pistoia; 227–31 for the contado; and 232 for the mountains.

46. ASF, Catasto, 260, 261, 262, 263, 264 and 265, and the "Sommario," vols. 282 and 283.

While our seven surveys reflect different methods of taxation, they are all fiscal documents and all give a full picture of the tax-paying population of rural Pistoia. It should of course be noted that the clergy were not included in any of them, and probably many homeless paupers escaped the notice of the tax assessors.[47] Such omissions, however, do not seriously compromise the value of these documents. They all show us the size of the economically active population of rural Pistoia. And, since they are all alike in the groups omitted, comparisons among them can still reveal accurately the direction and dimensions of demographic changes.

We must also note that the territory of Pistoia was larger when the Book of Hearths was redacted than when these subsequent surveys were taken, because of the surrender of several communes on the southern Monte Albano to Florence in 1329.[48] But this too can easily be adjusted, so that the surveys, in terms of the territory they include, will be nearly exactly comparable.

On the basis of these surveys, table 1 and graph 1 show the approximate population of Pistoia's countryside from ca. 1244, the date of the Book of Hearths, through 1427, the date of the Catasto. In order to illustrate not only changes in numbers but also shifts in rural settlement, the communes in each of the surveys have been classified as to whether their lands consisted chiefly of plain and low hills, middle hills, or mountains—the three regions, in other words, into which we are dividing Pistoia's medieval territory.

As the table and graph reveal, Pistoia's rural population plummeted at a shocking rate in the late Middle Ages. About 31,000 ca. 1244, it was less than 9000 in 1401—a scarcely believable fall of more than 70 per cent from its former size.

While all regions experienced a population decline, not all suffered these terrible losses to the same degree. The population catastrophe was in fact accompanied by a shift of major dimensions in the pattern of rural settlement. The region of the middle hills fell from 2882 to 734 households, a staggering loss of nearly three fourths of its people (74.5 per cent). Containing a substantial 43 per

47. A survey of ecclesiastical property, ASF, Catasto 189, has survived, and an estimate of the size of the clergy can be made from it for 1427. See below, p. 80.

48. See above, chapter 1, n. 59.

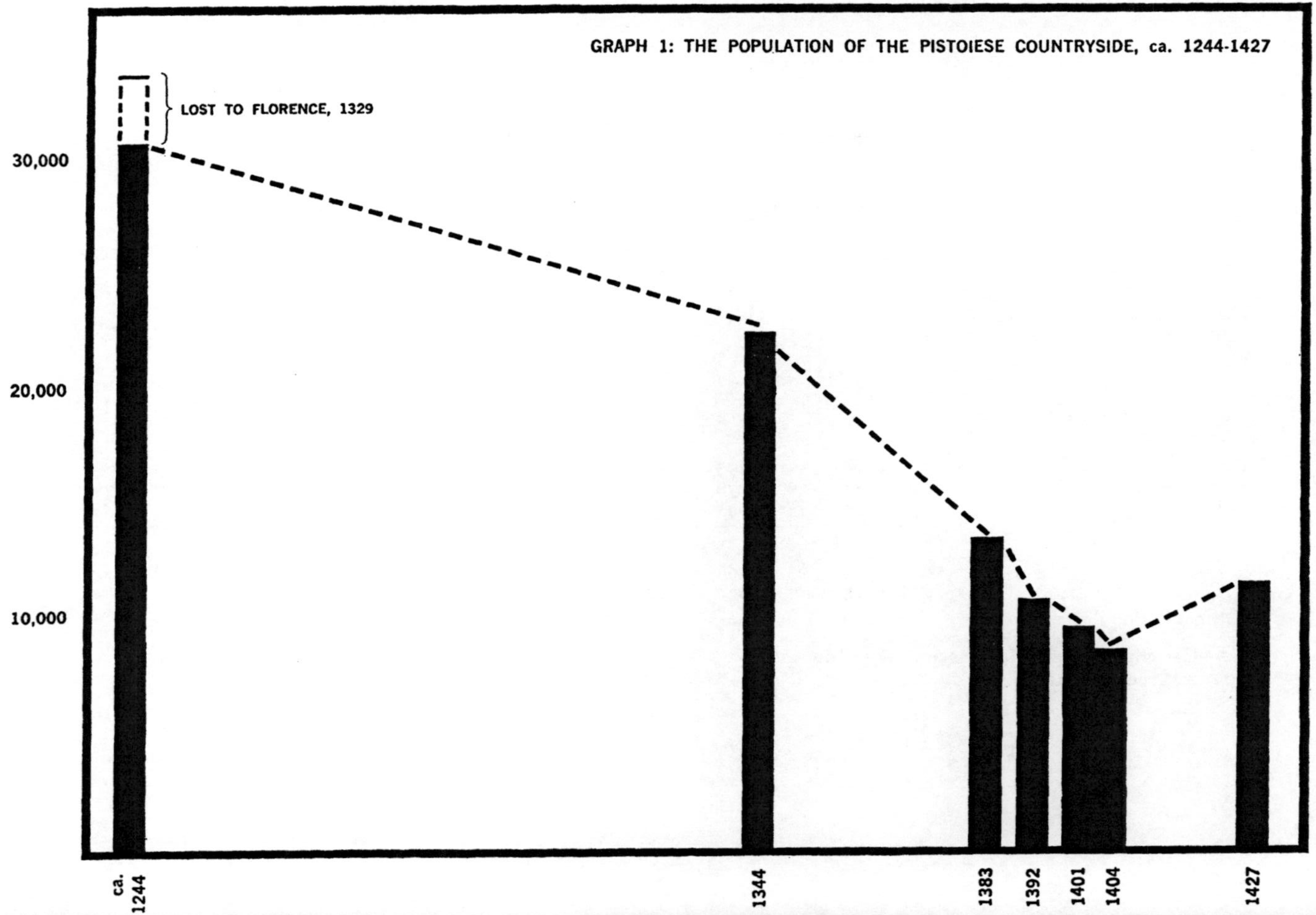

GRAPH 1: THE POPULATION OF THE PISTOIESE COUNTRYSIDE, ca. 1244-1427

TABLE 1 The Population of the Pistoiese Countryside, ca. 1244–1427

	ca. 1244		*1344*		*1383*		*1392*		*1401*		*1404*		*1427*		
	C	*H*	*C*	*M*	*C*	*M*	*C*	*M*	*C*	*M*	*C*	*M*	*C*	*H*	*M*
Plain and Low Hills	26	2309													
Middle Hills	69	3455													
Mountains	29	1548													
Totals	124	7312													
Adjusted to comparable territory:															
Plain and Low Hills	24	2284	12	7593	15	5180	10	4326	9	3752	13	4139	33	1170	5700
Middle Hills	65	2882	28	7278	19	3553	17	2792	15	2368	17	1912	17	732	3009
Mountains	29	1548	24	4772	19	2888	19	2197	20	2099	17	1317	19	605	2928
Adjustments														+ 29	135
Totals	118	6714	64	19,643	53	11,621	46	9315	44	8219	48	7368	69	2536	11,772
		× 4.65		× 1.22		× 1.22		× 1.22		× 1.22		× 1.22			
Estimated Population		31,220		23,964		14,178		11,364		10,027		8989			11,772

C = Communes, *H* = Hearths and *M* = Mouths.
Sources: See Appendix I.

cent of the population ca. 1244, the middle hills included only 26 per cent in 1404. The mountains fared better, as their losses between ca. 1244 and 1427, from 1548 to 609 households, amounted to a comparatively moderate 61 per cent. The plain and low hills bore the onslaught best of any region, falling from 2284 to 1193 households, a decline of less than one half (46 per cent). By the early fifteenth century, in other words, the plain and low hills had replaced the middle hills as the most populous region of the countryside. Even the mountains in 1427 had almost as many people as the middle hills, which once had been the heart of Pistoia's medieval settlement. These shifts in settlement are themselves a valuable commentary upon the simultaneous changes in the rural economy, which we shall examine later.[49]

This catastrophic population decline was accompanied by an equally drastic fall in the number of rural communes. Some of the depopulated rural villages were being combined into larger administrative units, while others were being entirely wiped out.

TABLE 2 The Rural Communes of Medieval Pistoia, ca. 1244–1427

Date	*Plain*	*Middle Hills*	*Mountains*	*Total*
1244	24	65	29	124
1255	14	63	31	108
1344	12	28	24	64
1383	15	19	19	53
1392	10	17	19	46
1401	9	15	20	44
1404	13	17	17	48
1427	33	17	19	69

Source: See Appendix I, pp. 271–82.

Between ca. 1244 and 1401, nearly two thirds of Pistoia's rural communes disappeared, and again the middle hills, with only 15 communes left out of 65, bore the brunt of the losses. Moreover, as table 2 includes data from the Book of Boundaries of 1255, it also shows that the number of rural communes was falling even then. No sooner do we possess our first full surveys of Pistoia's countryside than they register a declining population.

Massive population losses and the disappearance of two thirds of

49. See below, pp. 121–47.

Pistoia's rural communes must have meant an equally drastic contraction of the cultivated area, and the literary sources offer ample illustration of this. In 1415 one landlord complained that his houses in the rural village of San Giusto had been broken down to their foundations, and were good only to serve as latrines for little boys.[50] The village of Montagnana in 1428 was described as a "land laid waste."[51] Brandeglio was called "a deserted and a bad land."[52] At Montemagno, laborers could not be found "because of the plague."[53] Some lands had been abandoned for so long that even their owners had forgotten where they were located "because they are in deserted villages."[54] An acute shortage of workers is a universal complaint in the Catasto.[55] This contraction of the cultivated area and severe shortage of workers are two facts which must be kept constantly in mind in any consideration of the late medieval rural economy.[56]

Before examining further the causes and results of this great human catastrophe, we must consider the simultaneous changes in the urban population.

THE CITY

The city of Pistoia was not the subject of a surviving comprehensive survey until 1415, and our data concerning its population history are therefore much poorer than our rural figures. It is still possible, however, to make some rough judgments concerning the city's size, and to assess the impact of the late medieval population decline upon it.

50. Estimario, declaration of Niccolao di Tommeo di Reale, "i miei casamenti disfatti a San Giusto . . . sono fatti pisciatoio de' fanciulli."

51. ASF, Catasto 189, 165r, "paese guasto."

52. Ibid. 172r, "diserto e mal paese."

53. Ibid. 169v, "non si trova lavoratori per la mortalità."

54. Ibid. 169r, declaration of the hospital of San Gregorio of Pistoia: "Abbiamo in più luoghi terreni insalvatichiti e facti pruneti li quali si truovano per scripture di gran tempi. Non li sappiamo ne luoghi ne confini perchè sono in paesi abandonati. Non sena nulla."

55. Ibid. 165r, a tenant, Nanni di Chieri, has just renounced his lease, and the landlord comments "non so quel lo semina."

56. The extent of deserted lands and abandoned villages in Tuscany has perhaps not been sufficiently appreciated. Cf. Jones, "Lineamenti," p. 307, who comments that in the central and northern provinces of Italy "vi sono pochi indizi di *Wüstungen*."

In 1219 the adult, male, urban citizens of Pistoia swore to uphold a peace treaty with Bologna, and 3206 men participated.[57] These solemn oaths characteristically included all adult males, although the age at which a boy was considered an adult might vary from 14 to 19 years.[58] For such important agreements as a peace treaty, the government clearly sought to enlist the largest possible participation from among its citizens, in order to convince the other contracting city of the sincerity of its promises and probably also to impress it with the strength of its numbers. In basing population estimates upon such oaths, demographic historians commonly use the multiplier of 3.5.[59] This ratio in fact takes little account of possible absentees, and estimates calculated with its use should therefore be regarded as conservative.

On the basis of these 3206 adult male citizens who took the oath of 1219, Pistoia probably had an urban population of not less than 11,000. It was therefore, for the age, a sizable town. How sizable can be roughly discerned by comparing this oath of 1219 with similar oaths taken at nearly the same time by citizens of neighboring towns:

Town	*Date*	*Participants*	*Source*
Pistoia	1219	3206	*Liber censuum*, pp. 509–27
Bologna	1219	2187	Ibid. nos. 61–78.
San Gimignano	1227	1457	Fiumi, *San Gimignano*, p. 153.
Volterra	1227	1122	ASF, Dipl. Volterra, 25 Nov.–13 Dec. 1227.
Pisa	1228	4271	Herlihy, *Pisa*, p.36.

57. The oath, preserved in the State Archives of Bologna, has been published by Santoli, *Liber censuum*, pp. 509–27.

58. It was 14 years in the early thirteenth century, *Statuti*, ed. Berlan, cap. 75, p. 65. In the pacification of 1237, men from 15 to 70 swore, *Breve populi*, p. xviii. In the *Statutum potestatis*, II, cap. 18, the legal age for entering into contracts and binding agreements was given as 19.

59. Cf. the use made of the oaths of 1214 and 1227 by Fiumi, *San Gimignano*, p. 153, to estimate the population of San Gimignano. In 1427 in rural Pistoia, the number of the entire population (15,775 for whom ages were given) was 3.4 times the number of adult males aged 14 and over (5173).

In the early thirteenth century, in other words, Pistoia seems to have been twice the size of San Gimignano and Volterra. More remarkable yet, it was apparently larger than Bologna and three quarters the size of the great port city of Pisa. These comparisons of course cannot be pressed too far. But they strongly suggest that Tuscany in the early thirteenth century was a region of many large cities, no one of which, not the port city of Pisa nor Florence itself, had yet secured a marked population advantage over its neighbors.

Over the long and critical years from 1219 to 1351 we have only partial and indirect evidence of changes within Pistoia's urban population. These hints do, however, indicate that the city's size did not later surpass to significant degree the probable figure of 11,000 residents it had attained by 1219, although neither did it fall much below that number.

In 1171, for example, Pistoia assumed the burden of fielding 150 knights to aid its then ally Lucca.[60] In 1288 it assumed a similar responsibility for providing knights for Florence, and the figure remained at 150.[61] In 1312, to aid the Florentines against Emperor Henry VII, it fielded only 100 knights.[62] Over the same years, the number of knights supplied by Prato remained at 50 in both 1288 and 1312, while Lucca maintained 600 in 1312, as against only 300 in 1288. This suggests that Pistoia's military strength, and the resources and population which supported it, did not grow substantially in the late thirteenth century. In the light of the city's sad military performance, it would be hard to believe otherwise.

The evidence from the physical size of the city encompassed by its walls is unfortunately somewhat ambiguous. According to the seventeenth-century historian Salvi, Pistoia's third and final circle of walls was laid in 1240, suggesting that the city had by then attained its maximum medieval size.[63] The walls embraced about 117 hectares, making the town one of respectable size (the area encompassed by Pisa's third circle, for example, was about 185 hectares). But by the late thirteenth century many persons were living beyond

60. Tholomeus, *Annalen*, p. 71. The Pistoiesi agreed to supply each year for one month 150 knights and 500 foot soldiers.

61. G. Villani, *Cronica*, VII, cap. 120 (II, 319).

62. Ibid. IX, cap. 47 (IV, 43).

63. *Historie*, I, 185.

the walls, where a system of encircling canals called *circule* had been dug to protect them.[64] This was probably the most rapidly growing part of the city, but no evidence has survived to permit an estimate of the population living in it.

In 1569, Tedaldi mentioned that the city in 1300–10 had 2300 houses or a population of 11,000.[65] He does not cite the source of his information, but his estimate appears so reasonable as to suggest that he was drawing it from official records (he had been captain of the city, with easy access to the archives). Pistoia in the late thirteenth century seems to have enjoyed no remarkable expansion, but it kept its size and remained a moderately large town.

The population of the city, like that of the countryside, began to decline sharply from about the middle of the fourteenth century. In 1351, according to Matteo Villani, the city of Pistoia had 1500 citizens "o poco più" able to bear arms.[66] This would have meant a population shortly after the Black Death of no more than 6000 persons. The city remained about that size for the remainder of the century. In the plague year of 1400, a chronicler mentioned that one half the urban population died, "cioè bocche 4000."[67] In his estimate, therefore, the city counted some 8000 inhabitants shortly before 1400.

The first complete survey of the city, called the Estimario della città, dates from 1415.[68] It lists 1090 hearths, although it unfortunately tells nothing about the number of persons they contained. Urban households were usually considerably smaller than those of the countryside; in 1427 they averaged only 3.6 persons each. If the same ratio prevailed, as is likely, in 1415, the city included only about 3900 persons. In that year its population was only 35 per cent of what it had been two centuries before. In the city as well as in the countryside, the population losses in the late Middle Ages were staggering.

But in the city as in the countryside, the population decline was finally reversed during the opening decades of the fifteenth century.

64. Cf. the regulations concerning the "custodes portarum circularum," *Statutum potestatis*, I, cap. 12, p. 17.

65. "Relazione," p. 316.

66. M. Villani, *Cronica*, I, cap. 97 (I, 164).

67. Luca Dominici, *Cronache*, I, 233.

68. ASP, Provv. Tomus 699.

In 1427 according to the Florentine Catasto, the city possessed 1247 hearths and 4468 persons (excluding clerics). This shows a considerable increase of about 568 persons in a little more than ten years. The city proved unable to maintain this rate of growth, but at least by the 1420s the population was again moving upward, for the first time in perhaps 200 years.

Table 3 illustrates, in round numbers, the movement of population, both urban and rural, at medieval and Renaissance Pistoia. To give an idea of the long-term trends, Tedaldi's estimate of the size of the urban and rural population in 1569 has also been included.

TABLE 3 Population, Urban and Rural, 1219–1569

Date	*City*	*Countryside*	*Total*
1219	11,000		42,000
1244		31,000	
1300–10	11,000		36,000
1344		24,000	
1351	6000		20,000
1383		14,000	
1392		11,000	19,000
1399	8000		
1401	4000	10,000	14,000
1404		9000	13,900
1415	3900		
1427	4500	12,000	16,500
1569	8000	30,000	38,000

On the basis of this table and the other data we have presented, it is possible to divide Pistoia's population history into three rather well defined periods. From as far back in the thirteenth century as our surveys permit us to discern, to 1340 or 1348, the population remained very high both in the city and the countryside. Exact movements in this first period are difficult to determine, and fluctuations certainly occurred. On the whole, however, the population seems to have remained fairly stable, though perhaps experiencing some moderate losses.

The second period, from about 1340 to 1400 or 1404, was marked by huge losses, ranging from two thirds to as much as three quarters of the population. It should be noted, however, that not all areas suffered to the same degree. The city gained relatively; the urban population, which constituted about a fourth of the total population before 1250, made up about a third in 1427. So also in the countryside, the people of the plain and even of the mountains fared comparatively well. It was the population of the middle hills which suffered the steepest decline.

From about 1404, however, the population fall was reversed, and the numbers of people began to rise, slowly but fairly continuously. This growth—still slow but still continuous—apparently persisted through the fifteenth century and was particularly marked in the countryside. In 1569, according to Tedaldi's estimate, the rural population was again approaching its peak medieval size.

The central and most dramatic event in Pistoia's population history of the late medieval and Renaissance periods is certainly the great demographic plunge of the fourteenth century, which wiped out over two thirds of the community's inhabitants. These stupendous losses could only have been produced by powerful forces and must have had in turn a powerful impact upon the region's economy and society. An understanding of Pistoia's economic and social history in the late Middle Ages and Renaissance requires, in other words, a careful investigation of the factors behind this extraordinary demographic performance. To accomplish this successfully, we must first investigate the demographic behavior of the contemporary population, its patterns of mortality, habits of reproduction and the factors which influenced both. While such matters for most of our period remain poorly discernible amid the darkness, one source does permit a full investigation of these demographic patterns. That source is the Catasto survey of 1427, one of the oldest records in European history to offer reliable information as to how an entire population lived, reproduced and died.

4

Demographic Patterns, 1427

[The father] should note the hour, the day, the month and the year, and also the place, and write them in his domestic commentaries and secret books as soon as the baby is born, and keep them among his precious possessions. This for many reasons, but if there were no other reason, it demonstrates the great diligence of the father in everything. If it is reputed diligence to write the day and name the broker through whom you purchased a donkey, is it less laudable to write the day you became a father, and the day when a brother was born to your sons? Furthermore, many occasions may happen when it will be necessary to know [the date of birth]. . . .

—L. B. Alberti, *Famiglia* (1434–35), pp. 119–20

In studying the mortality experience of a population, one of the most useful demographic tools is the "life table." A life table shows the complete history of a segment or cohort of a population as it ages, giving, along with other information, the number of deaths each year, the mortality rate at each age, and, also for each age, the average number of years lived thereafter or, in more familiar terms, the expectation of life.[1] Ideally, a life table should be based upon precise information regarding deaths, but unfortunately, such data are not available for medieval populations. However, any census that records the ages of a population may be used as the basis of a crude life table, and also for an approximate calculation of the mor-

1. See George W. Barclay, *Techniques of Population Analysis* (New York, 1962), pp. 93–122.

tality rates and the life expectancies of its members. Strictly speaking, such calculations would be statistically valid only if the population remained stationary and closed, i.e. only if birth and death rates remained constant and equal and if the population was not gaining or losing members through immigration or emigration. These conditions rarely prevail for any population, still less for one in the Middle Ages. For this reason mortality rates and life expectancies calculated on the basis of a single census are only roughly approximate. But they still permit instructive comparisons of mortality experiences among various segments of the population—men and women, urban and rural residents, rich people and poor—and they also offer an invaluable insight into the conditions affecting mortality in medieval society. A consideration of age distribution can also cast light upon reproductive patterns, which could not be attained through any other approach.

THE DATA

In 1427, along with declaring their assets and liabilities, the taxpayers of the Florentine district had to name the residents of their households and also give their ages.[2]

Some groups were, however, omitted from the survey. According to the Catasto regulations, "an employee or servant, agent, factor or apprentice" was not to be considered a family member for tax purposes, and presumably some were not therefore included in the census.[3] But it is also evident that many families listed their young servants anyway, probably in the hope of winning a tax deduction for them.[4] Adult servants, of course, presumably made their own declarations. While it is not possible to judge exactly, the number of servants omitted from the survey because of this regulation was probably slight.

A more important omission was the clergy and wards of the Church—priests, religious, their household servants and the in-

2. Pagnini, *Della Decima*, I, 217. The "health, capacity, industry and skills" of all residents were to be included in the declarations.

3. Karmin, *Legge*, p. 27.

4. ASF, Catasto 265, 296r, a six-year-old girl is listed among the family members and identified as a "fanciulla per lavorare." Ibid. 246v, a twelve-year-old boy is mentioned with the annotation "tiene per fante."

digent poor and sick dependent upon them. The clergy, however, did not escape the tax burden but were included in a special survey of ecclesiastical property.[5] This survey names 64 beneficed priests, and describes endowments supporting 24 salaried priests, 15 "chierici" or boys in minor orders, 54 religious men and 81 religious women. Sick and infirm in the hospitals amounted to 75, although the beds available seem to have been substantially more numerous; servants in clerical households, chiefly female relatives of priests keeping house for them, numbered 45. The total ecclesiastical population thus was listed as 358 persons, although this is certainly an incomplete figure.[6] For some, though unfortunately not for all, of these members of clerical households, ages are given. They range from a six-year-old nun in the monastery of Santa Lucia to a 90-year-old mother of a priest, and the average age of the 26 for whom ages are given is 32.[7] This is higher, though not by much, than the average age of the lay population (29 years). Clerics did not, in other words, enjoy a particularly long life; because their work brought them into close contact with the sick, they seem to have fallen in disproportionate numbers victims of the plague. The omission of clerics, or at least the inadequate data given by the Catasto concerning them, has the result of making mortality rates calculated on the basis of the lay population alone slightly higher than they should be.

There are also indications that our data, particularly in regard to girls, is incomplete for the younger years. The sex ratio of the population, urban and rural, for children 15 years of age and younger is very high, 125 boys to every 100 girls. This may reflect a peculiarity in the sex ratio at birth. Giovanni Villani, for example, stated that at Florence in the 1330s, out of the 5500 to 6000 babies baptized yearly, the number of boys surpassed that of girls by from 300 to 500, but even this distribution, if accurately reported, would at the maximum result in a sex ratio during childhood of about 118.[8] Exposure of girl babies does not appear to have been a common prac-

5. ASF, Catasto 189, Pistoia e Prato. Beni ecclesiastici.

6. The declaration of the monastery of San Michele in Forcole, for example, seems to be missing from the survey, although an addition to it is recorded, ibid. 690r.

7. See ibid. 595r for the declaration of the convent of Santa Lucia. For the 90-year-old mother of a priest, see ibid. 670v.

8. *Cronica*, XI, cap. 94 (VI, 184).

tice; many surviving sermons provide a fairly complete list of the sins of the age, and that crime attracted no particular attention. Rather this imbalance seems principally due to a failure to report girl babies. Thus, the sex ratio for adults aged 16 years and over drops radically, to only 103. This sudden increase in the relative number of girls in the adult ages seems explicable only on the assumption that many were passing through their infant and childhood years uncounted by the tax surveyors.

While a few servants, all clerics and some girl babies are not included in the census, the omission of both babies and adults should tend to offset each other, at least for the calculation of mortality rates. The mortality rates and life expectancies of the lay population, as the Catasto permits us to calculate them, could not be far removed from the true figures for the entire community. Moreover, these omissions do not vitiate comparisons among groups within the lay population, and from such comparisons some of the most illuminating inferences can be drawn.

One other distortion in the data must be noted: the strong propensity to round ages, to report them, especially after age 25, as multiples of ten (30, 40, 50 and so forth), and also, though in a less pronounced way, as multiples of five and even two. This concentration around certain preferred ages is a characteristic of most censuses, and demographers have devised several ways of measuring it. We shall use here one developed by Professor Thomas Lynn Smith.[9] The unpreferred, unattractive ages are those not divisible by 10, 5 or 2, that is, they are the ages ending in 1, 3, 7, or 9. The number of persons reporting these unpreferred ages can be totalled up to age 100. If there is no rounding, the total should equal 40 per cent of the entire population, and if this is so the population receives a score of 100 for perfect reporting. If there is rounding, the total will be less than the 40 per cent, and a score is calculated on the scale of 100, showing what portion of the perfect figure the total represents. The populations of modern industrial societies characteristically score in the middle and high 90s. Pistoia's population of 1427 scores at the very low figure of 54.4, indicating a strong tendency to round off reported ages. This is, however, still a better score than that achieved by the Egyptian population in 1947, which is given by Smith as 47.5.

9. *Fundamentals of Population Study* (New York, 1960), p. 151.

While the accuracy of age reporting at Pistoia in 1427 is extremely low by modern standards, the more remarkable aspect of this Catasto census is that this age data was both sought by the communal government and that it could have been collected from the people even with the modest degree of accuracy achieved. With little prior experience with such censuses, and few cogent reasons for remembering ages, the population still achieved an admirable level of accuracy.

This accuracy in reporting ages is also an indication of the cultural level of the population. Interestingly, the city scores better than the countryside (55 to 53.5), but the difference is so small as to appear negligible. Age data alone, in other words, would not support the assumption that the urban residents had achieved a significantly higher cultural level than their rural counterparts. There is a marked difference, on the other hand, in the relative accuracy with which men and women report their ages. Men score fully 10 points better than women, 59 to 49. The reasons for this difference are not clear. Women did not have the educational advantages enjoyed by men, and this may have affected their interest in knowing and remembering when they were born. But more probably, ladies in 1427 were doing what women have often done in censuses; they were being less than frank about their ages.

This pronounced tendency to round ages particularly at age 40 and older does distort mortality rates and, to a lesser degree, life expectancies. Even if mortality rates are calculated for five-year rather than for single-year periods (the usual practice in historical demography), the preference for years divisible by ten is so great that, after age 40, the periods ending in 0–5 show an exaggerated mortality, and those ending in 5–9 a mortality much lower than the true. To offset this distortion, we can smooth the mortality rates for age 40 and older by twice taking running averages of three consecutive rates in the table.[10] Corrections of this sort are always to be used with caution, as they suggest an accuracy and consistency which the original data did not possess. But provided the risks in such procedures are recognized, they do make possible more pointed

10. Thus, to calculate a figure for the age interval 40–45, we average the rates for 35–39, 40–44 and 45–49; for the interval 45–49, we average those for 40–44, 45–49 and 50–54. To further smooth the resulting rates, we repeat the procedure a second time.

comparisons of Pistoia's mortality experience with those of other populations.

Appendix II gives three life tables illustrating Pistoia's population in 1427. The first shows age distribution by year for the entire population, both raw and smoothed mortality rates for five-year periods, and life expectancies for each year of life. The following two abbreviated tables contrast the mortality experience at Pistoia of men and women, and of city dwellers and rural residents.

The second life table presented in the appendix also illuminates a factor of considerable importance in Pistoia's social and cultural history: the distribution of its numbers between men and women or, in more technical language, its sex ratio.

THE SEX RATIO

For Pistoia's entire population, the sex ratio stood at 111 males to 100 females, but as we have mentioned, this high figure partially reflects an apparent under-reporting of female children. The sex ratio for the adult population alone, 103, probably gives a more accurate indication of what the true sex division was for the entire population.

That men should have outnumbered women in Pistoia's medieval population is partly to be explained by higher mortality rates for women, particularly during the child-bearing years.[11] But it may also show the impact upon Pistoia's population of emigration. The great city of Florence was only 21 miles away, and inevitably it exerted an attraction upon Pistoia's citizens who found the opportunities offered by their own city poor in comparison. In medieval Tuscany as indeed in many regions, women tended to emigrate more readily than men over comparatively short distances; in particular, they tended to congregate in large cities.[12] The loss of people, women more than men, to Florence may have been a factor tipping the sex balance in favor of men at Pistoia in 1427.

Within Pistoia's population, the sex ratio was strongly influenced both by place of residence and by age. In the city, women began to outnumber men from age 11 on. As the population grew older, in

11. See below, p. 90.

12. On the tendency of the sex ratio in cities to favor women, see Russell, *Medieval Population*, p. 17.

spite of higher female mortality rates, the preponderance of women in the city grew also, undoubtedly reflecting a continuous and substantial immigration of older women to the city. For urban residents aged 20 and over, there were 96 men for every 100 women, and for residents aged 50 and over, the proportion of men shrank to 91. The female majority within the adult urban population was further increased by the number of women religious (81), who substantially outnumbered the monks and friars (54) and who were, in even greater proportion than male religious, city dwellers. Clearly, many young women came to the city to enter household service. Older and wealthier women, especially widows, seem to have been attracted by the comforts and amenities of urban living.

The rural population, on the other hand, shows a strong male preponderance, particularly for the higher ages. For rural residents aged 20 and over, the sex ratio (men to women) was 105; for those 50 and older, it was 109 and for those 60 and over, 117. Parts of the countryside were dominated by males to an even greater degree. In the middle hills, for example, economically a depressed area in the late Middle Ages, the sex ratio of those aged 60 and over was 125.

The number of women within a community, as well as the social prominence they enjoy, strongly influences that community's society and culture. At Pistoia, not only were women numerous within the city, but many were also quite wealthy. Many indeed were the widows of prosperous peasants or rural landlords who sought out the comforts of the city after their husbands had died. Urban culture thus developed under strong feminine influence (urban residents were also, as we shall see, older on the average than those of the countryside). The importance in numbers and influence of women within the city is a factor which should not be ignored in any consideration of urban society and culture.

Rural society, on the other hand, was dominated by men, and rural life was lived in a milieu where women could exert only a comparatively weak influence upon customs and culture. This too is a factor not to be overlooked in any effort to analyze rural society and to explain its exuberance, brashness and seemingly irrepressible penchant for violence.[13]

13. For further comment on the possible influence exerted by women upon urban culture, see below, p. 257.

MORTALITY

The life tables of 1427 also illuminate the mortality patterns of the medieval population. To be sure, omissions and distortions in the data mean that the mortality figures we have calculated cannot be considered rigorously precise. But they do permit comparisons of two sorts. First, the mortality rates for various ages in the population (the "age-specific" rates) may be compared with those of other historic populations, and this should show the ways in which Pistoia's mortality experience may have been distinct or unusual. Secondly, the apparent mortality rates of different age, sex and social groups within Pistoia's population may also be compared; this in turn will isolate and clarify the factors which, in the Middle Ages, influenced longevity.

Historical demographers in recent years have assembled a considerable quantity of information concerning mortality rates in the Roman Empire, as revealed through numerous funereal inscriptions stating age at death. Two areas of the Roman Empire have yielded particularly full and reliable data: Egypt and Roman "Africa" (in the sense of the central and western provinces of Roman North Africa). For Egypt, M. Hombert and C. Préaux were able to collect data from 813 pre-Muslim mummies and inscriptions to provide the basis for a life table.[14] Even richer than the Egyptian—the richest in fact of all Roman data bearing upon mortality—are the funereal inscriptions of Roman Africa. We shall use here for purposes of comparisons the life table constructed from African inscriptions by A. R. Burn.[15] It should be noted that these two Roman life tables differ considerably one from the other. Mortality rates in Egypt were particularly appalling, among the worst in the Empire, while those of central and western Africa were among the best. Although they reveal sharp contrasts, the two tables serve excellently to illustrate pretty nearly the worst and the best life expectancies characteristic of ancient Roman civilization.

14. M. Hombert and C. Préaux, *Recherches sur le recensement dans l'Egypte romaine* (Leiden, 1952). The results of this and other studies based upon Roman inscriptions are summarized by Russell, *Medieval Population*, pp. 24–30, and by A. R. Burn, "Hic Breve Vivitur," *Past and Present*, 4 (1953), table 2.

15. "Hic Breve Vivitur," table II, based on 3004 inscriptions from both pagan and Christian North Africa.

Historical demographers usually assume that the mortality experience of ancient and medieval populations followed an "oriental" pattern, that is, that their high death rates make them more similar to recent oriental populations than to those of the modern West. While this contrast between "occidental" and "oriental" mortality patterns is somewhat rigid, the comparison of ancient populations with those of recent Egypt, India or China has undoubtedly proved instructive, and we shall make use of such a comparison here. Specifically, we shall cite for comparative purposes the census of the Indian population of 1901–10.[16]

Whether viewed alone or in comparison with the experience of these other ancient or recent populations, the most striking feature of Pistoia's life tables of 1427 is the terrible loss of children. At Pistoia, the apparent mortality rates for ages 1–4 was 17.7; the rate over the same interval was only 7.5 in Roman Egypt and 6 for both males and females in central and western Africa.[17] No Roman province had a higher rate for these young ages, and most show a figure only half as high as that of Pistoia in 1427.

It is, to be sure, difficult to judge deaths over the first few years of life, both because of the apparent under-reporting of babies and because, as we shall further see, there are strong indications that the birth rate at Pistoia had been unusually high in the few years preceding 1427. But the losses of children, even in the years over 5, are scarcely less appalling, and characteristically higher than those of these other comparable populations. In Roman Egypt, worst of all the imperial provinces, the mortality rate for ages 5–9 was 7.0 and for ages 10–14 it was 8.3. At Pistoia, the corresponding rates were much higher, 10.5 and 11.2 respectively. The comparison (see p. 87) of the percentages of those alive at age 5 who reached ages 10 and 15 respectively indicates that child mortality at Pistoia substantially surpassed the worst experience of Roman Egypt, as well as the rates of Roman Africa and recent India.

There is one, fairly obvious explanation for this sweeping carnage of children at Pistoia. Only four years before, in 1423, a plague, described as "gigantic," had struck the city, and the age distribu-

16. The results of this census are summarized in Burn, "Hic Breve Vivitur," table III.

17. Russell, *Medieval Population*, pp. 27–29, tables 23, 24 and 30.

Per cent of Survivors

Age	*Pistoia*	*Roman Egypt*	*Roman N. Africa*	*India (1901–10)*
5	100	100	100	100
10	89.5	93	94.5	90.5
15	79.5	85	90.2	85.2

tion of 1427 leaves no doubt that it carried off hundreds of children in its wake.[18] To gain an impression of its terrible toll is only to compare, in the census of 1427, the number of four-year-olds, who in 1423 were in their first year of life, with that of younger children, who in 1423 had not yet been born:

Age in 1423	*Age in 1427*	*Numbers*	*On Scale of 100*
Not born	1	726	100
Not born	2	700	95.5
Not born	3	735	101
0	4	483	61.5
1	5	356	49.1
2	6	289	40

The sharp fall between ages 3 and 4, from 101 to 61.5, is partially to be explained by a spurt in the number of births in 1424, as we shall see; but it also shows to what degree the plague was a killer of children.

If death, and the plague in particular, thus made frightful inroads into the ranks of Pistoia's children, the expectations of survival improved remarkably for those fortunate enough to reach age 15. For the age interval 15–19, the mortality rate at Pistoia (10.3) dropped below that of Roman Egypt (10.9). For the years of young adulthood, the contrast became even more favorable to Pistoia: mortality rates for ages 20–24 and 25–29 were 18.6 and 18.5 respectively in Roman Egypt, and only 12.9 and 13.0 at Pistoia. The following table illustrates the percentage of survivors after age 15 at Pistoia and gives comparable percentages for Roman Egypt,

18. Sozomenus, *Chronicon*, p. 14, mentions the plague of 1423 under the year 1424: "Pestis Florentie ingens; et plurimi Florentini Pistorium profecti sunt: ex eo quod superiori anno ibidem pestis fuerat ingens et iam cessaverat." Salvi, *Historie*, III, 246, describes the plague as follows: "Nell'estate [of 1423] la pestilenza fece straordinario flagello, perchè la Città restò quasi del tutto dishabitata. . . ."

Roman North Africa and recent India. Burn, in constructing his life table for Roman North Africa, selected the ages 22, 32 and so forth, at which to compare survivors; this he did to diminish the distortion due to rounding of ages at numbers evenly divided by ten. To permit comparisons with his data, we have done the same for survivors at Pistoia in 1427.

Per cent of Survivors

Age	*Pistoia*	*Roman Egypt*	*Roman N. Africa*	*India (1901–10)*
15	100	100	100	100
20	89.7	89	—	92.7
22	84.8	—	87.8	—
25	78.1	73	—	—
30	68.4	59.5	—	76
32	63.3	—	66.7	—
40	51	42.8	—	57.7
42	44.7	—	48.7	—
50	35.4	30	—	40.2
52	28.8	—	36.5	—

A young adult at Pistoia, although exposed to repeated plagues, thus had a better chance of surviving than his counterpart in Roman Egypt. His chances were, however, slightly less good than those enjoyed by young adults in Roman North Africa or in recent India. Here, however, some further points may be made. The tendency to round ages makes exact comparisons difficult. The number of young adults at Pistoia is certainly also under-reported, because some were passing into the ranks of the clergy who were not included in the census and some were emigrating. If compensation could be given to these losses not due to death, Pistoia's percentage of survivors might well surpass those of Roman North Africa and, as we have mentioned, the survival rates of Roman North Africa were among the best in the Empire. The population of young adults at Pistoia did not, in other words, suffer extraordinary losses due to the plague, and we must remember this fact when we attempt to evaluate the impact of the plague upon Pistoia's society.[19]

For Pistoia's older adults, however, chances of survival once more deteriorated. For the age interval 60–64, Pistoia's mortality rate

19. See below, pp. 111–12.

(smoothed) was 29.5; it was 26.1 in Roman Egypt, the bleakest of all Roman provinces. And Pistoia's mortality rate remains substantially higher than the Egyptian during the remaining years of old age. The following table shows Pistoia's survival rates over the ages 50–90:

Per cent of Survivors

Age	*Pistoia*	*Roman Egypt*	*Roman N. Africa*	*India (1901–10)*
50	100	100	100	100
52	81.7	—	81.7	—
60	62.6	55.8	—	61
62	45.2	—	58.5	—
70	30.5	26.6	—	27.8
72	17.4	—	35.5	—
80	9.6	15.6	—	5.45
82	3.1	—	14.7	—
90	1.1	5.2	—	—

Pistoia's survival rates in old age thus fell well below those of Roman North Africa, and even in Egypt old people had a better chance for a longer life, particularly after age 70. (Curious to note, however, expectation of survival in old age was better at Pistoia than in recent India.) The marked mortality in the higher ages again seems directly attributable to the plague, which was apparently far more lethal for older people than for young adults.

This then is probably the most distinctive characteristic of the mortality experience at Pistoia in 1427 in relation to age: the sharp contrasts between the high, nearly astronomic mortality rates of children and old people, and the moderate rates of young adults. The young adult in late medieval Pistoia had nearly as good a chance of survival and sometimes a better one than the ancient Roman or the recent Indian. Yet he lived, even more than these other persons, surrounded by death. This peculiar experience of life amid death may also have exerted some influence upon the age's culture.[20]

What other factors, besides age, influenced mortality? Sex, not unexpectedly, had considerable importance, though rather more surprisingly, women on the whole fared better than men.[21] At re-

20. See below, p. 267.
21. For the data upon which the following comments are based, see Appendix II (2), below, p. 287.

corded age 0 (which means, in the main, infants who had survived the first critical weeks of life), females had a higher life expectancy than males (29.8 to 28.4 years respectively), and show a lower mortality rate throughout childhood. Because of the under-reporting of girl babies, these figures are not worthy of unreserved confidence. At age 15, when the data for men and for women may be considered of equal quality, the life expectancy still slightly favored women (27.4 for men, 27.5 for women). It must again be noted that, because our figures take no account of persons who have entered the clergy or who have emigrated, they are somewhat lower than the true.

If females fared well in childhood, that situation changed in the adult years. Their mortality rates increased, finally surpassing those of men for the age interval 30–34, and women continued to die in comparatively greater numbers until ages 65–69. At the same time, of course, their life expectancy fell below that of men and remained below it from ages 16 to 61.

The risks of child-bearing naturally contributed to this deterioration of women's chances of survival, though perhaps not directly. The period of their lowest relative survival expectancy, approximately between ages 30 and 60, does not correspond exactly with the child-bearing years. The chief responsibility for the more numerous deaths of young women is probably to be laid to the generally hard life they led, particularly in the countryside from which they were so willing to escape. Then too, they were after all the community's nurses, and this brought them into frequent and dangerous contact with the sick.

The higher mortalities of women over the years 30 to 60 also had an important impact on Pistoia's family structure. It resulted in a proliferation of widowers in the community, and eventually in marriages in which the husband was considerably older than his wife. This too is of some importance in shaping the character of Renaissance society.[22]

Although the lot of women may seem harsh by modern standards, they still survived better than men in extreme old age and in

22. The aged husband, beautiful young wife and importunate young lover are, of course, stock characters in the period's *novelle*, and the situation may in fact have been a common one.

childhood, and apparently had a greater life expectancy at birth. These facts make Pistoia's society more nearly resemble a modern occidental population than the peoples of the ancient world or even of the earlier Middle Ages. In the Roman Empire, men could expect to outlive women by as much as 4, 5, 6 or 7 years.[23] Men never had at any age a comparable advantage over women in late medieval Pistoia. Even in the earlier Middle Ages, the high sex ratio favoring men, reaching into the 130s and apparently characteristic of the period's populations, indicates a substantially higher mortality rate among women than among men.[24] Late medieval, Renaissance society had created conditions far more favorable for the survival of women than most societies which had preceded it. When Robert of Anjou boasted that his age had achieved new levels of humanitarianism and refinement, women had reason to believe him.[25]

Surprisingly, residence too seems to have had some influence on mortality rates: for every period of life the city population shows a lower mortality rate and longer life expectancy than the rural people.[26] Here, however, another unfortunately uncontrollable factor is influencing our figures: emigration, the loss of rural residents to the town. Still, the fact that even young children survived better in the city suggests that conditions of life were indeed better in the town than in the countryside. It is of course true that diseases could be expected to spread more rapidly in the crowded town than in rural areas. On the other hand, the urban population included a much larger proportion of affluent people, who enjoyed a better standard of living and could afford to flee to the countryside at the earliest indication of approaching plague. Even the newly born infants of rich families were frequently placed in rural households, to be nursed for their first year of life in the countryside.[27]

23. See Burn, "Hic Breve Vivitur," p. 16, for life expectancies characteristic of Roman populations from age 15.

24. In the early ninth century, on the estates of the monastery of Saint Germain des Prés near Paris, the sex ratio was 132 (2438 males to 1842 females), cited in Russell, *Medieval Population*, p. 14.

25. See above, p. 2.

26. See below, Appendix II (3), p. 288.

27. This was characteristically done for the babies of the family of Antonio Rospigliosi in the fifteenth century, *Richordi*, p. 23 (1476), p. 48 (1480) and p. 61 (1481). One of his babies, Piero, was, however, accidentally smothered by his nurse (ibid. p. 23).

Did wealth and social position themselves influence longevity? The chroniclers do suggest that the poor were frequently the earliest and most numerous victims of famines and plagues, but it is hard to verify this statistically.[28] The difficulty with a statistical approach is that a person's wealth tended to change, and often to deteriorate, as he aged, and many people apparently paupers at 65 had in fact lived most of their lives in comfortable circumstances. The following table does, however, attempt to explore the possible correlation between residence in wealthier households and longevity at Pistoia in 1427.

TABLE 4 Wealth and Longevity in Pistoia, Countryside and City, 1427

Assessment	*Countryside*			*City*			*Totals*		
(*in florins*)	*Hh*	*P*	*Av*	*Hh*	*P*	*Av*	*Hh*	*P*	*Av*
0	282	156	0.55	222	121	0.55	504	277	0.55
1–50	1076	603	0.56	329	182	0.55	1405	785	0.56
51–100	497	297	0.60	154	86	0.56	651	383	0.59
101–150	275	190	0.69	107	66	0.62	382	256	0.67
151–200	141	109	0.77	82	47	0.57	223	156	0.70
201–250	73	60	0.82	49	28	0.57	122	88	0.72
over 250	131	140	1.07	241	121	0.50	372	261	0.70
Totals	2475	1555	0.66	1184	651	0.55	3659	2206	0.60

The table shows the number of households arranged in groups according to the ascending amount of their assessment, the number of persons 60 years of age and older residing in them, and the average number of old people per household. *Hh* = households, *P* = persons 60 years of age and older, and *Av* = the average number of such persons per household.

The table shows a clear correlation between residence in a wealthy household and the chances of attaining age 60, but only in the countryside. No such correlation between wealth and longevity is apparent in the city. The explanation for this discrepancy may be the greater instability in the wealth of urban residents, who were apt to grow poorer in old age. But perhaps more importantly, aged paupers in the countryside tended to come to the city, where charitable distributions were more common and available, and this influx

28. According to Salvi, *Historie*, II, 198, the plague of 1399–1400 initially carried off only the poor, "veggendosi perire quasi tutta povera gente," but as it worsened "né il povero né il ricco sapeva dove stare."

swelled the ranks of the aged poor. For the population as a whole, it is probably safe to say that wealthier persons did have a better chance of reaching age 60 than their poorer neighbors, although the influence of wealth upon longevity would have to be called only moderate.

BIRTHS

On the basis of the Catasto census alone, it is not possible to calculate exactly birth rates at Pistoia in 1427, although some comments may be made about them. The Catasto itself reports 646 babies less than one year of age. With a total population of 16,105, the crude birth rate must have been at least 41 per thousand. Of course, Pistoia's true birth rate must have been much higher. Many babies were almost certainly not being reported, although this distortion was partially offset by the under-reporting of young adults. Most importantly, however, babies who died in the critical first few weeks of life were not included in the count, and the true birth rate for 1427, if we could know it, would undoubtedly prove much higher than the already considerable figure of 41 per thousand.

In instances when data concerning births is unreliable, demographers make use of what is called a child–woman or "fertility ratio." This shows the ratio of children aged 0 to 4 years in the population to women of child-bearing age, usually taken as 15 to 44. At Pistoia in 1427, children so defined numbered 3364 and women 2877. This gives the astonishingly high fertility ratio of 1170 (or 1.17 children per woman). This astronomic ratio surpasses the highest ever achieved by an American population. According to the census of 1835, the state of Illinois had the highest ratio in the nation, 1165. Most contemporary American ratios were much lower, and ratios were lower still outside the then rapidly expanding United States. In England, for example, in 1821 when the population was growing at no mean pace, the comparable figure was 605.[29] Pistoia's fertility ratio of over 1100 would seem to assume a crude birth rate, at least for some years, of perhaps 65 per 1000. While this estimate of crude birth rate may appear almost incredibly high, medieval populations do seem capable of such phenomenal rates of

29. J. T. Krause, "Changes in English Fertility, 1781–1850," *EHR*, 11 (1958), 67.

reproduction, at least over short periods. According to Giovanni Villani, Florence in 1336–38 had a population of roughly 100,000 in the city and suburbs; in the same period, between 5500 and 6000 infants were being baptized each year at the church of San Giovanni.[30] The ceremony was held only once a year, so many babies died before ever being counted. Nonetheless, the birth rate must have been well over 55 or 60 per thousand so to crowd the baptismal font. Florentine women in 1338, and Pistoiese in 1427, must have been straining in their child-bearing the limits of the biologically possible.

The Catasto of 1427 not only shows that the population was capable of impressive feats of reproduction; it also reveals that the birth rate could and did vary quite sharply under different circumstances. Several factors could exercise a powerful influence upon it.

Somewhat paradoxically, the most effective of all factors in increasing the number of births was the number of deaths. In 1423 the plague had struck Pistoia, and the survey of 1427 catches the population in the midst of a successful effort to make good its losses. For both the onslaught of the plague and the extraordinarily rapid recovery from it have left indelible marks on the age distribution of Pistoia's young population. The number of children aged three is 735; in spite of the great attrition to be expected in the first four years of life, this figure substantially surpasses the number of children aged two (700), one (726) and babies less than a year (646). To create this pattern, births in 1424 must have been remarkably numerous, and then they must have fallen considerably and continuously over the subsequent years. The year in which this bumper crop of babies arrived, 1424, was the year after the terrible plague of 1423, which had left the city "almost uninhabited" in its

30. *Cronica*, IX, cap. 94 (VI, 184). For further comment upon Villani's figures concerning baptisms, see N. Rodolico, *La Democrazia fiorentina nel suo tramonto (1378–1382)* (Bologna, 1905), pp. 19 ff. Rodolico argued, I think correctly, that to produce so many babies the Florentine urban population must have included more than the 90,000 "bocche tra uomini e femmine e fanciulli" which Villani attributes to it. Assuming a rate of reproduction of 45 per 1000, he therefore calculated an urban population of 125,000. However, even with a population of 125,000, the rate of 45 per 1000 would probably not have been high enough to compensate for the great loss of babies in the first critical weeks of life.

wake.[31] The many births of 1424 seem unquestionably linked with the many deaths of 1423.

Increased births following upon increased deaths seems to be a fairly common demographic phenomenon, almost as if the population automatically sought to maintain its numerical equilibrium in the face of sudden losses. Greatly increased births can be noted, for example, following plagues at Augsburg in 1504–05, London in 1665–66, and Genoa in 1653–59.[32] A common demographic phenomenon, this quick replacement of lost numbers is also understandable. The plague, in largely sparing young adults, did not severely injure the population's capacity to procreate. Indeed, the plague helped make a larger percentage of young adults biologically effective. For one thing, it facilitated younger marriages. In sweeping away many older persons, it brought young people into early inheritances, which in turn gave to young men economic independence and the opportunity to start a family. Young women could also thereby gain the dowries they needed for marriage. Older men who recently lost their wives were apt, if they remarried, to seek younger and presumably more fertile spouses, and the ranks of spinsters would at all events diminish.

For married persons too, the plague encouraged reproduction. The deaths of so many persons enhanced the economic opportunities of the survivors and their ability to support more children. Moreover, perhaps the strongest reason for restraint in having children has always been other children. With the death of so many children in the plague, spouses had no longer reason for caution in producing more. A Pistoiese chronicler himself observed how, for a "long time" before 1399, the women of Florence had been barren. Then in the plague year of 1400, many became pregnant.[33] They seem not to have delayed in replacing the children they were losing.

31. See above, chapter 2, n. 18.

32. Russell, *Medieval Population*, p. 41. The Swiss statistician Johann Heinrich Waser (1742–80) considered that through augmented births following plagues the population could make good its losses in ten years ("Ein Menschenverlust durch die Pest kann in zehn Jahren wieder ersetzt werden"). Cited in Wilhelm Bickel, "Ueber die Pest in der Schweiz," *Studium Generale*, 9 (1956), 515.

33. Luca Dominici, *Cronache*, I, 197, "In questo tempo [1400] sono ingrossate molte donne, che è gran tempo non ne feceno fanciulli e similmente fatti molti fanciulli da donne [che] non ne feceno mai gran tempo è."

If deaths could strongly influence birth rates, and in fact push them to the limits of the biologically possible, those rates were also sensitive to residence. Women in the countryside, with a fertility ratio of 1200, were distinctly more prolific than their urban sisters, who score at 1090. Was the city population so poor in reproduction as to be dependent upon a constant influx from the countryside to maintain its numbers?[34] Unfortunately, the plague of 1423 worked so strongly to increase births as to obscure though not entirely to obliterate such contrasts, and to deprive us of the opportunity of judging the "normal" situation, if such a situation ever really existed. Whether or not the city was a demographic parasite of the rural areas, there can be no doubt that the countryside, far more successfully than the town, raised men.

Why was the countryside more prolific than the city? Perhaps the basic, and at least the most obvious reason is that young men in the countryside could gain their economic independence earlier than their urban cousins. Tenant farmers were in great demand, and the young peasant could not only easily secure land but also gain the capital and stock from the owner with which to work it. Even without an inheritance of his own, he could look forward to supporting a wife and family. The young artisan in the city, on the other hand, had to work with capital largely accumulated by his own savings, and had to wait until he could open his own shop before assuming the responsibilities of a family. If his economic prospects were in the long run better than those of his country cousin, they were slower in maturing.

Moreover, even within the countryside, residence affected fertility. On the plain—Pistoia's most fertile and in 1427 its most prosperous rural area—there were 1.32 children for every woman. The women of the plain, in other words, were producing four children for every three born to a like number of women in the city. The region of the middle hills, once Pistoia's most prosperous but by 1427 its most depressed area, shows a much lower ratio of only 1.11 children per woman, though even this was slightly higher than that

34. According to J. C. Russell, "Late Mediaeval Population Patterns," *Speculum*, *20* (1945), 164, cities in the late Middle Ages were characteristically failing to reproduce themselves and depended upon immigration from rural areas to maintain their size.

achieved in the city (1.09). The ratio for the mountain population was lower still, only 1.04, but here there may be some distortion because of the under-reporting of babies in isolated mountain villages.

This in turn suggests that births were influenced not only by residence but also by family wealth and social position. There are two ways by which the possible correlation between wealth and fertility may be investigated. We can count the number of children 15 years of age and under in Pistoia's families, arranged in categories according to the tax assessment they bore in the Catasto. And we can calculate the fertility ratio between children and women, again arranged in groups according to the tax burden borne by their families.

Table 5 presents the correlation between tax assessment and the number of children supported by Pistoia's families in 1427.

TABLE 5 Wealth and Child Support in Pistoia, Countryside and City, 1427

Assessment	*Countryside*			*City*			*Totals*		
(in florins)	*Hh*	*Ch*	*Av*	*Hh*	*Ch*	*Av*	*Hh*	*Ch*	*Av*
0	275	404	1.47	223	191	0.86	498	595	1.19
1–50	1108	1581	1.43	353	354	1.00	1461	1935	1.32
51–100	498	924	1.85	160	163	1.02	658	1087	1.65
101–150	274	588	2.14	110	113	1.03	384	701	1.82
151–200	141	344	2.44	84	108	1.29	225	452	2.00
201–250	72	177	2.46	51	75	1.47	123	252	2.05
over 250	136	439	3.21	257	582	2.26	393	1021	2.60
Totals	2504	4457	1.78	1238	1586	1.28	3742	6043	1.61

The table shows the number of households for each assessment group, the number of children 15 years and younger residing in them, and the average number of children per household. *Hh* = households, *Ch* = children, and *Av* = the average number per household.

As the table shows, city households were consistently supporting only two children for every three maintained in rural homes at the same assessment level. Residence had indeed a marked impact upon the number of children households were supporting. However, for both urban and rural families, there is an unmistakable progression in the number of children being reared between the poorest and richest families. The wealthiest households in both the city and countryside were supporting over twice as many children as their poorest neighbors.

In interpreting this table, it should of course also be noted that it is not strictly indicative of birth rates. Infant mortality too, which seems to have been higher in poorer houses than in the richer, would have influenced the distribution of children. Then too, wealthier families sometimes accepted poor children into their households, whether ultimately to work as servants or simply "for the love of God."[35] Moreover, the figures show the number of children per household, not per family. The large number of children in richer households to some extent reflects a tendency for the sons of richer families to keep their inheritance undivided and to raise their children together.

A more refined approach, which avoids the distortion due to combined families in a single household, is to examine the fertility ratio between children and women in Pistoia's homes, again arranged in groups according to tax assessment. A difficulty with this method is that the generally high birth rate of 1424 and following years tends to scale down differences, although not to the point of obliterating a correlation between the wealth of a household and the fertility of its female members.

TABLE 6 Wealth and Fertility in Pistoia, Countryside and City, 1427

Assessment	*Countryside*			*City*			*Totals*		
(in florins)	*Ch*	*Wo*	*Av*	*Ch*	*Wo*	*Av*	*Ch*	*Wo*	*Av*
0	247	222	1.11	127	117	1.09	374	339	1.10
1–50	898	801	1.12	201	202	1.00	1099	1003	1.10
51–100	503	405	1.24	89	87	1.02	592	492	1.20
101–150	322	252	1.28	60	58	1.03	382	310	1.23
151–200	186	161	1.15	62	59	1.05	248	220	1.13
201–250	100	77	1.30	36	33	1.09	136	110	1.24
over 250	259	178	1.45	274	225	1.24	533	403	1.32
Totals	2515	2096	1.20	849	781	1.09	3364	2877	1.17

The table shows for each assessment group the number of children aged 4 years and younger, the number of women aged 15 to 44, and the fertility ratio, or average number of children per woman. *Ch* = children, *Wo* = women and *Av* = average number of children per woman.

35. ASF, Catasto 265, 296r, a girl is identified as a "fanciulla per lavorare" although she was only six years old. Ibid. 532v, another six-year-old girl was kept by the household "per l'amore di Dio." Ibid. 534v, another young girl, of whom it is noted "tiene per l'amore di Dio."

Both in the city and the countryside, although on different scales, the richer the household the more likely its female members to show a high fertility, while the poor, to judge from the numbers of children they were supporting, must have had difficulty maintaining their numbers. That bad social conditions should have hampered reproduction, and good conditions favor it, while perhaps contrary to some modern experience, is not an unprecedented or even unusual demographic phenomenon. In the ancient world, Plutarch in his life of Tiberius and Caius Gracchus commented that the oppressed poor of the Roman Republic "neglected the bringing up of children so that soon all Italy was conscious of a dearth of freedom."[36] In the fourteenth century in England, a famous preacher, John Bromyard, denounced "fornicators" who refused to marry, claiming that they were too poor to support a wife and children.[37] Several theologians of the late Middle Ages, including St. Antoninus of Florence, condemned the husband who interrupted intercourse with his wife because he felt himself too poor to feed additional children.[38] In 1475, the Florentine government itself warned the Pisan commune that when working men could not find employment, "the number of mouths falls."[39]

In his *Discorsi*, Niccolò Machiavelli affirmed that the population grows faster in free and prosperous cities, "for people will gladly have children when they know they can support them."[40] In 1589 the political philosopher Giovanni Botero stated that "men without possessions who live from hand to mouth either do not want children or do not have desirable ones."[41] He further warned rulers that if they wished to govern a large population they must aid the poor.

At Pistoia in 1427 the Catasto itself partially shows how poverty could diminish fertility. Daughters of the poorest families appar-

36. "Tiberius and Caius Gracchus," cap. 7. *Plutarch's Lives*, transl. B. Perrin, X (London, 1921), p. 161.

37. Cited in John T. Noonan, Jr. *Contraception. A History of Its Treatment by the Catholic Theologians and Canonists* (Cambridge, Mass., 1965), p. 229.

38. Ibid. p. 220.

39. "scema il numero delle bocche," ASF, Provv. Tomus 167, 118, cited in Pöhlmann, *Wirthschaftspolitik*, p. 48, n. 5.

40. Book II, chapter 2; *The Prince and the Discourses*, Modern Library ed. (New York, 1940), p. 287.

41. *The Reason of State and the Greatness of Cities*, transl. P. J. and D. P. Waley (London, 1956), p. 154.

ently had no hope of marriage.[42] Those from slightly more prosperous backgrounds had to await a turn in their father's fortunes—perhaps a good harvest—before their dowries could be paid and they could join their husbands. In Pistoia's society, it was not unusual for girls to be betrothed at 14, 13 or even 12 years, but it was not unknown for them to linger in their father's house unable to join their husbands even to the age of 20.[43]

Within marriage too, limitations on procreation until circumstances should favor additional children seem widely characteristic of the medieval population. That Florentine women should have been so "barren" before 1400, and then so remarkably fertile as to attract the attention of a chronicler, must mean that they were consciously controlling the number of their offspring.[44] Contemporary sermons do refer to contraception, but probably the more common way of limiting births was sexual restraint within marriage.[45]

These then seem to have been the more notable characteristics of Pistoia's population as established by an analysis of the Catasto of 1427. There is no discounting the high death rates in this age of plagues, but the very young and the very old, far more than young adults, were their principal victims. Young adults in fact fared not markedly worse than their counterparts in many ancient, or recent

42. Cf. ASF, Catasto 307, 409r, commune of S. Maria Impruneta in the Florentine contado. "Nicholosa sua figliuola d'età 18. Nolla può maritare perchè è povero."

43. ASF, Catasto 264, 349v, commune of Tizzana. A girl aged 20 is "maritata" but still not living with her husband. Ibid. 265, 306r, a girl aged 18, of whom it is noted "avvisovi chell'o maritata e non la mando perchè non o da dare la dota."

44. See above, chapter 4, n. 33. On the importance of contraception in medieval society, see most recently Noonan, *Contraception*, pp. 200–30. Noonan concludes that while the practice of contraception was "not a large social problem," it remained "a reality of medieval civilization."

45. See, in the thirteenth century, the sermon of the archbishop of Pisa, Federigo Visconti (d. 1277), Cod. Laurent.–S. Crucis, XXXIII, Sin. 1, 27v, in the Laurentian Library at Florence. Federigo condemns the "malas et pessimas mulieres que non solum procurant abortum sed etiam venas [venena?] sterilitatis contra id, quod legitur in lege deut. vii, 'Non erit apud te sterilitas utriusque sexus,' quibus quasi homicidis penitentia imponi [debeat]." In the late fourteenth century, St. Catherine of Siena, in a vision of hell, noted a special class of sinners "who sinned in the married state," and later Bernardino of Siena declared, "Of 1000 marriages, I believe 999 are the devil's." See Noonan, *Contraception*, p. 227.

eastern populations. In regard to births, the population, even when decimated by the plague, retained a powerful capacity to reproduce and under favorable circumstances could rebound from enormous losses with an astounding rapidity. At the same time the birth rate remained highly unstable and critically sensitive to social and economic influences upon it. The most powerful stimulus to increased births was the plague itself, but the birth rate also varied widely according to place of residence and the social and economic position of the potential parents. Women in the countryside were much more fertile than those in the city. But in both countryside and city, the more favorable a family's conditions of life, the greater the likelihood that its women would show a high fertility.

In the light of what the Catasto has taught us about births and deaths in this fifteenth-century community, we can now examine and attempt to evaluate the several factors which combined to produce the great depopulations of the closing Middle Ages.

5

The Population Catastrophe: A Review of Causes

And place in your mind, and consider . . . how many more children there would be [if more young people married]. Do you not see that Siena is diminishing, that in Milan, when Brother Bernardino returned, it was told to him that twenty thousand young girls were there to marry, without counting those already married and those who had no time; and more young men than in all Italy?

—St. Bernardino of Siena, 1425

The first and most evident explanation for the huge population losses of the late Middle Ages is the great plagues and famines, which scourged the European peoples with such cruel frequency in the fourteenth and fifteenth centuries. Recently, however, many historians, perhaps unwilling to attribute so great a turning point in Western development to simple accident, have been questioning whether the plagues and famines should be considered the sole and exclusive causes of the great depopulations. Perhaps these disasters were only the manifestations of a deeper social and economic crisis within the European community.

Among the many scholars active in searching out possible economic factors in the great mortalities of the fourteenth century, the distinguished historian M. M. Postan has been especially prominent. Cautiously, and with great concern for terms, he has been advancing the argument that the demographic plunge of the fourteenth century was the consequence, even, as he says, the "nemesis," of the "inordinate expansion" of the earlier Middle Ages.[1] The high mortalities of the late medieval plagues and famines, in other words, are directly attributable to overpopulation. The younger English historian J. Titow similarly discerns "acute land shortage and severe overpopulation" in parts of England before the Black Death.[2] B. H. Slicher van Bath, in his recent *Agrarian History of Western Europe,* flatly attributes the high mortalities of the Black Death and other epidemics and famines to "prolonged malnutrition" brought on by excessive population growth.[3] The French historian Georges Duby includes within his own general agricultural history a section entitled "Overpopulation."[4] And numerous studies have recently been calling attention to the high levels of population density reached in many areas of Europe on the eve of the Black Death.[5]

We are, in other words, witnessing the emergence of an essentially Malthusian interpretation of the demographic collapse of the fourteenth century, which, while cautiously expressed and far from universally accepted, still promises to remain a major interest of historians in the forseeable future.[6] But to investigate possible over-

1. Cf. Postan's review of Georges Duby, *L'Économie rurale et la vie des campagnes dans l'Occident médiéval* (Paris, 1962), in *EHR, 16* (1963), 197, "The present reviewer [Postan] has been especially gratified to read the passages in the book wherein the depression of the fourteenth century is represented as the consequence, perhaps even the nemesis, of the inordinate expansion of the preceding epoch."

2. "Some Evidence of the Thirteenth Century Population Increase," *EHR, 14* (1962), 218–23.

3. *Agrarian History,* p. 84.

4. *L'Économie rurale,* II, 216–19, "Le Surpeuplement."

5. J. R. Strayer, "Economic Conditions in the County of Beaumont-le-Roger, *Speculum, 26* (1951), 277–87, concludes that the population of that Norman county was not greatly inferior in 1313 to what it is today. For bibliographies on recent regional studies, see Duby, *L'Économie rurale,* II, 216–19, and E. Carpentier, "Autour de la peste noire: famines et épidémies dans l'historie du XIVe siècle," *AESC,* 17 (1962), 1062–92. Italy has attracted relatively few regional studies, but see Fiumi, *San Gimignano,* esp. pp. 112–27 and pp. 170–74; idem, "La Popolazione del territorio volterrano-sangimignanese ed il problema demografico dell' età communale," *Studi in onore di Amintore Fanfani* (Milan, 1962), I, 249–90; idem, "La Demografia fiorentina di Giovanni Villani," *ASI, 108* (1950), 78–158; Cristiani, *Pisa,* pp. 162–88; Carpentier, *Orvieto;* and Bowsky, "Impact."

6. Russell, *Medieval Population,* p. 145, maintains that "for the most part"

population within the medieval community and the deaths indirectly attributable to it is necessarily to consider births as well, in an attempt to discern what role they too might have played in maintaining, or disturbing, the delicate balance of life.

This present chapter examines all three of these factors—the impact of natural disasters, the influence of overpopulation, and the role of births—in the light of the evidence which Pistoia's rich demographic sources have given us.

PLAGUES AND FAMINES

At Pistoia as at other Tuscan and European cities, plagues and famines struck with appalling regularity in the fourteenth and fifteenth centuries. Pistoia's late medieval chroniclers are relatively few and poorly informative, but, as table 7 shows, their works are still crowded with reports of disasters.

The frequency with which these ravishes decimated the city was matched only by their ferocity. At Pistoia, the combined famine and plague of 1339–40 carried away more than one quarter of the population, both in the city and countryside.[7] We are without surviving contemporary estimates of the losses attributable to the plague of 1348, but a later chronicler remarks that of the old and young "hardly a person was left alive."[8] At neighboring Bologna, a contemporary chronicler estimated the deaths at more than two thirds the population, and in his famous preface to the *Decameron,* Giovanni Boccaccio numbered the dead within the walls of Florence

---

the population of medieval communities remained well within available resources. See also the criticisms advanced by W. C. Robinson, "Money, Population and Economic Change in Late Medieval Europe," *EHR,* 12 (1959), 63–76, with a reply by Postan, ibid. pp. 77–82.

7. *Storie pistoresi,* p. 162. "E nella città di Pistoia fue grandissima e bastovi più d'uno anno continuo; e dicesi che quivi morio tra nella città e nel contado più che la quarta parte della gente."

8. Pandolfo Arferuoli, *Historiae* (written ca. 1628), I, 391, "This inflamation first broke out in people of tender age, and continued in the young and finally spread among the old people. Of these hardly a person was left alive, so that the city was undone, and the countryside destroyed." On the health regulations through which Pistoia sought to control the pestilence, see A. Chiappelli, "Gli Ordinamenti sanitari del comune di Pistoia contro la pestilenza del 1348," *ASI,* ser. 4, 20 (1887), 3–24.

TABLE 7 Plagues and Famines Recorded at Pistoia

Year	*Description*	*Source*
1313	Famine	Salvi, *Historie*, I, 315
1328–29	Famine	*Storie pistoresi*, p. 132
1339–40	Plague and famine; death of one quarter of population	Ibid. p. 163
1346	Famine	ASP, Provv. Tomus 19, 50v
1347	Famine and trace of plague	Ibid. 73r
1348	The Black Death	Ibid. 76v; Storie pistoresi, p. 224
1351	Scarcity	ASP, Provv. Tomus 20, 17v
1357	"Mortal fevers"	Salvi, *Historie*, II, 107
1369	Scarcity	Ibid. II, 124
1370	Scarcity	ASP, Provv. Tomus 30, 46v
1375	Famine	Salvi, *Historie*, II, 135
1383	Sickness	Ibid. II, 153
1388	Scarcity	ASP, Provv. Tomus 36, 37r
1389	Plague and famine	Ibid. Tomus 34, 8r
1390	Scarcity	Ibid. Tomus 37, 81v
1393	Famine and plague	Salvi, *Historie*, II, 172
1399–1400	Plague; death of one half the population	Luca Dominici, *Cronache, II*, 233
1410	Famine and trace of plague	Salvi, *Historie*, II, 232
1411	Scarcity	ASP, Provv. Tomus 47, 33v
1416	Plague	Salvi, *Historie*, II, 237
1418	Plague	Ibid. II, 246
1420	Scarcity	ASP, Provv. Tomus 45, 145r.
1423	Plague	Salvi, *Historie*, II, 242
1436–39	Plague	Manetti, *Chronicon*, p. 1048
1457–58	Plague	Salvi, *Historie*, II, 373–75

at over 100,000, although this latter figure surely exaggerates.[9] At Orvieto, in the judgment of E. Carpentier, at least one half the population was swept away.[10]

During the plague of 1400 at Pistoia, contemporary chroniclers

9. Matthaeus de Griffonibus, *Memoriale historicum*, ed. L. Frati and A. Sorbelli, RIS, new ed. 18, pt. 2 (Città di Castello, 1902), p. 56, "tam magna quod duae partes ex tribus partibus personarum firmiter decesserunt." Another Bolognese chronicle says "de cinque erano morte li tre et più," *Corpus chronicorum bononiensium*, ed. A. Sorbelli, RIS, new ed. 18, pt. 1 (Città di Castello, 1905), p. 585. For Boccaccio's estimate, see *Il Decameron*, ed. V. Branca (Florence, 1951), I, 25–26, "oltre a cento milia creature umane si crede per certo dentro alle mura della città di Firenze essere stati di vita tolti."

10. *Orvieto*, p. 135. Y. Renouard, "Conséquences et intérêt démographique de la peste noire de 1348," *Population*, 3 (1948), 459–66, estimates that the mortality rate in 1348 varied from one third to two thirds of the population according to region.

reported that one half the population was wiped out, and one enterprising citizen even set about counting the bodies in the city.[11] He arrived at the grim total of 3234, although he felt the true figure was more like 4500.[12]

There are in other words no grounds for doubting the high mortalities assigned by contemporaries to the great medieval plagues. But there still remain several unresolved problems concerning their nature and their impact.

Perhaps the greatest puzzle of all is the precise character of the diseases which exacted such terrible tolls.[13] An analysis of chronicle accounts from the Middle Ages, supplemented by modern medical experience with plague outbreaks among recent eastern populations, offers evidence that three distinct varieties exist: the bubonic, pneumonic and, a rarer type, the septicaemic. Alone among the three, the bubonic infection produces the characteristic glandular swellings or boboes, notably in the area of the groin, which most chroniclers associated with the plague victims in 1348. However, the bubonic variety does not seem contagious enough to spread so rapidly—"like fire" as Boccaccio says—as to wipe out one third or one half the population within a few months. Bubonic plague does not spread easily, because it cannot be carried directly from human to human. It is more truly a disease of rats or small mammals rather than of men. The bacilli responsible for it must first develop in rats, and then be carried to humans through fleas. A rapid spread of the bubonic plague requires an army of rats sickened by a true epizootic among them, and legions of fleas which enjoy rather easy access to human hosts. Moreover, recovery from a bubonic infection is not unknown or even unusual for an otherwise healthy victim. According to the observations made by a physician who in 1609–10 lived

11. Luca Dominici, *Cronache*, I, 233, "non fece mai peggio la moria: e' cci morta circa la metà della gente, cioè bocche 4000; e simile in contado." Sozomenus, *Chronicon*, p. 1170, "Et tamen dimidia pars hominum universaliter peste diem obiit." On the Book of Pestilence, see below, pp. 109–10.

12. Luca Dominici, *Cronache*, I, 288.

13. On the nature of the plague, see most recently J. M. W. Bean, "Plague, Population and Economic Decline in the Later Middle Ages," *EHR*, 15 (1963), 423–37; Carpentier, *Orvieto*, pp. 112–19; and Erich Woehlkens, "Das Wesen der Pest," *Studium Generale*, 9 (1956), 507–12. G. Sarton, *Introduction to the History of Science*, III, pt. 2 (Baltimore, 1948), pp. 1650–1733, provides a lengthy bibliography of accounts and medical treatises concerning the plague.

through an outbreak of the bubonic plague at Basel in Switzerland, the mortality rate of those infected was about 60 per cent.[14]

The medical characteristics of the bubonic plague thus correspond rather poorly with what chroniclers report about the Black Death, with the high contagion and terrible mortalities they attribute to it. In the face of such difficulties, many medical historians now feel that the real killer in many of the great historical epidemics was another variety of plague, the pneumonic (the septicaemic, while equally deadly, seems always to have remained relatively rare). While much obscurity still persists concerning it, pneumonic plague seems initially to develop as a secondary infection among victims of the bubonic variety. However, once developed in their human hosts, the bacilli of the pneumonic plague can spread through the air, directly infecting other humans, and hence run rapidly through a population. Moreover, infection with pneumonic plague seems to have been almost always fatal.

But the attribution of the high mortalities of the fourteenth-century epidemics to a form of pneumonia triggered by the bubonic plague does not remove all difficulties. Pneumonia is a wintertime sickness, spreading most rapidly when people are exposed to colds and chills and are living together in confined quarters. But the great plagues of the fourteenth century are characteristically described as diseases of the summer months. In 1348, the Black Death began to take noticeable tolls in the inland Tuscan cities only in March or April; it reached its peak virulence in high summer and dissipated with the cooler weather of September.[15] The plague of 1340 at Florence lasted from middle March through July.[16] At Pistoia, the plague of 1389 began in March and April and grew stronger as the weather warmed.[17] In 1400, while signs of approaching pestilence were noted at Pistoia the previous autumn, the highest mortalities

14. Cited by Wilhelm Bickel, "Ueber die Pest in der Schweiz," *Studium Generale*, 9 (1956), p. 514. Woehlkens, "Wesen der Pest," believes that it was not possible for the plague ever to have killed more than 35 per cent of the entire population.

15. Carpentier, *Orvieto*, pp. 99–101. At Siena, the plague reportedly lasted through June, July and August. See Bowsky, "Impact," p. 17.

16. *Storie pistoresi*, p. 162, "la mortalità fue grandissima e spezialmente in Firenze e nel contado, dove durò da mezzo marzo a tutto luglio."

17. Salvi, *Historie*, II, 165, "pestilenzia . . . incominciò per i mesi di Marzo e Aprile a sentirsi; anzi ogni di più augmentandosi. . . ."

were concentrated in the late spring and summer of 1400; deaths diminished after the feast of St. James (25 July) and by November the plague had spent its strength.[18]

That a pulmonary infection should have spread "like fire" in summer and disappeared in winter is difficult to explain, and this difficulty has set other historians to speculating that perhaps weather conditions in some way favored the spread of the contagion.[19] Pistoia's archives again yield some data directly indicative of weather conditions about the middle of the fourteenth century. These are the dates set by the commune for the beginning of the grape harvest (*vendemmia*), which show how early the grapes had ripened. Table 8 gives these dates from 1330 to 1355. After 1355, unfortunately for meteorological historians, the commune decided to abandon this policy of setting dates for plucking the grapes.

TABLE 8 Dates of the Grape Harvest at Pistoia, 1330–55

Year	*Date*	*Year*	*Date*
1330	8 Oct.	1338	30 Sept.
1331	23 Sept.	1342	1 Oct.
1332	20 Sept.	1345	26 Sept.
1333	18 Sept.	1346	24 Sept.
1334	3 Oct.	1347	24 Sept.
1335	4 Oct.	1352	1 Oct.
1336	1 Oct.	1353	23 Sept.
1337	6 Oct.	1355	25 Sept.

Sources: ASP, Provv. Tomi 5, 8, 9, 10, 11, 19, 21, 22 and 23.

Unfortunately, the records give no date for 1348; the commune had been too disrupted by the plague to be concerned with grapes.

18. Specimen historiae Sozomeni (ann. 1362–1410), *RIS*, XVI, 1057 and ff., records that "[pestis] incoepit de mense Aprilis, et perservavit usque ad et per totum mensem Octobris." According to Luca Dominici, *Cronache*, I, 233, "E la moria cominciò per S. Iacopo a restare e poi a poco a poco restette e per S. Maria di mezzo agosto pochi ci moriano e poi ristette prestamente."

19. Cf. G. Utterstrom, "Climate Fluctuations and Population Problems in Early Modern History," *Scandinavian Economic History Review*, 3 (1955), 3–47, who discerns a close connection between climate and demographic movements. For a more reserved evaluation of the role of weather in European history, see E. Le Roy Ladurie, "Histoire et climat," *AESC*, 14 (1959), 3–34; idem, "Climat et récoltes aux xviie et xviiie siècles," *AESC*, 15 (1960), 434–65; and idem, "Aspects historiques de la nouvelle climatologie," *Revue Historique*, 225 (1961), 1–20.

But the series as a whole, with half the dates in October, would suggest a sequence of unusually cool, humid summers about the middle of the fourteenth century—for cool, cloudy summers seem the principal factor in retarding the ripening of the grape. This corresponds well with current opinion concerning the climatological character of the fourteenth century: that it was an especially humid period.[20] But did this help diffuse the plague? If the cool wet weather of summer promoted contagion, why did that contagion cease in the cooler and wetter weather of winter? Perhaps there is a connection between climatic conditions and the great plagues of the fourteenth century, but more research is needed into the history of both weather and diseases before any firm conclusions can be reached.

In the light of our present knowledge (or ignorance) concerning the nature of the contagion and the physical conditions which promoted it, we can better explain the high mortalities by considering not the disease itself but its victims. Were some segments of medieval society particularly susceptible to infection? Here again, Pistoia possesses a relevant and for Tuscany an apparently unique source, a "Libro di Pestilenzia" or census of the dead.

In 1400 in the midst of a fierce attack of the plague, a notary, ser Paolo Dominici, made a count of the victims, and his inventory of bodies was incorporated into the chronicle of his brother ser Luca, also a notary.[21] To be sure, he was unable to register all bodies; he seems to have begun his count only in May, although the plague had been claiming victims since the preceding autumn. Moreover, the information he gives about the deceased is not entirely complete and consistent; the dead of one parish he does not identify by name, and the victims of four other parishes are named but no further indication is given as to whether they were fathers or mothers, sons or daughters, household heads or members. Ser Paolo says he saw 3234 bodies, though he identifies by parish 2301 and out of these he gives detailed information for only 1625.

Though ser Paolo's census of the dead is thus not complete, his list is still substantial and it offers a rare opportunity to identify with some exactness the characteristic victims of the plague.

20. Le Roy Ladurie, "Histoire et climat," p. 10.
21. Luca Dominici, *Cronache*, I, 288 and ff.

Of the 1625 dead, 430 are expressly called children (*fanciulli* or *fanciulle*) or are described by other names indicative of still tender years (*nipote, garzone, fante, giovane*). A still larger number of the deceased, 710, are identified not by their own names but as "sons" or "daughters" of the man in whose house they were living. Some few of these persons called sons and daughters may have been adults still living at home with their parents. But we know that the average size of the city household in 1427 was only 3.6 persons; it was obviously most unusual for married children or even adult children to continue living for long in the houses of their fathers within the city. These 710 victims of the plague, without households of their own and identified only by their fathers' names, must have been in the great majority children. Of the 1625 named victims, only 485 appear as masters and mistresses of their own homes and unquestionably adults.

Thus, according to the statistics given by the Book of Pestilence, nearly 1140 of the 1625 named victims of the plague, or 70 per cent of the total, seem to have been babies or children still living at home with their parents. With such carnage of children, whole families must have been wiped out, and in his list of the dead ser Paolo confirms this: "Currado his son and his five other children," reads one of his notes; "the wife of Lazzero his son with five children," another records. Of the 485 persons or 30 per cent who were certainly adults, many and perhaps most were older persons, and doubtlessly some of these were already weak and infirm.

Other plague descriptions similarly suggest, though with less statistical rigor, that the very young and the very old fell prey to the contagion in the largest numbers. At Siena in 1348, out of 52,000 plague victims, 36,000, or fully 70 per cent, were described as "vechi" or old persons.[22] In the same year the Sienese chronicler Agnolo di Tura buried with his own hands all five of his children.[23] At Pistoia in 1348, according to a description preserved by a later historian, the plague struck first "in people of tender years."[24] In

22. Agnolo di Tura, *Cronache senesi*, p. 555, cited in Bowsky, "Impact," p. 17.

23. Ibid. p. 15.

24. Pandolfo Arferuoli, *Historiae*, I, 391, cited in A. Chiappelli, "Ordinamenti," p. 6.

regard to the plague of 1400, ser Luca, in a somewhat garbled passage, seems to have said that there was "no remedy," specifically for "young children" and the "old of every generation."[25] And that the very young and the very old should have been characteristically the plague's victims is only what our consideration of the Catasto of 1427 should have led us to expect.[26]

Children and old people rather than young adults and (to judge from the Catasto) the poor probably more than the rich appear as the principal victims of the plague, and this pattern of mortality is of first importance in evaluating its impact. The plague, in other words, touched only mildly the young adults, who were at the same time the economically most active part of the population, the businessmen, workers, taxpayers, administrators and (perhaps most significantly) the child bearers. This explains why after the initial shock of the plague, the economy and government could so quickly regain their equilibrium. At Florence, for example, the plague had no lasting impact on urban revenues; indeed, by 1350 the revenues were substantially greater than they had been before the plague, and in spite of repeated later visitations they continued to grow throughout the century.[27] This would seem hardly possible if the number of taxpayers had in fact fallen from one half to two thirds. And with the child bearers largely spared, with the plague itself, as we have seen, offering a powerful incentive to fertility, the population should have, and in some instances did, replenish its numbers in a relatively brief period. This would help explain why the chronology of population decline does not exactly correspond with the chronology of the plagues and famines. At Pistoia, a noticeable if small population fall in the countryside had already begun before 1250, well before report of natural disasters crowd the annals. And the plagues of the fifteenth century seem to have given way little in virulence to those of the fourteenth; but they did not result in the

25. *Cronache*, I, 232, "e non ci è rimedio niuno: i giovani fanciulli, vecchi di ogni generazione gente."

26. See above, pp. 85–89.

27. Urban revenues at Florence for Nov. and Dec. 1347 were 41,585 pounds; for Nov. and Dec. 1348, 47,847 pounds. For May and June 1348 they were 48,282 pounds, and for May and June 1349, 75,970 pounds. For the same months in 1350, they were 137,262 pounds. See Herlihy, "Direct Taxation," p. 404.

kind of deep population plunge which those of the fourteenth century produced.

The impact of the plagues and other natural disasters upon Pistoia's medieval population is not a little paradoxical. There is no minimizing the huge losses directly attributable to them, and no discounting the shock suffered by society in their wake. But if the virulence of the plagues is unquestionable, there were certainly other factors at work in fourteenth-century society which magnified their impact and for long hampered efforts to recover from them.

Was one of those factors overpopulation?

THE MALTHUSIAN DIAGNOSIS

The more we learn of European populations before the plague, the more we must be amazed at the extraordinary numbers of people the medieval community had come to support.

Pistoia's population is no exception. At about 1244, the entire countryside of Pistoia was maintaining, as we have seen, about 34,000 persons settled within an area of about 900 square kilometers.[28] This represents a density of rural settlement of about 38 persons per square kilometer. The total population of medieval Pistoia, including approximately 11,000 then residents of the city, would be about 45,000, which means a density of settlement of about 50 persons per square kilometer. This remarkable density was achieved, it must be added, even before 1250 and within a contado where over one half the land was comprised of high and inhospitable mountains.

Tuscany's more favored towns and more fertile territories in the thirteenth century were even more densely settled, not to say glutted. According to E. Fiumi's reasonable calculations, the density of settlement, both urban and rural, at San Gimignano had surpassed 50 persons per square kilometer by 1227.[29] By 1277–91 it was more like 74 and by 1332 it had reached 85, making that area more densely settled in the Middle Ages than it is today.

For the Florentine contado, the largest in Tuscany, population densities can only be roughly estimated for the period before the Black Death. On the basis of salt consumption, Florence in 1318

28. See above, p. 70, Table 1.
29. *San Gimignano*, pp. 153–169.

seems to have counted about 25,000 families in the city and 30,000 in the countryside, exclusive of the rural nobles.[30] On the assumption that the average household was again about 4.65 persons, this would mean very roughly a population of about 116,290 for the city and 139,500 for the countryside, or a total of 255,700 persons settled in something like 3900 square kilometers. This gives a density of about 65.5 persons per square kilometer. The density of settlement at Siena may have been even higher.[31]

It is instructive to consider the implications of population densities which, even before 1250, reached and surpassed 50 persons per square kilometer. If all Tuscany shared the same density of population that Pistoia had attained by 1244—and since fully one half the Pistoiese contado was thinly settled high hills and mountains, that is not unlikely—the Tuscan province would have contained an astounding 1,200,000 persons even before 1250. Not until well into the nineteenth century would Tuscany again attain that figure.[32] According to E. Fiumi's not unreasonable estimate, the Tuscan

30. ASF, Provv. Registri, Tomus 15, 161–171, mentions that the distribution of salt for 1318 was 60,000 staia, 25,000 of which were distributed in the city, 30,000 in the countryside, and 5000 among the clergy. For non-noble families in the countryside, the distribution seems to have been made on the basis of one staio per family, as is explicitly stated for a later year (1323) in ASF, Provv. Tomus 20, 73r, 27 April 1324, "distributionem salis factam pro anno preterito in comitatu Florentie ad rationem unius starii pro qualibet familia ipsorum populorum et communium. . . ." The rural nobles had to accept 6 staia for every 100 pounds of their tax assessment. That the rural population consisted of about 30,000 families in 1318 fits in well with later estimates of its size. In 1350, right after the Black Death, the rural population, according to Fiumi's calculations, consisted of 31,386 families, but from this figure must be deducted the population of areas which were not part of the contado in 1318, notably Prato and the communes of the southern Monte Albano. The result is 26,717 families. On the survey of 1350, see Fiumi, "Demografia fiorentina," *ASI, 108* (1950), 119–58; but on the inadmissability of the data of the "Tavola Antica" supposedly of 1343, see Herlihy, "Population," p. 228. How the distribution of salt was accomplished in the city is not explained, but that the urban population consisted of about 25,000 families, or somewhat more than 100,000 persons, corresponds well with estimates concerning its size, about 90,000 according to Fiumi (ibid. p. 106) and 125,000 according to N. Rodolico (see above, chapter 4, n. 30).

31. Bowsky, "Impact," p. 11, estimates a population for Siena and its countryside from 100,000 to 150,000, which would mean for an area of about 950 square kilometers a density of over 100 persons per square kilometer.

32. In 1738, Tuscany still had only 890,608 inhabitants. In 1814 the population was 1,154,686 and in 1846, 1,565,751 inhabitants. See A. Zerbi, *Manuale storico di economia toscana* (Florence, 1847), p. 379.

medieval population at its height was "not less than" two million people.[33]

With a relatively low level of technology and inefficient transport, how could the medieval economy have fed and employed such enormous numbers? Only at the cost, it would appear, of forcing thousands and tens-of-thousands to eke out their living on the bare margin of subsistence. In 1302, a year of scarcity, the commune of Siena undertook a public distribution of food, and the poor and indigent were found to number 15,000.[34] The Florentine chronicler Giovanni Villani was himself shocked to surmise that in 1330 the paupers of the city of Florence seemed to surpass 17,000.[35] And poverty in the countryside was undoubtedly more gripping, if less conspicuous.

Poverty in turn brought poor nutrition, weakened physical stamina, and induced high susceptibility to disease. There can be little doubt that the great mortalities of the plague were closely linked to the poor nutrition and bad health of substantial numbers of the population. Many of the great plagues seem to have had the way prepared for them by famine and scarcity in the preceding years. The epidemic of 1340, first of the really great recorded killers, followed hard upon a year of want in 1339; two years of scarcity preceded the Black Death of 1348.[36] And death from the plague followed dearth again in 1388–89.

A huge population, massive poverty, endemic malnutrition, shocking mortalities and a catastrophic population decline—these are unquestionable facts, and the Malthusian diagnosis of the late-medieval crisis finds order and relationship among them. Does the fourteenth-century population plunge indeed present for us a true historical example of a classical Malthusian crisis?

Here, however, some reservation must be expressed. It is one thing to recognize the existence of a precarious balance between population and resources on the eve of the Black Death, and quite another thing to attribute the behavior of the demographic curve

33. "Popolazione del territorio volterrano-sangimignanese," *Studi in onore di Amintore Fanfani*, I, 290.

34. Bowsky, "Impact," p. 7.

35. *Cronica*, X, cap. 122 (V, 212).

36. See above, p. 105, table 7.

primarily to the impact of plague and famine upon an excessively swollen population. Rather, a careful examination of our data gives several substantial reasons for doubting that the shape of the curve does indeed follow the lines to be expected from an exclusively Malthusian diagnosis.

There is, to begin with, the pace and pattern of the population decline. The high mortalities of 1348 may with great plausibility be explained by malnutrition and by the inordinate numbers of consumers which induced it. But if Pistoia was overpopulated in 1344, was it still overpopulated in 1392, when the population was less than one half its former size? Yet its population continued to fall, well beyond the point where one may continue to speak of inadequate resources.

There is this further and, I think, decisive fact for rejecting an exclusively Malthusian interpretation for the depopulations of the fourteenth century. The plague of 1348 did not strike against a population blindly seeking to increase. The population had been stable or even declining at Pistoia for a century before the Black Death. The rural population of 1344, four years before the plague, had already shrunk by 23 per cent from what it had been one hundred years earlier. Moreover, for other Tuscan areas there are indications that the rural population was stagnant or declining well before the Black Death. At San Gimignano, the density of rural settlement had apparently reached its height by 1290 and by 1332 had already diminished.[37] It is more difficult to judge population movements in the Florentine countryside, for which surveys for only a few scattered rural communes have survived. But such surveys still convey the strong impression that rural population was stable or even declining for at least a half-century before the Black Death.[38]

37. Fiumi, *San Gimignano*, pp. 154–55.

38. San Lorenzo a Galiga, in the pieve of Sant'Andrea a Doccia, had 21 households in 1330 (ASF Not. A 351, 29 Aug. 1330) and 19 in 1340 (ibid. 1 Jan. 1340). Santa Maria Impruneta had 122 households in 1307 (ASF Not. B 1340, 234v–35r), 115 in 1319 (ASF F 308, 24 Aug. 1319), and 122 in 1330 (ASF B 1345, 154v). San Martino in Petroio had 42 households in 1332 (ASF A 351, 29 March 1332) and 39 in 1339 (ASF A 352, 11 Oct. 1339). Quarantoia (populus sancti Michaelis castri Quarantule) had 69 households in 1307 (ASF B 1263 55v) and 65 in 1340 (ASF Estimo, Vol. 55, 1340).

The great demographic crash of the fourteenth century was not triggered by nor was it a direct reaction against a population expanding too rapidly. If population size alone were the nemesis of the medieval community, it would be hard to understand why the Malthusian reckoning had not occurred in the middle thirteenth, rather than the middle fourteenth century.

Perhaps the chief weakness and omission of a purely Malthusian diagnosis of the fourteenth-century population collapse is its failure to recognize the importance of birth rates. It assumes that these rates were high and constant, and that the population would automatically and mechanically have continued to grow until its very size would have called down upon itself violent checks and readjustments. The picture in fact is more complicated. Our own consideration of the Catasto of 1427 has shown that birth rates were not at all fixed and stable, but were highly sensitive to a variety of influences. It is, moreover, a recognized demographic fact that even apparently small fluctuations in births can have profound effects on the direction and degree of population changes. No analysis of the great depopulations of the late Middle Ages can be complete without attention paid to the elusive but perhaps critical factor of births.

THE ROLE OF BIRTHS

We have two rough but useful indications of reproductive patterns in the thirteenth and fourteenth centuries: the long-term movement of the population and the apparent size of households.

The thirteenth century was comparatively free of major external checks upon population expansion. But even in the century's early decades demographic growth had weakened, ended or was already reversed. The birth rate in this epoch could have been only high enough to maintain the size of the community, and did not accomplish even that too successfully.

The plagues of the fourteenth century were terrible in their carnage, but they alone do not explain the failure of the population to rebound from them, as, in later periods, under more favorable circumstances, it was clearly able to do. Thus, in spite of plagues in 1416 and 1418, and another in 1423 which allegedly left the city deserted, the urban population actually increased between 1415 and

1427 by 20 per cent.[39] This must mean that the birth rate reacted quickly and effectively to the challenge of losses, and the population in 1427, with an astounding fertility ratio of 1170, shows the levels to which it could rise. So also, the losses due to the plague of 1400 are well-documented: one half the population in the city, and the same in the countryside. But even here, for all the dimensions of its losses, the population was able to make a quick recovery. The rural population was 11,364 in 1391; in 1401, only one year after the plague which carried off half its numbers, it was 10,027, almost regaining its former size.[40]

The fourteenth-century population, on the other hand, showed no comparable power to make good its losses. The failure of the birth rate to respond to the stimulus of deaths, more even than the deaths themselves, seems the root cause of the shocking population plunge of the fourteenth century.

More evidence of a comparatively low reproductive rate even in the thirteenth century comes from the apparent size of households in the Book of Hearths.

The Book, to be sure, records only the names of heads of households, not the number of persons they contained. However, the names themselves give indirect evidence concerning household size. Where women appear in large numbers at the head of households, the average size of the homes must be small, as some women were not marrying or remarrying and many widows were not living with their married children.[41] In 1427, for example, out of Pistoia's 2507 rural households, 191, or 7.6 per cent, were headed by a woman, and this corresponds to a household size of 4.65 persons. In the city, on the other hand, where the number of homes headed by women was substantially larger (264 out of 1247, or 21.1 per cent), average household size was correspondingly smaller, only 3.6 persons.

In the Book of Hearths of ca. 1244, the number of women appearing as household heads is high, approximately 714 out of 7312, or 9.8 per cent. This figure, it must be noted, cannot be considered exact; the sex of many of the persons listed in the Book cannot be

39. From 1090 to 1247 hearths. See above, p. 75–76.
40. See above, p. 70, table 1.
41. See the comments by Russell, "Mediaeval Demography," p. 90.

certainly established through their names alone.[42] And of course, upon this rough figure it would be impossible to base a precise estimate of average household size. But this high percentage of women at the head of hearths does show that the homes of ca. 1244 tended to be small, and probably could not have counted more than the 4.65 persons which they averaged in 1427. This was a small household in 1427 (the plague, after all, had struck only three years before, and the population was still in the process of recovering). It was also a small household in the thirteenth century.

The Book of Hearths shows further that in ca. 1244, as in 1427, the size of households, and presumably the birth rate, was affected by the social and economic status of their members. While the Book of Hearths gives no direct indication of a household's wealth, it does distinguish the homes of nobles from those of commoners. Noble households, which may be presumed to be the wealthier, appear also to have been the larger. Of noble hearths, 6.5 per cent were headed by a woman (17 out of 262), well below the 9.8 per cent representative of the entire community. The wealthy, even in the middle thirteenth century, were supporting larger households and presumably more children than the disadvantaged poor. One of Pistoia's noble and wealthy families, the Cancellieri, was so prolific as to attract the comment of chroniclers.[43] Appearing only in the early thirteenth century, it could boast, in three generations, of more than 100 men of arms.

We are not without contemporary comment stressing the critical importance of births in the growth and decline of the population. In 1425, St. Bernardino attributed the dwindling numbers of Siena and Milan specifically to the failure of many young people to marry, and implicitly to the low birth rate which their reluctance engendered.[44]

42. Such fairly common names as Gratia, Ventura or Vita could refer either to men or women, and only occasionally does the Book expressly identify the sex of a household head. J. C. Russell, "Mediaeval Demography," p. 90, says that 12 per cent of the householders in the Book of Hearths were women, but this appears to be too high.

43. Cf. G. Villani, *Cronica*, VIII, cap. 39 (IV, 54), "uno lignaggio di nobili e possenti che si chiamavano i Cancellieri, non però di grande antichità . . . e di loro nacquero molti figliuoli e nipoti, sicchè in questo tempo erano più di cento uomini d'arme, ricchi e possenti e di grande affare. . . ."

44. *Le Prediche volgari*, ed. C. Cannarozzi, O.F.M. (Florence, 1958), II, 107, "Non vedi tu che Siena viene meno, che in Milano, quando frate Bernardino

Leon Battista Alberti, in his *Libri della famiglia*, devoted a long section on how to make the family "populous."[45] He noted the problem of young men who refrained from marriage "because of poverty." He urged their older and richer relatives not only to encourage them with exhortation and example, but also to donate to them a "suitable sum" for their needs, "as if to purchase the growth of the family."[46] Otherwise, the family would fall in numbers and wealth, and perhaps disappear entirely, as many had.

These then seem to be the relative roles of plagues and famines, of overpopulation and of births in Pistoia's late medieval population history. The plagues, for which famines often enough prepared the way, took a fearsome toll, and mortalities from them were certainly heightened by poor nutrition stemming from overpopulation. The demographic plunge of the fourteenth century cannot, however, be taken as an example of a classical Malthusian crisis. A precarious balance between population and resources seems a fact of Tuscan rural life for as far back in the thirteenth century as our sources permit us to discern. The importance of overpopulation was probably greater in worsening social and economic conditions, and thus adversely influencing the birth rate, rather than as a direct provocation of plague and famine.

Although natural disasters clearly played a role of major importance in Pistoia's demographic history, their impact was apparently aggravated, and recovery from them delayed, by a low and unresponsive birth rate. The birth rate was in turn very sensitive to the social conditions under which Pistoia's families were living. In 1427, and undoubtedly too in the thirteenth century, poor people were having difficulty supporting children and maintaining their numbers. The willingness or ability of Pistoia's society to reproduce was strongly influenced by the extent and degree of poverty within it.

The evidence, scanty though it is, still suggests that bad and deteriorating social conditions under which numerous Pistoiesi had come to live by the late thirteenth century played a major role in

---

tornò, li fu detto che venti milia fanciulle v'erano da maritare, senza le maritate e quelle che non avevano tempo; e più fanciulli che in tutta Italia?"

45. *Famiglia*, pp. 104–10.

46. Ibid. pp. 108–109, "Contribuischi tutta la casa come a comperare l'accrescimento della famiglia. . . ."

halting the demographic expansion of the Middle Ages, and in worsening and prolonging the great depopulations of the fourteenth century. Conversely, the renewed if modest population growth of the fifteenth century implies that the conditions of life were then improving for an important segment of Pistoia's people.

These inferences, drawn from demographic evidence, will be examined in detail in the following chapters. It is at any rate certain that Pistoia's population history cannot be isolated from the changes experienced in the economy, society and culture of the medieval and Renaissance city.

6

The Agricultural Economy

And I am certain that whoever will note the returns and abundant fertility of a circuit of land which, as has been said, is no longer than 61 1/2 miles, will find it not only a most notable, but even a marvelous thing; for the province of Pistoia [is] most kind and most liberal in always returning to its cultivators the reward of their efforts. . . .

—G. B. Tedaldi, 1569

Pistoia, always more an agricultural than an industrial town, has preserved a rich fund of private acts, contracts chiefly, carefully written out on thousands of individual parchments or copied into hundreds of notarial chartularies.[1] These acts in turn can illuminate the performance of the agricultural economy under the contrasting conditions of high population density in the thirteenth, acute decline in the middle fourteenth, and slow growth and recovery in the fifteenth century.[2]

1. The parchments and the notarial chartularies upon which the tables in this and the following chapter are based are two deposits of parchments, those of San Michele in Forcole and the Badia a Taona, at ASP; and at ASF, Capitolo della cattedrale di P., Città di P., Domenicani di P., Monache da Sala di P., Olivetani di P., Patrimonio ecclesiastico di P., Potesterie di P., S. Bartolommeo di P., S. Chiara di P., S. Francesco di P., S. Gregorio di P., S. Lorenzo di P., S. Mercuriale di P., Ss. Michele e Niccolao di P. and Vescovado di P.

The ASP also contains, in the deposit "Spedali riuniti," several otherwise uncatalogued notarial chartularies, most of them the work of the notary ser Antonio di Puccetto Spada. The notarial chartularies at the ASF used here are: A 64–65, A 347, A 634, A 794, A 808–15, A 867–77, B 368, B 796–800, B 804, B 2305, B 2807–11, C 364, C 371, C 535–37, C 712, F 266, F 306–07, F 309, F 320, F 333–34, F 571, G 354, G 375, G 440, G 512, G 602, I 20, I 37, I 70, I 85, L 101–02, L 307–13, M 47, N 101–06, N 128, N 144–46, P 83, P 107–08, P 375, R 67, S 78–79, S 125–26, S 722–23, T 29–90, T 230–34, T 279, T 765, V 360, V 380, Z 80 and Z 92.

2. For reviews of recent publications on Italian agricultural history in the

No figures, to be sure, have survived to reveal for us total agricultural output, but we can reconstruct rather well the circumstances within which the landlord or cultivator had to operate his farm. Prices in particular are here most instructive, and concerning prices the documents permit the construction of fairly comprehensive series, regarding both the commodities the farmer sold and the costs of his own operations. Levels of rent, which cast light not only upon the productivity of the soil but also upon the relationships between landlords and tenants, can similarly be charted from as early as 1200. The documents can also illuminate the expected returns on capital invested in agricultural enterprise. These price and rent indices should further permit us to discern the changes in Pistoia's agriculture between the thirteenth and fifteenth centuries and in the life of the people who lived from it.

COMMODITY PRICES

The most important of all commodity prices is of course that of wheat, but its accurate reconstruction presents several formidable difficulties. Wheat sales are fairly common entries in the chartularies, but most call for future delivery of the grain and the price paid almost invariably concealed a substantial interest. Moreover, because of wide fluctuations in cereal prices from year to year, or even from month to month, the average price calculated on a few, chance survivals can easily give a misleading impression of the levels that actually prevailed. Perhaps our most reliable indication of wheat prices comes from what may be called its "exchange value," the price used to convert a staio of wheat into its equivalent value in money. Such exchange values are characteristically cited in court decisions, when the judge had to determine the present monetary value of an overdue rent, and they also figure in some agreements among private parties, as, for example, in leases where the tenant was allowed to pay either in grain or in money. Such citations are not, however,

Middle Ages, see E. Cristiani, "Città e campagne nell'età comunale in alcune pubblicazioni dell' ultimo decennio," *RSI*, 25 (1963), 829–45, and especially Jones, "Lineamenti." For a shorter statement of current scholarly opinions of medieval Italian agricultural development, see also P. Jones, "The Agrarian Development of Medieval Italy," *Deuxième conférence internationale d'histoire économique. Aix-en-Provence, 1962* (Paris, 1965), pp. 69–86.

numerous, and the possible margin of error in any series based upon them must be recognized as large. The following table gives average exchange values for a staio of wheat over the period 1201–1425, expressed in solidi of petty denarii (Pisan up to 1283, Florentine thereafter). Because the silver coinage was continuously being debased, we have also calculated wheat values in gold, with the price for 1201–25 taken as 100.

TABLE 9 Average Exchange Values of a Staio of Wheat at Pistoia, 1201–1425

Period	*Citations*	*Average price per staio*	*Value in gold on scale of 100*
1201–1225	3	5.6 sol.	100
1226–1250	3	5.0 sol.	91
1251–1275	11	8.7 sol.	125
1276–1300	1	20 sol.	204
1301–1325	6	25 sol.	170
1326–1350	7	21 sol.	125
1351–1375	10	28 sol.	146
1376–1400	15	32 sol.	150
1401–1425	29	30 sol.	134
(1427	Catasto	15 sol.	67)

The movement of wheat prices over these years seems divisible into four distinct periods. Prices were rising from the early thirteenth century into the 1280s (both 1282 and 1286 were years of acute famine in Tuscany, when cereal prices seem to have reached their maximum thirteenth-century levels). They then moderated, and the downward trend continued until about 1339 or 1340. After 1340, prices once again began to rise, and this new period of inflation lasted until the end of the century. Finally, in the early fifteenth century, cereal prices once more show a pronounced and protracted moderating tendency.

The strong inflation of wheat prices in the thirteenth century, continuing until about the middle 1280s, seems directly attributable to the powerful demand for cereals generated by the packed population in the city and countryside. Moreover, wheat appealed more than barley and millet to the refined tastes of affluent urban society, and these cheaper cereals seem to have declined in commercial importance.

The subsequent moderation of wheat prices between approximately 1286 and 1340 is likewise attributable to several factors. The vigorous growth of a long-distance trade in grain undoubtedly lowered local prices, as Tuscans came to consume in unprecedented quantities the cereals of Romagna, Apulia, Sicily and still more distant areas. Moreover, the Tuscan communes were characteristically exercising a strict supervision over the wheat market and vigorously intervening to prevent excessive price fluctuations in years of scarcity. The motives for these market controls, as a Pistoiese document explained them, were "the good of the city, its citizens and especially the artisans and the poor."[3]

At Pistoia, with the earliest indication of approaching scarcity, the commune would appoint special officials, usually eight in number, to assume supervision over the cereal market. If they deemed it necessary, the officials could forbid export of cereals, offer bounties to those who brought wheat to the city, and directly make large purchases of foreign wheat for resale and distribution to the people, at considerable costs to the city treasury.[4] Pistoia may have been, to be sure, less successful than wealthy Florence in providing its people an abundance of cheap cereal. A Florentine author, Antonio Pucci, who devoted a poem to the unlikely subject of the grain market, mentioned in it that Pistoia, Perugia, Siena and Lucca had all heartlessly expelled the poor from their territories during the famine of 1329; Florence, on the other hand, had welcomed them "like a mother."[5] But whatever the difficulties occasioned by severe famine, there can be no doubt that at Pistoia as in all the large Tuscan cities, low cereal prices were a major concern of governmental policy.

3. ASP, Provv. Tomus 12, 68v, 29 Oct. 1343, "ad ipsius civitatis et civium maxime artificum et pauperum utilitatem."

4. Cf. ASP, Provv. Tomus 5, 15v, 25 Sept. 1330, the "Capitula et ordinamenta super deveto blavi," and similar regulations in ibid. Tomus 8, 27r, 4 Jan. 1333. In 1339 Pistoia was offering a bounty of one solidus for every staio of wheat or millet brought into the city, ibid. Tomus 11, 21v, 18 May 1339. In 1340 the commune spent 12,000 pounds in the purchase of foreign grain for its citizens, ibid. Tomus 11, 30v, 11 Aug. 1340.

5. "Perugia, Siena, Lucca e i Pistolesi E altre terre assai per impotenza I poveri cacciar de' lor paesi. Ma la pietosa città di Fiorenza Tutti gli recettò, siccome madre I suoi figliuoi con umile accoglienza." Cited in V. Fineschi, *Istoria compendiata di alcune antiche carestie e dovizie di grano occorse in Firenze* (Florence, 1767), p. xi.

Moderate wheat prices from the late 1280s to the late 1330s were a pillar of the simultaneous prosperity of the Tuscan cities, then in the period of their peak medieval *fioritura*. Cheap food made possible the maintenance of large urban populations; cheap food also meant low wages and labor costs, and exerted a powerful and effective stimulation on urban industries.

The immediate impact of the population plunge of the middle fourteenth century was to introduce a period of inflation, involving wheat and most other commodities, which persisted until almost 1400. In 1390 the commune was selling wheat to its citizens for the substantial price of 35 solidi per staio.[6] In 1392, at its apparent peak value, a staio of wheat was estimated to be worth an astounding 60 solidi.[7]

Monetary factors seem partially responsible for this inflation. Men were dying, but coins were not. The volume of money available to the population increased, and prices may have reflected this new abundance of coins. On the other hand, the diminishing number of spenders, and presumably a declining velocity of circulation, must have partially offset the inflationary influence of a greater per capita volume of money. It is hard to know the exact weight to be given to these contrary pressures.

A factor of probably greater moment in provoking inflation in the middle and late fourteenth century was the widespread disruption of agricultural production, which must have fallen off even more rapidly than consumer numbers and demand. Over these years, the countryside was subjected not only to fierce and repeated plagues and famines and huge population losses but also to protracted wars, riots and terrible destruction. In 1364, for example, the city fathers bewailed the fact that through wars and taxes "the farms [poderi] of Pistoia's citizens remain uncultivated and not sown."[8] Inevitably, disrupted production brought high food prices, which added not a little to the city's woes.

By the late 1390s, but still more noticeably in the first quarter of the fifteenth century, wheat prices began again to fall, indicating a period of restored production and returning abundance. The official

6. ASP, Provv. Tomus 37, 85v.

7. ASF, Not. V 360 (3), 141r, 7 June 1392, the value of two *emine* of wheat is estimated at six pounds.

8. ASP, Provv. Tomus 28, 59v, 17 June 1364.

value assigned to a staio of wheat in the Catasto of 1427 was only 15 solidi—the cheapest price it had commanded since the early thirteenth century. This official price may have been artificially low, but there is still no doubt that the fifteenth century remained a period of cheap food. In the 1480s and '90s, Antonio Rospigliosi was paying for a staio of wheat between 30 and 32 solidi.[9] This price had hardly changed since the beginning of the century, in spite of a continuing deterioration of the money.

Citations of oil and wine prices, while not so numerous as those of wheat, still show a similar pattern:

TABLE 10 Exchange Value of a Quaderna of Oil at Pistoia, 1290–1427

Year	*Price in solidi*	*Value in gold on scale of 100*	*Year*	*Price in solidi*	*Value in gold on scale of 100*
1290	31	100	1410	65	104
1339	32	64.5	1411	60	97
1390	50	85	1427	50	81
1400	60	97			

Sources: ASP, S. Michele in Forcole, 28 June 1290. ASF, C 360 (4), 5 April 1390. L 309, 7 Feb. 1400. P 107, 29 March 1400. L 101 (3), 30 May 1411. ASF, Catasto 260–65.

TABLE 11 Exchange Value of a Barrel of Wine at Pistoia, 1347–1406

Year	*Price in solidi*	*Value in gold on scale of 100*	*Year*	*Price in solidi*	*Value in gold on scale of 100*
1347	12.5	100	1406	35	250
1362	22.5	175	1427	14–26	90–167
1395	40	266			

Sources: ASF, C 712, 4 April 1347. I 85, 204v, 18 Nov. 1362. L 102 (5) 6 Feb. 1395. L 312, 1 May 1406. ASF, Catasto 260–65.

Like wheat, oil was declining in value in the two generations immediately preceding the Black Death, confirming the character of the period as one of cheap food and apparent abundance. Like wheat too, the price of both oil and wine reacted to the disasters of the middle fourteenth century by climbing steeply, suggesting disrupted

9. *Richordi*, p. 70, 30 sol. in 1482; p. 108, 32 sol. in 1487; and p. 153, 30 sol. in 1495.

production and scarcities. In the better years of the fifteenth century, they returned to more moderate levels.

Pistoia's sources also give a rather full list of meat prices:

TABLE 12 Price of a Pound of Meat at Pistoia, 1296–1419

	1296	*1332*	*1389*	*1392*	*1398*	*1401*	*1402*	*1406*	*1407*	*1419*
Pork	6	9	18	26	19	18	18	20	18	22 d.
Beef, steer		14	26	32		26	26	28	26	23 d.
Beef, ox and bull		8		18			14		15	d.
Veal		14		36	30	25	25	30		24 d.
Mutton		7		20	16	16	15	16	14	22 d.
Lamb				24	28	20		24		d.

Sources: Based on maximum meat prices set by the commune. *Statutum pot.*, p. 166. ASP, Provv. Tomus 5, 58v, 3–6 Aug. 1332. ASF, L 308 (3), 8 June 1398. L 308, 4 Dec. 1392. ASP, Provv. Tomus 36, 64r. L 310, 13 April 1401. B 2809, 10 June 1401. L 310, 16 Sept. 1410. Ibid. 1 April 1402. Ibid. 22 July 1402. L 312, 2 May 1406. L 313, 1 Jan. 1407. B 2811, 2 Sept. 1419.

In terms of gold with the price of 1296 taken as 100, the price of a pound of pork over this period shows the following movements:

1296	*1332*	*1389*	*1392*	*1398*	*1401*	*1402*	*1406*	*1407*	*1419*	*1427*
100	93	162	222	158	150	150	167	150	183	100

Low and even declining prices before the Black Death, a strong upward movement after that disaster, then moderation following fifty years of scarcity: the pattern is the familiar one. Supplies of meat, as for that matter of cereals, oil and wine, could only have fallen off at Pistoia in the late fourteenth century. In 1378, in response to popular protests concerning the lack of meat and the prices it commanded, the city fathers appropriated 300 florins to subsidize its purchase.[10] In 1389 a still larger subsidy, 1000 florins, was voted to relieve the continuing shortage.[11] But again, in the early fifteenth century, meat production in the countryside must have improved enough to produce a steady and considerable fall in prices. A pound of meat in 1427 cost less than half the price of 1392.

Although all these series of commodity prices are incomplete and none can be considered rigorously precise, together they show

10. ASP, Provv. Tomus 27, 212r, 10 Sept. 1378.
11. Ibid. Tomus 36, 65r, 22 Jan. 1389.

the same sequence of four distinct periods in Pistoia's price history: inflation to about 1286; moderation and apparent abundance to approximately 1340; renewed inflation lasting to the end of the century, during which the prices of meat and wine reached better than twice their former levels; and renewed moderation, suggesting returning plenty, in the fifteenth century.

While the fifteenth century, like the early fourteenth, was an age of low prices, a new structure of market demand had by then emerged at Pistoia. This new structure can be illustrated by comparing the relative levels of commodity prices prevailing before the Black Death with those characteristic of the early fifteenth century.

In 1339 a Florentine citizen, Iacopo di Francesco del Bene, served at Pistoia as the Capitano di Custodia, the chief Florentine official in the city. A good administrator, he carefully kept an account of his expenses. In 1927 Armando Sapori published Iacopo's accounts to illustrate price levels at Pistoia in 1339.[12] The prices which Sapori calculated can in turn be compared with those prevailing a century later, specifically with the official prices assigned to the same commodities in the Catasto of 1427. Of course, there may be a certain distortion inherent in comparing prices actually paid in 1339 with official prices of 1427, as the latter may well have been somewhat lower than the true. But the comparison should still show the changes in relative price levels among the various commodities, and this is sufficient to illustrate shifts in market demand.

TABLE 13 A Price Comparison, 1339 and 1427

	Price in Pounds		*Value in gold on scale of 100*	
	1339	*1427*	*1339*	*1427*
Wheat, staio	19–22 sol.	15 sol.	100–116	63
Barley, staio	9 sol. 6 d. to 10 sol.	8 sol.	100–104	68
Wine, barrel (cheapest)	13 sol.	14 sol.	100	86
Oil, orcio	64 sol.	100 sol.	100	125
Pork, pound	11–12 d.	12 d.	100	87
Wood, soma	2 sol. 9 d. to 3 sol. 4 d.	4 sol.	100–121	116

Source: Sapori, "Prezzi," *BSP*, *30* (1928), 174, and ASF, Catasto, 260–65.

12. Sapori, "Prezzi."

By 1427, the price of cereals had settled to levels much lower than those they had held in 1339. The price of wine is more difficult to evaluate, because it could vary so greatly in quality. It seems, however, to have fallen much more moderately between 1339 and 1427 than had the price of cereals.

Oil, on the other hand, actually rose 25 per cent in value between 1339 and 1427, and it seems to have increased still further during the fifteenth century. Antonio Rospigliosi paid 51 solidi for a quaderna of oil in 1481, 72 in 1483 and 120 in 1498.[13] Wood too shows a relative price increase from 100 to 116 between 1339 and 1427. With a shrunken area of cultivation and a much larger portion of the land given over to forests and wastes, only a much wider demand for and use of wood, not curtailed production, could explain this strong price performance. Meat too held its price more firmly in 1427 than did wheat, indicating that consumers were demanding relatively more of it.

This then is the new shape of the market for agricultural commodities becoming evident by 1427: a diminished demand for wheat, but a much stronger demand for meat, wine, oil and wood. This new pattern thus suggests that Pistoia's consumers were eating a more balanced diet in 1427 than in 1339, and living in houses which were more commonly illuminated and heated than had been usual before the plague. In short, by 1427 the standard of living, insofar as consumption habits reflect it, seems to have improved from what it had been in the early fourteenth century.

How do these price movements compare with those of other areas of Europe after the Black Death? Characteristically in Europe, cereal prices fell in reaction to the contracting market for grain, while wages and the price of animal products held firm or even rose, as the diminished population worked for better wages and consequently enjoyed an improved standard of living.[14] The great depopulations, in other words, did confer some favors upon survivors.

Prices at Pistoia, however, only slowly came to show a similar pattern, and its economy only slowly benefited from the potentially higher per capita productivity which the depopulations made possi-

13. *Richordi*, pp. 60, 76 and 185.

14. Cf. Slicher van Bath, *Agrarian History*, pp. 137–44, and M. M. Postan in *CEH*, II, 191–216.

ble. The fourteenth-century plagues and famines initially produced a nearly universal inflation, which must reflect shattered production and prevalent scarcity. Only in the fifteenth century do prices at Pistoia show the characteristics common in Europe after the Black Death.

THE COSTS OF PRODUCTION

The prosperity of the rentier and peasant was influenced not only by commodity prices but also by the costs of production. Here we shall investigate two of the most important, the price of land and the price of farm animals, and we shall add a word about another cost equally important but more difficult to reconstruct: the price of labor.

Records of land sales have been preserved literally by the thousands in Pistoia's parchment collections and chartularies. Not all of them, to be sure, are suitable for price history. For many, it is not possible to differentiate the value of the land from the value of the buildings upon it. Not all contracts give the precise size of the land involved. However, most of the sales which do state measurements deal with land on the plain, and this lends the series a certain rough but real homogeneity.

Table 14 gives the average price per stioro of land, based upon sales preserved in Pistoia's parchment collections and chartularies.

TABLE 14 Average Price of a Stioro of Land at Pistoia, 1201–1425

Period	*Sales*	*Average price in pounds*	*Value in gold on scale of 100*
1201–1225	13	4.75	100
1226–1250	3	6.8	143
1251–1275	5	11	185
1286–1300	26	23.5	284
1301–1325	14	22.6	172
1326–1350	215	21.8	153
1351–1375	1191	25.6	157
1376–1400	2271	32.5	180
1401–1425	5373	21.8	115

The movement of land values thus parallels closely the price movements of agricultural commodities, especially wheat. In the thirteenth century land grew in value until about the middle 1280s, then moderated in the two generations preceding the Black Death, while most commodity prices were declining. The population collapse of the middle fourteenth century had the paradoxical effect of making land more valuable.

This growth in land values under conditions of a declining population is perhaps the most surprising fact revealed by our entire price series. With a contracting area of cultivation, with a growing abundance of land in relation to people, the price of real estate might have been expected to decline. In fact, abandoned lands seem rapidly to have lost their productive capacity, as buildings decayed, walls crumbled, ditches filled and natural vegetation spread over the terrain. To restore them to production characteristically required substantial investments. Even when they possessed some natural fertility, the proliferation of such decrepit farms did not in significant measure adversely affect the value of lands kept productive. Land values therefore continued to reflect commodity prices rather than the availability of real estate. Moreover, many investors after the Black Death preferred to place their money in land, even at high costs and low returns, rather than in risky commercial enterprises. Competitive bidding thus helped keep a high floor under real estate values.

The prices of farm animals show similar fluctuations, as table 15 shows. Citations of such prices are particularly abundant, as they are given not only in sales but also in leases (*soccide* as they were called at Pistoia) involving animals.

Before 1326, citations of livestock prices have not survived in sufficient numbers to support a full series, but the few we do have suggest that the value of animals was declining in the decades preceding 1340.[15] Moderating prices in turn imply that the animal population was growing, and evidence of this comes also from the fact that cattle sales and leases, rare in Pistoia's collections of contracts before 1325, proliferate thereafter.

15. An ass was worth 6 pounds in 1259 (ASF, Olivetani di P., 3 Dec. 1259), while its average value was less than 12 pounds from 1326–50. In real value, this represents a fall from 100 to about 66.7. An ox was worth 25 pounds in 1322 (ASF, Capitolo della cattedrale di P., 15 May 1322), but averaged less than 20 pounds from 1326–50.

TABLE 15 Price of Farm Animals at Pistoia, 1326–1425

	Sheep			*Pig*			*Goat*			*Horse*			*Mule*		
Period	N	*P*	*I*	N	*P*	*I*	N	*P*	*I*	N	*P*	*I*	N	*P*	*I*
1326–1350	12	1.8	100	8	5.4	100	8	2.1	100	12	24.7	100	6	75.9	100
1351–1375	15	2.2	111	5	13.9	233	11	2.8	120	36	36.4	130	17	76.1	92
1376–1400	22	3.4	147	24	8.5	128	9	3.3	124	40	38.3	126	14	81.6	86
1401–1425	28	2.5	105	21	7.8	108	13	3.2	114	45	41.2	126	30	62.3	63

	Ass			*Cow*			*Ox*			*Calf*			*Cow & Calf*		
Period	N	*P*	*I*	N	*P*	*I*	N	*P*	*I*	N	*P*	*I*	N	*P*	*I*
1326–1350	34	11.1	100	47	21.8	100	35	19.8	100	12	17.3	100	42	29.0	100
1351–1375	55	15.2	124	68	35.7	144	57	34.3	158	16	19.9	104	71	47.5	148
1376–1400	47	20.8	148	34	49.5	178	27	48.6	192	14	30.0	136	60	59.1	160
1401–1425	65	16.4	111	59	33.7	115	80	42.8	162	13	20.2	88	61	51.0	132

N = the number of citations upon which the averages are based, *P* = the average price in pounds, and *I* = the price index in terms of gold, with the prices of 1326–50 equalling 100.

The disasters of the middle fourteenth century were again directly responsible for an inflationary spurt in the cost of livestock, and prices remained high until the late 1390s. This high cost of animals appears somewhat paradoxical, as the marked contraction of the cultivated area should have freed an abundance of land for cheap grazing. In fact, as the price rise itself suggests, the population of farm animals must have fallen drastically in these war-wracked decades. And steep animal prices also hampered the restocking of farms, and helped deepen and prolong the bad times of the late fourteenth century. After this blighted period, however, animal prices once again moderate, apparently reflecting growing numbers of livestock in the more settled years of the fifteenth century.

A discussion of costs should also include some reference to agricultural salaries, but as documents on wages are few, whether in town or countryside, we shall consider all our information together in the following chapter on the urban economy.[16] Let it suffice to mention here that the movement in labor costs follows a sequence similar to these other price series: they were low in the early fourteenth century, high after the plague, and slowly moderating in the fifteenth century.

Having considered the price of commodities and the cost of land and of stock, we may now inquire into the profits, rents and returns which the landlord or cultivator could expect to gain from his enterprise.

RENTS AND RETURNS

Hundreds of leases have been preserved in Pistoia's archives, and these allow an accurate reconstruction of rent levels from the first quarter of the thirteenth century. To be sure, not all the surviving leases are suitable for such an investigation, as not all of them state the size of the rented properties. The dimensions are usually given only for the good and expensive lands of the plain and low hills, not for the poorer and cheaper properties at the higher elevations. This fact, however, again imparts to our series a certain rough and reassuring homogeneity.

16. See below, p. 150, table 22.

Table 16 gives the median rent in staia of wheat per stioro of leased land for 25-year periods from 1201–1425. Median rents rather than average rents are used here because they are not strongly influenced by leases with unusually high or low payments and they therefore yield a somewhat smoother sequence. In constructing the table, the rent per stioro of land was calculated for each lease. The leases for each period were then arranged according to ascending amounts of rent per stioro, and the rent in the median lease entered in the table.

TABLE 16 Median Rent in Staia of Wheat per Stioro of Land at Pistoia, 1201–1425

	Leases	*Rent*		*Leases*	*Rent*
1201–1225	9	1.50	1326–1350	66	2.50
1226–1250	5	2.30	1351–1375	230	1.60
1251–1275	10	2.67	1376–1400	269	1.50
1276–1300	14	2.50	1401–1425	394	1.40
1301–1325	15	2.50			

The results of this table are also illustrated by graph 2.

The table and graph should make manifest the prosperity of the rentier in the thirteenth and early fourteenth centuries, and also the powerful impact of the subsequent depopulations upon agricultural returns. From the middle thirteenth century to about 1340, with a huge population in the countryside and scarcity of good soil, landlords were able to demand astronomic rents from peasants eager to lease their properties. But with the demographic debacle of the middle fourteenth century, rents plunged by over 40 per cent. Now forced to compete in a depopulated countryside for takers of their land, landlords had little choice but to offer leases at low rents and, as we shall further see, favorable terms. Even in the early fifteenth century, there is as yet no indication that rent levels were once more beginning to rise.

The terms of tenancy also strongly reacted to changing population densities in the countryside. In the thirteenth century, leases characteristically called for a high, fixed rent, largely exonerating the landlord of the risk of a poor harvest and requiring from him no additional contributions in animals or capital to help cultivate the land. The population decline worked to alter such terms. Perhaps

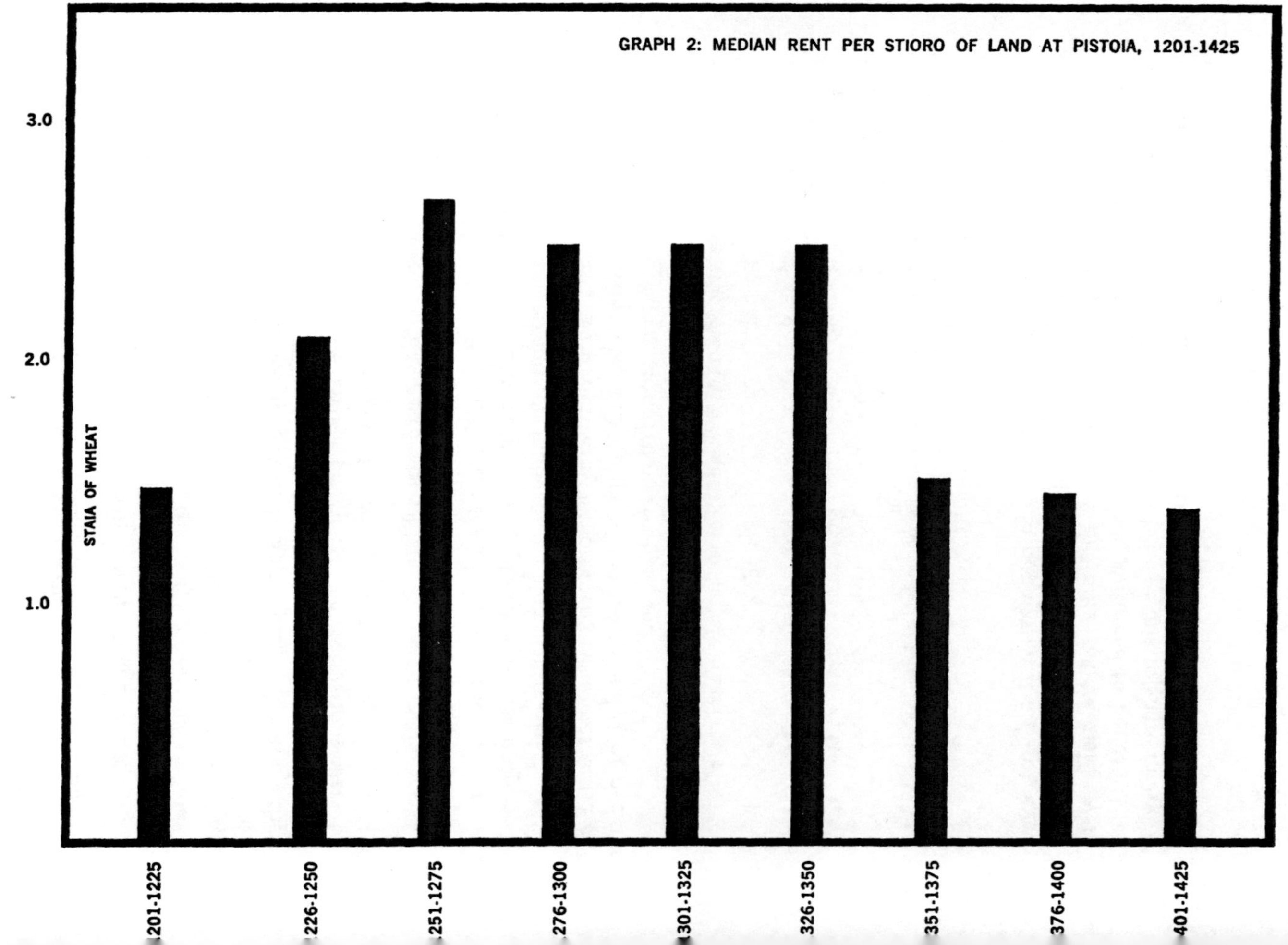
GRAPH 2: MEDIAN RENT PER STIORO OF LAND AT PISTOIA, 1201-1425
3.0
2.0
1.0
STAIA OF WHEAT
201-1225
226-1250
251-1275
276-1300
301-1325
326-1350
351-1375
376-1400
401-1425

the most significant shift was the growing utilization at Pistoia from the second quarter of the fourteenth century of the share-cropping lease, the famous Tuscan *mezzadria.* In 1349, for example, the monastery of Forcole, fearful "because of the plague" that a piece of its property would remain uncultivated, converted the rent due from it from 12 staia of wheat to one half the produce.[17] Several other similar conversions followed, as the monastery shifted its rent basis from high and fixed to flexible payments. Its motivations were to attract and encourage workers who were difficult to find

> because of the deadly pestilence which . . . raged in the year of the Lord 1348 in the city of Pistoia and its contado and in very many other cities and contados of the province of Tuscany, because of which many places, possessions and properties have remained and continuously remain uncultivated.[18]

Table 17 illustrates the growing importance of the mezzadria at Pistoia, by showing what percentage of the total number of poderi leased were for flexible rents, from 1201 to 1425.

TABLE 17 Proportion of Mezzadria Leases at Pistoia, 1201–1425

Period	*T*	*M*	*P*	*Period*	*T*	*M*	*P*
1201–1225	6	0	0	1326–1350	70	32	45.7
1226–1250	7	0	0	1351–1375	189	106	55
1251–1275	5	0	0	1376–1400	245	134	54.7
1276–1300	8	1	12.5	1401–1425	510	340	66.7
1301–1325	18	1	5.6				

T = the total number of recorded leases of poderi, M = the number of them which are mezzadria leases, and *P* = the percentage this represents of the total.

Although the mezzadria thus rose in popularity, it did not, even in the fifteenth century, dominate the entire countryside. It was an especially common arrangement in the hills, where risks were greater, while many poderi on the plain continued to be leased for fixed rents. But even these fixed-rent leases came to share many of the characteristics of the mezzadria contract favorable to the tenant,

17. ASP, S. Michele in Forcole, 25 March 1349.
18. Ibid. 26 May 1351. According to the lease, flexible rents would assure that the workers "magis sint pronti et efficientes ad laborandum et colendum."

such as requiring the landlord to contribute cattle or capital for the working of the farm.

The growing utilization of the mezzadria contract brought with it conditions of tenancy for the peasant much superior to those accorded him under the system of high, fixed rents which had formerly prevailed. Flexible rents protected the peasant from the high risks of a poor harvest, which now had to be borne primarily by the landlord. Moreover, under the mezzadria system, the landlord was committed to heavy and continuing investments upon his land, and this assured the peasant the cattle, tools, additional purchased fertilizers, seeds and cheap loans which he needed to work it well. Still in the early fifteenth century, landlords who did not advance loans to their workers had little hope of attracting them into their service.[19] The loans were free of interest and often in fact uncollectable.

The returns on agricultural investments, as well as rents and terms of tenancy, show a similar sharp contrast between the prosperous decades before 1340 and the hard times that followed.

Pistoia's archives have preserved by the hundreds contracts involving the creation or sale of perpetual rents. The investor who wished to place his money in agriculture would frequently buy from a peasant who needed the capital a perpetual rent upon his land. The rent might be in money, wine, oil, chestnuts or the cheaper cereals, but most commonly was in wheat. Sometimes the peasant or land owner would simply declare that a rent existed upon his land, which he then sold to the investor; at other times he would sell the land itself and receive it back in lease, often with an expressed right of repurchasing the land and extinguishing the rent after a stated number of years. Provided the interest was not manifestly exorbitant, such investments in rents were not considered usurious by canon law, and this explains the transaction's great popularity at Pistoia as elsewhere in medieval Europe.[20]

19. ASF, Catasto 189, 41r, "Item a in prestanza il detto Matteo [the tenant] da me fl. sei perchè lavori la terra. Altrimenti non si la vorrebbe." Ibid. 172v, "Dubito in fine non mi convegna lassarla [a vineyard] guastare. E s'io la volessi allogare me ne chiesto di prestanza florini da guastatori che anno di bisogno de la prestanza e non de la vigna." That these loans were largely uncollectable seems evidenced by the fact that the redactors of the Catasto refused to recognize them as true liabilities on the part of the workers.

20. On the relation of the perpetual rent to the usury prohibition, see John T. Noonan Jr. *The Scholastic Analysis of Usury* (Cambridge, Mass., 1957), pp. 154–70.

Table 18, together with graph 3, illustrates the median cost of a perpetual rent of one staio of wheat per year, for ten-year periods from 1201 to 1430. In calculating the median cost, the price per staio of rent was computed for each contract, the contracts were then arranged according to the ascending cost of the rent, and the median price cited in the table.

TABLE 18 Median Price of a Perpetual Rent of One Staio of Wheat at Pistoia, 1201–1430

Period	*Sales*	*Price (pounds)*	*Value in gold*	*Period*	*Sales*	*Price (pounds)*	*Value in gold*
1201–1210	6	2.80	100	1321–1330	19	8	89
1211–1220	13	2.75	98	1331–1340	31	8	93
1221–1230	17	2.60	93	1341–1350	60	9	100
1231–1240	28	2.80	100	1351–1360	62	10.30	107
1241–1250	13	3.00	107	1361–1370	52	12.80	139
1251–1260	6	3.00	107	1371–1380	56	15.00	145
1261–1270	19	4.00	114	1381–1390	58	16.00	150
1271–1280	33	6.67	160	1391–1400	90	20.00	184
1281–1290	37	10.00	203	1401–1410	90	14.00	125
1291–1300	41	9.00	160	1411–1420	121	15.50	139
1301–1310	17	8.20	107	1421–1430	37	13.33	83
1311–1320	28	8.00	104				

The price of perpetual rents in wheat thus rose strongly in the thirteenth century, reaching its peak in the 1280s when it was double the cost it had held in the century's initial decade. That price then began to moderate, and by the 1320s rents were actually cheaper than they had been a century before. Again, the onslaught of the great famines and plagues in the middle of the century reversed the movement of the price. It rose once more and maintained high levels until the 1390s. Then again, during the first decades of the fifteenth century it declined substantially; by the 1420s the price of a perpetual rent in wheat was at the lowest level attained during the entire 230 years surveyed in the table.

In its broad movements, the price of wheat rents corresponds rather exactly with the fluctuations of both the commodity price of wheat and of the value of land. This of course was only to be expected. The rent created was, after all, paid in wheat, and thus it responded to changes in the anticipated value of cereals. The rent

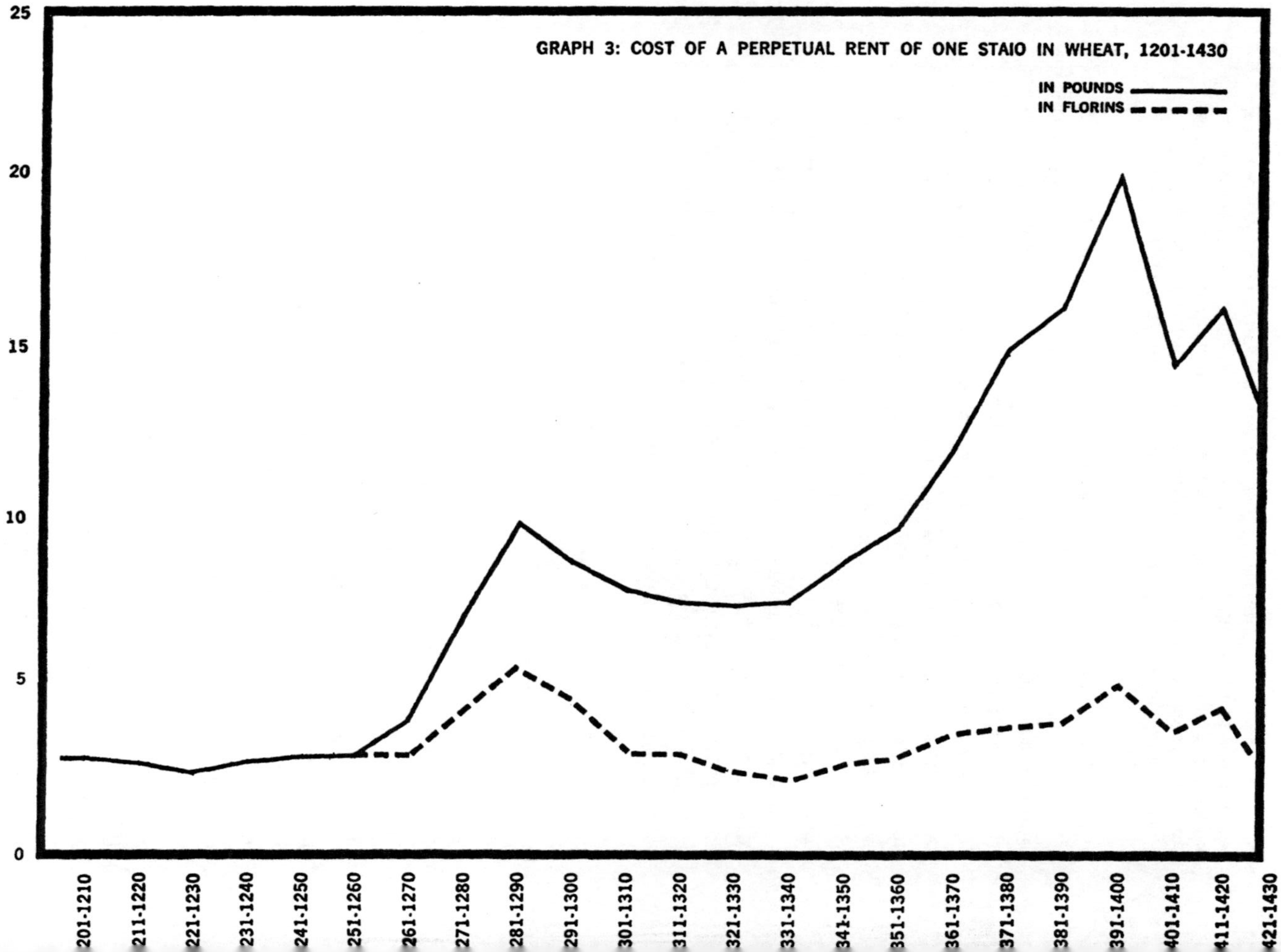

GRAPH 3: COST OF A PERPETUAL RENT OF ONE STAIO IN WHEAT, 1201-1430

was also secured by the value of the land over which it was established, and therefore fluctuated in harmony with the price of land. But the value of rents also reflected one other factor: the interest return to be expected from agricultural investments.

Before 1250, with wheat at about 5 solidi per staio, investors were gaining the good return from rent purchases of about 9 per cent, and as wheat prices rose after 1250, that percentage apparently held its own. In the 1280s, ten pounds was the usual cost of a rent of one staio, then worth about one pound; the return, in other words, was about 10 per cent. After the 1280s, though the price of both wheat and rents in wheat declined, the rate of interest actually rose; in the 1330s the going interest rate seems to have hovered around 15 per cent.

This handsome return indicates a strong demand for capital in Pistoia's countryside. Peasants, crowded on the land, many of them seeking to survive on farms of inadequate size, desperately needed credit to aid them in their labors and to tide them over years of scarcity.

This acute hunger for capital is also sadly apparent in the widespread practice of usury in the countryside. At Pistoia, it is possible to find notaries whose business consisted in little else but redacting thinly disguised usurious contracts, which wrung from the peasant rates usually as high as 20 per cent and sometimes as high as 50.[21]

With the depopulations of the middle fourteenth century, however, these conditions so favorable to investors dissipated. While the cost of both wheat and rents in wheat were rising and remained high for the fifty years following the plague, the rate of return on rents in wheat fell. In the 1390s the prevailing rate was no better than 7 per cent and often even less. In 1427 the redactors of the Florentine Catasto, in assuming that all rents represented a return of 7 per cent on the property's capital value, were being quite realistic.

While returns were falling for the agricultural investor after the

21. Cf. ASF, Not. I 29–30, Iacopo di Dino da Carmignano. Iacopo's work consisted largely in drawing up contracts in which peasants "sold" their land with a right to repurchase it within a few years. They then leased it from the new owners for the same term. The sum for which the land was sold was the loan, the rent paid the interest, and the land the security.

Black Death, the usurer also entered on bad times, at least in the countryside. Before the plague, notarial chartularies from everywhere in the Florentine and Pistoiese contados are packed with usurious transactions: fictitious sales of land and leases, and particularly sales of grain well in advance of the harvest for artificially low prices. In later chartularies, such transactions diminish to the point of disappearing; in the countryside at least, the reign of usury was ending.

In the course of the fifteenth century, however, interest rates slowly improved for the agricultural investor, reflecting better economic times. At the end of the century, Antonio Rospigliosi was buying perpetual rents of one staio of wheat for only 12.5 pounds. With a staio then worth about 30 solidi, the return was again about 12 per cent.[22] This was good interest, but still much below what would have been expected in the decades preceding the plague.

A fair number of contracts have also survived regarding perpetual rents in oil. The following table indicates the median cost of a perpetual annual rent of one quaderna of oil, for ten-year periods from 1201–1430.

The costs of oil rents did not swing so widely as those of rents in

TABLE 19 Median Price of a Perpetual Rent of One Quaderna of Oil, 1201–1430

Period	*Sales*	*Price (pounds)*	*Value in gold*	*Period*	*Sales*	*Price (pounds)*	*Value in gold*
1201–1210	—	—	—	1321–1330	—	—	—
1211–1220	3	6	100	1331–1340	1	26	144
1221–1230	5	6.25	104	1341–1350	7	28	145
1231–1240	—	—	—	1351–1360	3	28	137
1241–1250	1	6.15	102	1361–1370	4	33	167
1251–1260	—	—	—	1371–1380	11	41	184
1261–1270	1	10	113	1381–1390	15	38	167
1271–1280	4	10	113	1391–1400	27	40	171
1281–1290	1	11	105	1401–1410	34	40	167
1291–1300	—	—	—	1411–1420	20	37	154
1301–1310	—	—	—	1421–1430	11	32	133

22. *Richordi*, p. 139 (1492), rent of 7 staia purchased for 100 pounds; p. 171 (1497), rent of 12 staia bought for 150 pounds, and two other rents of 16 and 2 staia purchased for 200 and 25 pounds respectively.

wheat, but otherwise they performed comparably. They rose in the thirteenth century, and by the 1290s oil rents were giving returns at the rate of slightly over 13 per cent.[23] This probably was a little below what rents in wheat were yielding, and perhaps for this reason purchases of oil rents remain relatively rare before the Black Death.

The disasters of the middle fourteenth century produced a simultaneous rise in the value of and a fall in the return from oil rents. In the 1420s they were returning about 8 per cent, on the assumption that a quaderna of oil was then worth about 50 solidi. This appears to have been slightly better than the return from rents in wheat. At the same time contracts involving oil rents become considerably more numerous, showing that oil was indeed attracting the interest of investors.

In the light of this evidence concerning movements in prices, rents and returns, we can now attempt to identify the periods of prosperity and depression in Pistoia's medieval countryside.

PROSPERITY AND DEPRESSION IN THE MEDIEVAL COUNTRYSIDE

By most measures, the decades before the Black Death, and particularly the years from about 1290 to 1340, would have to be reckoned an age of brilliant prosperity, the culmination in fact of the great economic advance of the high Middle Ages. These years were prosperous as medieval men would have best understood the term: they were, on the whole, years of plenty. All our price series show a declining trend during this half-century, and this certainly indicates prevailing abundance.

Of the social groups associated with agriculture, landlords and rentiers were especially favored. Their fortunes were made and supported by a remarkably high level of rents, which more than compensated for the moderate commodity prices in the market place. The prevailing system of tenurial relations largely exonerated them from the risks of bad harvests, and did not require them to support with cattle or capital the labors of their tenants. Investors who

23. A quaderna of oil had an estimated value of 31 solidi in 1290, ASP, S. Michele in Forcole, 28 June 1290. At the same time a rent of one quaderna cost about 11 pounds. The rate of interest was therefore about 13.6 per cent.

purchased perpetual rents similarly enjoyed interest rates which reached 15 per cent, under terms which freed them from risks. Those of easier conscience, willing to flout the Church's repeated condemnations of usury, could gain for their money a still higher return.

This great prosperity of rentier and investor clearly had its principal foundation in the high population densities in the countryside. Competition in the crowded villages for land, capital and employment maintained high rents and interest rates and lowered wages, all for the greater profits of landlords, investors and employers.

But the economy of the countryside, even in this age of apparent plenty and prosperity, was still showing certain pernicious and ultimately destructive elements. Well before the Black Death, the rural population was coming to bear an insupportable weight in rents, interest rates and taxes.

For a century before the plague, rents demanded from the peasants were averaging, as we have seen, two and one-half staia of wheat for each stioro of rented land.[24] To support such a rent with any equity for the cultivator would have required a harvest for him of five staia per stioro of land, or about ten to one on his seed.[25] Ten to one on the seed was not beyond the technical capacity of the peasant working the good lower lands, aided by animals, utilizing the most intensive techniques and perhaps buying additional fertilizer outside his farm.[26] But such a return was undoubtedly well beyond the capabilities of the great majority of Pistoia's peasants.

In the middle thirteenth century, as shown by the Book of Hearths, most of Pistoia's rural population was settled not upon the

24. See above, p. 134, table 16.

25. We are assuming that an even division of the harvest between landlord and peasant was, for most of Pistoia's lands, the highest possible equitable rent. One-half staio of seed per stioro of land is the usual seeding ratio encountered at Pistoia. Cf. ASF, Dipl. Città di Pistoia, 4 Nov. 1392, a piece of land 7 coltre (28 stiora) in size was to be sown in 12 days with 14 staia of seed. ASF, Catasto 261, 97r, land 14 stiora in size required for seeding 6 staia.

26. A return of 5 staia per stioro (or about ten to one on the seed) is fairly commonly mentioned in the tax declarations of the Catasto of 1427. Cf. ASF, Catasto 267, 432r, 8 stiora in the commune of Bonnella on the plain return yearly 40 staia of wheat. In 1569, according to Tedaldi, "Relazione," p. 318, the average return for the entire countryside was seven to one on the seed.

fertile plain but upon the steep, dry and unpromising slopes between 500 and 1500 meters in altitude—the area we are calling the middle hills. They there inhabited over 70 small villages, working many, tiny plots often scattered widely over the infertile slopes. To judge from the many surviving agricultural contracts, they apparently made little use of cattle, or of the other aids in tools, fertilizers, seeds or hired labor which high capital investment might have secured for them.[27]

To improve their means of cultivation or, more usually, to tide them over famines, the peasants had to seek capital at high interest from the purchasers of perpetual rents, or to borrow under still more onerous charges from usurers. If the peasants suffered harsh terms from landlords and money lenders, they were similarly oppressed by the weight of city taxes. In spite of recent efforts to exonerate the town government of the charge of exploiting its rural citizens, it can be estimated that, in the 1280s, the countryside of Pistoia was supporting a tax six times as high as that paid by the city.[28]

To bear this mounting burden of rents, interest charges and taxes, the peasants had to seek high returns from the land. But the prevailing system of tenurial relations gave them little help in capital, while forcing them to assume the principal loss should the harvest fail.

Intensive cultivation of cereals with poor and primitive methods was an invitation to soil exhaustion and famine. Famines come with dreadful frequency even before 1348, and they introduce a note of ominous instability to the otherwise so prosperous pre-plague economy.

27. Sales and leases of farm animals and even mezzadria leases in which the landlord aided his tenant with a grant of animals or money, are scarcely to be found in Pistoia's sources in the thirteenth century. Only by the early fourteenth century do they become common. Cf. I. Imberciadori, *Mezzadria classica toscana con documentazione inedita dal IX al XIV secolo* (Florence, 1951), who discerns a growing use of cattle in the thirteenth century in Tuscany and attributes the spread of the mezzadria to the peasants' need for capital to make use of the new methods. On the spread of the mezzadria at Pistoia, see above, p. 136, table 17.

28. See below, chapter 8, n. 5. E. Fiumi, "Sui rapporti economici tra città e contado nell' età comunale," *ASI*, *114* (1956), 18–68, has recently argued that the countryside was fairly treated by the city. But see the comments of P. Jones, "Lineamenti," p. 347.

Destructive of the land, the agricultural system seems to have been destructive of people too. Poor and oppressed people, as we have seen, were not likely to produce and support sufficient children to maintain their numbers.[29] The deteriorating social conditions under which numerous peasants had to live, more perhaps than any other single cause, seems eventually to have undermined the great prosperity of the pre-plague period. Bad social conditions slowed population growth and obstructed recovery from plagues, and finally helped dissipate the high population densities in the countryside, upon which the prosperity of rentiers and investors primarily depended.

Giovanni Villani once tried to explain the serried disasters which had struck the Florence of his day.[30] Should they be attributed to inexorable natural forces, set in motion by celestial conjunctures? Or were they divine retributions for the sins of the Florentines, among which figured prominently their avarice, greed and usury? He concluded that the sins were responsible. Villani's society was indeed suffering from an acute imbalance in the distribution of social benefits, and to this extent at least the modern historian may concur with the chronicler's judgment.

By most measures, the period between approximately 1340 and 1400 must be considered an age of deep depression. These years were depressed as medieval men would have best understood the term: they were years of scarcity. High food prices, frequent famines, repeated protests in the sources concerning shortages of grain and meat within the city, present a uniformly somber picture of disrupted production and continuing want. The bad times were bred by the shock of drastic population decline and by destructive wars and social unrest in the countryside. Recovery was in turn delayed by the paradoxically high costs of land and stock.

Of all groups concerned with agricultural enterprise, those who had enjoyed the greatest prosperity in the preceding age now withstood the hardest blows. Landlords and rentiers watched their rent levels sink by 40 per cent, and many of them were fortunate to find any tenant at all for their lands. Through the spreading mezzadria system of tenancy they were forced to relieve the peasants of the

29. See above, pp. 97–100.
30. *Cronica*, XI, cap. 11 (VI, 5).

chief burden of risk. The new system of tenurial relations also obligated the landlord to provide capital in large amounts for his tenants, to pay for improvements on the farm or to purchase cattle, seed, tools or fertilizer. The land was becoming, and for long would remain, a sink for the city's wealth. Investors too watched their interest rates fall nearly in half, from about 15 to 7 or 8 per cent, as they had to compete to find takers of their capital.

But in this same bleak period, the foundations of a new agricultural system were slowly being laid. The declining demand for wheat made possible an increased concentration on oil, wine, wood and animals, and the new, more balanced agriculture helped assure a better treatment of the soil. Inevitably too, as their numbers declined, the peasants gained better terms from landlords, investors and tax collectors. The spread of the mezzadria contract, making up two thirds of farm leases by the early fifteenth century, is perhaps the best measure of the improved position of the peasants. Under this and similar contracts, they acquired well-stocked farms and the capital to work them; the landlords paid the direct taxes and met the larger share of losses due to failed harvests. Whatever the value of the mezzadria today (and this is much discussed), there can be no doubt that its triumph in Tuscany—a triumph nowhere really completed until after the Black Death—introduced a far superior system of cultivation and tenurial relations than the system of high, fixed rents which had formerly prevailed.

After about 1400, Pistoia's agricultural economy was attaining a new equilibrium, and was achieving a real if moderate prosperity. Declining commodity prices bespeak a returning abundance, and profits to investors, reaching 12 per cent by the century's end, registered a distinct if modest gain.[31] Among the factors which contributed to the new rural prosperity was the stabilization and then the steady growth of the rural population. Between 1427 and 1569 (if G. B. Tedaldi's estimate for the latter date is valid), the inhabitants of the countryside increased in number by two and one-half times.[32] This was a rate far surpassing that achieved in the city. Political and social tumult was largely, though not finally, calmed as

31. See above, pp. 123–26, tables 9–11, and p. 141.
32. See above, p. 76, table 3.

Florence, from 1402, brought Pistoia under its own, direct and strict supervision.[33] Moreover, over these same years, Pistoia witnessed a growing economic integration of its territory with that of the neighboring Florentine district, in a process which the following chapter will examine.[34] This acted as a powerful stimulus to Pistoia's agriculture. Freely serving the needs of populous Florence, that agriculture finally had a market worthy of its resources.

The prosperity of the thirteenth century, for all its brilliance and achievement, had come to rest in critical measure upon the oppression and exploitation of the poorest rural classes. This failure to achieve a more equitable distribution of social benefits proved to be, we have argued, its weakness and undoing. On the other hand, the new agricultural system of the fifteenth century, of which the mezzadria and the customs associated with it formed the cornerstone, offered distinctly improved if hardly enviable conditions for the peasantry. It was fairer to the land and to the people, and for this reason provided Pistoia's Renaissance society with a firm and stable basis for its political life and for its cultural growth. Indeed, to our own generation most peasants of both Pistoia and Tuscany have continued to live and work under an agricultural system which is essentially the product of the late Middle Ages.

33. See below, pp. 155–60.
34. See below, pp. 230–31.

7

The Urban Economy

In Tuscany even the knights give time to commerce.

—Cino da Pistoia

Surviving commercial records are not numerous at Pistoia, partially because rural more than urban enterprises consistently claimed the greater interest of its people. But they are enough to cast light upon the development of the urban economy between the thirteenth and fifteenth centuries, and illuminate the nature of the changes occurring within it. In investigating that development, we shall first consider the fluctuating business climate—the conditions, in other words, which enhanced or lessened profit expectations and which are revealed especially by prices. We shall then examine the geographical area within which Pistoia's merchants characteristically moved; here the chief object of interest must be the decline of the balanced localism and internationalism of the thirteenth century, and the slow but noticeable movement towards a Tuscan regional economy. And since economic history is the story of enterprise and people as well as prices and regulations, we shall then investigate the two chief sectors of the city's economy: its commerce and its artisan industries.

THE EXPECTATIONS OF PROFIT

For the city as for the countryside, no figures have survived to report total volumes of goods exchanged in commerce or total output from urban industries. But the sources again show fairly accurately the structure of prices within which the urban entrepreneur had to work, and do permit an assessment of his changing prospects for profit. Specifically they can illustrate the costs of his raw materials and of the labor he employed, as well as the prices of the manufactured articles he sold. Finally, the fluctuating costs of money rents help to show the changing profit levels to be expected from urban investments.

One of Pistoia's most important industries was iron and iron products—weapons, tools, pots, horseshoes, and so forth—and the chartularies have preserved some few citations of the price of iron smelted in the countryside. The following table illustrates the impact of the troubles of the fourteenth century upon it.

TABLE 20 Price of 100 Pounds of Iron at Pistoia, 1338–1427

Year	*Price in pounds*	*Value in gold on scale of 100*	*Year*	*Price in pounds*	*Value in gold on scale of 100*
1338	6	100	1399	7.2	96
1386	11	155	1402	6.4	86
1388	9.5	133	1420	6.5	86
1397	8	107	1427	6.5	86

Sources: ASF, A 347, 15 Dec. 1338. ASP, Not. 22 Dec. 1386. ASF, N 128 (4), 3 Aug. 1388. L 308 (2), 23 Oct. 1397. L 309, 10 July 1399. Ibid. 18 Feb. 1402. L 312, 4 Feb. 1405. T 232, 12 March 1420. Catasto, 260, 131r.

Like that of most agricultural commodities, the price of iron jumped to high levels in the two generations following the Black Death, indicating a partial breakdown of production in the troubled countryside. Then it moderated considerably in the opening decades of the fifteenth century, when it was cheaper than during the best years before the plague. This suggests that production in the fifteenth century, aided by high investments in iron works or *fabriche,* had regained and even surpassed its pre-plague levels.

No less important a raw material for the urban industries was wool, and its price movements follow a much similar pattern. Because no price citations have apparently survived at Pistoia for the years before 1348, we have added a citation from a comparable Tuscan area, Volterra, over the land of which many of Pistoia's sheep were taken on their way to the seaside pastures.

The price of wool, in so far as we can reconstruct its movements, remained low and perhaps even declining for at least fifty years be-

TABLE 21 Price of 100 Pounds of Raw Wool at Pistoia, 1363–1428

Year	*Price in pounds*	*Value in gold on scale of 100*	*Year*	*Price in pounds*	*Value in gold on scale of 100*
(1297	6	100)*	1413	11.4	95
1363	9.8	100	1415	14.7	122
1392	16.6	142	1417	14	117
1398	20	166	1420	12	100
1402	10.5	88	1421	14	117
1405	12	100	1423	14	117
1406	10	83	1423	14	117
1412	11	92	1428	14	117

* Volterra

Sources: ASF, G 403, 32r, 14 May 1297 (Volterra). A 64, 21v, 25 March 1363. G 602 (5), 4 Feb. 1392. ASP, Not. Paulus f. Fecti, 18 March 1398. L 310, 16 March 1402. L 312, 15 March 1405. B 2810, 18 Oct. 1405. L 101 (3), 17 Feb. 1412 and 1 March 1412. A 810, 5 Nov. 1413. L 101 (4) 155v, 8 April 1415. L 101 (7), 11 March 1417. C 535, 19 Feb. 1420. B 2811, 15 Oct. 1421. ASP, 4 Jan. 1423. C 535, 25 Feb. 1428.

TABLE 22 Some Typical Yearly Wages at Pistoia, ca. 1200–1428

Year	*Description*	*Wages in pounds*	*Value in gold on scale of 100*
ca. 1200	Treasurer "de foris"	3	100
1259	Agent in commercial company	3	100
1296	48 city guards	6	100
1332	Agricultural worker	12	133
1349	Helper in iron shop	21	219
1351–52	Helpers in wool shop	27.9	271
1353	Helper in iron shop	30	291
1359	Household servant	41	400
1360	Household servant	41	400
1370	Household servant	46	415
1397	Shepherd	54	462
1417	Helper in leather shop	36	300
1418	Factor in commercial company	40	333
1424	Shepherd	40	333
1427	Employees of urban hospitals	40–48	333–400
1428	Barber	40	333

Sources: Statuti, ed. Berlan, cap. 184. "Documento pistoiese," in Monaci, *Crestomazia*, p. 197. *Statutum postestatis*, I, 35. ASP, Not. Antonius Spada, 13 July 1349; 6 Feb. 1353; 13 Sept. 1359; and 23 April 1360. ASF, A 65, 28r, 5 April 1370. L 308 (1), 4 Nov. 1397. T 232, 16 Nov. 1417. A 811, 24 March 1418. C 535 (4), 16 Aug. 1424. ASF, Catasto, 189. Ibid. 261, 690v.

fore the Black Death. The impact of the disasters of the middle fourteenth century was again, characteristically, a price inflation which hung on for 50 years. Again too, the opening decades of the fifteenth century brought a considerable moderation.

Labor as well as raw materials of course represented a major cost for urban entrepreneurs, though because of wide variations in wage scales that cost is difficult to evaluate. Table 22 lists what might be called characteristic minimum wages at Pistoia, the salaries the less skilled members of the population were receiving.

Wages are difficult to follow in the thirteenth century, but our slim evidence suggests that they were low and fairly steady for most of the years preceding the Black Death.

There is, on the other hand, no obscurity at all concerning the impact of the mid-century calamities upon wages. They moved strongly upward; even a shepherd in 1397 could earn a handsome 54 pounds, or about 13.5 florins. Wages moderated somewhat in the early fifteenth century, but still remained at better than three times the levels of the middle thirteenth century—this in spite of cheapening commodity costs. In the Catasto of 1427, ten florins per year was the usual salary for a servant girl, and she was fed besides.[1] Complaints about the high cost of labor, especially servants, are common in the tax declarations. Bartholomeo di Battifolle, in describing his woeful economic circumstances to the tax officials in 1415, mentioned the "buono salaro" which a needed servant was drawing.[2] Lady Antonia, aged 78, needed two girls in 1427 to "govern" or care for her, "and she said they cost her a great deal."[3]

Along with the costs of labor and raw materials, the price of finished articles was similarly of importance in defining the entrepreneurial prospects of profits. One of the commodities for which a fairly extensive price series can be constructed is, rather oddly, bricks. Table 23 illustrates the price of lots of 1000 bricks at Pistoia from 1296 to 1395.

1. ASF, Catasto 261, 534r, "una fante chella ghoverna e dalla l'anno fiorini x."

2. Estimario, declaration no. 29 of the parish of S. Giovanni Fuorcività.

3. ASF, Catasto 261, 559r, "Tiene due femine ghovernano che dice le chostano assai." The high salaries spent on servants and the general affluence of the working class is a stock complaint of the moralists of the day; see especially Giovanni de' Mussi of Piacenza, in *RIS*, XVI (1730), 579–84.

TABLE 23 Price of 1000 Bricks at Pistoia, 1296–1395

Year	Price in solidi	Value in gold on scale of 100	Year	Price in solidi	Value in gold on scale of 100
(1280	55	209)*†	1376	145	261
1296	30	100*	1389	100	175
1332	45	100*	1394	150	256
1348	90	187	1395	150	256
1361	132	266			

* Official ceiling price
† Prato

Sources: Piattoli, *Consigli*, p. 270. *Statutum postestatis*, p. 188. ASP, Provv. Tomus 8, 7v. ASF, A 634, 7 March 1348. ASP Not. 4 March 1361 and 25 March 1376. ASF, C 360 (4), 2 Feb. 1389. L 307 (3), 2 May 1394 and 15 Feb. 1395.

The price of bricks remained low and, to judge from their cost at Prato in 1280, probably even declined for well over fifty years before the Black Death, helping to identify this period as one of generally moderating prices even for finished products. The troubles of the middle fourteenth century again engendered the familiar inflation. The point here especially to be noted is that while bricks grew in value by perhaps two and one-half times, wages over the same years were increasing by a much larger multiplier, by three and one-half or even four times. This could only have resulted in a squeeze on entrepreneurial profits and shows that these were not good times for businessmen.

Another finished product of great commercial importance was woolen cloth. Table 24 gives the price of a braccio of cheap cloth, called "panno albagio," made from local wool and woven in many places in the Tuscan countryside.

The price of this rough wool cloth thus seems to have fallen considerably in the late thirteenth and early fourteenth centuries. Low wages, cheaper production, and the competition of better cloths, probably all contributed to lowering its value. After the Black Death, on the other hand, prices rose, though again their increase by no means kept pace with the simultaneous rise in wages. The entrepreneur's revenues may have grown, but his expenses increased even more.

TABLE 24 Price of a Braccio of Panno Albagio at Pistoia, 1239–1382

Year	Price in solidi	Value in gold on scale of 100	Year	Price in solidi	Value in gold on scale of 100
1239	2.25	100	1375	10	120
(1249	2.8	127)*	1375	7.5	90
(1298	5	99)†	1376	9	108
1347	4.05	58	1382	11	129
1348	4.1	59			

* S. Gimignano
† Volterra

Sources: ASF, Patrimonio ecclesiastico di Pistoia, 19 Sept. 1240. I 106, 46r, 31 Dec. 1249. G 403, 59v, 5 Oct. 1297. F 571, 13 Jan. 1347. C 371 (2), 21 Jan. 1348. L 102, 13 Aug. 1375; 13 Jan. 1376; and 29 Dec. 1376. T 279, 23 March 1382.

We are unfortunately unable to follow these price fluctuations of finished articles into the fifteenth century, though the presumption would be that, like most other prices, they too moderated. We do, however, have one other indication of the varying returns from urban investments, which reflects directly upon the changing business atmosphere. This is the price of a perpetual rent in money. Rents in money were usually established upon urban properties, and their sale frequently provided capital for improvements upon them, such as the building or repair of houses or shops. Unfortunately, the number of rent sales which have survived from the preplague years is only three, and all of them date from the 1340s, when the best years for investors were already past. The series subsequently grows more ample, and at least from the late fourteenth and early fifteenth centuries it does convey an accurate idea of what

TABLE 25 Returns on Money Rents at Pistoia, 1326–1425

Period	Sales	Average price in pounds	Per cent of interest
1326–1350	3	13.6	7.3
1351–1375	11	15	6.67
1376–1400	19	18	5.55
1401–1425	37	11.85	8.45

an investor might hope to gain from the placing of his money in this conservative investment.

Because our sales for the period 1326–50 are few and late, the interest rate they show of 7.3 per cent is probably not at all indicative of what, before 1340, an investor might have gained. But this was still higher than interest rates later in the century. Rates fell for the following 50 years, reaching their lowest point in 1376–1400, when investors could expect scarcely more than 5.5 per cent from their capital.

But again, the economic picture brightens noticeably in the opening decades of the fifteenth century, when investments paying cash revenues came to yield more than 8 per cent of their capital value. Much later in the century, a return of 8 per cent remained the approximate figure which Antonio Rospigliosi was gaining from investments yielding a monetary income.[4]

It is worth noting that rents paid in wheat were simultaneously yielding Antonio the substantially higher return of 12 per cent. The reason for the difference was the chronic and acute shortage of available cash in Pistoia's fifteenth-century economy, concerning which we shall later say more.[5] Persons willing and able to pay a cash rent could sell it at a much lower interest than those who could only pay in agricultural produce.

While none of these series is complete and none rigorously precise, together they do make possible a reliable assessment of the periods of high and low profit expectations in the urban economy.

All the indicators which can be constructed declare that the 50 years before 1340 were favorable to commerce and enterprise. Raw materials and labor were both cheap; while the prices of finished commodities also showed a tendency to moderate, this seems primarily attributable to an expanding production. Many urban businessmen, who were also landlords in the countryside, were at the same time enjoying high agricultural rents and returns, which helped enlarge the capital they could invest in commercial and in-

4. In 1496 an investment of 200 pounds in a furnace was returning 16 pounds per year, *Richordi*, p. 165. A piece of land, purchased for 330 pounds, yielded 25 pounds per year (7.6 per cent), ibid. p. 167.

5. See below, p. 169. G. B. Tedaldi also mentions a "carestia dell'oro" at Pistoia in 1569 ("Relazione," p. 330).

dustrial enterprises. A favorable investment climate did not, of course, assure that all businesses would flourish and it did not offer immunity from destructive wars and sieges. But even these wars and sieges did not sensibly darken the economic atmosphere, as far as our sources show, before 1340.

The combined famine and plague of 1339–40 seem to have brought an abrupt end to this era of favorable profit expectations. As early as 1340, the city government noted that artisans and laborers were leaving the city "because of the lack of commerce, industries and employment," and repeatedly in the following years the commune had to offer generous tax concessions to those willing to make their homes in the city or countryside.[6]

In the latter half of the fourteenth century, as both raw materials and especially labor commanded inflated prices while finished articles lagged behind in value, the economic atmosphere turned uniformly gloomy. The business climate of the fifteenth century, on the other hand, might be described as falling halfway between the brilliance of the years before the plague and the depression of the half century which followed it. Raw materials and food moderated considerably in cost, in response to more stable political and social conditions and probably also reflecting heavy investments at least in some sectors of the economy. Wages, on the other hand, in spite of a slight decline, remained relatively high. This was not a climate favorable to the development of industries employing large numbers of men.

Against this background of high prosperity until about 1340, bad times from then until about 1400, then moderate revival in the early fifteenth century, the characteristic geographical confines of Pistoia's commercial activities were also showing some notable changes.

TOWARD A TUSCAN REGIONAL ECONOMY

In the thirteenth century, perhaps the most distinctive feature of Pistoia's commerce in a geographic sense was the movement of its

6. ASP, Provv. Tomus 11, 32r, 26 Aug. 1340, "propter defectum mercantiarum, artium et laborii." See also ibid. Tomus 27, 40r, 27 Aug. 1379, for a confirmation of the tax immunities offered to immigrants into the territory.

trade within two contrasting commercial areas: the one circumscribed by the narrow frontiers of its own district, and the other by the broad, almost limitless horizons within which Italy's great international merchants and bankers had established their primacy.

Even at the peak of its medieval prosperity, the territorial area within which most of Pistoia's citizens conducted their economic affairs did not extend much beyond the lands visible from the city's own campanile. The government of the free commune strove mightily to limit local trade to its own citizens and to prohibit foreigners from participating in it. It sought to accomplish this in two ways. It tried to concentrate all commercial exchange within its own walls, anticipating what under the later mercantilistic system would constitute "staple policy."[7] And in another exact anticipation of a mercantilistic idea—this time the "policy of provision"—it sought to prevent or limit export from its own district of things deemed essential for its own prosperity: food, raw materials and men.

The Statutes of 1296 thus required all inhabitants of the countryside to bring "all their salable wares and all their goods and especially wood" only to the city to be sold, and the men of the high mountains "from Brandeglio on up" were especially enjoined to take a solemn oath to obey the regulation.[8] The commune also insisted that iron ore, on its way to the mountain *fabriche* for smelting, be brought, weighed and offered for sale at the "venarium" of San Iacopo in the city—presumably to assure that Pistoia's citizens would have the chance to purchase it and to profit from the manufacture of iron.[9]

To assure an abundance of valued commodities within its own territory, the commune as early as 1162, and frequently thereafter, declared a *devetum* or export prohibition in regard to cereals whenever famine or scarcity threatened.[10] According to the Statutes of ca. 1200, all persons were obligated to swear that they would not sell

7. Cf. Eli Heckscher, *Mercantilism*, transl. M. Shapiro (London, 1962), II, 60–72.

8. *Statutum potestatis*, p. 125, "De pena foretanorum vendentium res suas alibi quam Pistorii."

9. Ibid. p. 36, "De officio illorum . . . qui sunt super venario."

10. According to Salvi, *Historie*, I, 95.

grain to a foreigner.[11] Similar export prohibitions were regularly imposed on pigs and even on sheep, although many of the latter were customarily wintered on the maritime plains of Lucca and Siena.[12] Wine, another essential food commodity, was likewise under a *devetum* in 1285.[13]

The export of raw materials was also discouraged. No wood could be taken at any time from the district, except tall pines suitable for ship masts.[14] Mountaineers, however, seem to have been especially prone to smuggle wood beyond the borders, and the city government clearly feared its export to Lucca, which also, in its mountains, was supporting an iron industry of some pretensions.[15] In 1334, in an effort to promote the local wool industry, the commune also forbade the taking of spun wool from the contado.[16]

Even workers were not supposed to pass beyond the borders in quest of more gainful employment. All rural inhabitants were required to take a solemn oath not to leave Pistoia's territory with intent of residing elsewhere, unless they first were able to secure the podestà's permission.[17]

In erecting all these walls hampering exchange with its neighbors, the commune was not aiming, it must be noted, at achieving a kind of economic isolation and autarchy. While limiting exports of food and raw materials, it favored imports of those same commodities. While forbidding its own workers to leave, it welcomed with attractive privileges skilled artisans from Verona and other Lombard towns, who might help in the development of a prosperous wool

11. *Statuti*, ed. Berlan, cap. 79, p. 66.

12. Enforcement of *deveta* on grain, pigs and sheep is treated as part of the regular duties of the podestà's "iudex super dannis datis," *Statutum potestatis*, pp. 154–55. This provision states "quod omnes castrones, que vernantur in plano nostro, sive in montibus, sint in deveto," but it seems to have been countermanded by a later chapter (ibid. p. 172), which allows citizens to maintain "quantas bestias voluerint" outside the boundaries of the district.

13. *Breve populi*, p. 169.

14. *Statutum potestatis*, p. 185, "De pena portantis lignamina extra districtum Pistorii." *Breve populi*, p. 81, exempts ship masts.

15. *Statutum potestatis*, p. 185, no one "de montanis districtus Pistorii" was allowed to sell wood "in districtu Lucensi" or to "alicui forestario de districtu Lucensi."

16. ASP, Provv. Tomus 9, 14r.

17. *Statutum potestatis*, p. 210.

industry.[18] Foreign merchants too, coming to Pistoia to buy cloth, were to be exempt from all tariffs and from any threat of reprisals against them for debts owed by their countrymen.[19]

The trade policies of the free commune envisioned a free flow of "the factors of production"—food, raw materials and labor—into its territory, and no flow at all of these same factors in the contrary direction. Exports would be limited to manufactured articles commanding high prices in foreign markets and earning an abundance of cash for the city. The flaw in these policies was, of course, that all the larger Tuscan communes were pursuing the same, proto-mercantilistic goals and were better able than little Pistoia to make their will effective. Fierce competition, strenuous efforts to develop much the same industries in all the many cities and to obstruct the progress of neighbors worked powerfully to restrict the flow of regional exchange and to lend to the thirteenth-century Tuscan economy its unmistakable character of localism.

Over these same years other merchants of Pistoia were penetrating into a much wider trading zone, the nearly boundless world of Italian international commerce and banking. Details of their history are reserved to the following section; suffice it here to note that their activities give the economy of the thirteenth-century free commune that balance between localism and internationalism which is one of its most distinctive features.

In the disturbed years of the late fourteenth century, Pistoia's merchants largely abandoned the arena of international banking and commerce, as we shall further see.[20] But with the growing political integration of Pistoia's contado within the Florentine state, the local restrictions on its trade also were breaking down, and Pistoia came to participate ever more actively within a regionally articulated economy.

The liberalization of commercial exchange, to be sure, progressed only slowly, and some historians doubt if it ever represented a con-

18. Ibid. p. 239. All "homines et personas forenses et extraneas, qui vel que sunt . . . de Verona . . . vel . . . de Lombardia vel undecunque" working at the wool trade were to be defended against prosecution for all crimes committed or debts contracted outside Pistoia.

19. Ibid. p. 219.

20. See below, p. 168.

scious and consistent policy on the part of the Florentines.[21] In gradually expanding its district, Florence did not abolish established tolls and tariffs and did not even curtail the authority of the now dependent cities to regulate them. The Florentine government might intervene, as at Pistoia in 1402, and assume temporary control over the city budget, but the usual policy was to leave fiscal administration under the supervision of the dependent communes.[22] Still in the fifteenth century, all the larger constituent communes of the Florentine district were collecting import and export duties at their gates and at other toll stations in their territories.

This chaotic system generated some striking anomalies. After taking Pisa in 1406, the Florentines retained until 1491 a tariff originally imposed against the products of their own wool industry.[23] In the late fifteenth century, iron ore could be shipped with lower tolls from Elba to Lucca outside the Florentine district than it could be taken to Pistoia within it. Finally in 1491, after Pistoia's iron makers protested this discrimination against Florence's own loyal subjects, the Florentine Signoria corrected this abuse—not by abolishing the internal tariff but by raising the charges on ore shipped to Lucca to equal levels![24]

But it remains incontrovertible that for Pistoia at least, political subjugation to Florence also brought freer commercial exchange with the latter city. As early as 1298, Pistoia, then under Florentine hegemony, was required to join a tariff union with Florence and its then ally Lucca.[25] According to its terms, the merchants of each of these three cities would be treated for tax purposes as citizens in the territories of the other two. The union could not have survived the

21. For an expression that the Florentines in the fifteenth century consciously pursued a policy of liberalizing trade, see especially Pöhlmann, *Wirthschaftspolitik*. But see also Carlo M. Cipolla in the *CEH*, III, 417, who states: "Curiously enough, the emergence of central power in states also often led to protective measures for the benefit of one city against competition from other cities of the same principality or kingdom."

22. Luca Dominici, *Cronache*, II, 65. From Jan. 1402 the Florentines assumed supervision of the "gabella maggiore delle porti" and of the salt tax at Pistoia. In later returning the administration of these taxes to the Pistoiesi, they still prohibited any additional imposts in the countryside (ibid. p. 85).

23. Pöhlmann, *Wirthschaftspolitik*, p. 122.

24. Loc. cit.

25. Davidsohn, *Geschichte*, III, 37.

protracted wars of the early fourteenth century, but after Pistoia once more submitted to Florence in 1328, the commercial bonds between the two cities were again tightened. In 1329 the Pistoiesi were permitted to drive their flocks and herds across Florentine territory, subject to taxes no greater than those paid by Florence's own citizens; in 1333 all restrictions on the flow of agricultural products between Pistoia and the Florentine communes of the Valdinievole were removed.[26] In 1357, in order to support a blockade they were imposing upon the port of Pisa, the Florentines permitted Pistoia's merchants to trade with and within their city without prohibitions.[27]

One of the most important steps toward a liberalized regional exchange was the freeing of commerce in cereals, wine, oil and other "grascia." In 1386, in response to a request from the Florentine government, Pistoia agreed to renounce all future export prohibitions (*deveta*) on all food commodities, in return for like action by the Florentines.[28] Moreover, both cities were to abolish all tolls on wheat. Tariffs on other agricultural commodities could be retained, but they were not to be raised higher than traditional levels.

Even before the fifteenth century, Pistoia's merchants were treated at Florence like the Florentines themselves. If tolls and tariffs still divided the cities, they were especially liberal regarding agricultural produce and for other commodities their purposes were exclusively fiscal. And the city governments were not unaware that lower tariffs could bring greater revenues.

By the fifteenth century, Pistoia had passed fully under the shadow of the Florentine market, and it would be hard to exaggerate the stimulus and influence which that market exerted upon its agriculture, commerce, banking and industry.

COMMERCE AND BANKING

The story of Pistoia's commerce is intimately connected with the development within the city of business and banking institutions.

26. *Capitoli*, I, no. 3, p. 5, 24 May 1329, and I, no. 9, p. 9.

27. Scipione Ammirato, *Istorie fiorentine* (Florence, 1647), II, 581, "ai quali [Pistolesi] era perciò stata levata ogni prohibizione che havessero di mercanzie con la città di Firenze. . . ."

28. *Capitoli*, I, no. 28, p. 25, 7 Aug. 1386.

At Pistoia as commonly in medieval Europe, three types of businessmen fulfilling banking functions may be distinguished: pawnbrokers, money changers, and the great merchant bankers.[29] Little can be known specifically about pawnbroking at Pistoia, other than that numerous brokers were already doing a lively business in the thirteenth century.[30] In 1397, two Jews came to Pistoia specifically for its practice, and their activities were welcomed and encouraged by the communal government.[31] Ecclesiastics appear among the brokers' frequent customers, but credit from pawnshops seems to have played no role of evident importance in financing business ventures.[32] More important in a commercial sense were the money changers or *cambiatores*.[33] The first important Tuscan city to be encountered by travellers coming from Bologna beyond the Apennines, Pistoia was ideally placed to change foreign money into the local Tuscan coinage. "Consules campsorum," consuls of a guild of money changers, are mentioned already in 1218.[34] In 1257, twenty tables or "banks" of money changers were doing business on the city's principal square.[35] By the end of the century if not before, these changers were also accepting deposits at their tables. The Statutes of 1296 required that each "table" post with the podestà the substantial bond of 2000 pounds, to assure the protection of

29. On the various types of banking institutions, see the comments of de Roover, *Medici Bank*, pp. 14 ff. and the more extended treatment by the same author in the *CEH*, III, 70–105.

30. A. Sapori, "L'Usura nel dugento a Pistoia," *Studi di storia economica medievale* (2nd ed. Florence, 1947), pp. 117–25.

31. L. Zdekauer, "L'Interno di un banco di pegno nel 1417 (con documenti inediti)," *ASI*, ser. 5, 17 (1896), 91, n. 1.

32. ASF, Catasto 189, 3r, the chapel of San Bartolomeo owed a debt of 80 pounds "al giudeo." Ibid. 635r, two priests, Iacopo and Antonio, sons of Vanni Buonacorsi, owed 14 pounds "al prestito de' giudei di Pistoia per uno pegno." On the other hand, in the tax declarations of businessmen in the Catasto, I was unable to note debts to Jews.

33. On the history of Pistoia's banks, besides the works of Sapori and Zdekauer cited in nn. 30 and 31 above, see Guido Zaccagnini, "I Banchieri pistoiesi a Bologna e altrove nel sec. XIII. Contributo alla storia del commercio nel medio evo," *BSP*, 20 (1918), 26–55, 131–44 and 188–204; 21 (1919), 35–46, 96–108 and 117–30.

34. Zaccagnini, "Banchieri," p. 28, n. 1.

35. *Liber censuum*, no. 344, p. 240, 1257. The document is cited by Salvi, *Historie*, I, 162, but misdated 1225.

their depositors and their own honesty.[36] This provision would make little sense unless the *cambiatores* were also working with or re-investing their depositors' funds.

While money changers thus acquired an early and large importance at Pistoia, their profession did not provide the foundations for the greatest mercantile fortunes. The twenty *cambiatores* named in 1257 did not apparently include a single representative of the great families of merchant bankers, although many of these families were already settled within the city and at work building their fortunes. Rather than local money changing, the long-distance trade to Bologna, Lombardy and France seems to have been the road which led the greatest mercantile families to their enormous affluence.

Like all the inland Tuscan communes, Pistoia was much behind the great ports of Venice, Pisa and Genoa in developing a vigorous long-distance trade. "Consuls of merchants" are not even mentioned in the Statutes of 1107, although they do appear in the later redaction of ca. 1200, where they are accorded a respectable role in the communal constitution.[37] From 1212 a list of these consuls, broken but still valuable, has survived.[38]

The area which initially attracted these merchants was the lands beyond the Apennines, to which the mountain passes offered easy contact: Bologna and the other Lombard towns, and France. Bologna with its great university, gathering scholars from all over the Christian world, offered a marvelous market for skilled businessmen able to change money, transfer funds, and carry the scholars' precious books to school.[39] By the late thirteenth century, Pistoia's many bankers at Bologna were organized into fifteen companies and were the most prominent of all Tuscan merchants in the great

36. *Statutum potestatis*, p. 244. "Quilibet campsor et qui tenet bancum in civitate Pistorii" must deposit 2000 pounds with the podestà, to offer assurance "de ipsa arte fideliter exercenda et de restituendis depositis sibi factis."

37. *Statuti*, ed. Berlan, cap. 164, p. 110, "Habebo in communi consilio omnes Consules Negotiatorum. . . ."

38. The first appearance of "consules Pist. mercatorum" is *Liber censuum*, no. 25, p. 20, 7 Sept. 1212. The list of consuls given by Salvi, *Historie*, I, 125 and ff. is taken from citations in the *Liber censuum*.

39. See the documents reflecting the banking activities of Pistoiese merchants at Bologna published by Zaccagnini, "Banchieri," *BSP*, 21 (1919), pp. 105 ff.

university town. Their activities have left a deep imprint in Bologna's surviving sources.[40]

But Pistoia's bankers were no strangers in other cities too. In 1209 they are mentioned among the Italians trading at the Champagne fairs.[41] From a not much later date, business records have survived to enrich our knowledge. On December 8, 1227, for example, a company of four Pistoiesi advanced to Sienese merchants 200 "strong" pounds of Provins, and directed that the money be repaid them at the fair of Lagny in Champagne, the opening date of which, January 2, was only a month away.[42] In 1242, several Pistoiese merchants were waylaid along with other Tuscan travellers near Piacenza in Lombardy, presumably on their way to France; one of them was Chiarente Chiarenti, whose name would identify one of the city's largest banks.[43] In 1255 at Milan, another Pistoiese company, including thirteen partners, contracted to sell northern cloth to a merchant from Mantua—a demonstration of how these merchants could function in an international market with no tight ties to their native city.[44]

Pistoia's proximity to the mountain passes had helped carry its merchants to prominence in the Lombard and French trade, but by the late thirteenth century the sea route from Pisa to Marseilles or Nice was gaining in importance. This must surely be considered an unfortunate shift for Pistoia, but the city's merchants were not slow in frequenting the new avenue to France. They appeared at Marseilles from 1248, and even before, in 1240, the commune had prudently struck a commercial treaty with Genoa.[45] In 1272, Pistoiese merchants were carrying on a Pisan ship purses, silk and linen hats, clothing and spices to Marseilles, only to lose their cargo to pirates

40. Zaccagnini's study, cited in n. 33 above, is largely based on the volumes of "Memoriali" in the State Archives of Bologna, which seem to be richer in this regard than any surviving documents in Pistoia's own archives.

41. Zaccagnini, "Banchieri," *BSP*, 20 (1918), 31.

42. *Imbreviature notarili. Il Liber imbreviaturarum notarii MCCXXVII-MCCXXIX*, ed. M. Chiaudano (Turin, 1938), p. 22.

43. A. Schaube, *Handelsgeschichte der romanischen Völker des Mittelmeergebiets bis zum Ende der Kreuzzüge* (Munich and Berlin, 1906), p. 363.

44. *Documenti del commercio veneziano nei secoli XI-XIII*, ed. R. Morozzo della Rocca and A. Lombardo, II (Turin, 1940), no. 826, pp. 352–54.

45. Schaube, *Handelsgeschichte*, p. 363.

from Nice.[46] In 1268 Charles of Anjou granted to six companies of Pistoiese merchants safe conduct through his lands, though it remains uncertain whether Provence or Sicily was the attraction for them.[47] A Pisan document of 1283 mentions merchants of Pistoia upon a Pisan ship, carrying four bundles back from France, containing paper, perhaps intended for Bologna's busy scholars, and felt hats, white and dyed, to the number of 86.[48]

Many in number, ranging widely in the lands they visited, these companies were also growing in size and complexity. A document, notable for its age, has survived from 1259 to cast some light on developing business structure.[49] It describes the "new capital" invested in the company "dei Boni," which seems to have been undergoing one of the frequent reorganizations characteristic of these enterprises. Five partners—Ciunta Kerardi, Iacopo Foresi, Thakaria Jacopi, Arriko and Fucio sons of Dolciamori, and Lambertino de lo 'segna—invested 3853 pounds in fairly equal shares ranging from 500 to 800 pounds. An additional 1555 pounds 7 solidi were placed with the company by eight other investors, minors and a woman, to constitute a total capitalization of 5408 pounds 7 solidi.[50] The exact division of future profits is not altogether clear in this terse document. Investors could apparently expect a fixed return of 7 per cent per year. Profits among the active partners were, on the other hand, quite unevenly divided. Arriko was conceded profits to the proportion which 200 pounds would bring; Iacopo, what 150 pounds would gain; Lambertino, 100 pounds; Fucio, 50 pounds; and a hitherto unmentioned Francesco the same. It appears that in this quite disproportionate profit division, services to the company were also being considered. If the mysterious Francesco is not to be identified with the partner Ciunta, otherwise unprovided for in the profit division, he might perhaps have been the company's manager or agent.

46. *Registri della cancelleria angioina, ricostruiti da Riccardo Filangieri,* X (Naples, 1957), no. 644, p. 164.

47. *Relazioni,* nos. 56, 57, 58, 59, 60 and 61.

48. Archivio di Stato di Pisa, Not. 2545, 30v, 16 Jan. 1283. The cargo consisted of "ballas duas cartarum cum carpitis octo circa ipsas ballas et ballas duas feltrarum numero lxxxvi inter albos [et] tinctos" among other items.

49. Edited in Monaci, *Crestomazia,* no. 73, pp. 197–99.

50. The document itself gives the total as 5408 pounds 8 solidi, an error of one solidus.

Perhaps the most interesting aspect of this reorganization of 1259 is the flexible structure the company "dei Boni" had acquired; while its name suggests that it was originally a family enterprise, it was welcoming as partners and investors persons who had no evident blood ties among them. It was also large, as its 5000 pounds of capitalization was, for the age, no paltry sum.

By the late thirteenth century, several of Pistoia's companies had attained spectacular dimensions. Five of them in particular were to win renown on the international scene: the Ammanati, Chiarenti, Panciatichi, Reali and Visconti. For all of them, the great period of expansion was the late thirteenth century. The Ammanati house, until the 1290s the largest of them all, seems to have been first brought to tremendous size by a Bartolomeo who died not long after 1274. In the Book of Hearths of ca. 1244, he is mentioned with two other members of his family among the nobles of the rural commune of Montemagno, still not permanently settled within the city.[51] In its breathless expansion, the company had established branches or was maintaining correspondents at Bologna (from 1261), Genoa (1269), England (1266), Orléans (1267), Paris and Montpellier (1277), Acre in the Levant (1290), as well as at Rome, Milan and Avignon, not to mention Tuscan towns.[52] From 1283 they were also "following" the Roman curia.[53] The fall of the Ammanati was almost as spectacular as their rise. As faithful Ghibellines, they were exiled from Pistoia in 1290, although it is hard to know if the exile really injured their banking operations. They apparently indulged heavily in the risky practice of extending loans to prelates and princes widely scattered throughout Europe. In 1302, caught without funds to satisfy importunate depositors, they fled both Rome and Bologna in bankruptcy. In 1304 they addressed an appeal to Pope Benedict XI to force their French debtors among the higher clergy to pay and also to persuade King Edward of England to meet his obligations, but their pleas brought no evident results.[54]

51. *Liber focorum*, p. 110, no. 397, "Bartolomeus Amanati."

52. Zaccagnini, "Banchieri," *BSP*, 20 (1918), pp. 37 ff.

53. The relations of Pistoia's bankers with the papacy are treated in Yves Renouard, *Les Relations des papes d'Avignon et des compagnies commerciales et bancaires de 1316 à 1378* (Paris, 1941), passim.

54. The letter seems to have survived only in Salvi, *Historie* I, 285, but there is no reason to doubt its authenticity.

The size of the company is attested by the debts of King Edward, which alone reached a gigantic 150,000 florins.[55]

Over the next decades the popes made repeated if sporadic efforts to recover at least part of their deposited funds; as late as 1358, Innocent VI was still demanding restitution.[56] The fact that the popes recovered almost nothing is testimony to the magnitude of the Ammanati collapse.

The Chiarenti, who replaced the Ammanati as Pistoia's greatest bankers after the latter's failure in 1302, were commoners in origin, though like the Ammanati they came from Montemagno and moved to the city, probably in the early thirteenth century. The real founder of the family's fortunes was Anselmo di Chiarenti, who served as *anziano* or elder of the people in 1265.[57] The Chiarenti were active in Genoa from at least 1253, and had branches at Bologna from 1265, Paris from 1269, Viterbo from 1271, and also served the Roman curia. By the early fourteenth century their range of operations extended to Aragon and Navarre, and the archbishops of Trèves and Mainz in Germany figured among their debtors. Closely associated with the Ammanati in the papal service, they followed them into failure at Rome, probably in 1305, and the popes had with them no more success than with the Ammanati in recovering their lost deposits.

The Visconti, Reali and Panciatichi were all old noble families,

55. Loc. cit.

56. Renouard, *Relations*, p. 575. See also A. Flinaux, "La Faillite des Ammanati de Pistoia et le Saint-Siège (début du XIVe siècle)," *Revue Historique du Droit Français et Étranger, 3* (1924), 436–72.

57. Zaccagnini, "Banchieri," *BSP, 20* (1918), pp. 131 ff. A Chiarenti d'Anselmo, apparently the father of Anselmo, appears as a conjuror in the oath of 1219 to uphold the peace with Bologna, and is mentioned again in 1232. For Anselmo di Chiarenti at Genoa in 1253, see R. Lopez, "L'Attività economica di Genova nel Marzo 1253 secondo gli atti notarili del tempo," *ASLSP, 64* (1935), p. 162. By 1259 the Chiarenti company had eleven partners, who are named in a document of 13 December of that year. See R. Doehaerd, *Les Relations commerciales entre Gênes, la Belgique et l'Outremont d'après les archives notariales génoises aux XIIIe et XIVe siècles* (Institut historique belge de Rome. Études d'histoire économique et sociale, 2; Brussels and Rome, 1941), no. 1125, p. 617. The Chiarenti were the most active of all Pistoia's merchants at Genoa, and participated vigorously in the cloth trade with France. See the comments of A. Ferretto, "Codice diplomatico delle relazioni fra la Liguria, la Toscana e la Lunigiana ai tempi di Dante (1265–1321)," *ASLSP, 31* (1901), p. 187, n. 2.

whose banks were organized somewhat later and grew more slowly than the Ammanati and Chiarenti. Vinciguerra Panciatichi, founder of the Panciatichi fortunes, presents a good example of the glamorous career possible for these great merchants.[58] He left Pistoia in 1281 as an exiled Ghibelline, established himself in Avignon, pursued a flourishing business and married a French lady. He then attended the court of Philip the Fair, served as a royal official in Normandy and was knighted by the king in 1301. His son Giovanni became the leader of one of the powerful factions of Pistoia and for a brief period (1350–51) was ruler of the city. These latter three banking families did not enter papal service and avoided the spectacular growth and collapse of the Ammanati; most reached their heights of size and prosperity in the early fourteenth century.

This survey has mentioned only a few of Pistoia's great banking houses and described only part of their activities. But enough has been said to support the following comments about them. The banks were of colossal size, recruiting capital not only from the patrimonies of the founding families but from partners and numerous depositors. Their affairs carried over an enormous geographic range, making them true manifestations of the economic internationalism of the medieval world. Even contact with their native city seems surprisingly unessential to their success. Exile not only did not visibly injure their operations; in the case of the Panciatichi, it helped inspire and promote it. They were also remarkably unspecialized in their business activities, and a large element of commercial opportunism figured in their policies. The Ammanati, for example, were landlords in Bologna and an official stationer (*stazionario*) to the Studio there. They bought, sold and transported books, exchanged and transferred funds, traded in cloth and apparently almost any other article from which profit might be made, advanced loans, farmed taxes and served the pope.

Intense localism and a brilliant internationalism were thus the slightly paradoxical characteristics of Pistoia's thirteenth-century commerce, and for long the city, for all its mountainous contado and modest size, was able to prosper by it. But the system also fomented a fierce and wasteful competition among the Tuscan towns,

58. Zaccagnini, "Banchieri," *BSP*, 21 (1919), pp. 38 ff.

for which in the long run Pistoia was ill-equipped. The effort to advance production within an exclusively local framework further hampered regional exchange, delayed the regional development of resources, and threatened the local economies with early saturation.

The precise impact of the age of low profit expectations in the late fourteenth century upon Pistoia's commercial companies is hard to reconstruct, but the Estimario of 1415 and the Catasto of 1427 do allow us to discern some of the results and to note some of the weaknesses inherent in these great enterprises. The period worked havoc with most of the greatest thirteenth-century commercial houses. Three branches of the Ammanati family are mentioned in the Catasto, with assets of 284, 343 and 37 florins respectively.[59] These sums would rank them on the level of prosperous artisans, hardly of international financiers. The one representative of the Reali family similarly bore the modest assessment of only 220 florins.[60]

Only one of the old houses may be said to have weathered the storm with relative success: the Partini. Its founder, Partino di Deodato, was a commoner active in trade from 1254.[61] The four brothers Partini (Lapo, Bartolomeo, Rinieri and Antonio, sons of ser Niccholaio di ser Lapo) constituted the richest household at Pistoia in 1427, with an assessment of 12,309 florins.[62] Nearly half this sum represented investments in land (5358 florins) and animals (217 florins). The Partini were, however, still quite active commercially. They were partners in a company for dyeing wool cloth, with credits worth 913 pounds, and offered for sale at their haberdashery cloths, shoes and cloaks (*cappucci*) valued at 843 florins. The volume of their affairs is measured by the fact that their tax declara-

59. ASF, Catasto, 260, 710r (Nanni di Giovanni Amannati), 712r (Nanni di Giovanni di Churrado Amannati) and 261, 183v (Bona di Niccholuccio Amaneti).

60. Ibid. 260, 720r (Niccholaio di Tommeo Reali).

61. Zaccagnini, "Banchieri," *BSP*, 21 (1919), 41. He is mentioned in a document of 1237, *Liber censuum*, no. 305, p. 212. The Partini were quite active in France in the early fourteenth century and suffered, along with other "Lombards," from the discriminatory policies of Philip the Fair. Cf. the letter written in 1330 by a member of the company in France, complaining of the royal oppression, in *Medieval Trade in the Mediterranean World*, ed. Robert S. Lopez and Irving W. Raymond (New York, 1955), pp. 394–400.

62. ASF, Catasto, 260, 298r and ff. The father, ser Niccholaio, was called a "riccho huomo" in 1401 by Luca Dominici, *Cronache*, II, 22, and he was also identified as a supporter of the Panciatichi faction.

tion gives abstracts of 17 separate account books, listing no less than 824 debtors, most owing small sums between 5.5 and 20 pounds, and carrying a total book value of 9700 pounds.

This extraordinary credit structure illustrates one of the characteristics, and one of the points of weakness, of these great commercial houses. They had to operate to a large and precarious extent on credit, extending it not only to a few great customers but even to petty purchasers of their wares. This shortage of customers able to buy in cash was surely pronounced in a small town like Pistoia, with no mint and no great markets of its own. But difficulties encountered by the agricultural economy—famines, wars, plague—could make these credits uncollectable for long periods and sometimes forever, to the jeopardy of the company. "They [the Partini brothers] say," reports the Catasto, "that their business is entirely in credit, and many are lost which they think we will never recover, and others [only] after a great length of time."[63] The book value of their accounts had to be reduced by 50 per cent to arrive at a fair tax assessment, and reductions by 50, 75 or an even higher percentage seem almost a characteristic way of handling mercantile account books in the Catasto.[64]

This difficulty of attaining cash payments seems to have influenced the Partini brothers in the management of their own enterprises. They appear to have invested most heavily in those products easily salable in the Florentine market, with its better possibilities of securing cash receipts. They had come to operate two iron founderies (*fabriche*) in the mountains, one at least of which, called "la fabbricha nuova a San Felice," seems to have been recently built. And of course, much of the produce from their many farms, their largest single investment, would be marketed at Florence. Florence attracted not only their products but their capital too. Their greatest single monetary asset was a deposit of 1500 florins, but it was placed not with Pistoiese but with Florentine bankers.[65]

63. Ibid. 311v. "Dichono i loro trafichi sono tutti in hredenze e sono assai perdute che pensono non rischoteramo mai e l' altre si risquotono chon grande lunghezzo di tempo."

64. The account books of Lodovicho d'Angnolo Taviani, ASF, Catasto 261, 38v, were similarly reduced by 25, 50, 75 or 80 per cent, according to the varying prospects of collection.

65. Deposits with Leonardo e Franco di Marcho Bartoli of Florence, along with those in other Florentine banks, amounted to over 2000 florins.

The Partini accounts thus suggest two things: that Pistoia's commercial economy was showing vitality in the early fifteenth century, but that its character was ever more strongly influenced by the demands of the Florentine market.

Certain evidence of considerable commercial growth and prosperity at Pistoia in the early fifteenth century comes from a comparison of our two tax surveys, the Estimario of 1415 and the Catasto of 1427. The merchant Batista di Marco, for example, in 1415 had in his shop stock worth 2500 pounds (about 625 florins); in 1427 the value of his stock was assessed at over 5000 florins.[66] Not all Pistoia's merchants show so great an increase in the value of their goods, but wherever comparisons are possible, some gains are usual. In 1415 the spice merchant Giovanni di Michele Lippi had invested in his shop 1750 pounds; his son Michele di Giovanni Lippi had over 4000.[67] The business investments of Lando di Simone jumped over the same period from 300 to 542 pounds.[68] Filippo de' Fabbroni had "in bottega" only 50 pounds in 1415, and 300 florins in 1427.[69] These comparisons could be prolonged, but the trend seems clear enough: the twelve years between 1415 and 1427 had witnessed a considerable business recovery.

The character of Pistoia's businesses was also changing. The huge, sprawling, unspecialized deposit banks of the earlier period had entered upon bad days and were not recovering. One of the city's richest merchants, Batista di Marco mentioned above, was still operating a "banco" in 1415; there is no mention of a bank in his declaration of 1427, and new among the commodities in which he was trading was iron.[70] In 1415 Rinforzato Mannelli expressly declared to the tax officials that he had abandoned the banking business, and another merchant, Andrea d'Aldobrandino, similarly referred to his bank in the past tense.[71] Two factors explain this

66. Estimario, San Michele in Bonaccio, no. 3; ASF, Catasto 261, 687r.

67. Estimario, Santa Maria fuor le porti, no. 17; ASF, Catasto 261, 590v.

68. Estimario, Santa Maria fuor le porti, no. 21; ASF, Catasto 261, 574r.

69. Estimario, San Giovanni fuor cività, no. 50; ASF, Catasto 261, 421v.

70. Estimario, San Michele in Bonaccio, no. 3, "botegha e traffico di mercantie e banco." ASF, Catasto 261, 687r, "traffico in panni e ferro."

71. Estimario, Santa Maria fuor le porti, no. 39, "o di meo traffico quantunche non faccio più banco pure o davere d'altrui con alcuni denari e a riscuotere nell'arte della lana lire 500." Ibid. San Paolo, no. 4, "aveo insul bancho quando io lo faceo. . . ."

abandonment of banking: the competition of the great Florentine houses, and the attraction of other investments.

In the fifteenth century, a merchant of Pistoia who wished to transfer funds or invest abroad found it convenient to make use of the large and efficient Florentine houses. Antonio Rospigliosi and his brother Milanese, for example, deposited 1000 ducats in the Venetian branch of the Medici bank, and another large Florentine bank, that of Filippo Strozzi, handled for Antonio a letter of exchange with Naples.[72] Other Pistoiesi were depositing money with their own Opera di San Iacopo, with Florentine banks and companies or even with the Florentine Monte, as the funded public debt was called, but in 1427 hardly any of Pistoia's own companies were functioning as deposit banks.[73]

The favored business enterprise of the fifteenth century at Pistoia was small, specialized with no foreign interests, and largely concerned with the exploitation of local resources. If the merchant of the thirteenth century was apt to put all his capital in a single, large company, his counterpart in the fifteenth century would probably be a partner in several, separated enterprises, each with its own distinct capital, partners and purpose. Antonio Rospigliosi at various times in his life was a partner in ten companies, usually in several at a time, trading in cheese, food, wool cloth, spices, shoes, silk, tile and earthenware.[74]

The special interests of these companies are best examined as part of a consideration of Pistoia's artisan industries.

72. *Richordi,* p. 27, 15 Feb. 1477, "Noi Antonio e Milanese di Taddeo aviamo rimeso in Vinegia duchati mille, cioè D. M. viniziani a Lorenzo e a Giuliano de' Medici e chonpagnia di Vinegia per le mani de' loro di Firenze. . . . Ce ne ponghino creditori per chonto a parte, chon condizione e chommisione che e' detti denari esercitino e trafichino per noi in tutte quelle chosse che a loro parrà. . . ." Ibid. p. 87, 1484, a "lettera di chanbio" sent to Filippo Strozzi e conpagnia at Florence, drawn on their Naples branch.

73. Cf. ASF, Catasto 261, 593r, madonna Verde donna fu di messer Antonio Baldinotti (himself a jurist of some reputation) reported that her dowry of 1000 florins was "in disposito nelle mani degli operai di San Iacopo . . . de' quali n'a l'anno a ragione di fl. viiii per chento che sono fl. 90." Besides depositing with the Medici bank (above, n. 72), Antonio Rospigliosi also kept deposits with the Florentine Monte to assure dowries for his two daughters. *Richordi,* p. 51.

74. Ibid. pp. 13, 18, 28, 34, 36, 58, 73 and 145.

ARTISAN INDUSTRIES

Pistoia, while it acquired considerable importance as a commercial town already by the middle thirteenth century, was much slower in developing artisan industries of any size. Of the 3206 urban residents who took the oath of 1219, only 41, or not even 2 per cent, bear an artisan's title.[75] (At Pisa in 1228, about one fourth of the 4271 conjurors may be identified as artisans.)[76] Pistoia's 41 artisans were further occupied in 25 separate skills; the largest single group, iron workers or *fabri*, numbered only seven. No industry by 1219 had yet attracted a large concentration of specialized artisans.

The history of Pistoia's artisan guilds also shows that industries at Pistoia were growing only slowly in the thirteenth century. The Statutes of ca. 1200 do mention a "council of the rectors of all the arts of the city of Pistoia," but the "arts" or guilds are not identified and the power accorded them seems to have later been rescinded.[77] Even with the establishment of a permanent popular regime at Pistoia from 1267, the guilds gained only a moderate influence upon communal government. Only two of the eight elders or anziani had to be artisans; the guilds are not specifically identified either in the *Breve populi* of 1284 or in the *Statutum potestatis* of 1296.[78] Even under the popular commune, Pistoia could not be considered, as could Florence, a guild republic.

The great age of growth for Pistoia's artisan industries seems to have been the decades following 1296, the period when, as we have seen, price structure was particularly favorable to enterprise. These years do at any rate witness the formation of the city's recognized guilds, which the Statutes of 1330 finally permit us to identify. The guilds numbered eight, and included some 46 rather oddly assorted professions. They are as follows:

(1) Judges and notaries (*iudices et notarii*).

75. *Liber censuum*, pp. 509–27.

76. Herlihy, *Pisa*, p. 129.

77. *Statuti*, ed. Berlan, cap. 33, p. 35. The podestà or consuls were forbidden to impose taxes or loans in the city and countryside "nisi communicato consilio Rectorum omnium artium civitatis Pist. vel maioris partis." But this requirement seems contradicted by a later one, ibid, cap. 158, p. 107, in which the phrase reads "nisi comunicato consilio C. hominum civitatis Pist., omnium vel maioris partis."

78. *Breve populi*, p. 8.

(2) Dealers in spices, gold, silks, girdles and money changers (*medici, speziarii, setaiuoli, cambiatores, merciarii, aurifices et corregiarii*).

(3) Merchants and workers in cloth and porters (*mercatores francigeni et ritalli, lanaioli, linaioli, testores, sartores, cimatores, stracciaiuoli, farsettarii, calzaiuoli et vectarii*).

(4) Butchers, leather workers and furriers (*beccharii, galligarii et pelliparii*).

(5) Iron workers and merchants (*fabri, ferratores et omnes qui laborant fabricam, videlicet: armaioli et ferrovecchi*).

(6) Stone masons and wood workers (*magistri petre et mercatores et magistri lignaminis soppedanorum vegetum barlectariorum astarum stradorum et cuiuscumque lignaminis*).

(7) Shoemakers, painters and barbers (*calzolarii novi et veteres, pictores, barbitonsores*).

(8) Vintners, innkeepers and food salesmen (*vinacterii, hospites et fornarii, venditores casei, olei et carnium salitarum et biadaiuoli*).[79]

To compare this list with the 41 artisans mentioned in 1219 is to recognize the continued importance of the crafts of wood and iron at Pistoia, masters of which had already been cited as early as 1107.[80] Leather workers and furriers were also present in the oath of 1219, although in small numbers.[81]

The industry which shows the most remarkable growth in the late thirteenth century is wool manufacture. Only one cloth worker, a *pectinarius* or comber, is mentioned in the oath of 1219. In the late thirteenth century, eager to promote the growth of a cloth industry, the commune had welcomed workers from Lombardy and even from France itself.[82] By 1330 specialties and skills had clearly multiplied; the sources mention weavers, finishers, tailors, stocking and

79. Listed by Zdekauer, *Breve populi*, p. liv.

80. In 1219 there were six *fabri*, two *scudarii* or shield makers, one *ferarius*, probably a blacksmith, and one *spadarius* or swordsmith. See above, p. 41, for artisans mentioned in 1107.

81. There were four shoemakers, two *pelizarii* or furriers, one *selarius* or saddle maker, one *erbaiolus* and *galigarius*, also tanners, and one *pelaio* or leather worker.

82. A "Iontorinus, cimator pannorum de Piccardia," is mentioned in 1288, *Breve populi*, p. liv.

doublet makers as well as merchants in linen and in new and used woolen cloth; significantly, however, these skills did not constitute an autonomous guild but were still in 1330 subject to the "art" of cloth importers. In 1334 the commune enacted special "Ordinamenta lane," which removed all taxes on raw wool, thread, woad, alum or dyes imported into the city or on looms within its walls; export of spun wool was at the same time prohibited.[83] In 1344 the government further decreed that an "ars lane" should be established at Pistoia, by which was apparently meant an independent guild of wool workers no longer subject to the cloth importers.[84]

With relatively few sources, it is hard to judge the size of these industries before the plague. But the conclusion seems reasonable that Pistoia, on the eve of the great disasters of the fourteenth century, had succeeded in developing fairly diversified if perhaps not large artisan industries.

It is also hard to follow the fate of these industries in the bad times of the late fourteenth century. Salvi, apparently impressed with the number of fulling mills in and about Pistoia mentioned in the documents, declared that in the year 1380 the city was "flourishing and rich through the art of wool," but this judgment is difficult to test.[85] After an extended period of darkness, however, the Estimario of 1415 and the Catasto of 1427 cast a flood of light upon Pistoia's commercial and industrial enterprises. Table 26 gives the number of merchants, artisans and shops described in the Catasto, arranged according to the eight guild divisions of 1330. The figures both for the persons involved in these various trades and for shops are undoubtedly somewhat understated in the Catasto, but they should at least accurately reflect the relative importance of these commercial and industrial activities at Pistoia.

In the early fifteenth century, one of the most active of all Pistoia's industries was that of iron and metal products. It clearly was attracting new and heavy investments. Batista di Marco, one of Pistoia's richest merchants, had operated a bank and dealt in dry goods in 1415; by 1427 he had, as we have mentioned, abandoned

83. ASP, Provv. Tomus 9, 14r, 17 April 1334.

84. Ibid. Tomus 13, 29v, 29 Nov. 1344, "Quod ars lane fiat in civitate Pistorii. . . ."

85. Salvi, *Historie*, II, 145.

TABLE 26 Merchants, Artisans and Shops at Pistoia, 1427

	Persons	*Shops*
(1) Notaries	24	
(2) Dealers in spices, gold, silks, girdles and money changers	24	12
(3) Cloth merchants, cloth workers, and porters	43	16
(4) Butchers, leather workers and furriers	25	9
(5) Iron workers	51	10
(6) Stone masons and wood workers	24	1
(7) Shoemakers, painters and barbers	64	10
(8) Vintners, innkeepers and food salesmen	13	4
Unspecified laborers	22	

The table shows the number of persons involved in the various trades, and the number of shops mentioned, in the Catasto of 1427.

the bank and his "traffico" was declared to be "in panni et ferro."[86] Fioravante Fioravanti, from a famous Pistoiese family, was similarly a merchant in dry goods in 1415, but by 1427 had acquired substantial investments in several *fabriche.*[87]

According to the Catasto of 1427, the metal products industry was employing, besides 34 *fabri,* coppersmiths, makers of knives and pots, and dealers in old iron. The industry was also strong in the countryside, where the *fabriche* were located which smelted the iron. One of the richest men in the mountains was an arms maker, Iacopo di Ciata of Lizzano.[88]

Iacopo's affairs also show the stimulus to Pistoia's iron industry exerted by the nearby Florentine market. He was in fact a partner with Piero di Cintonio "e chonpagni," lance merchants (*lanciai*) of Florence, to whom he had recently delivered 2000 "lancie da chavallo."[89] Another Florentine merchant of lances, Piero d'Antonio, also owed him 880 pounds, while he himself was in debt to Marcho di Iachopo Salvetti, dealer in cloths, from the same city.

To secure the iron ore needed for arms and other iron products in turn required close contact with Elba. The shipping of the ore was still hampered in the fifteenth century by high internal tariffs, but

86. See above, n. 66.

87. Estimario, San Giovanni fuor cività, no. 50.

88. ASF, Catasto 265, 284r.

89. Loc. cit. "[Da] Piero di Cintonio e chonpangni lanciai in Firenze debbo avere certa quantità di danari . . . d'una conpangnia ferri chol detto Piero di dumila lancie da chavallo."

at least it was spared the total interruptions of the former, frequent Pisan-Florentine wars. And Pistoia's rich families were not adverse to investing in *fabriche* in the territory of Lucca, where the tariff situation was apparently more favorable. One such *fabrica*, built at Pietrabuona in the Lucchese mountains, was financed by Fioravante di Piero Fioravanti, Piero Cancellieri, and Giorgio di Iacopo Tonti, and was valued at the impressive figure of 2800 pounds.[90]

Much evidence thus suggests that the iron industry was growing and prospering in the fifteenth century as it had not grown and prospered even before the plague: the high investments it was attracting and the number of persons it was employing; the willingness even of Florentines such as the Medici to place their money in it; the appearance of water-powered *fabriche*, hitherto unknown, in the mountains.[91] And the most effective stimulus to its growth, apart from possible technical improvements, seems to have been the closer integration of Pistoia within the Tuscan regional economy, making it possible for the industry to gain the material, capital and markets it needed for development.

In 1427, even more numerous than metal workers within the city were artisans producing leather goods, who in fact constituted the largest single industrial group. Shoemakers alone numbered 45, and they were joined by tanners (6) and saddle and pack makers (15).

Two factors help explain the importance of leather working at Pistoia. Near the great sheep runs between the Apennines and the sea, the town could conveniently acquire cheap supplies of animal products, cheese, wool and skins. The sinking price of animals in the early fifteenth century further suggests that local herds and flocks were growing. The industry also used Pisan, Sardinian or even Catalan pelts, which were purchased by the hundreds at Pisa and taken to Pistoia.[92] Moreover, the transhumance of those who guarded the

90. ASF, Catasto 261, 428r.

91. See above, chapter 2, n. 35.

92. Cf. ASF, Catasto 261, 155v, Iacopo di Bartholo Guidi has bought at Pisa fl. 110 of "certe pillicerie" for which he cannot pay. For other sales mentioned at Pisa, see ibid, 264v, involving 400 "pelli sardeschie," and ibid. 687r, involving 150 "pelli catalani." In 1569 Tedaldi, "Relazione," p. 325, stressed the importance of the business brought by the shepherds to Pistoia: "E perchè Pistoia è terra di passo e molto frequentata, e sempre vi si riducono assai persone, e maggiormente quando i pastori et i mietitori vanno e tornano dalle Maremme (i quali usano tutti di far capo quivi a fornirsi de' lor bisogni e lasciandovi assai buona quantità di denari). . . ."

flocks between the mountains and the sea also brought regularly to Pistoia men and customers needing leather shoes and boots, saddles and saddle packs, and iron equipment. This demand from shepherds would seem to explain the considerable number of saddle makers employed in the city.

The making of wool cloth was also an important industry at Pistoia in 1427, as the number of shops, sixteen, more than for any other branch of trade, testifies. If artisans were less numerous, the reason is perhaps that much of the work was done in the countryside. Here too the close commercial ties with Florence acted as a stimulant, as Pistoiese peasants, or at least their wives, seem to have worked on even Florentine cloth.[93]

The shops selling spices and luxuries, numbering twelve, were also important at Pistoia, and one of the new luxuries was silk. Here too, the significance of trade with Florence becomes evident. One of Antonio Rospigliosi's companies traded in silk; specifically, it raised the silk worms and spun the thread, but the weaving of it into expensive cloth was left to Florentine masters.[94]

Another of Antonio's enterprises shows the importance of free exchange with Florence upon Pistoia's economic activities. Earthenware had not been an old skill within the city, whether in 1219 or 1330. For Tuscany as a whole, the great center of the craft since Roman times had been Arezzo, and the region stretching through the Chianti hills in the direction of Florence. One commune in that area with a long tradition of pottery making was Santa Maria Impruneta, which lies in the Florentine contado a few miles south of the city. In 1481, Antonio Rospigliosi and Piero di Giovanni Astesi struck a partnership with a master *fornaciaio* from Santa Maria Impruneta, named Antonio di Giusto.[95] With capital supplied by the two Pistoiesi, Antonio was to bake tiles and oil jars (*chopi da oglio*)

93. Iacopo di Ciata of Lizzano (see above, n. 88), for example, was in debt to a Florentine cloth dealer for cloth owed him, "salva lavorazione," which must mean that he was putting out the cloth for some work in the mountains, perhaps for fulling at mills built along the mountain streams.

94. *Richordi*, p. 36, July 1479. Antonio makes a "chonpagnia" with Antonio di Pino fiaschaio, "cioè di bozoli di seta." The company was to buy the "filugello," or the silk worm, and collect the silk. In the same year Antonio sold 32 pounds of raw silk to a Florentine, ibid. p. 40. By 1569 the silk trade was one of Pistoia's most important businesses. See Tedaldi, "Relazione," p. 319, where its total volume was estimated at a sum of 25,000 scudi per year.

95. *Richordi*, p. 58.

at Pistoia, in return for an equal share of the profits. The freer movement of labor within the Florentine district was giving Pistoia an industry it had not previously possessed.

This then seems to be the broad outline of the city's commercial and industrial history between the thirteenth and fifteenth centuries. The great prosperity which had illuminated the years between about 1290 and 1340 gave way, in the wake of plagues, famines, wars and a plunging population, to over a half century of bad times, from about 1340 to 1400. In the opening decades of the fifteenth century, however, a slow but noticeable recovery was occurring, making the period one of real if modest prosperity. Although labor costs remained high, the downward movement of most other prices bespeaks a returning abundance. The slow, upward swing of the population curve, after nearly two centuries of stagnation or decline, is perhaps an even surer indicator of the advent of better times.

Against this sequence of brilliant prosperity, dark depression, and returning good times, the structure of Pistoia's economy was also changing. Both the broad internationalism and intense localism of the thirteenth century disappeared, and Pistoia became ever more tightly integrated within a Tuscan regional economy dominated by the Florentine market. The city lost its former international prominence and abandoned both long-distance trade and large-scale deposit banking to its Florentine competitors and masters. But tight commercial ties with Florence also stimulated an intensive development of those resources in which Pistoia's countryside was well endowed: its fertile soil, its mountain meadows, its timber and water power. Pistoia became a principal supplier of agricultural commodities, iron and iron products, wool, skins, cheese, wood and raw silk to its great and populous neighbor. Its economy drew substantial benefits from this enlarged regional market, from the more rational division of economic activities within it, and from the curtailment of the former fierce and wasteful competition. With a smaller population to support, this increased efficiency and rationalism almost certainly assured Pistoia's economy a higher per capita productivity than in the thirteenth century.

The new tone of Pistoia's fifteenth-century economy was stability and a moderate prosperity. Great fortunes were harder to accumulate, but were more easily maintained and defended. The brilliant years of the thirteenth century, when daring and resourceful merchants could compete for enormous riches in international markets, were forever ended at Pistoia. But the bulk of the people did not lose by their passing.

8

Social Transformations

And especially in the beautiful and charming, and unhappy little city of Pistoia, the sects and parties were more than in other lands. The one sect and party was of the Cancellieri, and called itself the party and sect of Saint John; it was filled with great and grand citizens more than the other. And the other was the party of the Panciatichi, and this called itself the party and sect of Saint Paul. It was filled with merchants and artisans and people of low station more than the other.

—Luca Dominici, describing Pistoia in 1401

In examining and, in some degree, measuring social change at Pistoia between the thirteenth and fifteenth centuries, one of our best indicators is the distribution of wealth, which surviving tax records illuminate in some detail. These and other records also permit a close consideration of Pistoia's patriciate in the fifteenth century, its composition, its wealth, and its social ideals. Finally, no study of Pistoia's society can be complete without an examination of the bitter factional and social conflicts which, in the fourteenth and fifteenth centuries, disturbed the city's history and which constituted perhaps the greatest single problem which its government had to confront.

THE DISTRIBUTION OF WEALTH

To judge the distribution of wealth in Pistoia's society before the Black Death, we can make use of surviving tax surveys, called *libre* or *estimi.*

From the late twelfth century, the Tuscan communes imposed direct taxes not by a flat charge upon each household but proportionately according to ability to pay.[1] They therefore drew up lists of families within a community, estimated the worth of their patrimonies, and entered a sum in pounds alongside each name. The sum given, it should be noted, represented not the exact total of a family's wealth but its relative ability to pay, measured against that of the other families in the commune. The tax could then be declared, usually in terms of so many solidi per each pound of assessment.

At Pistoia, one such estimo has survived for the rural, nearly suburban commune of Piuvica.[2] Its interest is its date, 1243, which makes it one of the most venerable of such surveys in the Tuscan archives, and its size, as it includes a substantial 238 households. The distribution of wealth at Piuvica, as shown in this estimo of 1243, can be compared with the distribution in the same commune nearly 200 years later, according to the Catasto of 1427.[3] Table 27 and graph 4 give the results of this comparison.

These two surveys, to be sure, cannot be considered exactly comparable. The assessment methods used in 1243 are not precisely known, but those of 1427 were certainly more sophisticated. Moreover, the estimo of 1243 did not include the entire rural population, as the nobles of the commune paid their taxes with the city.[4] If these had been included on the surviving tax roll, a much greater contrast in wealth would undoubtedly be apparent. While the comparison is crude, the distortion is still not so great as to vitiate its results. While assessment methods certainly changed, they agreed in their fundamental philosophy, that the tax should reflect ability to pay. If nobles were considered urban residents for tax purposes in 1243, the community in 1427 was similarly without representatives of the most prominent families, which by then, in fact as well as law, were located in the city. The ranges of society included in both surveys are thus not dissimilar.

Between 1243 and 1427, Piuvica's rural society was apparently

1. On the nature of these early estimi, see E. Fiumi, "L'Imposta diretta nei comuni medioevali della Toscana," *Studi in onore di Armando Sapori* (Milan, 1957), 329–53; B. Barbadoro, *Le Finanze della repubblica fiorentina* (Florence, 1929), pp. 53–144; and Herlihy, "Direct Taxation."

2. ASF, Dipl. Comune di Pistoia, 20 Aug. 1243.

3. ASF, Catasto 262, 332 ff.

4. There are 24 "nobiles istius loci de Piuvica" named in the *Liber focorum*, p. 51.

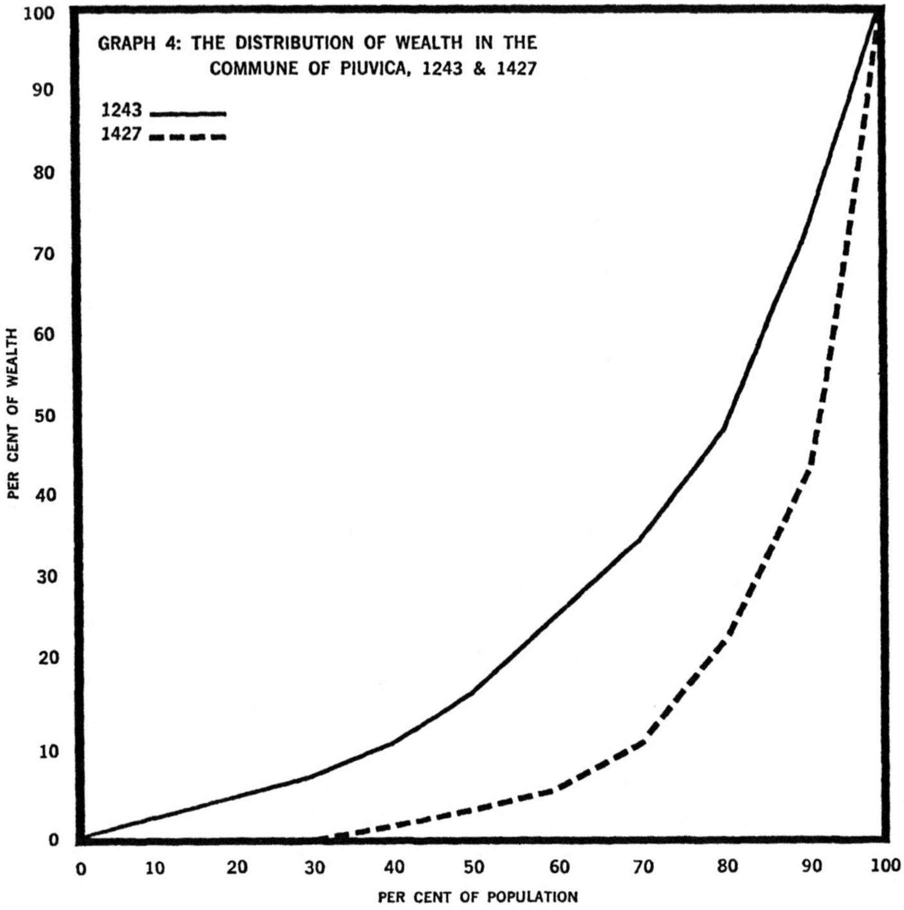
GRAPH 4: THE DISTRIBUTION OF WEALTH IN THE COMMUNE OF PIUVICA, 1243 & 1427
1243
1427
PER CENT OF WEALTH
PER CENT OF POPULATION
0
10
20
30
40
50
60
70
80
90
100

TABLE 27 The Distribution of Wealth in the Commune of Piuvica, 1243 and 1427

Per cent of population	*Per cent of wealth, 1243*	*Per cent of wealth, 1427*
10	1.7	0
20	4.4	0
30	7.7	0
40	12.4	0.7
50	18.3	2.9
60	25.5	7.1
70	36.0	12.9
80	50.0	26.1
90	67.9	45.0
100	100.0	100.0
	238 households (Assessment: 775 pounds 17 solidi)	96 households (Assessment: 5814 fl.)

Lowest ____ per cent of population owns ____ per cent of taxable wealth.

struck by an advancing wave of poverty. In 1243 no family was completely without taxable wealth (although one was assessed only one solidus); as land was the most important single asset in this society, most if not all the residents of Piuvica probably owned some real property. In 1427, more than 30 per cent of the population had no taxable wealth at all. At the same time, the proportion of the commune's wealth owned by its richest families registered a substantial gain. In 1243 the most affluent 10 per cent owned only one third of the wealth, but by 1427 its share was well over half.

Whether considered objectively or comparatively, the most distinctive feature of this rural society in the thirteenth century was the importance of the middle levels of its social pyramid, the numerous group of moderately prosperous peasants and landlords. This group constituted what may justifiably be called a rural middle class. The existence of such a class fits in well with what we know of the weight of the tax assessment in the countryside. It can be estimated that, in the 1280s, the rural communes of Pistoia were supporting a tax six times as high as that paid by the city.[5] The

5. In 1287 the town government imposed on the city a tax of 3.5 per cent of its assessment, which in 1284 had been 200,000 pounds and could not have

fairness of the distribution may of course be questioned, but the ability of the countryside to support such a tax burden indicates the presence of large numbers of fairly prosperous residents.

Unfortunately, our defective sources do not show how these wealthier inhabitants of Piuvica initially gathered their modest fortunes. Piuvica was, however, close to the city, and it may be assumed that many of its residents took advantage of the urban market for agricultural produce and even for labor. Piuvica's inhabitants were also conveniently located to serve as administrators or mesne tenants for urban landlords, and even a little capital could provide the basis for engaging in the profitable if risky business of agricultural loans.

The social character of this rural middle class is of special interest, as it contributed beyond the weight of its own numbers to emigration to the city, and thus to shaping the quality and interests of the growing urban population. This was a point first strongly emphasized by the Danish historian Johannes Plesner. Plesner reacted strongly against an older assumption which held that the urban population was recruited largely from escaped serfs and the rural poor. These penniless persons, fleeing the land, supposedly amassed capital in the city through commercial pursuits and only belatedly began to acquire property in the countryside. His own studies, although limited to a single region of the Florentine contado (Passignano), showed that the emigrants were more often than not property owners, who kept their holdings and continued to maintain close ties with their rural homes even after settling in the city.[6]

Pistoia's sources offer a further opportunity to examine the character of rural emigration, at least for the middle thirteenth century. The redactors of the Book of Hearths, in order to keep the list of rural taxpayers current, added after many names such phrases as "dicunt se esse cives" or "habent libram cum Civitate." These com-

---

been much different in 1287. See *Statutum potestatis*, p. xlviii. This impost thus probably returned about 7000 pounds. In the same year the commune imposed a tax of 5 pounds 15 solidi upon each rural hearth. If the number of hearths had remained at about the 7300 listed in the *Liber focorum*, this tax would have netted 42,000 pounds.

6. *L'Émigration de la campagne à la ville libre de Florence au XIIIe siècle* (Copenhagen, 1934). For recent, largely favorable comment upon Plesner's argument, see Cristiani, *Nobilità*, pp. 175–78.

ments thus noted a change in the status of the taxpayers and indicated a recent emigration to the city. For the commune of Piuvica, thirteen residents are so described, and their relative wealth can be checked in the estimo of 1243, to see from what level of rural society they were drawn. Two of the emigrants had been the second and third wealthiest members of the commune in 1243.[7] The entire group carried an average assessment of 7.8 pounds, better than twice the average assessment for the entire commune (3.6 pounds).[8] In disproportionate measure, the city was attracting the wealthy.

Besides the amenities and the opportunities of the city, fiscal pressures too were working to promote emigration from among the prosperous rural residents. The system of taxation, based upon a flat assessment levied against the rural communes on the basis of their hearths, but actually collected on the basis of wealth, inevitably required the rich to assume responsibility for the taxes which their poorer neighbors were unable to pay. As the burden of taxes mounted, the rural wealthy were threatened with the ruin of their fortunes.

The flight of the rich to a more favorable tax climate had important results both for the countryside and the city. Rural areas suffered from it, as they were gradually deprived of their most enterprising and affluent residents. But as the emigrants turned their interests and their capital to building new careers in the city, the urban economy enjoyed a powerful stimulus. Emigration was one foundation of the great dynamism and brilliance of the thirteenth-century Tuscan town.

Unfortunately, no tax surveys have survived to show us exactly the distribution of wealth within the city. The provision in the statutes, ordering that all old estimi be burned, was evidently scrupulously respected.[9] But given the certain attractiveness of the city for the rural middle classes, it seems a safe assumption that the city too was becoming crowded with many, moderately prosperous residents, who controlled an important portion of its wealth.

7. *Liber focorum*, commune of Piuvica (pp. 44 ff.), nos. 21 and 71.

8. The sums borne by the emigrants were 8.5 pounds (no. 160); 8 pounds (no. 161); 13 pounds (no. 162); 3.5 pounds (no. 191); 8 pounds (no. 193); 7 pounds (no. 195); 9 pounds (no. 196); 2.5 pounds (no. 199); 5 pounds (no. 200); 5.5 pounds (no. 239); and 1 pound (no. 240).

9. *Statutum potestatis*, p. 212.

The importance of the middle class in the free city seems evidenced by the entire trend of its political development. The late thirteenth century witnessed the victory of the popular regime known as the *Popolo*. The circumstances of that victory, and the institutional changes it wrought, are discussed in the following chapter; here we confine ourselves to its social implications. The emergence of the Popolo was not a democratic success by any modern comprehension of the word. But it did admit a broader segment of society to participation in government, while subjecting many of the older and powerful families to disenfranchisement and legal disabilities. And the contribution of rural emigration to the rise of the Popolo seems clear. The Council of the Popolo, for example, met not within the confines of the old city, in neighborhoods dominated by the old families, but in the church of San Giovanni Fuorcittà, "outside the city," in an area which recent emigration was building.[10]

Perhaps the most distinctive feature of the society of the free commune in the thirteenth century was the apparent importance of the middle ranges of its social hierarchy, the numerous group of moderately wealthy landlords, merchants and artisans. Pistoia's middle class, in other words, appears to have been more numerous, wealthier and more influential in the thirteenth than in the fifteenth century, and this should warn us against interpreting the humanism of the latter period too exclusively as a "bourgeois" phenomenon.

By the early fifteenth century, the community's wealth had come to be concentrated in much fewer hands. Table 27 has already shown that in 1427, within the territory of Piuvica, 30 per cent of the population had no taxable wealth at all. Table 28 and graph 5 illustrate the distribution of wealth in the same year for the entire population. On the graph, the distribution curve for the middle hills has not been entered separately, because it so closely follows that of the mountains.

By 1427, urban residents had come to bear the larger part of the tax assessment. In the 1280s, as we have mentioned, the city was apparently supporting only about one seventh, or 14.3 per cent, of the weight of the direct tax.[11] In 1427 it was supporting 58 per

10. See the comments by Zdekauer in *Breve populi*, pp. xvi–xvii.
11. See above, n. 5.

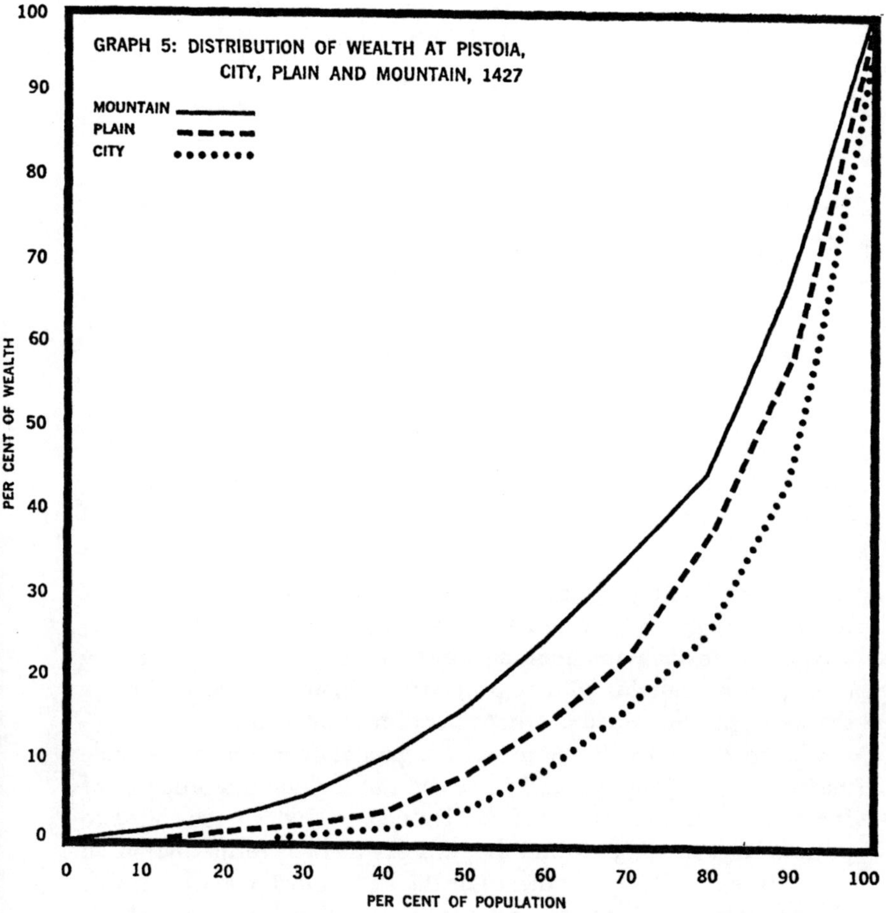

GRAPH 5: DISTRIBUTION OF WEALTH AT PISTOIA, CITY, PLAIN AND MOUNTAIN, 1427
MOUNTAIN
PLAIN
CITY
PER CENT OF WEALTH
PER CENT OF POPULATION
0
10
20
30
40
50
60
70
80
90
100

TABLE 28 Distribution of Wealth at Pistoia, City and Countryside, 1427

Per cent of population	Per cent of wealth				
	City	*Plain*	*Middle Hills*	*Mountains*	*Total Population*
10	0	0	0.1	0.3	0
20	0	0.2	1.4	1.8	1.3
30	0.5	1.1	3.9	4.7	3.3
40	1.8	3.2	7.7	8.9	6.2
50	4.1	7.1	13.0	14.6	11.2
60	7.9	12.9	20.3	22.2	17.9
70	14.3	21.2	30.5	32.3	27.1
80	23.9	33.8	44.0	45.1	28.4
90	41.0	53.3	62.7	62.8	43.7
100	100	100	100	100	100
Households	1247	1193	734	609	3729
(Assessment)	(263,085 fl.)	(81,847 fl.)	(67,473 fl.)	(45,716 fl.)	(458,121 fl.)

Lowest ____ per cent of population owns ____ per cent of taxable wealth.

Source: ASF, Catasto, 260–65.

cent (approximately 263,000 out of the total of 458,000 florins). Or rather, comparatively few of the city's families possessed these assets, as the urban population also included the largest relative percentage of households with no property at all, and the richest 10 per cent of its people owned nearly 60 per cent of its wealth.

Wealth was concentrated to an even greater degree than this table indicates, as the Catasto of Pistoia did not include the property of families which had emigrated to Florence, but which continued to possess large holdings within the territory of their former home. In 1427, for example, two branches of the Panciatichi, one of Pistoia's old magnate houses, were permanently settled in Florence. Gabbriello di messer Bartolommeo Panciatichi was in fact Florence's third richest citizen, with an assessment only slightly less than that of Giovanni di Bicci de' Medici, the famous founder of the Medici bank.[12] Gabbriello's assessment of 78,166 florins was higher than that carried by Pistoia's entire population either of the middle hills or of the mountains. The eight richest families at Florence (including the two Panciatichi branches) bore a combined assessment

12. See the list of assessments of Florentine citizens given by Martines, *Social World*, pp. 365 ff. On Bartolommeo, Gabbriello's father, see below, p. 204.

higher than that supported by Pistoia's entire city and countryside.[13]

Perhaps the most significant novelty in the distribution of wealth at Pistoia in 1427 is the evident weakening in numbers and collective assets of the middle class, that once large group of moderately prosperous landlords, merchants and artisans, which in the thirteenth century had lent to the society of the free commune its most characteristic stamp. In the city and on the plain—the economic heart of the territory—a few families with great wealth had come to confront many with few assets or none. The troubles of the fourteenth century had not been favorable to the growth or even the defense of small fortunes.

The contrasts in wealth distribution among the various areas of the countryside can be further illustrated, and partially explained, by a consideration of a related problem: the ownership of the land. Pistoia's Catasto, as it does not include the extensive lands owned by Florentine residents, does not give a complete picture of the distribution of real property in 1427. Moreover, even in regard to lands described, size is not all the time stated, and exact calculations are thus impossible. But the relative importance of at least one type of property can be examined—the land owned by ecclesiastical institutions, especially the urban hospitals, which were the most important and the most typical of the great landlords. In the Catasto the surveyors, to identify the location of property listed, characteristically named the owners of land contiguous to it. These references to contiguous owners, amounting in number to the tens of thousands, constitute a huge catalogue of landlords, and the frequency with which a given name appears within it should give a rough measure of the importance of his or its holdings.

This method of estimating the distribution of ownership shows quite clearly that the concentration of ecclesiastical property was influenced by two factors: the quality of the soil, and the proximity of the city. On the fertile plain and low hills, 20.3 per cent of the land belonged to religious corporations, and the percentage was even higher on the rich plain lands near the city.[14] At Piuvica, for

13. According to the assessment sums given by Martines, *Social World*, pp. 365–78.

14. Specifically, 2181 out of 10,762 references to contiguous owners in the

example, a third of the land was under ecclesiastical ownership. On the other hand, the percentage of ecclesiastical property fell off as one moved south of the city, toward the poorer lands of Tizzana. Among laymen, the distribution of land apparently followed a similar pattern; the more fertile and more expensive the lands, the greater percentage likely to be held by the wealthy families of the city. The Partini brothers alone, for example, owned land at Piuvica worth more than twice the value of that possessed by the richest local resident.[15]

Amid the poorer soils of the middle hills, the percentage of ecclesiastical property fell off, averaging only 15.5 per cent.[16] But here again, proximity to the city was influential in affecting the size of great properties. At Brandeglio, in the hills just above the city, about 25 per cent of the land was under ecclesiastical ownership, while at Lamporecchio, on the other side of the Monte Albano away from the city, the portion was only 10 per cent.

In the mountains, the percentage of ecclesiastical property was even slightly less, only 15.1 per cent of the total.[17] Urban investors, while they were interested in mountain lands to provide wood and carbon for iron works and to support their large flocks and herds, were little inclined to place their money in large stretches of poor mountain soil.

In 1427, the best lands of Pistoia were dominated by great landlords, ecclesiastical corporations and the wealthiest urban families. This concentration of property is partially explained by the flow of bequests and inheritances. In an age of frequent plagues, religious institutions, especially the hospitals, were showered with bequests. The shrinking of the population also undoubtedly favored with accumulated inheritances a few lucky survivors. But the wealthy were also able, as smaller landlords were not, to keep their farms in operation. This required, as we have seen, continual outlays of capital

---

surveys of the plain communes are to ecclesiastical institutions. On the considerable increase in ecclesiastical property at San Gimignano, from 12 per cent of the total in 1315 to 25.7 per cent in 1419, see Fiumi, *San Gimignano*, pp. 216–23.

15. The value of their lands at Piuvica was assessed at 1765 florins. The richest resident owned lands assessed at 705 florins.

16. Out of 13,079 contiguous owners mentioned, 2030 are ecclesiastical institutions.

17. 2010 out of 13,251 owners cited.

in cattle, equipment, seeds and loans to attract scarce laborers.[18] Under the extending mezzadria system of tenure, the landlord had also to assume high risks and possess the resources to survive disasters. The property owner of modest means, unable to meet these expenses, had either to watch his lands go to seed or sell them to a more resourceful neighbor. The new conditions of cultivation, in other words, requiring high investments at modest returns and considerable risks, were disadvantageous to the middle-class landlord. The great property owner, on the other hand, while he hardly prospered under the new conditions, at least was not destroyed by them.

Within the city too, the high costs required in economic enterprises, the low return from them, were similarly hostile to the growth or defense of moderate fortunes, and similarly worked to erode the prosperity and importance of the urban middle class.

Great concentrations of wealth, an extension of fiscal pauperism, and a weakened middle class were thus the dominant features of Pistoia's society by the early fifteenth century.

Here, however, one further point must be made. While the ranks of those with no taxable assets were growing, it would be wrong to equate these fiscal paupers with the authentic and oppressed poor, and to conclude that the fifteenth century had brought an increase of misery. While many of the families with no assessment were indeed in hapless economic circumstances, many others were in fact tenants and workers upon large and fertile farms, which they leased under the mezzadria or similar, favorable contracts. The poderi which supported them were well-stocked and productive; with capital to aid them and risks largely removed from them, with good food to nourish their families, it would be hard to call these mezzadri disadvantaged. Most were better off than the independent peasants of the sterile hills and mountains who, because they owned property, stood above the mezzadri on the assessment scale. This probably explains why, in the countryside at least, households with no assessment were supporting more children than households with an assessment of 1–50 florins.[19]

Moreover, the concentration of land in the hands of relatively

18. See above, p. 72. For a similar concentration of property in fewer hands at San Gimignano after the Black Death, see Fiumi, *San Gimignano*, pp. 192–216.

19. See above, p. 97, table 5.

few great lords imparted, or perhaps restored, a distinctly paternalistic note to property ownership, which the provisions of the mezzadria contract themselves reflect. The lord was thus supposed to protect his workers against disasters and to aid them in need. The disruptions of the late Middle Ages were bringing a return of quasi-feudal, or at least of paternalistic relationships within Pistoia's society.

We may now look more closely at the few wealthy families which, by the fifteenth century, had emerged as the social leaders of the Renaissance town.

THE PATRICIATE

Table 29 lists the fifteen richest families at Pistoia according to the Catasto of 1427.

TABLE 29 The Fifteen Richest Families at Pistoia, 1427

	Name	*Catasto Reference*	*Assessment*
(1)	Lapo, Bartolomeo, Rinieri e Antonio di ser Lapo Partini	260, 298r	12,309 fl.
(2)	Batista di Marcho merciaio	261, 687r	5452
(3)	Matteo e Andrea di messer Giovanni Panciatichi	260, 154r	4909
(4)	Fioravante di Piero Fioravanti	261, 428v	4718
(5)	Pippo di Paolo de' Rossi	260, 505r	3400
(6)	Nanni di Rinieri Bracciolini	260, 578r	3104
(7)	ser Taiuolo di Piero Taiuoli	260, 729v	2587
(8)	Gherardo di Bartolomeo	260, 180v	2553
(9)	messer Bartolomeo Bracciolini	260, 736v	2531
(10)	Piero di Bartolomeo di Meglio	261, 164r	2521
(11)	Antonio, Leonardo, Iacopo e Baldassare di messer Nicholo di Bartolomeo Gualandi	261, 60r	2441
(12)	Iacopo di messer Piero Cancellieri	261, 555r	2439
(13)	Lodovico di' Agnolo Taviani	261, 38v	2420
(14)	Franchino d'Agnolo Taviani e mona	260, 214v	2400
	Valeza donna di Giovanni sua nuora	260, 214v	2400
(15)	Iachopo e Nicchola figliuoli d'Antonio di Michele lanaiuoli	261, 602r	2142

Sums are given to the nearest florin.

In the early fifteenth century, Pistoia's patriciate was not entirely closed to new men. The career of the second wealthiest citizen in

1427, Batista di Marco, presents a good example of a continuing social mobility in the fifteenth century. Batista was already a successful merchant in 1415, with merchandise and a "banco" worth 2500 pounds.[20] In his tax declaration of that year, he warned the officials that he had better be "measured with the same rod as the others"—a clear allusion to the favoritism of factions that often influenced tax assessments.[21] If he was not measured by the same rod, he threatened to leave the city. "And it does not appear to me," he added with some satisfaction, "that the pursuit of [my] trade is to the damage of our city; rather is it useful and pleasant to every citizen."[22] Batista apparently was implying that the "trades" exercised by some members of the old, turbulent families often brought anything but happiness to the city. Batista did elect to remain at Pistoia, and the years were good to him. By 1427, although he was no longer a banker, the value of his "traffico" had increased to over 5000 florins.[23]

Of the fifteen wealthiest houses, four were apparently new families. Although it cannot be certainly ascertained, most seem to have made their fortunes during the comparatively good economic years of the early fifteenth century.

But it must also be noted that nearly three quarters of the families, the majority and the core of the patriciate, represented old houses, the fortunes of which had been established at least since the late thirteenth century. The founder of the Partini family, which headed the list of the wealthy in 1427, was Partino di Deodato, who was active in commerce from 1246.[24] A "dominus Ugolinus Partini" was a member of the commune's great council in 1267, but with the victory of the Popolo the family was considered to be of popular status.[25] In 1342, Vanni di Gualando Partini held the Popolo's chief

20. Estimario, San Michele in Bonaccio, no. 3. See also above, p. 170.

21. "Fate cioche volete in piacere pure che io sia misurato con quella canna che gl' altri. . . ."

22. Loc. cit. "che non mi pare fare tal mestieri che sia danno della nostra città piutosto utile e piacere di ciascheduno cittadino."

23. ASF, Catasto 261, 687r.

24. In that year he was lending money to the commune. See Barbi in *Storie pistoresi*, p. xx, n. 1. The history of the house is discussed by Zaccagnini, "Banchieri," *BSP*, 21 (1919), pp. 39 ff.

25. *Relazioni*, no. 18, p. 9, 4 May 1267.

office as *gonfaloniere*.[26] A branch of the Panciatichi family held third position on the scale of wealth in 1427, and the Panciatichi, as we have mentioned, were one of Pistoia's oldest magnate houses and the one-time leader of its Ghibelline faction.[27] As for the Fioravanti (fourth on the scale), a Feravante Accursi appeared among the commune's counselors in 1267.[28] The family was quite active in the councils of the Popolo, and members served as gonfalonieri no less than seven times between 1332 and 1347.[29] The Rossi, ranked fifth, were originally a magnate house; one of their number had served as captain of the knights in 1215.[30] But in 1429 they sought and were accorded popular status.[31] The Bracciolini in ninth position were also originally a magnate family closely related to the Panciatichi, but they were early given popular status and contributed a gonfaloniere in 1334.[32] Finally, the Cancellieri sprang from the merchant ser Cancelliere di Sinibaldo who from about 1210 had begun amassing a large fortune in the city.[33] Some of them had been knighted by 1237. Although Guelf in allegiance, they were reckoned as magnates by the popular commune.[34]

These leading families of the fifteenth century were thus indiscriminately drawn from magnate and popular origins, and represented both Guelf and Ghibelline sympathies. What distinguished them all was age, and this predominance of old houses illustrates the considerable stability of the patriciate in the fifteenth century. One basis for this stability was the nature of the patrimonies which supported them.

There is little doubt that at least by the early fifteenth century, investments in land were much preferred over commercial ventures.

26. No. 118 in the list given by Salvi, *Historie*. On the character of the office, see below, pp. 218–19.

27. Zaccagnini, "Banchieri," *BSP*, 21 (1919), pp. 38–39.

28. *Relazioni*, no. 18, p. 9, 4 May 1267.

29. Nos. 49, 62, 66, 95, 110, 135 and 139 in the list published by Salvi, *Historie*.

30. Rinieri di Spettare de' Rossi, according to Salvi, *Historie*, I, 132.

31. C. Paoli, "Capitoli dei 'Paciali' di Pistoia del MCCCCLV," *BSP*, 1 (1899), 20. The Taviani also acquired popular status in the same year.

32. Margugliese di Andrea Bracciolini, no. 65 in Salvi, *Historie*.

33. Zaccagnini, "Branchieri," *BSP*, 21 (1919), pp. 39 ff. See also below, p. 201.

34. They are among the magnate families excluded from holding office according to the Statutes of 1330, ASP, Provv. Tomus 22, 15r.

In 1415, for example, Iacopo di Lottiere di messer Guelfo de' Taviani asked for mercy from the tax assessors, because he was supporting his large family "without a house and without land and vineyards."[35] "We must nourish ourselves," he explained, "[exclusively] from the fruit of this money."[36] The money he mentioned amounted to almost 1200 florins in outstanding loans, which was hardly a pauper's patrimony. But for a man to live exclusively from the fruit of liquid capital still seemed to Iacopo deserving of pity.

To judge from tax declarations, Pistoia's great families tried, insofar as they were able, to keep a major portion of their patrimonies in real property, the attractiveness of which was also greatly enhanced by the presence of the great Florentine market for agricultural commodities. Several of the older houses, the Bracciolini and the Rossi for example, had no commercial investments at all.[37] The Partini, who appear to have been the most active commercially of the old families, still retained nearly one half of their assets in real property.[38]

The larger and the more stable part of Pistoia's aristocracy of wealth was thus comprised of old families, with patrimonies firmly founded upon the solid earth. Commercial interests apart from trade in agricultural products were for many peripheral and for some negligible. A career in business could still carry some few new families to fortune, but for the established houses, commerce was viewed with caution.

The life and interests of a patrician of Pistoia in the fifteenth century were thus tightly bound up with the defense of the patrimony and fidelity to the traditions of his family. His primary economic concern was the management of land, and here he could not easily assume the posture of an idle rentier. His properties were best su-

35. Estimario, San Mazzeo, no. 16, "Sono con dieci in famiglia sanza casa e sanza terra e vigna."

36. Loc. cit. "e convienci noturare del fructo di questi denari e tucti son fanciulli e non possono pure l'uno l'altro."

37. ASF, Catasto 260, 578r.

38. See above, p. 168. In 1569 Tedaldi, "Relazione," p. 325, noted that the nobles confined their business interests to agricultural speculations. "I Nobili attendono a multiplicare le lor richezze . . . ponendo ogni loro studio et industria per empiere i lor granai . . . per conservarli a smaltire a pregi più alti e maggiori, per il che non votano prima i lor grannai [*sic*], che non si assicurino molto bene d'haverne a empiersene le borse loro."

pervised personally, and this usually required him to spend each year several months in the country.[39] Rural life was thus intimately familiar to him and to his family. His children were occasionally placed to be nursed in peasant households, and for some of them their earliest memories would have been of a rural home.[40] The idealization of country life, so strong an element in Renaissance literature, may owe something to this common and early experience and memory of the countryside, preserved from childhood and associated with its happiness.

The ownership of extensive lands also brought with it, as we have mentioned, a paternalistic responsibility for tenants and mezzadri, and it would be wrong to discount the strength of the obligation and the bond it created. It was not unknown for peasants to stand as godparents for the children of their rich and powerful landlords, and for this to occur the personal ties between the families, however different their social levels, must have been intimate.[41]

One other interest occupied the attention and the time of the rich *paterfamilias:* public affairs. For many aristocrats, commitment to communal politics was an integral part of the defense of their fortunes, for the power to tax in the hands of enemies might well mean the power to destroy. But for others, higher motives were not excluded. Men such as Antonio Rospigliosi, educated to the defense of family, friends and dependents, accepted a responsibility too for promoting the community's interests, and the community was grateful for it.[42]

To be sure, a large if diminishing number of the old magnate houses were still in the fifteenth century excluded from office, but many nobles could gain respectable and remunerative employment as professional officials in foreign communes and courts. The career of messer Giovanni Francesco Panciatichi well illustrates the importance that public service in foreign communes could play in the

39. Personal supervision of one's property is strongly recommended by Piero de' Crescenzi, *Opus*, I, cap. 13, "De officio patrisfamilias."

40. Cf. Antonio Rospigliosi, *Richordi*, p. 48, Antonio's infant son Vincenzio given "a baglie a Lanporecchio a Orlando di Pasquino Maxi." Ibid. p. 61, another son Domenico given to Ulivo del Ghanba da Ramini.

41. Ibid. p. 61, "Ghabriello di Forte nostro lavoratore" mentioned as a "chonpare" for the baby Domenico.

42. See below, chapter 9, n. 56.

life of a great family. Giovanni was podestà at Perugia (1399), Rieti (1401), Ferrara (1403–04), Orvieto (1407), Perugia again (1408), Ancona (1408), Genoa (1416), Siena (1431), Fano (1434), Recanato (1435) and elsewhere.[43] In his tax declaration of 1415, he gave a colorful account of his career for the benefit of the tax assessors. While in the service of the court of Ferrara, he had been wounded in battle, robbed of his horses and armor, and disabled for ten months.[44] He frequently was not paid for his services, and one time had to accept his wages in salt worth 2700 florins, but this was apparently confiscated when he tried to sell it at Rome.[45] To restore his bruised fortunes, he was selling in 1415 a portion of his lands at Pistoia. This, he assured the tax assessors, he would never do, unless dire need were pressing him.[46]

Many of Pistoia's aristocrats, with old and resonant names and reputations, could boast of similar careers, and perhaps also of better luck.[47] Even Giovanni's own mournful biography given to the tax assessors in 1415 may have been less than honest. His two sons, Matteo and Andrea, formed in 1427 Pistoia's third richest household and, like their father, they were embarked upon public careers of some distinction.

This close association of Pistoia's patricians with government service, whether as office holders or as appointed members of a professional staff, also greatly influenced the lay culture of the Renaissance city, as shall later be discussed.[48]

43. On Giovanni, see L. Passerini, *Genealogia e storia della famiglia Panciatichi* (Florence, 1858), p. 40, and L. Chiappelli in the *BSP*, *18* (1916), 91–92.

44. Estimario, San Giovanni fuorcività, no. 57. "Io fui a Ferrara el marchese me mandò a Cento ove fui ferito et stetti infermo di dieci mesi et fui rubato tra denari cavalli panni e ariento et arme il valsente di più di fiorini secento et mai non fui ristorato. . . ."

45. Loc. cit. "fumi poi dato in pagamento sale per dumila settecento fiorini . . . e tolse a me et a molti altri tutto il sale . . . dicendo era sale del comune di Roma et lui era signore dovea esser suo."

46. Loc. cit. "Et siate certi signori del catasto che s' io avessi denari io non starei qui a cerchare di vendere terra. . . ."

47. On the many Pistoiesi who served as high officials in foreign communes, see especially L. Chiappelli, "Studi storici pistoiesi, I: I Pistoiesi come rettori in altri comuni fino al secolo XVI," *BSP*, *18* (1916), 78–113 and 149–92; *19* (1917), 1–44; 121–222; and 129–60.

48. See below, p. 258 ff.

FACTIONAL AND SOCIAL CONFLICT

In these centuries of transition from free commune to Florentine dependency, Pistoia was continuously occupied with the critical problem of controlling the factional and social violence of its citizens. It is not too much to say that the suppression of private warfare constituted the greatest single problem faced by the community in its effort to attain a new, more ordered and more stable form of political life.

Pistoia seems even to have surpassed all other cities of Tuscany in the ferocity of its factional struggles. The chroniclers recognized this, and explained it by the myth that the Pistoiesi had descended from the Roman conspirator Catiline and his rebellious men, who had been defeated near the site of the future city.[49]

Several features of Pistoia's geography, economy and society combined to accentuate the violent tenor of its medieval life. Its government was chronically weak. It not only labored under the encumbrances common to medieval regimes, but it also faced the difficult task of policing a sizable mountain area. This was the region most prolific in private wars (and in social revolts), and even factions and parties from the plain could easily find there nearly impregnable retreats. The extensive and accessible mountains gave a promise of security to those who wished to gamble on the sword.

Economic conditions could also favor factional outbursts. The relatively primitive economy characteristic of the high hills and mountains placed few penalities on social feuding. As we have seen, the inhabitant of the uplands usually owned his own farm.[50] But the poverty of his livelihood gave him little need for outside capital and rewarded him with little produce to sell in outside markets. Free from the discipline of commercial commitments and obligations, he was also free to form his associations on the basis of those most elemental considerations, blood and friendship.

The shape of the social pyramid also influenced the formation of factions. A society in which relatively few great families monopo-

49. Cf. G. Villani, *Cronica,* I, cap. 32 (I, 46). "e però non è da maravigliare, se i Pistolesi sono stati e sono gente di guerra fieri e crudeli intro loro e con altrui, essendo stratti del sangue di Catellina e del rimaso di sua così fatta gente, sconfitta e tagliata in battaglia."

50. See above, p. 188, table 28.

lized property and power, in which a middle class was weak or nonexistent, was especially prone to factional divisions and alignments. Particularly in the absence of a strong government, the great families acted as points of attraction for the community's weaker members who sought from them protection and favors.

To appreciate the nature of factional struggles at Pistoia is first to recognize the extraordinary character of these family alliances. Membership in them was by no means limited to the great houses. A faction was a vertical as well as a horizontal association, linking great men and small, cutting across class lines and working to obscure them. The famous schism between the Blacks and the Whites, which broke out in the Cancellieri family probably in 1286, soon divided the city, and the countryside too, into warring factions.[51] The subsequent feud between the Cancellieri and the Panciatichi similarly engulfed nearly the entire city and swept into the countryside, to set village against village and family against family.[52] Factions could reach remarkable size, uniting and dividing distant cities and entire provinces. Like electric wires, the lines of "friendship" which the Cancellieri laid throughout Tuscany, carried the tension between Blacks and Whites through all corners of the province and nearly sparked civil wars in Lucca and Florence.[53] In 1401, according to the chronicler Luca Dominici, the Panciatichi family of Pistoia had enlisted as their friends and supporters 30 Florentine families, including many of the most prominent.[54] Their rivals the Cancellieri similarly had recruited many allies at Florence, and were even more strongly represented at Lucca, where their friends included many of the dominant houses.[55]

51. Tholomeus, *Annalen*, p. 209 (1286), "divisa enim est domus inter Albos et Nigros et tota civitas. . . ." *Storie pistoresi*, p. 6, "Questo fue lo cominciamento della divisione della città e contado di Pistoia. . . ."

52. Luca Dominici, *Cronache*, II, 14, "quasi tucte famiglie di Pistoia e di gentiluomeni et popolani fosseno divise." Ibid. pp. 27–28, gives a list of Pistoia's rural villages and the factional party they supported.

53. Tholomeus, *Annalen*, p. 210, "divisa enim est . . . ac tota per consequens Tuscia secundum amicitias, quas in civitatibus habebant, et precipue de Florentia et Luca. . . ."

54. *Cronache*, II, 11. "E per non dire molto, quasi tucti li predecti reggienti, et maximamente i maggiori, erano amici de' Panciatichi da Pistoia et ellino loro, et a uno stato concorrevano."

55. Ibid. II, 12.

The struggle against these large and powerful private alliances is as old as the free commune and forms a major theme of its history. The climax of that struggle came in the late thirteenth century, with the emergence of the commune of the Popolo.[56] The Popolo, largely recruited from the new middle class, sought energetically to limit the private violence of the magnates. At Pistoia, the popular commune from 1272 demanded that the magnates provide compensation for damage caused from their feuding and offer guarantees for their peaceful behavior; in 1292, in imitation of the "Sacred Ordinances" of Bologna, the commune drew up a "liber securitatum nobilium," which forbade under heavy penalties any violation, on the part of the magnates, of the public peace.[57]

Historians today still discuss the extent to which the policies of the popular commune were motivated by class interests, specifically by the desire of the "popolani," representing the middle classes, to create within the city a political and social milieu favorable to their interests.[58] But concerning this point at least there seems no disagreement: the popular commune took as a major goal of its internal policies the repression of private warfare. Success here would have assured the commune a new and more ordered form of political behavior. This aspiration certainly corresponded to the interests of persons, popolani and some magnates too, who identified their own advantage with peaceable and successful commercial and industrial enterprise.

The experience of the free, popular commune in the late thirteenth century thus included an early, vigorous effort to discipline the old, unruly magnate factions and control their destructive egoism. At Pistoia, that effort enjoyed a partial though not a final success. The difficulties of policing its rugged contado excessively burdened the commune's thin resources. Moreover, the city itself, with a relatively small population and no great industries, lacked a sufficiently strong and aggressive middle class to offset the power of the great magnate houses. The violent and disastrous schism of the

56. See below, p. 216.

57. See Barbi in the *Storie pistoresi*, pp. lvi–lvii.

58. The recent works of E. Fiumi, "Sui Rapporti economici tra città e contado nell' età comunale," *ASI*, *114* (1956), 18–68, and of Cristiani, *Nobiltà*, have tended to discount the importance of class conflict in the history of the commune.

Blacks and the Whites in the last decades of the thirteenth century proclaimed the free commune's crowning failure to discipline its own society.

Because it came eventually to involve Italy's greatest poet, this battle between the Blacks and the Whites is perhaps the most famous incident of Pistoia's medieval history. It has therefore been intensively studied, although much obscurity still surrounds its origins.[59] The chroniclers unanimously place its beginnings in a factional division within the numerous and wealthy Cancellieri family. The Cancellieri were a relatively new house of popular status, which had been carried to wealth in the great commercial expansion of the thirteenth century. In the early decades of that century, the founder of the family, the merchant ser Cancelliere, had rapidly accumulated an enormous fortune and sired three sons (Amadore, Ranieri and Sinibaldo). They in turn fathered a large progeny and spun webs of factional friendship throughout Tuscany. By 1300, according to Giovanni Villani, the family could boast of 100 men of arms.[60] Like many new families struggling to rise in traditionally Ghibelline Pistoia, the Cancellieri were Guelf, and they also contributed one of the first "captains of the people."[61] But their large numbers seem to have weakened their cohesiveness and prepared the way for factional division.

Probably in 1286, two cousins of the Cancellieri house, Dore di messer Guglielmo and Carlino di messer Gualfredi, fell to arguing while drinking and gaming in a tavern.[62] Violent words led to violent acts, blows were struck, blood spilt and revenge demanded. In the growing struggle, Vanni, brother of Carlino, lost three fingers and Dore his entire hand. The family divided in support of the contenders. The descendants of Ranieri Cancellieri supported their own Vanni and Carlino; the offspring of Amadore rallied behind the injured Dore. For reasons still not explained, the Amadori were known as the Whites, and the Ranieri as the Blacks. Through their

59. See the detailed reconstruction of Davidsohn, *Geschichte*, II, pt. 2, pp. 523–33, and of S. Barbi in the introduction to the *Storie pistoresi*.

60. *Cronica*, VIII, cap. 39 (IV, 54).

61. Cialdus de Cancelieriis was captain in 1267, *Breve populi*, p. xlix.

62. Tholomeus of Lucca is the only chronicler to give the date of the altercation, *Annalen*, p. 209.

many alliances, their feud was carried through the city, the countryside, and the whole province of Tuscany.

Almost predictably, historians have discounted the importance of the barroom altercation of 1286. The two branches of the Cancellieri must already have been distinct in 1236–37. In those years Ranieri di Cancelliero had lent money to the corporation of *pedites*, the commoners, while his brother Amadore was at the same time banker to the corporation of knights.[63] This shows not only a division of property between the brothers, but a difference in policy too, with the brothers apparently taking opposite sides in the growing feud between the knights (or magnates) and popolani. Moreover, the dispute gained strength by subsuming earlier factions and continuing earlier struggles. The Cancellieri were traditionally Guelf and originally popolani. But the Whites of Ranieri were moderate if not cool in their Guelf allegiance. They ultimately absorbed the remnants of the Ghibelline and magnate forces—this in spite of the fact that Ranieri had apparently been aligned with the *pedites* in 1236–37. The Blacks, on the other hand, were the more committed Guelfs; they also represented the interests of the new, popular families favoring a strong enforcement of the anti-magnate legislation.[64] In real measure, the battle between Blacks and Whites carried on, in a new form, the traditional and still unsettled conflicts between Ghibellines and Guelfs, and between the magnate and popular parties.

The power of the White Guelfs at Pistoia was for the moment crushed when the armies of the Black powers Florence and Lucca took the city in 1306. But the factional forces soon regrouped under other names. The Cancellieri, once more united, absorbed the remnants of the Guelf and Black parties of former years. The old noble house, the Panciatichi, formed a faction which united the defeated Whites and Ghibellines. It was the victory of Giovanni Panciatichi in the city in 1350 which, as we shall see, provoked Florentine intervention and the final loss of Pistoia's liberty in 1351.[65]

63. *Liber censuum*, no. 305, p. 212, and no. 318, p. 216. Barbi, *Storie pistoresi*, p. xxxix.

64. According to Barbi, *Storie pistoresi*, p. lxxi, "E allora, più che una lotta interna di Parte guelfa, divenne battaglia generale fra la 'gente nuova' . . . e la 'cittadinanza antica' di tradizioni ghibelline . . . e quella prese il nome di Neri, e questa di Bianchi."

65. See below, p. 228.

Amid the other troubles of the middle fourteenth century, the competition of these factions grew more bitter and their violence worsened even under Florentine rule. In real measure, Pistoia's society was lapsing back to older and more primitive, really feudal forms of social organization and behavior. The social changes of the age which we have already considered—the growing concentration of wealth in the control of a few great families, the weakening of the middle levels of the social pyramid, the proliferation of the poor in need of aid and protection—all tended to enhance the strength of factions. Economic factors also played a role. If communal government was weak, it still offered employment and patronage, which was valuable if not essential to the defense of family fortunes in an age of otherwise poor commercial opportunities. This *gara di uffici,* this competition for office among the factions, is one of the most common explanations advanced by the chroniclers to explain their violence. The perspicacious observer, Dino Compagni, identified the battle for patronage as the root cause of the fighting between the Blacks and the Whites at Florence.[66] At Pistoia, another chronicler placed the source of contention between the Cancellieri and the Panciatichi "in civil suits, and in the choosing of magistrates by lot, and criminal cases and condemnations."[67] Pistoia in the fourteenth century presents the paradox of a government too weak to control the violence of its citizens, but still possessing a patronage worth fighting for.

Disagreement over public policies also sharpened the rivalry, and here a remarkable shift is evident. The Panciatichi, as an old Ghibelline and White family, had been traditional opponents of the Florentines, and as late as 1350 the assumption of power in the city by Giovanni Panciatichi had brought quick Florentine intervention.[68] By the end of the fourteenth century, however, the Panciatichi had come to favor loyalty and continued submission to Florence, supporting a pronounced "Florenizing" policy. In 1378 one of

66. *Cronica,* I, cap. 2, p. 11. "Piangano adunque i suoi cittadini sopra loro e sopra i loro figliuoli; i quali, per loro superbia e per loro malizia e per gara di uffici, anno cosi nobile città disfatta . . ." and I, cap. 20, p. 82. "La città, retta con poca giustizia, cadde in nuovo pericolo, perchè i cittadini si cominciarono a dividere per gara d'ufici. . . ."

67. Giannozzo Manetti, Chronicon, p. 1070, "in civilibus causis, et in sortitionibus magistratuum, sed de criminalibus et condemnationibus."

68. See below, p. 228.

their number, messer Bartholomeo Bandini, had received Florentine citizenship, and in 1401, according to Luca Dominici, he was Florence's richest inhabitant.[69] Still according to Luca Dominici, the family then maintained close personal ties with the ruling Florentine families.[70] The Cancellieri, on the other hand, originally Guelf and pro-Florentine in the thirteenth century, shifted completely by 1401 to an anti-Florentine position; Ricciardo Cancellieri led, as we shall see, the great uprising against Florentine power in 1401–03.[71]

This reversal of policy seems best understood in the light of the social character these factions possessed. As described by Luca Dominici, the Panciatichi in 1401 had the support of "merchants, artisans and persons of low station," including many peasants.[72] Close ties with commercial interests were almost traditional for them; even in the thirteenth century, the Panciatichi themselves, and most of the great banking and commercial families, had been joined together as Ghibellines. And those families such as the Partini, which the Catasto of 1427 show to have had considerable commercial investments, do indeed appear in the list of Panciatichi supporters as given by Luca Dominici.[73]

The shift in policy from an "anti-Florenizing" to a "Florenizing" position thus seems to correspond to a change in attitude of the commercially minded elements of Pistoia's society over the same period. In the thirteenth century, the Florentines were viewed only as rivals, and the policy favored by Pistoia's business families was therefore hostile to them. By the late fourteenth century, as rivalry with the Florentines in the international market was abandoned and cooperation strengthened on the regional level, these families

69. Salvi, *Historie*, II, 142. *Cronache*, II, 20. "Messer Bartholomeo Bandini cavalieri, il più riccho huomo di Firenze, stava a Firenze."

70. Ibid. II, 10–11.

71. See below, pp. 229–30.

72. *Cronache*, II, 13, "era copiosa di mercatanti et artieri et gente di bassa mano più che l'altra."

73. Of the fifteen wealthiest families in 1427 (see above, p. 000, table 29), at least nine were supporters of the Panciatichi and only two were certainly associated with the Cancellieri. The nine families supporting the Panciatichi were the Partini (no. 1), the Panciatichi themselves (no. 3), the Fioravanti (no. 4), the Rossi (no. 5), the Bracciolini (no. 6), the Taiuoli (no. 7), the Bracciolini (no. 9), the Taviani (nos. 13 and 14), and Michele di Lapo (grandfather of Iachopo and Niccholo, no. 15). The two supporters of the Cancellieri were Batista di Marco (no. 2) and the Cancellieri themselves (no. 12).

identified their own interests with close political and economic ties with Florence. They were joined in this attitude by many peasants and landlords producing for the Florentine market. These same groups also benefited from the enhanced security and more stable political order which Florentine power made possible. Much the same shift in policy is evident also at Pisa, where business families, hostile to Florence in the thirteenth century, became the chief Florenizers in the late fourteenth and fifteenth centuries.[74] In other words, the growth of the Florentine state and its greater political and economic integration attracted no little sympathy and support from within the communities it was absorbing.

Florence, however, for long remained reluctant to involve itself directly in local feuds, and the social history of Pistoia in the late fourteenth century is steeped in violence. The Panciatichi, exiled in 1351, were allowed to return in 1353.[75] Fighting erupted again in 1354, and a short-lived compromise was hammered out in 1357. But the battle was soon thereafter renewed, and the Florentines could not indefinitely watch this strategic city decimated by internal warfare. They intervened in 1373, and again in 1376 and 1383 they sought to end the continuing struggle over elections by themselves preparing the purses which decided them.[76] In 1376 the entire city was divided into two companies, with the benign names of San Paolo (representing Panciatichi interests) and San Giovanni (supporters of the Cancellieri), each with its own set of electoral purses.[77] The offices would be filled by choosing first from one, then from the other set, in peaceful alternation.

But the factions were not ready for compromise, and the local government was too weak and the Florentines unwilling to impose it upon them. The bloodiest of all Pistoia's factional outbursts occurred in 1401–03; its history presents a good example of the com-

74. On the effort of Pisan merchants to liberalize trade with Florence, against the opposition of the local wool manufacturers, see P. Silva, "Intorno all'industria e al commercio della lana in Pisa," *Studi Storici*, new ser. 1 (1910), 329–400, reprinted in *Storia dell' economia italiana*, ed. C. M. Cipolla (Turin, 1959), pp. 123–62, and my own comments, *Pisa*, p. 185.

75. Salvi, *Historie*, II, 83.

76. *Capitoli*, I, nos. 18, 21 and 24.

77. Salvi, *Historie*, II, 138.

plex combination of personal, family and policy issues upon which factional peace or war depended.

Prime responsibility for the civil war of 1401–03 is attributed by the chroniclers to a dispute over an inheritance.[78] A young heiress of Prato, Datina, daughter of Stefano Guazzalotti, had been betrothed by her guardian to Biceccho Bracciolini, who was related to the Panciatichi and a warm supporter of their interests. He quarreled, however, with the girl's guardian, who sought then to marry the girl to Paperino Cancellieri. Faced with the loss of a good inheritance, the Panciatichi appealed to the Florentine officials at Pistoia, who decided in their favor. Ricciardo Cancellieri, then the leader of the Panciatichi's opponents, was enraged at the decision, and he also had further reasons for chagrin. One day on the streets of Pistoia, some young blades of the Panciatichi had whistled and hooted at his wife.[79] This affront might have been answered by calling out his supporters to do battle in the streets, but Ricciardo was an ambitious and not untalented leader, who dreamed of ridding himself of his rivals and restoring freedom to Pistoia in one gesture. He planned to assassinate the head of the enemy faction, Giovanni Panciatichi and his sons, seize the city, and demand that Florence recognize its independence. If it refused, he would appeal for help to Giangaleazzo Visconti, the great tyrant of Milan and dedicated enemy of the Florentines.

But word of the conspiracy somehow leaked to the Florentine government. On August 3, 1401, Nanni di Sinibaldo de' Cantasanti, who had agreed to commit the murders, was arrested at Florence. He revealed the plot, although his confession did not save him from execution. Ricciardo, warned at once of the arrest of his fellow conspirator, fled to the mountains, where the castle of Sambuca revolted in his favor. Two years of bitter and destructive fighting ensued, but Ricciardo successfully warded off the expeditions sent against him. However, the death of Giangaleazzo Visconti (1402) dissipated the prospects of a Milanese victory over Florence, upon which Ricciardo's own hopes depended. In September 1403 he made peace with the Florentines; he was allowed to return to Pistoia

78. Luca Dominici, *Cronache*, II, 25; Manetti, Chronicon, p. 1070; and Sozomenus, *Specimen*, p. 1122.

79. The incident is mentioned by Manetti, Chronicon, p. 1070.

with all his property restored to him. He thus went unpunished for his betrayal and revolt, in the wake of which, the chroniclers agree, an "ingens numerus" of persons had been killed and extensive areas of the countryside left in ruins.[80]

The revolt did, however, force the Florentines to maintain a now constant vigilance over Pistoia.[81] Other factors too, besides the power of the Florentine state, helped introduce in the early fifteenth century a new era of relative social peace at Pistoia. Better economic times strengthened the wealth and influence of such men as Batista di Marco and Antonio Rospigliosi, whose welfare depended upon peaceful conditions.[82] Even for the older families with a tradition of turbulence, good times lessened the need to battle over government patronage. And the influence of the new humanism, which stressed the moral responsibility of service to the entire community, should not be ignored.[83] The Cancellieri and Panciatichi, to be sure, continued their rivalry, sometimes violently, but at least the city was spared the disastrous experience of total civil war.

The century between the breakdown of the free commune and the establishment of an effective Florentine hegemony was also marked by class conflicts, especially in the countryside, although it is often hard to distinguish these from factional struggles with which they were often related. The mountain communes again compiled the longest record of violence, for reasons we have mentioned: the rugged terrain offered natural defenses against punitive expeditions sent from the city, and the poor and primitive mountain economy left most highlanders with little to lose by rebellion.[84]

Mountain communities had offered the stoutest resistance to the advance, in the twelfth century, of the city's authority in the countryside. The commune had to put down uprisings in Sambuca in

80. The most detailed contemporary account of the rebellion is Luca Dominici, *Cronache*, II, Cronaca seconda. For the destruction caused see Manetti, Chronicon, p. 1072. "Tantum enim variis interemtorum hominum caedibus, et tam magnum caesorum numerum vulgo exstitisse creditur, ut ex duarum armigerarum personarum millibus . . . multo pauciores cives reperirentur, colonis et agrestibus praetermissis, quorum ingens numerus interesse dicebatur."

81. See below, p. 230.

82. On Batista, see above, p. 193.

83. See below, p. 260.

84. See above, pp. 198–99.

1128, San Marcello and Gavinana in 1140, Treppio and Fossato in 1159—all castles or villages in the high mountains.[85]

The thirteenth century, on the other hand, was an age of relative rural peace, even in the mountains. Peace was maintained primarily by the city's power, but that power in turn conferred certain real benefits upon the rural communities. It helped control banditry and repress factional warfare. Its advance was a factor of major influence in the disappearance of serfdom, under which most peasants had been living in the high Middle Ages. In claiming the rights to judge, to punish, to tax and to levy soldiers, the commune slowly absorbed seigneurial jurisdiction and left the status of serf devoid of meaning. Thus, the Book of Hearths of ca. 1244 distinguishes nobles from commoners but not free men from serfs.[86] In the commune's view—the one view that mattered—all commoners were equal for all were equally its subjects. At the same time, acts of emancipation grow rarer in Pistoia's diplomatic collections, and apparently are not to be found at all after 1250. The freeing of a serf had by then become meaningless.

But if the thirteenth century was an age of relative social peace, the crisis of the free commune, its government and economy, filled the fourteenth century with violence. Acute population fall and changing conditions of production had disturbed the relations and the equilibrium between the classes, and city officials and landlords for long remained reluctant to grant the concessions to the peasants which the new situation required.

The first great rural uprising occurred in the summer of 1303. The city government, warring at once with Florence and Lucca, had tried to impose a new universal tax upon the countryside which, according to Salvi, "greatly disturbed particular persons."[87] A rebellion broke out in the mountains, led by one Musone della Moscacchia, who with about a hundred followers raided the countryside and harassed the highway to Bologna. The communal government was still strong enough to defeat Musone, but his uprising was only an omen of worse to come.

The decade of the 1340s, crowded with famines and plagues, wit-

85. Salvi, *Historie*, I, 69, 77 and 92.
86. On the Book, see above, pp. 58–63.
87. *Historie*, I, 280.

nessed still more protracted and serious outbursts, and until the 1370s it would be hard to say that peace was ever successfully restored in the mountains. In 1346, a year of famine when Pistoia was also distracted by the feud between the Cancellieri and Panciatichi, a wave of "robberies, murders and killings" swept over the mountains, and a special force of 200 men had to be dispatched to repress them.[88] The results proved ephemeral. Again in 1349, the "most grave excesses" brought another force of 100 men from the city, attempting to pacify the mountains.[89] In 1351, 1352 and 1356, the mountains were again in turbulence, and by 1358 the entire region had broken into rebellion.[90] The city, to mollify the mountaineers, offered them tax exemption for four years, and extended the privileges of urban residence to their "first families," even though they continued to live in the mountains.[91] In 1369 bandits were again infesting the mountains, and rebellions were reported at Piteglio in the mountains, Cecina in the hills and even Montemagno on the plain.[92] In 1371 so many outlaws were roaming the uplands that the government feared an attack on Pistoia itself, and ordered that the walls be strengthened.[93]

The authority of the commune over the mountains had clearly broken down. Again it appears that amid the chaos Pistoia's society was reverting back to older, more primitive forms of social organization. In 1356 the urban government complained that certain rural lords were holding peasants "quasi sub iugo dominii," and collecting taxes from them, much to the damage of the city.[94] The ebbing of the city's power over the countryside was permitting a resurgence

88. Ibid. II, 72 and 82.

89. Ibid. II, 82. ASP, Provv. Tomus 20, 21r, 15 April 1349, also mentions the "novitatibus ortis in montanea superiori."

90. Ibid. Tomus 20, 34r, 16 Dec. 1351, for discussion by the anziani of the "multe inimitie et discordie inter cives et districtuales." Salvi, *Historie*, II, 97 and 118.

91. Ibid. II, 114.

92. ASP, Provv. Tomus 30, 42v, 23 July 1369. Salvi, *Historie*, II, 124.

93. Ibid. II, 130.

94. ASP, Provv. Tomus 31, 10v, 20 Nov. 1356, the anziani complain "quam in aliquibus partibus comitatus Pistorii comitatini . . . tractantur tirannice per aliquos nobiles circumstantes et quod ipsi comitatini indebite congiunti quasi sub iugo dominii per dictos nobiles adsolvere indebitas factiones cum hoc redundet in dannum civitatis et civium."

of serfdom, which its rising authority had once so nearly swept away.

This period of nearly continuous uprisings and fighting in the countryside, falling between 1346 and 1371, corresponds with the years of most rapid population fall. It also lies within the interlude between the breakdown of the power of the free commune, and the effective submission of Pistoia's mountains to the authority of the Florentine state.

For the Florentines could not remain forever indifferent to the reigning chaos in the mountains, which offered their best natural defense against Visconti power from beyond the Apennines. In 1373 they finally intervened, and insisted that the office of captain of the mountains be conferred upon a Florentine citizen.[95] This extension of Florentine power over the highlands seems to have resulted in an immediate if still not permanent pacification. While bandits were again pillaging and murdering in 1384 and 1390, the years were free of major uprisings.[96]

But the peace proved to be only the calm before the storm. Mountain communities joined enthusiastically in the revolt of Ricciardo Cancellieri from 1401–03; their territory was the scene of the principal fighting and also bore the brunt of the considerable destruction.[97] The warfare of these years, while originating in a factional feud, took on overtones of a class conflict. According to the chronicler Luca Dominici, work all but ceased in the countryside.[98] Many peasants, taking advantage of the troubles of the city, renounced their leases, and many landlords were themselves forced to gather at their own expense, their portion of the harvest. Some peasants negotiated for lower rents, while others abandoned altogether the cultivation of the soil.

95. *Capitoli* I, no. 18, p. 13, 23 Nov. 1373.

96. Salvi, *Historie*, II, 154 and 168.

97. In 1404, 21 communes of the mountains and the middle hills had to be granted tax exemptions of three years because of the destruction they had suffered. ASP, Provv. Tomus 43, 164r, 26 May 1404.

98. *Cronache*, II, 130. "Testeso quasi tucti li lavoratori mutavano quistione a' cittadini delle terre: chi le rifiutava in tucto, chi volea menimare l'affícti, chi volea prestanza, chi vantaggi di qua, chi di là, chi se ne andava, et chi ssi fuggiva, et più che a molti conveniva ire o mandare a sue spese per la sua parte della ricolta."

The constitutional reforms of 1402, bringing stronger Florentine control over the countryside, made the opening decades of the fifteenth century years of relative quiet.[99] But rural dissatisfactions were not yet overcome, and a final great outburst occurred in 1455. As the contemporary Sozomenus describes it, the peasants were exasperated by the violence and unpunished crimes which factional strife was continuing to perpetrate in the countryside.[100] They therefore marched upon the city, beating and (according to Salvi) even killing the urban residents they encountered, and eventually took possession of the city square. To restore order, the Florentines sent four commissioners who, together with the podestà and captain, also Florentines, acted to meet the peasant demands for more social discipline in the countryside. They greatly strengthened the laws against murder and other violent crimes, imposing on all violators what Sozomenus calls "most severe penalties."[101] Apparently satisfied with the reform, the peasant bands dispersed.

This pacification of 1455 was the culminating event in the extension of Florentine power over Pistoia's countryside, and the achievement within it of a new level of public order. Other factors also contributed to the new social peace. Times were better economically, fiscal pressures less exasperating, and the new tax system, represented especially by the Catasto, not unfair to rural residents. Moreover, relations between landlords and tenants had come to be pretty well stabilized with the extension of the mezzadria and similar leases, with terms not unfavorable to the peasants.

The history of factional and social conflict at Pistoia thus divides into three rather distinct periods. In the thirteenth century, the government of the free, popular commune had sought to limit fac-

99. See below, p. 230.

100. Sozomenus, *Chronicon*, p. 53. "Rustici comitatus Pistorii, cum diu inter se pessimo more ferarum multos homines interfecissent propter seditiones, sectas et divisiones bestiales eorum, tandem oratores Pistorienses Florentinorum patrocinium implorantes, magnifici domini florentini elegerunt [six commissioners to reform the laws at Pistoia]."

101. Loc. cit. "Qui omni cum diligentia posuerunt omnes in pace et statu tranquillissimo, roborantes gravissimis statutis et penis, ut de cetero nullus homicidium commictere auderet. Et sic reformata fuit civitas et eius comitatus, dummodo contigat ipsos seditiosissimos more sue patrie stare in pace et cessare ab homicidiis." See also C. Paoli, "Capitoli dei 'Paciali' di Pistoia del MCCCCLV," *BSP*, 1 (1899), 11–24.

tional and social disorders, with partial though not final success. The disruptions of the middle fourteenth century brought a resurgence of private and social warfare and, for Pistoia's society, a true relapse into earlier, distinctly feudal patterns of social behavior. By the fifteenth century, however, considerable political integration with the Florentine state, aided by better economic times, largely restored social peace. Factional and class antagonisms were by no means eradicated, but at least one aspiration of the free commune, the suppression of private warfare, was pretty well achieved for Pistoia within the fabric of the fifteenth-century, Florentine state.

9

Political Transformations

But laws, and the scholars who study them, are honored above all doctors and philosophers.

—Coluccio Salutati, *De nobilitate legum et medicinae*

Since the time Jacob Burckhardt advanced the famous thesis that the state of the fifteenth century in Italy was a work of art, rationally constructed and administered by a new kind of ruler, the nature and even the existence of a "Renaissance state" has been debated by the historians. Recent research, successfully establishing that both in its administrative practices and in its legal assumptions the Italian state of the fifteenth century had deep medieval roots, has been on the whole critical of this key Burckhardtian concept.[1] But while it may be time to banish the term "Renaissance state" from the historical vocabulary, it does not necessarily follow that constitutional change was slight and negligible in the fourteenth and fifteenth centuries.

The political history of Pistoia, free commune in the thirteenth century, subject city in the fifteenth, offers an exceptional opportunity to study constitutional change in the Renaissance period. Specifically, Pistoia's history may help illustrate and measure the trend away from the jurisdictional multiplicity of the Middle Ages toward a more integrated, centralized, if not quite modern territorial state within the Florentine domain. Administration over these

1. Cf. P. J. Jones, "Communes and Despots: the City State in Late-Medieval Italy," *Transactions of the Royal Historical Society*, 5th series, 15 (1965), p. 95, "not the least striking resemblance between [republics and despotisms] is their unqualified failure, in common with other forms of European government, to support the fashionable concept of 'Renaissance state' or 'Renaissance monarchy.'"

same centuries was also changing, transformed in fact by the growth of a class of professional civil servants, specialists and experts in the art of government. If the Italian state of the fifteenth century may no longer be considered a work of art, as Buckhardt maintained, it was still relying on professional, trained administrators to a degree which the free commune had not achieved for most of its history. This bureaucratic expansion, offering employment and support for large numbers of literate laymen, in turn exerted a profound influence upon the secular culture of the Renaissance.

FROM FREE COMMUNE TO FLORENTINE DEPENDENCY

To understand the processes and degrees by which the land of Pistoia was joined to and integrated with the Florentine territorial state is first to investigate the principal institutions and offices of the free commune, which continued to function even under the Florentine hegemony.

Those institutions, cumbersome in character and complex in operation, may be classified into three categories: the great executive offices, a parallel skein of councils associated with them, and the "staff," the growing body of professional assistants and experts who aided both officers and councils in the performance of their duties. This last category of staff becomes so important and characteristic a part of the fifteenth-century state that we shall consider its development in a separate, subsequent section.

The earliest supreme magistrates of the free commune were the five consuls, first mentioned in 1105.[2] Serving for one year, at first apparently without salary, which goes unmentioned in the Statutes of 1107, the consuls in every respect represented and embodied the commune's growing sovereignty. Their first and primary duty seems to have been judicial. Initially they held their own court and, when growing business led to the establishment of separate courts for matters involving Roman law ("de lege") and local custom ("de usu"), they supervised the subaltern judges set over them.[3] They managed the commune's property, spent its funds, gathered its taxes, maintained the roads, supervised the trades, led the army and

2. *Libro croce*, p. 250, August 1105.
3. *Statuti*, ed. Berlan, cap. 130.

conducted foreign relations. Their considerable powers were in theory limited only by the requirement to consult a council of unstated size in important matters; in practice their powers must also have been restricted by the difficulty of securing agreement within their own cumbersome board of five.

Toward the end of the twelfth century, the consular regime gradually gave way to a new form of executive organization. Growing factional and class conflicts made selection of this multiple executive difficult, and probably also the complicated business of government was demanding an undivided and more expert direction.[4] Certainly from 1188, and perhaps as early as 1158, a new, single supreme magistrate appeared at the head of the commune, the podestà.[5] The new officer did not at once replace the consuls; the older multiple executive continued to appear sporadically, but ever more rarely after 1210 and not at all after 1248. At first a native, the podestà from at least 1219 was regularly a foreigner, and his term, originally one year, from about the same time was reduced to six months.

As the commune's supreme magistrate, the podestà assumed all the former consular functions. He was the commune's chief judge, supervising not only courts hearing criminal and civil cases but also a special tribunal, "de dannis datis," "on damage caused," concerned, among other duties, with adjudicating Pistoia's chronic outbursts of violence among families and factions. Administration of taxes, supervision of subordinate officials, maintenance of the army and conduct of foreign affairs were all committed to his care, subject only to the supervision and, in weighty matters, to the approbation of a complicated system of councils presently to be reviewed. The podestà was also the head of the commune in a ceremonial sense, leading processions, receiving ambassadors and approving treaties. Even after he lost supreme power to newer officials, he remained an important figure, though with duties which by the fifteenth century were largely limited to the administration of civil justice.

Much earlier, however, in the latter half of the thirteenth cen-

4. According to the Statutes of ca. 1200, three of the five consuls had to be "de popularibus," and this indicates a dispute over their selection. See ibid. cap. 154.

5. See Barbi's preface to the *Storie pistoresi*, p. xv, n. 5.

tury, the podestà surrendered the distinction of the supreme magistracy first to the "captain of the people" (first mentioned 1263), who in turn (from about 1295) saw it pass to the *gonfaloniere* or standard bearer of justice.

Both these officers were agents not strictly of the commune itself but of a special organization within it, the *Popolo*. The Popolo, the corporation of common citizens from which knights and nobles were excluded, was a kind of commune within a commune, really a state within a state, which dominated and directed but did not replace the government of the podestà. Popular associations, and popular agitation against the rule of the knights, go far back into the thirteenth century. In 1236 at Pistoia a major disturbance broke out between the corporations of knights and people, which was finally settled the following year through a pacification imposed by the Florentines.[6] At almost the same time, similar disturbances were dividing Pisa and other towns.[7] But the popular parties were not yet strong enough to establish permanent regimes. However, a little more than a decade later, following the death (1250) of Emperor Frederick II Hohenstaufen and the abeyance of Ghibelline power it brought, popular upheavals broke out in many Tuscan cities (Florence, Pisa, Lucca, Volterra, Siena), and the Popolo was able to claim for itself a more lasting power.

It appears likely that Pistoia too passed under a popular regime in the 1250s, although we are without certain evidence for this.[8] A captain and elders (*anziani*) of the Popolo are mentioned at Pistoia only in 1263, and they were then still clearly subordinate to the authority of the podestà.[9] A popular government, if it had been established, probably lost much of its power with the Guelf defeat at

6. The relevant documents concerning the pacification are in the *Liber censuum*, nos. 303–18, pp. 206–16, and the *Breve populi*, pp. xv–xviii.

7. Cristiani, *Pisa*, pp. 13–63; R. Davidsohn, "Die Popular-Bewegung in italienischen Städten bis zur Mitte des 13. Jahrhunderts," *Forschungen*, IV, especially pp. 22–24.

8. Between 1252 and 1254, men who had been or were to be associated with the Popolo in other cities were serving as podestà at Pistoia. See Barbi in the *Storie pistoresi*, p. xxi.

9. *Liber censuum*, nos. 356–357, p. 246, 7–9 April 1263. But as late as May 1267, the podestà and council promised the city's loyalty to Charles of Anjou, without the participation of the captain or the elders, showing that these latter officers were still subordinate to the podestà.

Montaperti. In 1266, however, Guelf and popular fortunes were revived with the victory of Charles of Anjou, younger brother of King Louis IX of France invited into Italy by the pope, over the Hohenstaufen Manfred at Benevento. Guelf and usually popular regimes assumed authority in the Tuscan communes, including Pistoia, by 1267.[10] Pistoia's *Breve populi,* or Statutes of the People, which survives only in a redaction of 1284, was in fact largely written between 1267 and 1271, in the first flush of the Guelf-popular victory.[11]

According to those Statutes, the captain of the people served as the chief executive officer of the Popolo. He had to be at least 30 years of age and could not be a Tuscan, and his term of office was six months.[12] His principal responsibility was the defense of the Guelf and popular privileges against any Ghibelline and aristocratic resurgence. He was therefore primarily a police or peace officer, with his own staff of soldiers and with the right of summoning 300 "good men of the people" to "follow and maintain" him with arms when needed.[13] His relations with the podestà were slightly ambivalent and must in practice have been delicate. He was to support the podestà in all his efforts to maintain the statutes, and he was also to help him enforce his judicial decisions. But the captain was also to make sure that the podestà did not encroach upon popular liberties. To this end, the captain maintained a court of appeals in civil cases, which sat in the open under the cathedral's great bell tower open to all comers, and he likewise held criminal hearings and meted out punishments. The captain, unlike the podestà, also sat with the powerful councils of the Popolo and served as a liaison officer among them; he therefore had a voice, although only a restricted one, in legislation.[14] After about 1295, the captain lost his status as leader of the Popolo to the standard bearer of justice, but he con-

10. By 22 August 1267, Charles of Anjou was addressing himself to the "potestas vel capitaneus comunis et populi" and to the anziani as chief officers of the commune, *Liber censuum,* nos. 368 and 371, pp. 257–59.

11. Book 1 and Book 2 up to the fifth rubric were then composed. See Zdekauer, *Breve populi,* p. xiii.

12. *Breve populi,* p. 11.

13. Ibid. p. 38.

14. The council of elders or anziani could meet without the captain, and the captain was in turn obligated to report the decisions of the anziani to the larger popular councils, ibid. p. 18.

tinued to serve as the commune's chief peace officer, a sort of city sheriff. He still retained a hand on the sword, and this explains his continuing importance.

It is not certain when the office of this new leader of the Popolo, the *gonfaloniere della giustizia* or *vexillifer iustitie,* was established. Salvi names a standard bearer for 1291, but the office seems clearly modelled after the Florentine magistrate of the same name, which dates only from 1293.[15] This makes 1296, the year from which a fairly complete list of gonfalonieri has survived, a more likely date for its foundation.[16]

At Florence, the standard bearer was primarily responsible for the enforcement of the new harsh laws directed against the magnates, the famous Ordinances of Justice, and at Pistoia too the new officer appeared in the wake of sterner measures taken against the noble class, the "liber securitatum nobilium" of 1291 and the "Liber exbannitorum" of 1292.[17] His primary duty, and the explanation of his name, was to marshal the armed citizenry to defend the popular rights. Bearing the *vexillum* or standard of the people, he would lead them to the houses of refractory nobles, to enforce court decisions carried against them. His presence was also essential for a meeting of the Popolo's council of elders, and in it he advised on legislation. He drew the lots by which the chief magistrates were selected, and received oaths of loyalty from subject communes. As bearer of the popular standard, he also assumed the position of ceremonial head of the commune in all civil functions, and was officially recognized as such from 1417, when he replaced in this capacity the senior anziano or prior, as the officer was then called.[18] His office alone of the three great magistracies could be held by a man born in the city, and was therefore considered a high dignity for the incumbent. However, his short term (two months) and the

15. *Historie,* I, 243, no. 1.

16. A gonfaloniere is still not mentioned in the solemn act by which the commune of Pistoia surrendered full powers to reform its constitution to Florence, *Liber censuum,* no. 683, pp. 389–92, 3 May 1296, but the officer is mentioned in a document of 29 August 1296, ibid. no. 684, p. 392. This means almost certainly that the office was created with the Florentine reform of the constitution in 1296.

17. On this legislation, see Barbi, *Storie pistoresi,* pp. lvi–lvii.

18. Fioravanti, *Memorie,* p. 15.

manner of his election, presently to be discussed, assured that his power would constitute no threat to the fundamental oligarchic character of the communal constitution.

Supervising and advising these officers was a system of numerous councils, of quite diverse size, character and power.

According to the Statutes of ca. 1200, the podestà had already two councils, a smaller one of 24 members, from which he sought advice, and a larger council of 100, which approved major decisions concerning war, peace and taxes.[19] With the triumph of the popular regime, the podestà and his two councils largely lost their legislative functions. The fate of his smaller council is difficult to follow. In the fifteenth century he was being advised by 14 counselors, all of whom were lawyers, and the professional character of this council shows the podestà's exclusive concentration on civil justice.[20] His larger council, or the "General Council of the Commune" as it came to be called, expanded to include fully 600 members in 1273, but by 1296 had been reduced to 300 and by 1330 to 100, perhaps reflecting a shrinking urban population.[21] After 1330, its composition was evenly balanced with 50 popular members and 50 magnates (including knights, judges and doctors). The chief business of this General Council of the Commune was to hear proposals for changes in the statutes or on other grave matters of public policy, as presented to it by the podestà, who in turn acted on direction of the Popolo's board of elders. The General Council did retain the theoretical right to reject such proposals, but its powers were in fact largely illusory. The same proposals, if approved by the exclusively popular councils, would be entered into the *Breve populi* and be binding anyway.[22] The General Council of the Commune did, however, provide a forum in which the decisions of the elders of the people could be promulgated, and their approbation helped add a certain solemnity to them.

Under the popular commune, the real seats of power were the councils associated with the organization of the Popolo. Of these the smallest and most powerful was the council of anziani or elders,

19. *Statuti*, ed. Berlan, cap. 65 and 126.
20. Fioravanti, *Memorie*, p. 15.
21. *Breve populi*, p. 82; *Statutum potestatis*, p. 10.
22. *Breve populi*, p. 63, "Quod statuta populi prevaleant statutis comunis."

whose name, at Florentine insistence, was changed to priors in 1402. Originally twelve, then (after 1286) eight in number, the anziani had to be at least 30 years of age, could not be members of certain proscribed noble families, and served two months.[23] Two of the eight had to be artisans. They sat with the standard bearer of justice and with the captain of the people, although the latter's presence was not required for a valid meeting. They supervised the activities of the captain, heard appeals from his condemnations, and directed the podestà in the performance of his duties. They alone could propose, by two-thirds vote of their members, *reformationes* or *provisiones*—changes in statutes or policies—which then were taken by the captain to the larger popular councils for approval.[24]

The anziani could further seek the advice of a Council of Forty, the members of which had to be over 40 years of age and served a six-month term. This was a true deliberative council, comparable to the "Senate" in other towns (its members, it should be noted, had to be older than the "elders" themselves). It also heard every two months the report of the two communal treasurers. It was, however, specifically excluded from approving changes in laws and policies, unless the General Council of the People had authorized it to do so.[25]

The largest of the popular councils was the "General Council of the People," to be distinguished from the still more numerous but less powerful "General Council of the Commune" discussed above.[26] It included, in the late thirteenth century, 200 members, but by 1330 it had been reduced to 100.[27] Its members could be as young as 20, and they served one year. With this council sat also the standard bearer of justice, the elders, the members of the Council of Forty and the rectors and counselors of the guilds. They approved proposals brought to them by the captain, and participated in or at least witnessed elections. This was an important council, the decisions of which mattered. Its meetings could be occasions of some drama, as in 1398 when the council sat for fifteen hours,

23. Ibid. p. 8.
24. Ibid. p. 18.
25. Ibid. pp. 9 and 67. It also arbitrated disputes between the podestà and captain.
26. See p. 219.
27. *Breve populi*, pp. 10–11. Fioravanti, *Memorie*, p. 15.

listening to and finally accepting the demands of Florentine ambassadors, who were insisting that the city henceforth elect only Florentines as podestà, and thus surrender its last pretense to independence.[28]

The Popolo was also divided into twelve armed companies, three in each quarter, which had been established by 1267.[29] Each had its own standard and standard bearer, two captains and four counselors. Their primary function was to defend, by force if necessary, the rights of the people.

One other council appears fleetingly in the sources: the assembly of the entire populace, gathered "in arringo" or "in contione." According to the Statutes of ca. 1200, this assembly was to be held, if possible, at convenient times, that is, during the months of March, May, July or September.[30] This peculiar selection of months may perhaps show the extent to which the urban population was still occupied with agricultural labors. To call the populace together, according to the *Breve populi* of 1284, the largest bell was to be sounded, and it was to be struck rapidly with a hammer so that the people could recognize the summons.[31] But apart from these stipulations, we hear not at all of full assemblies in the thirteenth century. Meetings of the entire citizenry had obviously become impractical in the larger city, and their functions were pretty much assumed by the general councils of the commune or of the people.

Both the great officers and their counselors served only for brief terms, two months to a year, and the methods of holding the frequent elections needed constituted one of the most disputed features of communal government. The earliest statutes are unfortunately vague on this vital point, but the operative principle seems to have been that the smaller councils selected the larger. The new consuls were themselves chosen by a special board of electors, nominated by the out-going consuls and enlarged by cooption.[32] Oligarchic domination of the elections continued even under the popular com-

28. Salvi, *Historie*, II, 177.
29. See the "Ordinamenta de societatibus populi," *Breve populi*, p. 172.
30. *Statuti*, ed. Berlan, cap. 56.
31. *Breve populi*, p. 21.
32. According to the Statutes of 1107 (*Statuti*, ed. Berlan, cap. V), five "potiores et idoniores homines" were chosen, who in turn selected three electors to choose the consuls.

mune. The large councils witnessed the elections, added solemnity to them, and learned who their new chiefs would be; but they had no assigned voice in the outcome. Boards of electors continued to function in the thirteenth century, although, in some instances at least, their entire number was selected by lot.[33] Finally, by 1330, clearly in imitation of the Florentine electoral reform of 1328, the selection of the gonfaloniere and anziani was directly left to lot, though subject to arrangements that assured few surprises in the outcome.[34]

The electoral system as described in a reform of 1373 well illustrates how this cumbersome method of choosing officers functioned.[35] To choose the chief officials (the standard bearer, the eight elders and their notary), four "ordinary purses" were to be prepared, one for each quarter of the city, each containing the names of ten eligible men. Three days before the beginning of the new term, the standard bearer then in office was to choose one name from each of the four purses in a prearranged sequence, until the ten offices were filled. At the next election, the sequence would be continued until all the purses were emptied. The purses, with their total of 40 names, thus served for four years, and similar purses were to be prepared to select the then 128 members of the General Council of the People.

If, however, a person whose name was drawn from the purses should prove ineligible, dead or absent, another name could not be taken from the same purses, as this would disrupt the sequence, shorten the period for which the purses could serve, and leave the quarter under-represented. A second series of "subsidiary" purses had to be prepared, and if again the lot should yield the name of an ineligible, dead or absent citizen, still a third group of "extraordinary" purses had to be used. These purses, over the four years of their service, were carefully guarded; they were kept in a special

33. Thus, to select the 300 members of the general council of the commune, the podestà, standard bearer and the elders first selected four to six men from each quarter, and then together with them named 75 persons from each quarter, *Statutum potestatis*, p. 10. On the other hand, the notary who served the captain was to be named by a board chosen by lot, *Breve populi*, pp. 85–86.

34. For details of the Florentine reform, see Davidsohn, *Geschichte*, III, 862–64.

35. *Capitoli*, I, no. 18, p. 13, 23 Nov. 1373.

chest, locked with three keys held by the commune's three chief officials, and placed in the august and protected sacristy of San Iacopo.

Upon the preparation of these electoral purses control of the communal government obviously depended, and the issue regularly summoned the factions to battle. The duty of scrutinizing the citizens, determining eligibility and filling the purses fell usually to special commissioners selected by the anziani for the task. But the results of their work could well mean civil revolt on the part of a dissatisfied faction, and the Florentines were forced repeatedly to intervene, to prepare the purses themselves or to impose ingenious if unworkable schemes for balancing and pacifying the factions. Florentine commissioners thus reformed the offices and prepared new purses in 1373, in 1376 (repudiating a reform made shortly before by factionally inspired Pistoiesi) and in 1383 (again repudiating another local reform).[36] After another intervention in 1402, Florentines prepared the purses continuously up to 1420.[37] However unfortunate Pistoia's own loss of freedom, there can be no doubt that Florentine power at Pistoia was a buttress of civic peace.

These great offices and councils of Pistoia's communal constitution were changed hardly at all as the city passed ever more extensively under Florentine control. From an institutional viewpoint, the Florentine "district" in the fifteenth century remained thoroughly decentralized, divided by a multiplicity of local and apparently autonomous jurisdictions. In fact, however, more integration was being achieved than a consideration of institutions alone might suggest. Florence was characteristically insisting that the great offices of its subject cities be filled with its own citizens; this bureaucratic integration of the Florentine state assured, at Pistoia as elsewhere, both loyalty and a favorable hearing to whatever "requests" Florentine "ambassadors" might present.

Indeed, the best measure of Florence's growing domination of Pistoia is exactly its control of the great traditional offices of the city. Table 30 marks the years during which Florentines served at

36. Ibid. I, no. 18, p. 13; I, no. 21, p. 19; I, no. 24, p. 22. See also Salvi, *Historie*, II, 133 and 138.

37. Luca Dominici, *Cronache* II, 67, reporting that Florentine "riformatori" burnt the old purses on 12 Jan. 1402. See also Salvi, *Historie*, II, 244.

Pistoia whether as podestà or as captains of the people; in order to illustrate the context of these dates, the table also cites some major events of Florentine and Tuscan history.

TABLE 30 Florentine Officials at Pistoia

Podestà	*Captain*	*Comparative Events*
1222		
		Dispute between knights and people at Pistoia, 1236.
1237		Florence imposes pacification, 1237
		Florentine "Primo Popolo," 1250–60.
		War with Pistoia, 1251–54; Peace of Empoli, 1254. Pistoia agrees to accept Florentine podestà, 1258
1258–60		
		Guelfs defeated at Montaperti, 1260.
1277		
	1280	
1289		
		"Secondo Popolo" at Florence, 1292.
1294–1301	1293–94	Ordinances of Justice at Florence, 1293.
		Authority over Pistoia given to Florence, 1296.
	1296–1301	Civil war between Whites and Blacks at Pistoia and Florence, 1301.
1305*	1303–05*	Pistoia besieged by Florence and Lucca, 1305.
1306–10	1306–10	Pistoia under rule of Florence and Lucca.
1328–30		Pistoia taken by Florence, 1328.
		Peace between Pistoia and Florence, 1329.
	1331–42	Authority over Pistoia given to Florence, 1331.
1343	1343	Tyranny of Walter of Brienne at Florence, 1342–43.
	1351 on	Authority over Pistoia given to Florence, 1351; all subsequent captains Florentine.
1369		
1399 on		Florence demands that Pistoia choose only Florentines as podestà, 1398.
		All subsequent podestà Florentines.

* Held by Florentine White exiles.

Sources: Liber censuum, nos. 170, 303, 348, 354, 457, 552, 555, 683, 684 and 688. R. Davidsohn, "Florentiner an der Spitze auswärtiger Kommunen," *Forschungen* IV, 557–77, and Salvi, *Historie.*

As the table clearly shows, Pistoia came only belatedly to accept Florentines as podestà, certainly for the reason that citizens of so powerful a neighbor could not be trusted, it was felt, in so exalted an office. In 1237, however, taking advantage of a rift between the knights and people of the city, Florence imposed a pacification upon them and forced the acceptance of a Florentine in the city's highest office.[38] This initial period of Florentine dominance did not, however, last beyond 1239, although the circumstances of its ending are not clear.[39]

In 1250, the establishment of an aggressive popular regime at Florence, the famous Primo Popolo, brought a stronger challenge to Pistoia's liberty. War broke out almost at once between the two cities (1251–54), the Florentines were brilliantly victorious, and Pistoia, at the Peace of Empoli (1254) was forced to admit a Florentine garrison into the city.[40] Its humiliation was completed in 1258, when it agreed to accept a Florentine podestà.[41]

The defeat of the Guelfs at Montaperti (1260) and the overthrow of the Primo Popolo at Florence enabled Pistoia to recover its freedom. But with the outbreak of fighting between the Blacks and Whites from perhaps 1286, the communal government proved unable to pacify its own citizens.[42] Riots occurred again in 1290, their violence leading directly to the anti-magnate legislation of 1291 and 1292. But warfare continued for the next three years, and in 1295 the Florentines intervened with force to establish a fragile peace. The Popolo at Pistoia, exasperated by the magnate violence but unable to contain it, appointed special officers, the "Posati," whose function seems to have been to deliver Pistoia under Florentine power, in hopes of restoring order. On May 5, 1296, the Florentine government accepted full power over Pistoia, to last until July 1, 1301.

The Florentines, however, instead of restoring order, rather absorbed the feud of their subject town. The Whites of Pistoia were

38. *Liber censuum*, no. 303, pp. 206–11.

39. By 1239 the podestà, Ugo de Castello, was no longer a Florentine, ibid. no. 319, p. 216.

40. R. Davidsohn, "Die erste Unterwerfung von Pistoia, Poggibonsi, Volterra und San Gimignano (1253–57)," *Forschungen*, IV, pp. 115–21. L. Zdekauer, "La Guerra con Firenze dal 1251 al 1254," *BSP*, 5 (1903), 51–72.

41. *Liber censuum*, no. 348, pp. 241–43.

42. On the Blacks and Whites, see above, pp. 201–02. For the events recounted in this paragraph, see Davidsohn, *Geschichte*, III, 34–38, and Barbi, *Storie pistoresi*, pp. lv–lxvii.

linked with the Florentine faction led by Vieri de' Cerchi, the Blacks with the followers of Corso Donati.[43] In May 1301, prompted by their Florentine friends and eager to act before Florence gave up its power over the city, the Whites of Pistoia drove out the Blacks. But the tables were turned the other way at Florence. Charles of Valois, brother of the king of France, papal agent supposed to reconcile the Florentine factions, entered the city on November 1, and the result of his intervention was a complete Black victory. In January 1302, faced with answering trumped-up charges before the victors' tribunal, the leading Whites, including Dante Alighieri, fled the city.

War at once broke out between White Pistoia and Black Florence, and in 1305 the allied armies of Florence and Lucca laid destructive siege to the city. Pistoia was no match for such a coalition, and in 1306 accepted a harsh peace. Its territory was partitioned, and its two chief offices, those of podestà and captain, were alternately to be given to Florentines and Lucchesi. Finally in 1310, with some papal aid and with Florentine acquiescence, Pistoia reassumed control over its own territory and regained a precarious liberty.

In the following years, that liberty was constantly jeopardized in the course of the wars waged against Florence first by Uguccione della Faggiola, lord of Pisa then of Lucca (1314–16) and by Castruccio Castracane, the magnificent and terrible lord of Lucca (1316–28). Within the city the factions battled over whom Pistoia should support in the protracted wars. Uguccione and then Castruccio had the support of the exiled Whites and their numerous sympathizers in the city, while Florence remained the champion of the Black Guelfs.

In 1321 Ermanno di Iacopo Tedici, abbot of the monastery of Pacciana, supported by the peasants and artisans who were exasperated by the ruinous fighting, forced the commune to seek peace with Castruccio.[44] From late 1322 or early 1323, Ermanno himself

43. On the extension, probably from the spring of 1300, of the names White and Black to the Florentine factions of the Cerchi and Donati respectively, see Davidsohn, *Geschichte*, III, 128. The events in the following paragraphs are recounted according to ibid. III, 143, 169, 195, 316 and 374.

44. Ibid. III, 678–83.

became tyrant of the town. But the aged and somewhat vacillating abbot was overthrown the following year by his more determined and ambitious nephew, Filippo Tedici, a man of pronounced White and Ghibelline sympathies, who in July 1324 replaced his uncle as tyrant of Pistoia. In 1325 Fillippo delivered the lordship over Pistoia to Castruccio, receiving in exchange a reported 10,000 florins, the title and pay of the captain of the people, the hand of Castruccio's daughter, and a lasting reputation as a traitor.[45] The acquisition of Pistoia brought Castruccio to the height of his power, and made the vision of a unified Tuscan state under his command seem on the verge of realization.

The tenacious Florentines did not, however, abandon the struggle. Taking advantage of Castruccio's absence at Rome, they retook Pistoia (January 1328). Although the great lord of Lucca, rushing back to Tuscany, was able to recapture the town (August 1328), his own death on September 3 undid his labors and left Pistoia defenseless before the Florentine power. Peace was concluded between the two communes in 1329, at which time Pistoia was forced to surrender the southern third of the Monte Albano.[46] In 1331, authority over the city was surrendered to the Florentines for one year, and the grant was later regularly renewed.[47]

Between the death of Castruccio in 1328 and the overthrow of Walter of Brienne, Duke of Athens and tyrant of Florence, in 1343, Pistoia remained under Florentine hegemony. While allowing the Pistoiesi after 1331 to choose their own podestà, the Florentines insisted that the captain of the people (or, as he had by then been renamed, the "capitano della custodia") be a native of their own city. This assured them control of police authority within Pistoia, and meant that a faction hostile to their interests could not easily seize power over the commune. Since the captain also presented the proposals of the elders to the General Council for approval, this Florentine official had an implied right of veto over legislative enactments.

The overthrow of Walter of Brienne in 1343 again led to a brief

45. Ibid. III, 713–15 and 728–29.

46. *Capitoli*, I, no. 3, p. 5.

47. Ibid. I, no. 6, p. 8 (1331), and renewals in ibid. I, no. 7, p. 8 (1332), I, no. 9, p. 9 (1333), and I, no. 12, p. 12 (1335).

restoration of Pistoia's liberties, and brought a quick revival too of its bitter and damaging factional feuds. By 1350 Giovanni Panciatichi had emerged victorious from among the contenders, but this member of a traditionally Ghibelline family was not the person to reassure Florence of the city's continuing loyalty. Beyond the Apennines, the power of Giovanni Visconti, the Ghibelline bishop of Milan, loomed large, and the Florentines feared, not without reason, that Pistoia under Panciatichi rule might welcome a Visconti army from beyond the mountains. To preclude such a disaster, the Florentines seized the city (March 1351), in time to view from its walls the arrival of a frustrated Milanese army (July 1351).[48] Challenged by the power of a growing territorial state beyond the Apennines, Florence had little choice but to reorganize its own region in a similar fashion.

Florentine rule over Pistoia was permanent after 1351, and it falls rather clearly into two periods or phases. From 1351 to 1398, Pistoia continued to choose its own podestà, who was only once a Florentine, and this assured the city a large measure of autonomy. The agreement of 1351, by which authority over the city was conceded to the Florentines for an initial period of fifteen years, expressly guaranteed the liberty and autonomy of the town as long as it remained under a Guelf and popular regime.[49] But again, the captain had to be a Florentine, and this gave to Florence police authority within the city, power to prevent the establishment of unacceptable regimes, and a veto over unwelcome proposals. Further, the Florentines were accorded the right of garrisoning the strategic castles of Sambuca and Serravalle, and they also could maintain a small force within the city itself.

In later renewals of this agreement, Florentine authority was measurably strengthened. In 1373, as part of a general reform of the communal offices, the "captain of the mountains," the official responsible for the vast area of Pistoia's Apennines wherein lay the strategic passes to Lombardy, had also to be a Florentine, as well as the castellans at Sambuca and in the city itself.[50] To select them along with the capitano della custodia, the names of 200 "popular

48. M. Villani, *Cronica*, I, cap. 96 and 97 (I, 161–67).
49. *Capitoli*, I, no. 14, p. 11.
50. Ibid. I, no. 18, p. 13, 23 Nov. 1373.

and Guelf" Florentines were to be placed every two years in purses, and the purses kept at Florence where the drawings would be held. The reform expressly stipulated that proposals from the elders could not be taken before the General Council without the captain's agreement, confirming the right of veto of this Florentine official.

But as long as the podestà was not a Florentine, the entire area of civil justice, a large part of criminal justice, and the supervision of governmental operations escaped Florentine control. Collisions between the still autonomous local authorities and the new integrated bureaucracy of the Florentine state were inevitable. In 1397 an official of the Florentine captain was imprisoned by an agent of the podestà, and the enraged captain retaliated by having some of the podestà's officers beaten.[51] The following year, three ambassadors came from Florence to demand that in the interest of internal peace Pistoia's podestà should thereafter be a Florentine. After a tumultuous fifteen-hour session, the General Council submitted, and in 1399 the first of an unbroken line of Florentines assumed the office of podestà. This not only established Florentine control over civil justice and governmental operations, but it also turned Pistoia more firmly than ever toward the Arno city. The tradition of summoning podestà from Lombardy or Romagna had given Pistoia direct contact with these distant areas and lent a note of cosmopolitanism to its government. After 1399 Pistoia could look only to Florence for its great officers and for the decisions affecting its fate.

At the same time, Florentine influence and control over Pistoia's internal affairs, notably fiscal matters, was being noticeably strengthened. In the period of relatively loose Florentine rule, from 1351 to 1398, the Florentines directly imposed no taxes upon Pistoia and did not intervene in its fiscal affairs. Florence did, however, request subventions, both in money and in paid soldiers, and these were often substantial: 7000 pounds in 1354; 22,000 in 1375; 8000 in 1377; 70,000 in 1386; 45,500 in 1388; and 32,000 for three consecutive years from 1397.[52] This capricious and often chaotic system broke down completely shortly after the turn of the century. In

51. Salvi, *Historie*, II, 176.

52. ASP, Provv. Tomus 21, 45r, 6 Oct. 1354; ibid. Tomus 39, 38r, 8 April 1397; and Salvi, *Historie*, II, 135, 141, 161, 164.

1401–03, Pistoia was paralyzed by the civil war between the Cancellieri and Panciatichi, and was unable to meet payments of 1000 florins per month demanded of it. Commissioners at once set forth from Florence to investigate Pistoia's fiscal management. Surprise and shock awaited them. As Luca Dominici put it, the Florentines, after inspecting "all our revenues and expenses and tariffs and ordinances . . . found things so miserable that they marveled at them and could not believe it."[53] They therefore removed "all the revenues of the tariffs and all authority [from Pistoiese control], and thus [the men of Pistoia] were slowly reduced to slavery."[54] The commissioners proceeded to reform the entire constitution, incidentally changing the name of the board of elders from "anziani" to "priors," as the comparable officers were called at Florence. While the administration of indirect taxes was shortly returned to Pistoia's control, Florence forbade the introduction of any new direct taxes on the countryside and continued to exercise a close supervision over Pistoia's fiscal behavior.

The reigning fiscal chaos at Pistoia, the inability of the town to regulate its own taxes without provoking often violent opposition, may be considered steps in the preparation of that epoch-making fiscal reform: the introduction of the Catasto of 1427.[55] The Catasto brought the same methods of assessment, and an unfamiliar efficiency and justice, to all parts of the Florentine district, and achieved a real measure of fiscal integration, at least in regard to direct taxes. The fact that we know so much concerning Pistoia's population and economy in 1427 must be credited to the skill and care with which this great survey was accomplished.

With its two chief offices held by Florentines, with its other offices closely supervised, with a large part of its fiscal autonomy surrendered and matters of high policy removed from its consideration, Pistoia from the early fifteenth century was in large measure integrated within the new Florentine state. But it would be wrong to

53. Luca Dominici, *Cronache*, II, 60. "E volleno sapere tucte le nostre entrate et uscite et gabelle et statuti, et truovarono le cose si misere, se ne maravigliarono et non lo poteano credere."

54. Sozomenus, Specimen, p. 1174, "removendo ab eis omnes introitus gabellarum, et omnem auctoritatem . . . et sic ad servitutem paulatim redacti fuerunt." See also Luca Dominici, *Cronache*, II, 65–67 and 84–87 for the further reforms of April and May, 1402.

55. On the Catasto, see above, pp. 66–67.

imply that local offices had become powerless, and local political life moribund, with the extension of Florentine power. The Florentines themselves respected traditional forms, and to gain acceptance for their proposals in Pistoia's councils, they still dispatched "ambassadors" and presented formal requests. To the Pistoiesi themselves, the offices still open to them, in the salaries they drew and the patronage they commanded, offered a means of buttressing the fortunes of family and faction, at a time when commercial opportunities were few and uncertain. On a higher level, service to the commune, even a patriotic regard for its welfare, was still considered the duty and the honor of the best citizens. When Antonio Rospigliosi died in 1498, his family noted that the entire city grieved "for he was a worthy and a good man for his commune, defender always of his community; he was always found in the governments of our republic, alongside every other citizen."[56] Antonio did not consider service in this subject government nugatory, and his family and city honored him for it.

THE GROWTH OF STAFF

The changing character of communal government over these same centuries may be illustrated not only by considering the great offices and councils, but also by examining the numbers and training of the men who aided them, that group of professional administrators we are calling staff. The growth of a class of men, educated for, living by and committed to the art of government service is one of the most significant political and social developments in the period's history.

The Statutes of 1107 make provision for no staff at all. Some "custodes" of unstated number guarded the commune's forest of Ursinia, but there is not even indication that they were paid for their efforts.[57] It is hard to believe that the commune could have functioned without any professional help, but help, if it existed, attracted no attention from the redactors of these early statutes.

By about 1200, however, the commune, with a more expert direc-

56. *Richordi*, pp. 188–89. Antonio was described by his sons as "uno demgnio e uno buono huomo per il suo chomune, difensore sempre della sua chomunità, trovosi senpre in ne' ghoverni della nostra ripublicha apreso a omgni altro citadino."

57. *Statuit*, ed. Berlan, cap. XVII.

tor, the podestà, at its head, was likewise procuring more expert assistance. The podestà had his own staff, including two judges, one presiding over cases in Roman law and the other over cases in customary law.[58] Each received the then handsome salary of eight pounds per year—testimony to their professional skill. Two advocates were also employed to aid in the trials, "pro causis ventilandis" as say the statutes.[59] Two *castaldi* were in charge of criminal justice. The communal treasury was under the direction of two officials, although it is not clear how they divided their labors. One was called the "publicus camarlingus" and the other, somewhat mysteriously, the "camarlingus de foris." A "dominus" is mentioned as the podestà's representative at the castle of Serravalle and magistrates with undefined responsibilities were also serving at the rural villages of Cerbaia and Barga. A "treuganus" or special judge to arbitrate factional feuds, also appears, and he was further entrusted, with no evident logical consistency, with supervising the bakers and the wine salesmen.[60] In all, the podestà's staff, which was tantamount to the staff of the entire communal government, included fourteen persons, at least eight of whom (the two judges, two advocates, two castaldi and two notaries) required some professional training.

In one hundred years, the commune had moved a long way toward enlisting professional help in its administration. But its staff still seems minuscule when measured against the task of governing Pistoia's already considerable population and extensive territory. In fact the podestà had little choice but to requisition services from citizens, who received no pay and had no particular training for the tasks imposed on them.

This reliance on nonprofessional, unsalaried, part time and probably often reluctant citizen administrators is nowhere more apparent than in the communal system of tax collection. The podestà, without professional administrators to replace them anyway, for long continued to permit the great feudatories—the bishop and many nobles—to collect tolls and tariffs, although he did claim the right to review their administration and to receive accountings of

58. Ibid. cap. 36 and 130.
59. Ibid. cap. 185.
60. Ibid. cap. 42, 128 and 180.

their stewardship.[61] In drawing up surveys for the imposition of direct taxes, the communal government had to rely upon local "recitors" of hearths, who reported the number of homes in their communes and swore on the gospels that they told the truth.[62] In the surviving Book of Hearths, these "recitors" seem usually to have been the village priests, but the locally elected consul sometimes served or, in the absence of both, a simple "rusticus."[63] But the task of these amateur tax officials was not finished yet. On the basis of the hearths reported, the city government set a sum to be paid by the rural villages, but also insisted that the sum be distributed not by a flat charge levied against each household but proportionately according to relative wealth.[64] The rural communes had therefore to prepare their own local assessments, *libre* or *extima*, examples of which have survived.[65]

The disadvantages of this system seem evident enough. It cost the taxpayers themselves time in redacting their own assessments, and for the city the resulting tax distribution was probably often poorly remunerative and of dubious equity. Hostility to the communal government, common enough by the late thirteenth century, was apt to produce a nearly total breakdown in tax collections. Administrative difficulties were surely one reason why, by the early fourteenth century, the city abandoned entirely a direct tax on rural property, preferring the more easily administered tax on mouths.[66]

From the late thirteenth century, however, paralleling the emer-

61. Ibid. cap. 175, p. 114. All "qui habent passagium" had to swear "ut faciant . . . secum rationem de omnibus iis rebus, que ad eos pervenerint pro passagio vel guida."

62. See the regulations governing "recitors" in the *Statutum potestatis*, p. 217.

63. *Liber focorum*, p. 60, no. 150, "nescit presbiter an solvat cum civitate." Ibid. p. 164, "presbiter Iohannes de Plebe dixit istos esse pauperes. . . ." Ibid. p. 256, "consul renunciavit infra scriptos propter absentiam sacerdotis." Ibid. p. 255, "Non est presbiter. Venit rusticus et renuntiavit istos."

64. According to the Statutes of ca. 1200 (*Statuti*, ed. Berlan, cap. 67), the cost of the new city walls was to be imposed upon the "pauperi . . . tamquam pauperi et diviti tamquam diviti."

65. See above, pp. 180–81.

66. The effort to impose a direct tax had resulted in a rural uprising in 1303; see above, p. 208. At least by 1330, Pistoia had abandoned the direct tax on rural property; see the list of communal revenues given in ASP, Provv. Tomus 5, 11v. On the declining importance of the direct tax in the early fourteenth century, see Herlihy, "Direct Taxation," pp. 397–99.

gence of the popular commune and continuing even in the face of plagues and famines, a transformation occurred which was destined to alter radically the character of the communal government. That transformation was the professionalization of governmental service, the progressive replacement of unpaid, untrained and part time administrators by men educated for and largely living by government employment.

By 1296 the staff of the podestà had expanded to include four judges, instead of the former two.[67] All had to be "legistas expertos." One supervised criminal justice (replacing the castaldi), two judged civil cases, and one was placed "super dannis datis," "on damage caused." This last judge replaced the older treuganus, who in the Statutes of ca. 1200 did not have to be a legist. The number of notaries in the podestà's *familia* increased from two to twelve, and he also had the service of two knights, eight servants and a guard of twenty "beroarii."[68] The size of his staff, expanding from 14 to 46 persons, had more than tripled since the early thirteenth century, although the podestà's responsibilities had been considerably curtailed with the triumph of the popular commune.

The captain of the people, whose office did not exist in the early thirteenth century, also possessed a large and growing staff. In 1268, soon after he came to lead the commune, the captain was assisted by one knight, one judge and one notary; by 1286, his staff included one knight, two judges, two notaries and a guard of six—expanding, in other words, from three to eleven persons in less than twenty years.[69] His guard at least must have continued to grow, as the statutes stipulate that it should be no smaller than that of the podestà, which in 1296 numbered twenty.[70]

Another official with a growing staff was the "sindicus," who reviewed the administration of the podestà, captain and anziani after they left office, inspected their financial accounts and heard appeals from their judicial decisions. In the Statutes of ca. 1200, this important function was performed by three men, chosen in the general

67. *Statutum potestatis*, p. 8. Cf. the contemporary expansion of the corps of judges and notaries at Padua, given by Hyde, *Padua*, p. 49. In 1254, only 14 judges and 86 notaries could be found to take a solemn oath. Forty years later, there were at least 100 judges and probably 500 notaries in the city.

68. *Statutum potestatis*, pp. 9 and 54.

69. See the *Breve populi*, p. lxiv.

70. Ibid. p. 31.

assembly of the people ("in arringo"), who again had no particular training, went unpaid and had no staff.[71] By 1296 only a trained judge was eligible for the post, and because of its importance, only a foreigner could be appointed.[72] Two notaries and a guard of six assisted him.

The staff serving the elders or anziani also witnessed a considerable expansion. The elders of course needed a notary, and two chancellors also took minutes at Council meetings and carried on correspondence with foreign towns.[73] The tax system was administered by two treasurers, special officials in charge of the salt and wine monopolies, toll collectors at the gates, and notaries to assist all these officials. In the countryside too, government was growing. By 1296 ten rural podestà were holding office, all of whom probably needed some legal training and required the services of notaries.[74]

The number of men employed by the city in public services defies an exact count. By the late thirteenth century, a rudimentary fire department had been organized; it included the part time services of twenty men, masters in the art of wood and iron, whose primary tactic of fire fighting seems to have been to dismantle a burning building before the blaze could spread.[75] The statutes mention numerous guards stationed at the gates and bell tower or patrolling the quarters, night and day. One special contingent was to prevent men and women from making love in the cathedral of San Iacopo during the nights of the saint's uproarious festival in July; the task took ten men.[76] In all, the city guards numbered well over 200 men.

A good indication of the new character of communal government is its employment, by the late thirteenth century, of fully 100 *precones*, heralds or messengers.[77] Clearly, this was a regime based upon intensive communications and wide use of written instruments.

Table 31 summarizes the growth of professional staff in Pistoia's

71. *Statuti*, ed. Berlan, cap. 60.
72. *Statutum potestatis*, p. 76.
73. Ibid. p. 15.
74. Ibid. p. 17.
75. Ibid. p. 37.
76. Ibid. p. 35, "ut infra illam ecclesiam non fiant aliqua illicita vel conversio illicita maris et mulieris in prima nocte festivitatis predicte et in aliis sequentibus."
77. *Statutum potestatis*, p. 31.

government; it is hard to be exact about the figures, as some of the chapters in the statutes may have been superseded by later ones, but the direction of the trend still strongly emerges.

TABLE 31 The Growth of Staff in Communal Government

	1107	*ca. 1200*	*1284–96*
Judges	0	2	10
Notaries	0	2	35
Administrators	0	10	29
Captains	0	0	8
Totals	0	14	82

The table shows the number of paid officials mentioned in the Statutes of 1107, of ca. 1200, and in the *Breve populi* of 1284 and the *Statutum potestatis* of 1296. Guards and military personnel are excluded.

Another measure of this bureaucratic expansion is the increase in the salaries earned by the great officers. Initially the podestà, as a native, seems not to have been paid at all, but by the early thirteenth century he was given 35 pounds per year and gifts of food at Easter.[78] By 1267 his salary (from which his staff was also supported) had climbed steeply to 800 lire for his six-month term, and by 1296 it had again more than doubled (even though the coinage was deteriorating) to 2500 pounds.[79] By 1306 he was earning 3000 pounds for six months.[80] The captain enjoyed a similar boost in salary, reflecting both the increase in his staff and the better appreciation of his skills. He was paid 600 lire in 1267, and 2000 in 1306, again for a six-month term.[81] The sindicus, whose office was allocated no salary at all in the Statutes of ca. 1200, earned in 1284 500 pounds per year.[82]

Both the number of communal officials and the salary they received continued to grow in the early fourteenth century. In 1296 there were ten rural podestà, who were then drawing a combined salary of 180 pounds for six months.[83] In 1332 there were 30 such officers, and their salaries added up to 794 pounds for the same

78. *Statuti*, ed. Berlan, cap. 176.
79. *Breve populi*, p. xxv; *Statutum potestatis*, p. 7.
80. Salvi, *Historie*, I, 290.
81. *Breve populi*, p. 11; Salvi, *Historie*, I, 290.
82. *Breve populi*, p. 76.
83. *Statutum potestatis*, p. 17.

period. Their numbers and wages had tripled, in spite of a continuing deterioration of the money.[84] And it should be noted that this count of officials and of salaries takes no account of the numerous temporary commissions, which were becoming a characteristic part of communal government in the early fourteenth century.

The late thirteenth and early fourteenth centuries emerge as the period in which this growth of staff was most pronounced. The subsequent population crash seems to have slowed but it did not stay this bureaucratic expansion. In 1358 a single captain, the *capitaneus montanee superioris*, was appointed to govern the mountain communes, and this permitted a reduction in the number of rural podestà.[85] In 1373 there were only six such officers and by 1427 only three (serving at Tizzana, Montale and Larciano-Serravalle).[86] However, the staff even of these rural officials remained large. The podestà of Tizzana, for example, was served by a chancellor, treasurer, three counselors and an unstipulated number of soldiers and messengers.[87] The days when the rural communes were largely self-governing were ended.

Over these same years, the governmental staff within the city was growing in professional competence if not so dramatically in numbers. As described by Iacopo Maria Fioravanti, the staff of the podestà came eventually to consist of fourteen men—a decline in numbers from earlier years but an increase in technical proficiency, as all had to be university graduates, "dottori" or "avvocati."[88] The staff of the board of priors under Florentine rule included a *fiscale* or fiscal officer, an assessor who had to be "versato nella facoltà legale," the captain of the priors' guard, two managers (*operai*) of their palace, an administrator of food supplies (*grascia*), a chancellor presiding over the old tribunal "on damage caused," a master of ceremonies (*maestro di casa*), and 26 servants.

The government under Florentine hegemony came to include no less than 37 bureaus or magistracies, which administered among

84. ASP, Provv. Tomus 8, 24r, 18 Dec. 1332.

85. Fioravanti, *Memorie*, p. 16.

86. Six according to *Capitoli* I, no. 18, p. 13, 23 Nov. 1373, but only three at the time of the redaction of the Catasto of 1427.

87. The expenses of his administration are listed in ASF, Catasto 264, 389v.

88. The following reconstruction of the offices under Florentine administration is based on Fioravanti, *Memorie*, pp. 15 ff.

other activities the college (the Pia Casa di Sapienza, founded in 1473), rivers and streams, the Monte della Pietà or credit institution for the poor, public schools, health (il Magistrato sopra la Sanità) and the poor. Many of these responsibilities, such as those regarding education, health and the poor, had received only sporadic official attention before the plague; the creation of special offices to supervise them is a good example of the growing range of governmental interests, even in this small, subject city of from six to eight thousand people.[89]

This professionalization of communal administration has important implications in regard to other aspects of Pistoia's political and social history. To support so large a professional staff required abundant cash revenues and the complete conversion of the communal budget to a monetary basis. By the 1330s the city's budget was running about 36,000 pounds per year.[90] It remained at about the same levels one hundred years later. But as the population in the interim had fallen by more than two thirds, the amount of cash collected in taxes must have tripled on a per capita basis. At Florence over the same years, in spite of substantial population losses, the government enjoyed a continuous and considerable growth in cash revenues.[91] The ability to maintain and even increase monetary income in spite of huge population losses probably reflects a greater per capita productivity among the surviving taxpayers. But it seems also to indicate more skillful and remunerative fiscal management.

This administrative transformation was also made possible by, and in turn helped promote, the growth in numbers of educated, professional laymen, especially lawyers and notaries, within the community. At a time when business opportunities were restricted, the still expanding services of government offered Pistoia's young men attractive, honorable and rewarding careers.

The great increase in the professional civil service was not, to be sure, an unmixed blessing. It could only be supported by astro-

89. On education at Pistoia, see A. Zanelli, *Del Pubblico insegnamento in Pistoia dal XIV al XVI secolo* (Rome, 1900).

90. For the sources of the estimate, see Herlihy, "Direct Taxation," pp. 387–88.

91. Ibid. pp. 403–05, giving the bi-monthly accountings of the Florentine communal treasurers from 1240.

nomic tax levels, which helped slow if not stifle vigorous economic development. Moreover, as we have seen, competition for office was a major, and perhaps the most important, cause of factional disputes within the commune.[92] The violence of these feuds is itself a measure of the extent to which Pistoia's great families had become dependent on patronage for the support of their fortunes.

At the same time, it would be difficult to appreciate the lay culture of the Renaissance without recognizing the influence exerted upon it by these men "nourished," as Flavio Biondo put it, "by civil office."[93] That influence the following chapter will examine.

92. See above, p. 203.
93. See above, introduction, n. 16.

10

Directions of Cultural Change

I should like to live a while longer, to do a little good—for of harm I have done a great deal.

—Francesco di Marco Datini, merchant of Prato, 1396

Pistoia was not a major center of artistic and literary production in the Renaissance, although many of its monuments, such as the great silver altar of San Iacopo dating from the fourteenth century or the Ospedale del Ceppo well merit attention. It was also the homeland of Cino da Pistoia, renowned jurist and gifted poet, one of the first masters of the *dolce stil nuovo*.[1] Even the humanist chancellor of Florence, Coluccio Salutati, might by extended courtesy be considered a Pistoiese, as his birthplace, Stignano in the Val di Nievole, is today part of Pistoia's province, although it lay just beyond its boundaries in the fourteenth century. But while poor in major figures, Pistoia did produce a fair number of minor writers, who helped support and enlarge the humanist movement. A consideration of their careers should add to our knowledge of the social, economic and professional strata for which the new humanistic learning exerted the strongest appeal.

But perhaps the chief value of Pistoia's sources is the opportunity they offer to study Renaissance culture in its more popular manifestations, specifically in the religious life and in the secular interests of the people. The new directions evident in the period's popular culture were not without paralells with and influences upon even the most elevated expressions of Renaissance art and letters.

1. See below, p. 261.

CIVIC CHRISTIANITY

The extent and importance of religious influences upon Renaissance culture have in recent years attracted considerable attention, although research has perhaps been too narrowly concentrated upon segregating and balancing critical or sympathetic comments upon religion in the writings of the great humanists.[2] Much more attention needs to be paid to the varying forms of devotional exercise and to the changing ideas and styles of sanctity illuminated by them. It is here, on the level of religious practice, that the sources of a small town like Pistoia can make the most valuable contribution.

By the early fifteenth century, the Church at Pistoia was beset by multiple difficulties, which gravely hampered it in the fulfillment of its pastoral mission. Not the least among its troubles were economic problems, and the Catasto of Church property (1428) leaves little doubt that the ecclesiastical endowment was in a sorry state.[3]

To be sure, the portion of the soil owned by the Church was large—between 15 and 20 per cent of the total—and apparently even expanding. But revenues remained poorly distributed among the individual churches and religious corporations. Most churches and even some monasteries had only modest possessions, while the urban hospitals, as we shall see, controlled the greatest part of the ecclesiastical endowment. The churches, as small landowners generally, had suffered from the declining rent levels following the Black Death. Moreover, many of these ecclesiastical revenues were in the form of perpetual rents, as these did not require close managerial supervision, which could be a distraction from religious duties. But perpetual rents, usually placed upon mediocre soils, were especially vulnerable to population shrinkage, as rent payers disappeared with no one to replace them. The descriptions of ecclesiastical properties overflow with comments like the following: "[This rent] has not been had for more than ten years. . . . They are dead

2. On the place of religion in the Renaissance, see the excellent survey by C. Angeleri, *Il Problema religioso del Rinascimento. Storia della critica e bibliografia. Introduzione di E. Garin* (Florence, 1952).

3. ASF, Catasto 189, contains the survey of ecclesiastical property for the diocese of Pistoia, including Prato.

the men who answered for it."[4] "For twenty years it has not been given."[5] And like other landlords, the clerical owners had difficulty finding workers to farm their lands. One ecclesiastic reported that a house in San Quirico would cost 24 florins to repair, but the investment would be lost, "because it is a deserted place."[6] Another complained that he could lease his land only if he advanced substantial loans to "guastatori" who were more interested in the loan than in the property.[7]

The fiscal policies of the secular government also injured the ecclesiastical endowment. In 1282 the popular commune had abolished the compulsory tithe, still an important support for parish churches.[8] When the bishop protested, it was even proposed in the communal council that a strike, a sort of anti-interdict, be organized against the clergy; no one should sell priests wine or cut their beards.[9] But more serious still was the crushing burden in taxes which, by the early fifteenth century, the Florentine state was demanding from Church lands. One cleric remarked in his tax declaration of 1428 that over the last twenty years his church had helped meet imposts upon the clergy to the sums of 30,000, 25,000, 100,000, and 80,000 florins.[10]

Both in the city and countryside, many churches were in ruins in 1428. The rector of San Giusto in the city declared that with a tax of seven florins imposed upon him out of the 35,000 demanded from the clergy, "never had a greater injury been done and the church is falling to earth."[11] San Vitale, also in the city, similarly threatened collapse, although the parish, with 109 families, was one of the

4. Ibid. 417r, "più di anni dice non se auto . . . sono morti gli uomeni che rispondeano."

5. Loc. cit. "Da anni xx non ce la dato."

6. Ibid. 175v, "ghostami fiorini xxiiii e di più per aconciare la casa . . . e sia perduta perchè è luogo solitario."

7. Ibid. 172v, "Dubito in fine non me convegn' lassarla guastare e s'io la volessi allogare me ne chiesto di prestanza fiorini da guastatori che anno di bisogno de la prestanza e non de la vigna."

8. *Breve populi*, p. 111.

9. Ibid. pp. 114–15. Compare the similar troubles over the compulsory tithe and the strike against the clergy at Reggio in 1280, Salimbene, *Cronica*, II, 207.

10. ASF, Catasto 189, 757r, declaration of the property of Santa Maria da Santomato, pieve of Vigliana.

11. Ibid. 508r, "Non si fa mai maggiore ingiuria ella chiesa chade in terra."

city's largest.[12] Urban monasteries, particularly the convents, were also in miserable straits. Three of them—San Mercoriale, Santa Lucia and San Desidero—had to ask for mercy from the tax officials.[13] The rural churches present, if anything, an even more somber picture. "Because of taxes" the church of the castle of Sambuca had been abandoned and left to decay, "for [the priest] does not have [anything] with which to live."[14] The church of San Niccolaio at Vergiole was similarly "chaduta e disfatta."[15] No less than four churches in the pieve of Santa Maria a Limite were described as ruined and without a resident priest.[16]

But in spite of the fiscal difficulties confronting the parish churches and monasteries, the great ecclesiastical offices still offered attractive livings, and not surprisingly, the same intense competition for office, the "gara d'uffizi" which disturbed communal politics also waged around ecclesiastical appointments. In 1428 the bishop of Pistoia was Ubertino degli Albizzi, from a prominent Florentine family; among his eight canons was Tommaso di Tommaso di Soldo degli Strozzi, from another great Florentine house, and Andrea di Iacopo Fioravanti, from a prominent local family. With shrunken revenues, however, suitable salaries for these great officials could be assured only through the simultaneous holding of several benefices and livings, through a "pluralism" technically forbidden by church law. Canon Fioravanti, besides the prebend provided from his canonry, held four other benefices in the city and countryside.[17] Canon Tommaso Strozzi was also piovano or presiding priest at Carmignano and held the same office at the distant pieve of Santa Maria a Piteccio in the mountains.[18] Messer Tommaso did try to gain tax relief for the mountain village: "You see this poor pieve . . . ," he told the assessors, "let it have mercy for the love of God for it is poor and poor also are its people." But it is hard to

12. Ibid. 782r, Opera di Santo Vitali, "La detta opera a di bisognio che sia aiutata dalle persone del popolo e se non chaderebbe tosto la chiesa perchè non si potrebbe mantenere."

13. Ibid. 47r, 595r and 620r.

14. Ibid. 891v, "Per le gravezze de' sopradetti la detta chiesa chade. Non vi sta prete perchè non a di che vivere."

15. Ibid. 796r.

16. Ibid. 838r.

17. Ibid. 81r.

18. Ibid. 480r.

believe that his mountain flock saw much of their pastor. Many of these rural churches, which were technically held by urban clergy or which were too poor anyway to support a priest, were served only by chaplains, who visited them once a week and left the people for most of the time without religious direction or solace.[19]

The chaotic state of the ecclesiastical endowment and the maldistribution of ecclesiastical revenues between the great clerics and the priests who served the people inevitably compromised the pastoral and spiritual life of the church. Many of the lower clergy lived on the edge of poverty. A priest in the Estimario of 1415 had to beg for mercy, describing himself as "povero che e sanza beneficio e salaro."[20] Even the number of priests seems to have been woefully inadequate to meet the spiritual needs of the people. The surveyors in 1428 took declarations from only fourteen secular priests, not even enough to staff all the city's 29 parishes. This number did not include the religious clergy or priests without benefices, but the latter group at least was probably not numerous. An acute shortage of parochial clergy seems also to have added to the Church's troubles.

Moreover, the great ecclesiastics, often careerist and spiritually lukewarm men, were not always distinguished by edifying lives. In 1416 Pistoia's Council of Priors felt compelled to protest to the commune of Florence concerning the behavior of their bishop Matteo, then absent from the city attending the Council of Constance.[21] He was accused of visiting a convent, and soliciting the nuns to join him in "illicito coitu."[22] He had also allegedly kept a concubine and raised several daughters, one of whom was married and living in the city—all this to the scandal of the faithful.

These then were the chief troubles of the Church at Pistoia in the fifteenth century: a poorly remunerated and apparently numerically

19. Cf. ibid. 803r, church of Santa Maria del Ceretto, "per uno capellano una volta la settimana lire 15." Canon Tommaso Strozzi similarly paid a chaplain 20 staia of wheat per year for similar services.

20. Estimario, no. 78 of the parish of San Paolo, prete Iacopo di Paolo Braccini.

21. The letter directed to the priors of Florence is printed in F. A. Zaccaria, *Bibliotheca pistoriensis* (Turin, 1752), p. 31.

22. Loc. cit. "dum episcopus sub visitationis umbra pergit ad monasterium, temptavit quamplures moniales de illicito coitu requirere."

inadequate lower clergy, a careerist hierarchy often marred by unedifying lives, and a faithful whose pastoral needs were often poorly fulfilled.

But in spite of the institutional chaos, the piety of the people remained authentic and fervent. The researcher encounters it in unexpected places. In the midst of tax declarations, usually dry as dust, a citizen may add a note of gratitude to God, the spirit of which cannot be mistaken:

> I find [declared the wool merchant Antonio di Michele in 1415] of my own stock and capital from good [debts], subtracting all old and bad debts from two years and older and subtracting loans to workers as the statutes say, 2000 pounds or thereabouts, for which I thank God as much as I am able, for from Him, I recognize, comes this and every good.[23]

And the researcher encounters it in unexpected dimensions, as with the movement known as the "Grand Company of the Whites," presently to be discussed. The argument could even be made that religious piety was more intense, or at least more manifest, in the fifteenth century than it had been in the thirteenth.[24]

This piety of the fifteenth century, however, had its own characteristic tone, much different from that of the preceding Middle Ages. Piety of course, as a mood and expression of the spirit, cannot be measured statistically. But some of its social results can be, specifically by noting the kinds of religious institutions and activities favored by the faithful in their donations and bequests. We can, in other words, compare the distribution of ecclesiastical wealth in the fifteenth century with that of an earlier period, to discern what kind of religious work the age had come to favor.

Fortunately, we have suitable sources for such a comparison. In 1276–77 and again in 1296–97, the churches, monasteries and hospitals of Pistoia were subjected to a papal tithe, and the record of

23. Estimario, no. 6 of parish of S. Maria fuor le Porte. "Truovo di mio proprio ceppo e capitale di buoni trattone tutte credenze vechie e cattive da due anni a drieto e trattone prestanze di lavoratori come diceno i capitoli lire dumilla o quasi della quale cosa ringrazio idio quanto posso perchè dal lui ricognosco questo e ogni bene."

24. For "trufatoribus et illusoribus" in thirteenth-century society, who made fun of religious piety and practices, see Salimbene, *Cronica,* I, 107 et passim.

their payments has survived.[25] The size of the tithe collected gives a rough idea of the relative wealth of churches and religious institutions in the thirteenth century. It would of course be wrong to assume that payments were exactly proportionate to endowment, but it remains true that the tithes do allow a just if crude differentiation between large and small ecclesiastical establishments, and this rough differentiation is all our comparison really requires. To judge relative wealth among ecclesiastical institutions in the fifteenth century, the Catasto of ecclesiastical property of 1428 is similarly serviceable, and even more accurate. Here again, the figures of revenues and expenses we calculate from it cannot be considered entirely exact; there are doubtless many omissions, and the total figures are much affected by the values assigned to revenues stated in agricultural products, which are difficult to determine. But here too, a reliable picture of the relative wealth of religious corporations emerges, and this is all that is needed in our comparison.

Table 32 lists the ten richest ecclesiastical institutions in 1276–77 and 1296–97.

Between 1276–77 and 1296–97, the order of relative wealth, in so far as we can judge it with some omissions in the later tithe, changed only slightly; the episcopate, fourth in 1276–77, rose to second position later in the century. The table shows quite clearly that in the thirteenth century, the great tithe payers, and presumably the great owners of property, were the canons, the bishop and the old Benedictine monasteries. Particularly to be noted is the absence from this group of wealthy landlords of any hospitals or religious companies.

By the early fifteenth century, the distribution of ecclesiastical wealth had become vastly different, as table 33 illustrates.

The years between 1276–77 and 1428 thus witnessed a remarkable growth in the relative wealth of hospitals and of the Opera di San Iacopo, the peculiar functions of which shall presently be described. The hospital of the Ceppo did not even exist in 1276; according to Salvi, it was founded about 1277 by Antimo di Teodoro and his wife Bandella.[26] By 1428 not only was it the richest of all Pistoia's

25. Published in the two volumes of *Tuscia.*
26. *Historie,* I, 228.

TABLE 32 Relative Wealth of Religious Institutions at Pistoia, 1276–77 and 1296–97

	1276–77			*1296–97*		
	Institution	*No.*	*Payment*	*Institution*	*No.*	*Payment*
(1)	Canonica	1156	92	Canonica	1262	46
(2)	Mon. S. Bartolomei de Pistoia	1162	72	Episcopatus	1248*	45
(3)	Mon. S. Maria de Pacciana	1146	66	(Mon. S. Bartholomei de Pistoia	1264	non solvit)
(4)	Episcopatus	1143*	50	Mon. S. Maria de Pacciana	1251*	35
(5)	Mon. S. Salvatoris vallis Agne	1335	45	Mon. S. Salvatoris vallis Agne	1461	23
(6)	Mon. S. Barunti	1361	40	Mon. S. Barunti	1488	20
(7)	Mon. S. Michelis de Forcole	1144*	40	(Mon. S. Michelis de Forcole	1249	non solvit)
(8)	Plebes S. Iohannis de Villiana	1328	37	Plebes S. Iohannis de Villiana	1454	18
(9)	Plebes S. Michaelis de Carmignano	1247	24	Plebes S. Michaelis de Carmignano	1371	12
(10)	Mon. S. Salvatoris Fontane Taonis	1147*	23	Mon. S. Salvatoris Fontane Taonis	1252*	12

* technically exempt

The table shows relative wealth only for religious institutions within Pistoia's district. Those of Prato, while part of the diocese, are not included. "No." refers to the number of the entry in *Tuscia* reporting the tithe collected. Payments are rounded to the nearest pound.

TABLE 33 Relative Wealth of Religious Institutions at Pistoia, 1428 (in pounds per year)

	Institution	*Approx. Income*	*Approx. Expenses*
(1)	Ospedale di S. Maria de' Poveri del Ceppo	3354	5454
(2)	Opera di San Iacopo	2029	3678
(3)	Vescovado	1981	2636
(4)	Spedale della Misericordia di S. Gregorio di Pistoia	1550	1394
(5)	Badia di S. Bartolomeo di Pistoia	1312	434
(6)	Canonica	1069	1768
(7)	Fratri humiliati	813	844
(8)	Monastero di S. Lucia	498	
(9)	Fratri di San Lorenzo dell' Ordine di S. Francesco	358	
(10)	Compagnia della Trinità de' Preti	350	198

Source: ASF, Catasto 189.

religious corporations, but also its budget was nearly twice the size of the bishop's. The Hospital of St. Gregory had by the same time surpassed all the older monasteries in wealth. Hospitals were increasing in number as well as wealth; there were eleven in 1428, more than twice the number (four) listed in the tithe of 1276–77 for the district of Pistoia. Besides these hospitals there were nine religious companies or "disciplines," most of which included laymen as well as ecclesiastics and which also assumed numerous charitable functions.

Pistoia, a town of only 4500 in 1428, was spending what seems an extraordinary amount of money in works of public charity. The hospitals and religious companies aided the sick of course, but they also helped orphans, the insane, the homeless, the poor and girls without sufficient dowry to marry.

For the sick, the Hospital of the Ceppo alone maintained 70 beds, and supported usually 25 persons permanently infirm.[27] It spent 600 pounds per year on "medicine and sugar" for the sick, 500 pounds on wheat, 300 on wine, and 50 pounds just for the purchase of barley to make aquavita. The Hospital's professional staff included two physicians, eight nurses (four male and four female) as well as several other servants, attendants and messengers. The Hospital of St. Gregory had 33 beds for the old and insane, and took care of 17 persons permanently sick.[28] The other hospitals were smaller, with about 10 beds each.[29] In rough estimate, there were over 200 beds available to the sick and aged in this tiny town of 4500.

Distributions of food and clothing to the poor were also a common and expensive activity of these hospitals. The Hospital of the Ceppo gave a meal of bread, wine and meat to all the poor who presented themselves on the feast of All Saints (1 November) and on Holy Thursday, and the same meal to prisoners on the Sunday within the octave of the Assumption (15 August). Every week, on

27. The information on the services performed by the hospital of the Ceppo is based on its tax declaration in ASF, Catasto 189, 81r and ff.

28. Ibid. 162r and ff.

29. The Hospital of Sant'Antonio in Porta Lucchese (ibid. 863r) kept 10 beds. The Spedale di Santo Spirito al Ponte della Brana spent yearly 50 pounds on maintaining its beds, which, in comparison with what other hospitals spent, must have numbered about 10, ASF, Catasto 189, 604r.

Monday, Wednesday and Thursday, six ounces of meat, two pieces of bread and a glass of wine was sent to the "poveri vergognosi" of the city—those too ashamed to present themselves publicly. Every Monday morning, all paupers who came received a piece of bread, and were similarly fed on the vigils of six feasts; wine was added to the meals in August. The smaller hospitals made comparable distributions of food and clothing to the poor, in keeping with their resources, as did many of the religious companies.

Poor girls were not forgotten, and the Hospital of the Ceppo contributed 100 pounds per year to their dowries; the opera di San Iacopo gave another 200.

This amazing growth in the wealth of hospitals between the thirteenth and fifteenth centuries was made possible only by the donations and bequests of the faithful. It therefore suggests a new direction in Christian piety, a new form and tone in the expression of Christian sanctity. The practice of charity, to be sure, is a virtue that has always been required of the good Christian. It seems not unfair to remark, however, that for most of the Middle Ages charity was largely considered a secondary goal and fruit in the pursuit of holiness. The monks were to welcome the sick and the homeless, but not to go out to seek them. The worship of God and contemplation of His works, the atonement of sins, were the foundations of medieval piety, from which all virtues, including charity, would flow.

The medieval, Christian stress on contemplation, asceticism and penance seems to have lost ground in the fourteenth century before a new, charitable and social emphasis in religious practice. To the hundreds of people who showered their wealth upon these hospitals rather than upon monasteries or even churches, Christian piety seemed primarily to impose a pressing responsibility for the socially disadvantaged, and made necessary an active effort to alleviate at least some of their sufferings. Francesco di Marco Datini, the rich merchant of Prato, while urged to give his wealth to a monastery, chose rather to endow a hospital, and the choice was characteristic of his age.[30]

It is not too much to say that the great novelty in the religious spirit of the fourteenth and fifteenth centuries was a more sensitive

30. Iris Origo, *The Merchant of Prato: Francesco di Marco Datini* (London, 1957), p. 321.

moral and social consciousness, a new awareness of the responsibility of the Christian in regard to the present world and its troubles. The spirit which built and enriched these hospitals, reflecting an active involvement with human society and a greater compassion for its ills, we may justly call "civic Christianity."

Another movement also reflects the intense religious devotion of the age: the "Grand Company of the Whites." While many areas of Italy were affected by it, one of the most detailed accounts of the movement has been left by a chronicler of Pistoia, ser Luca Dominici.[31]

According to ser Luca's account, the company was first formed in Dauphiné in southern France in 1399 (other chroniclers place its origins in England, Scotland or Spain).[32] A peasant, having just finished his midday meal, was approached by a noble young man, who asked for some of his bread. The peasant replied that he had eaten all he possessed, but when ordered to look again, he found three pieces, which he knew had been miraculously produced. The young man then told him to throw the three pieces into a nearby stream, which was also produced by a miracle. But as he sought to do so, a weeping lady, dressed in white, asked him to refrain, but on the insistence of the young man, he threw the first piece into the water. The weeping lady then made known her identity. She was the Virgin, and the noble youth was Christ, who was intent on destroying the world for its sins. The casting of the one piece of bread into the stream meant that one third of mankind would die; if the remaining two were also thrown, the entire human race would perish.

The peasant then pleaded with the Virgin to tell him what might be done to avert this dreadful fate. She told him that he should go from city to city and from village to village throughout Christendom, preaching that all men, women and children, clerics and laymen alike, should dress in white linen garments inscribed with a crimson cross. They should then go on pilgrimage for nine days,

31. "Cronaca della venuta dei Bianchi," *Cronache*, I, 49–228. The Whites are, however, mentioned in numerous chronicles of the period. See the references collected by G. Gigliotti in Luca Dominici, *Cronache*, I, 50, n. 2. On the character of the movement, see G. M. Monti, *Le Confraternite medievali dell'alta e media Italia* (Venice, 1927) I, 289–92.

32. *Cronache*, I, 50–57.

during which time they were not to change their white garments, sleep in beds or remain at night within a walled town. As they marched from city to city they were to beat themselves and chant: "mercy, mercy, mercy, peace, peace, peace." If this was done, Christ might revoke his terrible sentence against mankind, or at least against those who participated in this pilgrimage of Whites.

The peasant at once gathered eighteen followers and went to preach this saving message. At Genoa, the first city in Italy to hear of the movement, more than 20,000 participated in the pilgrimage, and peace was restored among the warring families of the countryside, where men, fighting like beasts, had killed up to then, according to ser Luca, 10,000 persons. In August 1399 the first pilgrims arrived at Lucca, their procession accompanied by many miracles. On Sunday, August 10, the Grand Company set forth from Lucca, and on the following Tuesday evening they arrived at Pistoia. Ser Luca, who had a taste for figures, put their number at 1700 and noted that they were everywhere received with enthusiasm, by the peasants who gave them food and by the city folk who took to heart their message of pity and peace. The company, never inclined, it seems, in its exhilarated mood to linger in the work of saving the world, moved on the next day to Prato, where, incidentally, the rich merchant, Francesco di Marco Datini, joined their number.[33] By the time the company approached Florence, it included perhaps 5000 persons.

At Pistoia, in the enthusiasm of this moment, an "infinite" number of reconciliations were struck among the city's long-warring families and factions, giving substance to the pilgrims' cry for peace.[34] Their cry for pity too was not without effect. Pistoia's supreme council permitted the return, under lenient terms, of banished criminals and debtors, gave amnesty to prisoners and borrowed 100

33. Origo, *Merchant of Prato*, pp. 316–20. Francesco carefully kept an account of the expenses he incurred while on pilgrimage, which has been published in C. Guasti, *Lettere di un notaio ad un mercante del secolo XIV*, I (Florence, 1880), pp. xcix–ciii.

34. Luca Dominici, *Cronache*, I, 67–71. Luca expressly describes by the names of the families involved 16 reconciliations, and adds "e così infinite paci, le quali non potrei dire, nè contare. . . ." Four special officials, called Paciali, were elected by the commune to arrange for these agreements, and their work progressed "miracolosamente."

pounds for distribution among the poorer pilgrims. When all these charitable acts were carried unanimously, the Florentine captain, Andrea di Neri de' Vittori, fell to his knees and began to cry "peace and mercy." The entire council took up the chant, and their voices, says ser Luca, were heard through half the city.[35]

It is easy to be cynical about the results of such religious movements. Two years later, hardly before the memory of the Whites and their message of pity and peace could have died in people's hearts, Pistoia was rent with the most violent factional battle it had ever experienced. "The Whites went out who are now turned black," remarked Luca Dominici.[36] But it would be hard to deny that the pilgrimage of the Whites gave expression both to the devotion and to the spiritual aspirations of the people.

Such outpourings of religious enthusiasm were of course not without precedent in Italian religious and social history. In the thirteenth century, several movements of comparable dimensions had occurred. In 1233, the movement known as the "great alleluia" had swept through Italy's cities—so named from the shouted response which great throngs gave to fiery preachers, exhorting them to show their honor for God.[37] In 1260 there had similarly spread the "devotio verberatorum," the "devotion of the flagellants"; under its inspiration, even great officials ran through the streets of Italy's towns, beating themselves to the point of drawing blood, in retribution for their sins.[38]

Less massive by measure of public participation, but still indicative of religious mood, was the movement organized at Vercelli and Novara by Fra Dolcino, a leader of the sect known as the *Fratelli Apostolici,* whom Dante was to place in hell.[39] With a community of perhaps 3000 persons (mostly rural folk and mountaineers

35. Ibid. I, 73, "e così tutto il Consiglio a uno grido unitamente fece che s'udi per mezzo Pistoia."

36. Ibid. II, 37. "A dì XVII d'ogosto, mezedima, in qual simile di XVII d'ogosto, ora è due anni, andorono fuori i bianchi che ora sono facti neri."

37. Salimbene, *Cronica,* I, 98–107. On the religious movements described in Salimbene's chronicle, see H. Hefele, *Die Bettelorden und das religiöse Volksleben Ober— und Mittelitaliens im XIII. Jahrhundert* (Leipzig and Berlin, 1910).

38. Salimbene, *Cronica,* II, 146–48.

39. *Inferno,* xxviii, 55. On Dolcino, see most recently E. Anagnini, *Dolcino e il movimento ereticale all' inizio del Trecento* (Florence, 1964).

according to Villani) who recognized neither property nor marriage and who lived their "beastly" lives (the term is Villani's) for two years in the mountains, Fra Dolcino defied the papal crusaders sent against him.[40] But cold and hunger tempered their enthusiasm, and Dolcino surrendered on March 26, 1307, to end his brief career at the stake. Then in 1310, beginning in Piedmont and spreading throughout Lombardy, Liguria, Tuscany and all Italy, new bands of *gente minuta*, common people, had marched.[41] Uncounted numbers of men, women and children, says Villani, left their occupations and went flagellating themselves from town to town, crying for mercy (Florence, however, refused to admit them). In their wake much devotion was kindled and many reconciliations inspired. The year 1349 was also one of marching religious bands, clearly moved to acts of penitence by the great mortalities of 1348.[42]

The Grand Company of the Whites, while closely resembling these earlier movements, also shows some differences from them. The great alleluia of 1233, while resulting in a temporary restoration of peace among some warring communes, had little social content and message. The "devotion of the flagellants" of 1260 was a pilgrimage of expiation, typically medieval, primarily intended to bring the people to penitence. Fra Dolcino's unhappy experiment with a millenary society also bears little resemblance with the company of the Whites, who seem to have had no expectations of an imminent, total renewal of society and who counted many rich in their numbers. The Grand Company most closely resembles the bands of *gente minuta*, which in 1310 had marched through Italy's cities, beating themselves and crying for mercy and peace; but it differs too in that it was not primarily a pilgrimage of expiation. The pilgrims were, to be sure, to dress after the manner of the *Battuti* or flagellants, and beat themselves. But ser Luca and other chroniclers hardly mention acts of expiation in their accounts of the movement. They are concerned to record the reconciliations achieved and the numerous acts of charity performed in its wake, by individuals and governments alike. The mood and style of piety was shifting, subtly

40. G. Villani, *Cronica*, VIII, cap. 84 (III, 161).
41. Ibid. VIII, cap. 121 (III, 200).
42. In October 1349 Pope Clement VI forbade the formation of these associations of flagellants; see Monti, *Confraternite*, I, 289.

but distinctively, away from the older emphasis on penance and expiation. Into prominence had come the plea for the alleviation of the notorious and scandalous failings of contemporary society: its cruelty, heartlessness and violence.

This new human and humane involvement in civic society was not the only novelty in fifteenth-century religious practice. Somewhat paradoxically, it developed side by side with a new taste for splendor in the Church's liturgical life.

At Pistoia, another quasi-ecclesiastical institution which grew remarkably in wealth after the Black Death, surpassing even the episcopal see in endowment, was the Opera di San Iacopo. By 1428 it was, to be sure, already a venerable institution. Pistoia was the center of an ancient cult of San Iacopo, the apostle St. James the Greater, although the origins of this devotion remain somewhat obscure. According to Salvi, the intercession of the saint had protected the city from a Saracen invasion in 866; one of the churches within the old circle of walls was San Iacopo in Castellare, showing that the saint had indeed been honored at Pistoia since early in the Middle Ages.[43] This devotion to St. James brought the city into close and intimate contact with the apostle's great western shrine at Santiago de Compostela in Spain. Atto, the saintly bishop of Pistoia in the first half of the twelfth century, was a Spaniard born at Badajoz; one of his great services to the city was the securing of a relic of the body of St. James from Santiago, which he enshrined in the cathedral. This relic, as the church's and city's most precious possession, became the nucleus of a treasury, and in 1174 an "opera" or special magistracy was established to maintain the chapel and guard its treasure. According to the *Breve populi,* two operai were responsible for it.[44] They could not be required to accept any other communal office while serving the chapel, and were excused from marching with the communal army. But because they guarded a treasury, they had to leave with the podestà a bond to guarantee their honesty. By the late thirteenth century, the operai had the help of two guards to protect the treasury, into which the commune was

43. *Historie,* I, 31. On the history of the Opera, see A. Chiappelli, "Storia e costumanze delle antiche feste patronali di San Iacopo in Pistoia," *BSP,* 21 (1919), 1–34; 65–95; and 157–86.

44. *Breve populi,* p. 68.

also placing its precious possessions and important records. The Opera di San Iacopo thus came to form a kind of adjunct to the communal treasury, and the operai were frequently ordered by the commune to expend funds for civic purposes, as, for example, the purchase of grain or meat in years of shortages.[45] By 1428 they were also supporting numerous charitable activities, giving money to girls for their dowries (200 pounds per year), helping support poor students studying away from home (84 pounds), distributing clothes among the poor (400 pounds), and aiding pilgrims who were going "all the year" to Compostela (100 pounds).[46]

But the chief duties of the operai were liturgical and ceremonial. They had to maintain and embellish the chapel of San Iacopo, pay for the liturgical services performed there, and arrange for the great celebration of the feast of St. James in July.

The considerable growth in the income and expenses of the Opera in the late Middle Ages is thus primarily indicative of the increasing demand for splendor and magnificence in the chapel and the ceremonies through which the saint was honored. In the tithe of 1276–77, the Opera paid only 12 pounds, not a fourth of the bishop's assessment (50 pounds).[47] But the Opera's income grew rapidly in the fourteenth century, in spite of the period's economic difficulties. In 1329 its revenue was more than a thousand pounds, and 25 years later it was about 517 florins (1750 pounds).[48] In 1395, the bishop of Pistoia, Andrea Franchi, won from the pope a permanent indulgence attached to the chapel, and this helped bring an accelerated growth in the Opera's wealth.[49] By 1428, according to the Catasto, its revenue amounted to over 2000 pounds, although some rents were certainly omitted and the figure we have used to estimate the worth of wheat payments—15 solidi per staio—may be too conservative. Chiappelli says that by 1433 the Opera's total income probably reached 8000 pounds, and the endowment continued to expand through the fifteenth and into the sixteenth centuries.[50]

45. See above, p. 127.
46. ASF, Catasto, 189, 153r, "Spese e incharichi sopra detti beni."
47. *Tuscia*, I, nos. 1190 and 1143.
48. Chiappelli, "Storia," *BSP*, 21 (1919), 5.
49. Loc. cit.
50. Ibid. p. 6. Toward the end of the sixteenth century, the income of the Opera reached 7000 staia of wheat, 200 staia of millet and 200 scudi every

The Opera at the same time was spending substantial sums to enhance the majesty and magnificence of the chapel and ceremonies honoring St. James. Over these years (between 1287 and 1399 according to Salvi), the great silver altar of San Iacopo, still one of the city's artistic masterpieces, was constructed—an amazing accomplishment at a time when Pistoia's citizens, individually and in community, were desperate for money.[51] To illuminate the chapel and, during the saint's festival, the entire cathedral in a great *luminaria* held since the thirteenth century, the Opera spent yearly no less than 100 pounds on wax, importing it from North Africa, Spain, Corsica, the Adriatic and the Byzantine Empire.[52]

The feast of St. James (25 July) was also Pistoia's great holiday; public celebrations are first mentioned in 1213. By 1296 the mood was so festive that ten guards, as we have mentioned, had to protect the cathedral for the entire week from vigil to octave, to prevent couples from making love in the shadows.[53] The celebrations grew in lavishness in the fourteenth and fifteenth centuries. By 1428 the Opera was spending on the feast almost 544 pounds, and of course, this sum does not include the additional amounts expended by individuals and societies. The great procession held in the saint's honor included not only city officials, representatives of the guilds, companies and rural communes, but numerous ambassadors from foreign towns, whose presence added considerably to the splendor. A "palia" or horse race, run in competition for an expensive cloth (*palium*), was also held in conjunction with the feast, and here too the trend was toward even greater spending. According to Chiappelli's calculations, the race cost the Opera 30 pounds in 1313, 100 in 1348, 300 in 1366, 350 in 1445, finally reaching 686 pounds in 1561.[54]

The taste for ceremonial and liturgical splendor is also evident in the activities of numerous religious companies. These companies, usually including both priests and laymen, performed many chari-

year. In 1569, according to Tedaldi, "Relazione," p. 322, the Opera over 22 days each year distributed 1700 staia of wheat to the poor.

51. *Historie*, II, 178.

52. ASF, Catasto 189, 153r. See also Chiappelli, "Storia," *BSP*, 21 (1919), 12.

53. *Statutum potestatis*, p. 35; see above, p. 235.

54. *BSP*, 21 (1919), 164.

table services, but they also characteristically supported liturgical ceremonies, both for themselves and for the public.[55]

The civic Christianity of Renaissance Pistoia was thus marked by a huge investment in works of public charity, bespeaking a consciousness of responsibility for the destitute of the city, and by a new taste for liturgical splendor. Social factors, while they do not fully explain, at least can help make understandable these somewhat paradoxical developments. The adult, urban population in the early fifteenth century was made up in the majority by women, many of whom were heads of their own households, widows with some property who were able to exert much influence upon the character of religious practice. In 1427, women headed no less than 21.4 per cent of the urban households (264 out of 1247).[56] A form of piety which stressed sympathy and service ahead of contemplation and the often brutal atonements of the Middle Ages seems to reflect no little feminine influence. Moreover, urban women, many of them living in small families, had to seek diversion and spiritual restorations beyond their households. The splendid religious ceremonies, often enhanced by the dramatic preachers of the age, must have appealed to an audience, the majority of which, like the majority of the adult urban population itself, was probably women.[57]

Moreover, the strongly paternalistic note of Pistoia's civic Christianity may well reflect the peculiar structure of its urban society. The presence of a narrow and largely stable patriciate controlling most of the wealth, the poor representation of a middle class, the evident need of many of the poor, could not fail but inculcate in the privileged a sense of paternalistic responsibility. *Noblesse oblige,* and so also, even according to traditional Christianity, do wealth, advantage and privilege. Pistoia's patriciate, a *de facto* if not a *de iure* nobility, could not be deaf to the demands of social conscience.

Social experiences as well as social factors also played a role in defining the character of the new religious spirit. A growing commitment to charity may justly be considered a reaction to the fre-

55. On the religious and liturgical practices of the confraternities and religious companies, see Monti, *Confraternite,* II, 53–54, and 79–91.

56. See above, pp. 117–18.

57. It was customary to invite famous preachers to give sermons on the great feast days or during Lent. In 1428 the bishop's share of the expenses for this "predichatore da duomo" was 120 pounds per year, ASF, Catasto 189, 65r.

quent disasters of plague, famine and war and to the misery they spread. The taste for ceremonial magnificence is less easy to explain, particularly since it diverted money and attention from needed charitable endeavors. But it was in a way a charity itself, a public display of magnificence, a distribution of awe and wonder among the people, most of whom saw few such qualities in their private lives. As the most common and most popular of entertainments, it offered psychological release from the still plentiful human miseries which, even with charity, would never be entirely corrected. Finally, liturgical splendor imitated and reaffirmed the existence of an ideal, celestial world; it offered a depiction, at once refreshing and reassuring, of that magnificence and glory for which men were intended, and which many could hope to achieve, in spite of present woes, if only beyond the grave.

CIVIC HUMANISM AT PISTOIA

One of the colorful customs of fifteenth-century Pistoia was the summoning at the birth of a baby of an expert to predict, apparently through consulting the afterbirth, the child's future. Antonio Rospigliosi secured such analyses twice, at the birth of his sons Iacopo in 1461 and Tommaso in 1466. Commercial success and brilliant marriage were the common ingredients of such predictions, but the expert said also concerning Iacopo that the boy would not die a "bad death" but would grow up to be a "beautiful speaker," a fortunate man and a "spender."[58]

Beautiful speech and a willingness to spend may not appear the most appropriate virtues for sons of a mercantile family, but Iacopo's father was pleased to hear this future foretold for his baby; "may God grant it to him" he wrote in his *Richordi.*

Good speech and spending, an admiration of rhetoric and of splendid living, are indeed two of the outstanding characteristics of the lay culture of the fifteenth century.

Rhetorical skill and a magnificent presence were useful if not essential to a patrician son for three reasons. The defense of his family and friends and the upholding of the dignity of his house still

58. *Richordi,* p. 3. "Alderotto Brunelleschi vide l'asiendente di Iacopo suddetto e dice non morrà di mala morte e che serà bel parlatore e serà aventurato e spendente, che Idio li conceda della sua grazia."

required, in the fifteenth century, participation in communal government even in a subject city such as Pistoia, and rhetoric and magnificence helped make that participation effective. Moreover, for many patricians, particularly from the older families, government service offered a honorable and remunerative career at a time when other professional opportunities were few and unrewarding. Finally, for the patriciate as a whole, rhetorical theory was at the basis of a new concept and standard of nobility, to which the great families could aspire, in spite of their disparate backgrounds, and which in turn could offer them justification for the privileges they enjoyed and the distinctions they claimed.

For beautiful speech, according to traditional theories of rhetoric, included not only verbal dexterity, *eloquentia,* but learning and wisdom as well, *sapientia.*[59] In humanist thought, the most useful and honorable of men were those who could apply abstract learning to particular human situations, convince their fellows of the proper course of actions to be taken, and so serve their communities.[60] They were the experts in politics, the moral philosophers, and the lawyers, who combined their general knowledge with the persuasive rhetoric needed to make it socially beneficial.

> For how great is the dignity of those who judge or govern others or who assist the governors, who teach the judges, and how great the dignity of patrons, who prosecute or defend in cases, is clear to all.[61]

Moral philosophy and law, made effective by rhetoric, assured

59. Cf. Cicero's *De Oratore,* II, cap. 1, "neminem eloquentia non modo sine dicendi doctrina, sed ne sine omni quidem sapientia florere umquam et praestare potuisse." This idea that *philosophia* or *sapientia* was essential for the orator was frequently expressed by Cicero and may have originated with him. See K. Barwick, *Das rednerische Bildungsideal Ciceros* (Berlin, 1963), pp. 35–42.

60. Cf. Coluccio Salutati, *De Nobilitate legum et medicinae. De Verecundia.* Ed. E. Garin (Edizione nazionale dei classici del pensiero italiano, 8; Florence, 1947), p. 162. So important, says Coluccio, is active participation in the political life of the community that even monks "cannot live" without serving society: "Cuius rei tanta vis est, ut etiam qui monasticam et solitariam eligunt vitam, sine servitiis humane societatis nequeant vivere, nec suis contemplationibus indulgere."

61. Ibid. p. 66. "Quanta tamen sit iudicantium dignitas, qui ceteris president vel presidentibus assistunt quique docent iudicaturos, quantaque dignitas patronorum, qui causas agunt atque defendunt, omnibus clarum est. . . ."

the conservation of human society, the formation of good citizens, and thus embraced all virtues.[62]

The great dignity attached to community service could also be used to justify the position, privileges and distinctions of the fifteenth-century patriciate. As we have seen, that patriciate, while largely stable, had been recruited from disparate origins, from old magnate houses, from old *popolani* families, and was still in the fifteenth century not entirely closed to new men. Claims of birth and lineage alone could not confer distinction upon such a group, particularly since many originally noble families were abandoning their former status in order to assume the politically more advantageous position of *popolani*. But the humanists were simultaneously developing a concept of nobility which applied to and appealed to such men. In the early fifteenth century a humanist of Pistoia, Buonaccorso da Montemagno, stated that ideal as well as any contemporary writer.[63]

The history of Buonaccorso's own family was itself fairly typical. It had orginally been a magnate house. But it adopted popular status in 1332 and thus, like many other once noble families, consciously abandoned the pretense that blood or birth alone brought social superiority.[64] Buonaccorso himself produced, among many writings, a tract "On Nobility." It was posed in the form of a debate between two Romans of the classical period, both arguing before the Senate for the hand of the beautiful Lucretia. One of the suitors, Publius Cornelius, spoke of his distinguished ancestors; the other, Gaius Flaminius, described only his services to Rome:

> For when I understood that human skills are so much the more glorious when placed at the service of the Republic, I gave myself entirely to my fatherland. Never thereafter did I cease to think of its safety and prosperity, fearing no labor and no danger, which might bring it glory and security.[65]

62. Ibid. p. 170. "Nam si virtutes queris, legalis iusticia cunctas virtutes amplexa est."

63. His tract, "De Nobilitate," is edited in *Prosatori latini*, ed. Garin, 142–65. For further details on his family, see below, p. 262.

64. Salvi, *Historie*, II, 18. Lapo di Currado Montemagni was gonfaloniere in 1332 (no. 50 in Salvi's list).

65. *Prosatori latini*, ed. Garin, p. 156. "Etenim cum intelligerem praeclariora

Gaius' public service thus proved his superiority as a man, and of course he was given Lucretia's hand.

All this, of course, has the redolence of oil, and Buonaccorso's views were no more than a humanist commonplace. But the strength of its appeal to the social and professional pride of the patriciate is understandable. When Antonio Rospigliosi died, the chief consolation for his sons was not even so much his religion and piety, but the gratitude shown by the city for his public service.[66] In other words, the patricians, most of them now of relatively assured position, were given an ideal to justify their privileges, and the best of them were not remiss in living by it.

To review Pistoia's own small but perhaps not unrepresentative band of authors and humanists is at once to recognize their close social ties with the city's patriciate and a frequent, professional association with government service.

The most famous and probably the most gifted of Pistoia's writers was Cino de' Sinibaldi (d. 1336), usually called simply Cino da Pistoia.[67] The scion of an old magnate family, Cino became a doctor in law, and in 1317 served his commune as the podestà's judge of civil cases. He wrote nine books, lectured and interpreted the law at Florence, Siena and Bologna. He counted among his students Bartolo of Sassofratto, one of the most renowned legists of the age, and even Petrarch attended his lectures for four years. He was also one of the first practitioners of the new style of Tuscan lyric love poetry, the *dolce stil nuovo*. Dante, no poor judge in such matters, complimented Cino for the excellence, clearness, completeness and polish of his style.[68] The lady he loved, of course not his wife, was Selvaggia Vergiolesi from another magnate family. In praise of her he

---

tantum fore mortalium ingenia cum ad rempublicam accommodantur, totum me meae patriae concessi. Neque unquam postea illius salutem et amplitudinem cogitare desii, nihil laboris pertimescens, nihil periculi, quod illi gloriam et incolumnitatem parare posset."

66. See above, chapter 9, n. 56.

67. On Cino, see most recently Domenico Maffei, *La Lectura super Digesto veteri di Cino da Pistoia: Studio sui MSS Savigny 22 e Urb. lat. 172* (Quaderni di "Studi Senesi" No. 10) (Milan, 1963). On the relationship between the administrative class and the coming of humanism in Padua, see Hyde, *Padua*, pp. 283–303.

68. *De vulgari eloquentia*, cap. 14.

was able to bring a new freshness and sincerity to the stilted and mannered courtly love tradition. But for all his literary gifts and achievements, Cino was bitterly disappointed when Petrarch deserted law for the exclusive study of letters, and chided him for his decision.[69] Cino evidently felt that eloquence alone, when not founded on the knowledge and wisdom which legal studies afforded, would be barren.

Later in the century, another doctor of law from Pistoia, Zelone Zeloni, wrote a Latin epic called "Pia fons," which today rests in a perhaps not unmerited oblivion.[70] A man with some taste for the new learning was Tancredi Vergiolesi, who engaged in an active correspondence with Coluccio Salutati.[71] He too was from an old magnate house, and pursued a career of public service in foreign communes; in 1361 he was employed by the commune of Lucca and he also served at Pisa.[72] A Tancredi Vergiolesi, perhaps his son or grandson, also appears in the Estimario of 1415.[73] His properties, while large, were hardly enough to support him, and he had no commercial interests. Government service was thus probably essential for the maintenance of the family's fortunes.

Similarly from an old family, and similarly engaged in careers of law, government service and letters, were the Montemagni. Buonaccorso da Montemagno the elder is remembered for some *canzoni* written in honor of the lady Lauretta, and his grandson, also named Buonaccorso, became a professor of law at Florence and author of several literary works.[74] His treatise, "On Nobility," has already been quoted.[75] Law and literary interests similarly marked out the careers of the Baldinotti family. Antonio Baldinotti (d. 1423) was a jurist of considerable prominence who lectured at Florence; his tax declaration is in the Estimario of 1415.[76] From the same family later came Amerigo Baldinotti, another jurist well known in his day, and

69. Cino's letter to Petrarch is printed in Salvi, *Historie,* II, 40–42.
70. Salvi, *Historie,* II, 134, under the year 1374.
71. *Epistolario,* I, no. 2 (I, p. 5) and Appendice, no. 1 (IV, p. 275).
72. Loc. cit.
73. Estimario, 330r.
74. The younger Buonaccorso died in 1429. Zaccaria, *Bibliotheca,* p. 208.
75. See above, p. 260.
76. Estimario, parish of S. Maria fuor le Porte, no. 1. Antonio Baldinotti e Benedetto suo nipote.

Bartolomeo, who taught law at Pisa.[77] Another Baldinotti, Tommaso, studied at Paris and was the author of several literary works in Latin and Italian.[78] Even Sozomenus (d. 1458), perhaps the best known of Pistoia's fifteenth-century humanists, had a background in legal training.[79] His father was a notary. While Sozomenus took orders, he studied canon law for several years at Florence. He also lectured on letters there, and collected one of the first and finest of the humanist libraries.[80] His universal history we have several times cited.[81]

The high prestige accorded by the humanists to public service seems to have been something more than a reflection of their own social and professional associations. May we not also discern in it a parallel with the contemporary changes in religious piety? One of the most marked developments of the age was, as we have seen, the growth of social conscience, the effort to define Christian responsibility in the light of existent social conditions. In secular culture too, there is evident an effort, through the art of politics, to apply another body of largely traditional, abstract learning, philosophy and law, to the concrete problems of social life. The culture of the Renaissance, in both its religious and secular manifestations, included a common effort to place the accumulated knowledge and wisdom of the Middle Ages at the service of the community, in the interest of achieving a higher, more ethical, more virtuous and more rewarding form of civic life.

This fundamental idea, that the end of learning should be the service of men in their present world and society, was expressed with some passion by Coluccio Salutati:

> I, however, to speak the truth, would say boldly and freely admit that I would leave you and to those carrying speculation up to the sky all other truths without envy or argument, if the truth and reason of human things would be left to me. You

77. Zaccaria, *Bibliotheca*, p. 166.

78. Loc. cit.

79. On Sozomenus, see Zaccagnini's introduction to his edition of the *Chronicon*.

80. The inventory of his library, dated 29 Oct. 1460, is published in Zaccaria, *Bibliotheca*, pp. 37–45.

81. No complete edition exists, but sections have been published in Sozomenus, *Chronicon*, and idem, Specimen.

> may be full of speculation, but I would abound in the goodness by which I may be made good. . . . I would always be engaged in doing things, I would consider the final end: whatever I do, am I helping myself, my family, my relatives and (what above all is to be preferred) am I helping my friends, am I useful to the fatherland? And I would so live that I would contribute by both example and works to human society. In all these things I shall always think is that supreme happiness, which we cannot but wish for, and which we cannot desire for any reason other than itself.[82]

The secular culture of the Renaissance also shares with the religious a pronounced taste for splendid display. This is the age when the commune of Pistoia, along with the governments of other cities, waged an uneven battle against the luxurious fashions of its citizens, especially its women. In 1332, 1360, 1439 and 1558 sumptuary laws were passed to restrain the lavishness, each one sterner, though apparently no more successful, than the last.[83] According to G. B. Tedaldi, the women of Pistoia were among the worst offenders in Tuscany.[84]

The great events in the history of the patrician families—births, knightings, marriages, even funerals—were all occasions for public exhibitions of magnificence. In April 1388 the celebrations accompanying the knighting of Giovanni Panciatichi lasted seven days.[85] Weddings were no less lavish. Agniola, one of Antonio Rospigliosi's daughters, was married in a multiple wedding the like of which, her father recorded with satisfaction, Pistoia had never seen before.[86] Agniola's groom and his three brothers were all married on the same day, and all conducted their brides to the same house. At the principal tables at the wedding feast, there were seated no fewer

82. *De Nobilitate legum et medicinae*, p. 180.

83. See A. Zanelli, "Di Alcune leggi suntuarie pistoiesi dal XIV al XVI secolo," *ASI*, ser. 5, 16 (1895), 206–24. According to Salvi, *Historie*, II, 173, a special commission of 32 citizens was appointed to "publicare certi capitoli e bandire alcuni divieti per correzione e riforma" of the "immodest" customs of the city.

84. "Relazione," p. 325, "vestendosi richissimamente e superbissamente quanto in altra città di Toscana. . . ."

85. See Gigliotti's note in Luca Dominici, *Cronache*, I, 66, n. 1.

86. *Richordi*, p. 51, 4 June 1480. Her groom was Luigi d'Abram di Batistia.

than 94 men and women, "not counting some of their brothers, because they did not sit at table."[87] At the lower tables 300 persons and more "of every type" ate and drank to the health of the spouses. The festivities lasted a week, and Antonio had reason to call this a "dengnio paio di noze."

In 1415, the scion of one of Pistoia's most distinguished patrician families, Lotto di Gualfredi Cancellieri, made an accounting of his own wedding expenses, which well illustrates the extravagant façade a great household presented to the world. The accounting is edited in Appendix III.[88] The context in which this document has survived is itself noteworthy: it was part of Lotto's tax declaration. His motives in listing these large expenses for the benefit of tax assessors are less than clear. To present one's self as wealthy and a great spender is rarely advisable at assessment time. Was it sheer pride that prompted Lotto to reveal the fortune that his wedding had cost him? It is more likely that Lotto believed that the assessors would recognize that these were necessary expenses for a great family, without which it could hardly expect to maintain its station.

To present a proper appearance at his bride's house when the wedding agreement was signed, Lotto needed a company of eight horsemen, and this and other visits made to the girl cost him in all 18 florins—more than a year's salary for a well-paid artisan. Clearly, Lotto did not appear casually at his fiancée's home. In wedding gifts he gave his bride six dresses, some embroidered with silver and lined with fur, and all—he carefully noted—of excellent cloth, a petticoat, doublet and cloak, several chests filled with girdles and garlands, a silver chain, rings of diamond, sapphire and pearl, an inlaid bedstead, mattresses, bed clothes, towels, pans and other bedroom furnishings, and additional girdles, which his bride gave as gifts to her relatives.

The culminating ceremony in a Renaissance wedding, following a Mass in the morning (the "messa dei congiunti"), was the procession of the bride to the house of the groom.

87. Loc. cit. "e ferano un dengnio paio di noze in modo che alle prime mense furano a taula tra donne e hominni novantaquatro persone non chontando alquno di loro fratelli perchè non sederano a taula."

88. See below, p. 289.

> Also I spent [Lotto related in his ungrammatical statement] in the marriage when I brought her when I made the marriage of my own expense in sending for her and on the way and through the rooms and for horses in all I spent 65 florins.

The cost of bringing Lotto's bride to her new home would have paid the salaries of perhaps six servants for an entire year. The total cost of his marriage, not including celebrations afterwards, was 574 florins. Such a sum would have made a man wealthy according to the Catasto of 1427.

This public extravagance of Pistoia's great families is the more remarkable, as it often concealed a mean existence behind the locked doors of their homes. Lotto Cancellieri, describing how he had embellished his bedroom with new furnishings for his bride, stated that there had been "gran bisogna"—"great need"—for the refurbishments. His furniture had been lost when soldiers were garrisoned in his house during the "war of Sambuca." But the war of Sambuca had been fought more than a decade before his declaration, in 1401–03![89] For all the intervening time, his bedroom and house had apparently been left in shambles.

Public exhibitions of splendor were, for many of Pistoia's patrician families, quite clearly a matter of social and even professional need. A magnificent presence might influence the decisions of councils, upon which family welfare could depend. And men who wished to represent cities and princes in high public office had to cultivate a brilliant appearance. When messer Bartolomeo Bracciolini journeyed to Perugia in the early fifteenth century, apparently to assume public office, he had to borrow 500 florins from Florentine merchants, to assure himself a dignified and impressive "andata" and entry.[90] Messer Giovanni Panciatichi, whose knighting in 1388 had been celebrated for seven days, similarly spent 500 florins while serving at Ferrara, undoubtedly to maintain a splendid household, and comparable sums in the other cities where he held office.[91] At an-

89. This was the revolt of Ricciardo Cancellieri; see above, p. 205.
90. Estimario, parish of S. Maria Pretanselmi, no. 2. "Item debbo dare a cittadini fiorentini i quali achattai per fornirmi per l'andata feci a Perogia fiorini cinquecento."
91. Estimario, parish of S. Giovanni fuor cività, no. 57. See above, p. 196.

other point in his colorful career, he was robbed of "money, horses, cloth, silver and arms" worth more than 600 florins.[92]

Moreover, this love of magnificent display, which parallels a similar taste for a sumptuous liturgy in the age's religious life, may also be considered a kind of diversion and escape, not only for the patrician families themselves but for the populace which witnessed their processions and often participated in their feasts. In spite of frequent plagues, the young adult of Pistoia did not need, as we have seen, to be excessively troubled by the prospect of his own imminent demise; children and the aged accounted for the bulk of the population's tremendous losses.[93] Still, his life was led in the midst of death, and could this have failed to impress him? Not terror of his own immediate departure, but awareness of death's ultimate, inevitable triumph, of old age and decrepitude which would prepare its way, seems to have weighed upon his thoughts. The psychological antidote for this melancholy experience was to be a fortunate man and a spender, to live, in pretense and imagination if not in reality, a magnificent life.[94] And so, for example, in Giovanni Boccaccio's *Decameron*, the young narrators sought solace from the plague by telling tales largely concerned with youth, nobility, love, wit, humor and success. Franco Sacchetti, in his own preface to the *Trecentonovelle*, similarly stated that people wished to hear pleasant tales which would "bring comfort" amid so many human miseries.[95] Italian life as depicted in the abundant *novelle* literature of the fourteenth and fifteenth centuries, for all its earthy flavor, remains an idealized reconstruction, in which the cruel realities of the age, the appalling death of children, the *maninconia dei padri*, the

92. Ibid. n. 44.

93. See above, pp. 85–93.

94. Cf. the prediction regarding Antonio Rospigliosi's son (above, n. 58), in which to be a "bel parlatore" "aventurato" and "spendente" are placed in opposition to "mala morte."

95. *Trecentonovelle*, "Proemio": "Considerando al presente tempo, ed alla condizione dell'umana vita, la quale con pestilenziose infirmità, e con oscure morti, è spesso vicitata. . . ." Sacchetti goes on to note that under these conditions people are desirous to read things "agevoli a intendere, e massimamente quando danno conforto, per lo quale tra molti dolori si mescolino alcune risa. . . ."

ravages of time, the ill-concealed miseries, the harshness and the violence, find scant attention.[96]

In the fourth part of his great book, Jacob Burckhardt defined the essence of Renaissance culture as "the discovery of the world and of man." When measured against the experience of this one small town of Pistoia, the phrase has a certain validity, although only in part. Pistoia's citizens (or at least, the more sensitive of them) showed in their charity and service a new commitment to the welfare of their fellows and their community. By their actions they were implicitly accepting the humanist proposition that both religion and learning imposed a primary obligation to benefit society. To this extent, it may well be said that they showed a new consciousness and awareness of their social surroundings. But at the same time, in their festivals and ceremonies, their literature and art, they strove not to depict the world as it was, but rather to construct diverting and refreshing visions of an idealized, sublime and splendid life. And, in cultural history, it is for their imaginative and enchanting explorations of ideal worlds, rather than for any supposed rediscovery of the harsh nature which surrounded them, that the men of this age deserve to be remembered.

96. In Leon Battista Alberti's *Famiglia*, pp. 30–35, the melancholy of fathers, provoked by the diseases and death of their children, is advanced as an argument for avoiding marriage. Although the argument is refuted in the course of the dialogue, this melancholy is still treated as a common experience here and elsewhere in the work.

Appendixes

Appendix I

Population Surveys of Pistoia's Countryside, ca. 1244-1427

1. The *Liber focorum*, ca. 1244. For the date and nature of the *Liber focorum* or Book of Hearths, see above, pp. 58–63. The rural communes mentioned in the survey are classified here according to quarter and according to the three regions of the plain (lands up to approximately 200 meters in altitude), the middle hills (between 200 and 500 meters) and the mountains (over 500 meters). Because many communes included terrain within two or even three regions, these classifications are necessarily somewhat rough. In making them, not only the altitude of the principal center of habitation but the general lay of the commune's territory were considered. The numbers given for each commune represent the correct number of its hearths, not the number given by the notary, which is often in error.

Plain		*Middle Hills*		*Mountains*	
Porta Caldatica:					
Agliana	231	Artimino	43		
Canapale	13	Baccareto	202		
Capraia	5	Buriano	54		
Castellina iusta Arno	20	Carmignano	280		
Pacciana	17	Castra	39		
Piuvica	264	Celle, S. Lorenzo de	23		
Quarrata	67	Conio	30		
—, Lucciana de	32	Vitolini	48		
—, Montorio de	24				
—, Pancole de	31				
Tizzana	163				
Vizzana	8				

Totals for quarter: 21 communes, 1691 hearths

Porta Lucchese:

Plain		*Middle Hills*		*Mountains*	
Casalguidi	343	Carlatico	10	Avaglio	40
Collina and Farneto	35	Castellina Lombardorum	30	Calamecca	45
Gabbiano	25	Castellina Molazani	71	Casore del Monte	41
Groppoli	79	Castellum de Celle	18	Crespole	26
Montemagno	431	Castrum Novum super Vinacianum	68	Fagno	60
S. Pantaleo	26	Cecina	63	Lanciole	10
S. Pietro and Solaio	17	Cupano	11	Momigno	50
		Fabbrica	18	Serra	35
		Gugliano	19	Verruca	47
		Lamporecchio	245		
		Larciano	199		
		Marliana	28		
		Montagnana	38		
		Orbignano	63		
		Petruolo de Celle	18		
		S. Baronto	42		
		Serravalle	183		
		Urazano de ultra Umbrone	21		
		Urazano Monacorum	16		
		Vignano	13		
		Vinacciano	69		
		Vizzano vallis Celle	20		

Totals for quarter: 38 communes, 2573 hearths

Porta Sant'Andrea:

Plain		*Middle Hills*		*Mountains*	
Gello	54	Arcigliano	12	Batoni	41
		Brandeglio, Campiglio	78	Gavinana	88
		—, Castellina	82	Lizzano	202
		—, Pieve	83	Piteglio	84
		Brilliano	14	Popiglio	194
		Gegno	21	Pornechium, Saricone and Grimilliano	29
		Isola	11	Sammomme	59
		Piazza	49	S. Marcello	117
		Piteccio	170		

Plain		*Middle Hills*		*Mountains*	
		Prombialla	18		
		Sarripoli	40		
		Saturnana	71		
		Scapato	9		
		Vergiole	29		

Totals for quarter: 23 communes, 1555 hearths

Porta Guidi:

Plain		*Middle Hills*		*Mountains*	
Brugianico	39	Alfiano	16	Cantagallo	58
Candeglia	48	Baggio	22	Castello Averardi	33
Montale	113	Caloria and Gello	29	Castiglione v. Bisentii	34
Santomato	95	Casese	18	Fossato	33
Sarloco	32	Casore	36	Luicciana	32
		Chiapore	18	Luogomano	25
		Cignano	15	Migliana	22
		Colle, Gaiono, Maiano	28	S. Stefano	8
		Dagnana	6	S. Cristina	23
		Fermiano	22	Sezzana	21
		Gerexano	54	Torri and Monticelli	53
		Germinaia	35	Treppio	38
		Lupicciana	19		
		Montecastiglione, Codelupo, Carmignana and Pratale	35		
		Mozano	20		
		Picugna	33		
		Pulica	55		
		S. Moro	21		
		S. Quirico de Carnechia	129		
		S. Romano	44		
		S. Simone	15		
		Sieta	14		
		Staggiano	25		
		Usella	11		
		Uzzo	66		

Totals for quarter: 42 communes, 1493 hearths

Totals for countryside: 124 communes, 7312 hearths

Plain: 26 communes, 2309 hearths
Middle Hills: 69 communes, 3455 hearths
Mountains: 29 communes, 1548 hearths

2. The *Liber finium seu confinium comitatus seu districtus Pistorii,* dated 1255, published in *Liber focorum,* pp. 269–367. The communes named in the Book of Boundaries have been arranged according to region, as in the preceding section.

Plain	*Middle Hills*	*Mountains*
Porta Lucchese: 31 communes		
Casalguidi	Belvedere	Avaglio
Gabbiano	Carlatico	Calamecca
Groppoli	Castellina	Casore del Monte
Montemagno	Celle	Crespole
	Cupano	Fagno
	Fabbrica	Lanciole
	Gugliano	Momigno
	Lamporecchio	Serra
	Larciano	Verruca
	Marliana	
	Montagnana	
	Orbignano	
	Petruolo	
	S. Baronto	
	Serravalle	
	Varazzano	
	Vignano	
	Vizzano	
Porta Guidi: 42 communes		
Brugianico	Alfiano	Cantagallo
Candeglia	Baggio	Carmignano v. Bisentii
Montale	Caloria and Gello	Castello Averardi
Santomato	Casese	Catugnano
Sarloco	Casore	Fossato
	Chiapore	Luogomano
	Chiano	Migliana
	Cignano	Monticelli
	Cirigiano	S. Stefano
	Dagnana	Sezzana
	Fermiano	Torricella
	Germinaia	Treppio
	Lupicciana	
	Montecastiglione vecchio	
	Mozano	
	Picugna	
	Pulica	
	S. Moro	

Plain	*Middle Hills*	*Mountains*
	S. Quirico	
	S. Romano	
	S. Simone	
	Sieta	
	Staggiano	
	Usella	
	Uzzo	
Porta Sant' Andrea: 22 communes		
Gello	Arcigliano	Batoni
	Brandeglio, Castellina di	Gavinana
	Brandeglio, Pieve di	Lizzano
	Campiglio	Mammiano
	Icio	Piteglio
	Isola	Popiglio
	Piazza	Pornechio, Saricone and Grimilliano
	Piteccio	Sambuca
	Saturnana	Sammomme
	Scapato	S. Marcello
	Vergiole	
Porta Caldatica: 13 communes		
Agliana	Artimino	
Piuvica	Baccareto	
Quarrata	Buriano	
Tizzana	Carmignano	
Vignole	Castellina	
	Castra	
	Conio	
	Vitolini	
15 communes	62 communes	31 communes

Total for countryside: 108 communes

3. The *Taxa boccarum* of 16 April 1344, ASP, Provv. Tomus 12, 13v. The following list shows the number of mouths for Pistoia's rural communes again arranged according to region. For the meaning of a "mouth," see above, p. 66.

Plain		*Middle Hills*		*Mountains*	
Agliana	1120	Brandeglio	900	Calamecca	209
Canapale	169	Buriano	192	Cantagallo	119
Cappanella and Santomato	270	Candeglia and Valdibura	602	Castello Averardi	84
Casalguidi	795	Carmignanello	24	Casore	284
Chiazzano	121	Castellina	175	Catugnano	75
Groppoli	60	Castiglione Merlini	48	Crespole	193
Montale	1319	Castra	120	Fagno	206
Montemagno	931	Cecina	207	Gavinana	177
Piuvica and Pacciana	981	Celle, Pieve	41	Lanciole	91
Quarrata	519	Conio	120	Lizzano and Cutigliano	918
Tizzana	973	Dagnana	41	Luogomano	73
Vignole	335	Fremiano	53	Mammiano	64
		Isola, Piastreto and Gello	56	Migliana	155
		Lamporecchio and Orbignano	1289	Momigno	189
		Larciano	770	Piteglio	122
		Marliana	196	Popiglio	391
		Montagnana	125	Sammomme	141
		Piazza (S. Felice)	72	S. Marcello	338
		Piteccio and Castagri	219	S. Stefano	56
		S. Quirico	188	Serra	107
		S. Romano	52	Sezzana	82
		Sarripoli and Scapato	56	Torri and Monticelli	189
		Saturnana	375	Torricella	258
		Serravalle	985	Treppio and Fossato	251
		Usella	73		
		Uzzo	37		
		Vergiole	49		
		Vinacciano	213		
12 communes 7593 mouths		28 communes 7278 mouths		24 communes 4772 mouths	

Totals for countryside: 64 communes, 19,643 mouths

4. The *Taxa boccarum* of 1 April 1383, ASP, Provv. Tomus 26, 7v.

Plain		*Middle Hills*		*Mountains*	
Agliana	700	Brandeglio	210	Calamecca	130
Canapale	100	Castellina	100	Casore del Monte	130
Casa al Vescovo	60	Castra	50	Crespole	106
Casalguidi	600	Cecina	120	Cutigliano	390
Castelnuovo	20	Celle, Pieve	8	Fossato	62
Chiazzano	100	Conio	40	Gavinana	140
Masiano	120	Isola	15	Lanciole	70
Montale	600	Lamporecchio	860	Lizzano	400
Montemagno	700	Larciano	600	Luicciana	354
Piuvica	680	Marliana	120	Mammiano	40
Quarrate and Buriano	370	Montagnana	60	Momigno	80
Ramini	60	Piazza (S. Felice)	10	Piteglio	40
Santomato	170	Piteccio	60	Popiglio	230
Tizzana	680	S. Quirico	140	Sammomme	60
Vignole	220	Sarripoli	20	S. Marcello	240
		Saturnana	110	Serra	40
		Serravalle	410	Torri	80
		Valdibura	500	Treppio	120
		Vinacciano	120	Val di Bisenzio	176
15 communes 5180 mouths		19 communes 3553 mouths		19 communes 2888 mouths	

Totals for countryside: 53 communes, 11,621 mouths. (Survey gives incorrect total of 11,711 mouths.)

5. The *Taxa boccarum* of 10 Feb. 1392. ASP, Provv. Tomus 38, 109r.

Plain		*Middle Hills*		*Mountains*	
Agliana	743	Brandeglio	235	Calamecca	114
Casalguidi	506	Castellina	99	Casore del Monte	75
Chiazzano	96	Castra	63	Crespole	74
Montale	500	Cecina	71	Cutigliano	300
Montemagno	565	Conio	37	Fossato	55
Piuvica	590	Lamporecchio	690	Gavinana	153
Quarrata and Buriano	308	Larciano	321	Lanciole	65
Santomato	113	Marliana	97	Lizzano	329
Tizzana	643	Montagnana	42	Luicciana	204
Vignole	262	Piazza (S. Felice)	15	Mammiano	30
		Piteccio	54	Momigno	42
		S. Quirico	123	Piteglio	47
		Sarripoli	16	Popiglio	186
		Saturnana	82	Sammomme	63
		Serravalle	404	S. Marcello	163
		Valdibura	338	Serra	42
		Vinacciano	105	Torri	55
				Treppio	97
				Val di Bisenzio	103
10 communes		17 communes		19 communes	
4326 mouths		2792 mouths		2197 mouths	

Totals for countryside: 46 communes, 9315 mouths. (Survey gives the correct total of 9315 mouths.)

6. The *Taxa boccarum* of 20 June 1401. ASP, Provv. Tomus 43, 29r.

Plain		*Middle Hills*		*Mountains*	
Agliana	619	Brandeglio	184	Calamecca	110
Casalguidi	439	Castellina	61	Casore del Monte	59
Chiazzano	103	Castra and Conio	108	Crespole	60
Montale	483	Cecina	85	Cutigliano	358
Montemagno	583	Lamporecchio and Orbignano	650	Fossato	31
Piuvica	514	Larciano	312	Gavinana	105
Quarrata and Buriano	305	Marliana	86	Lanciole	42
Santomato	145	Montagnana	40	Lizzano	214
Tizzana	561	Piazza (S. Felice)	8	Luicciano	162
		Piteccio	62	Mammiano	29
		S. Quirico	104	Momigno	33
		Sarripoli	12	Piteglio	39
		Saturnana	81	Popiglio	190
		Serravalle	233	Sammomme	303
		Valdibura	265	S. Marcello	143
		Vinacciano	77	Serra	33
				Torri	27
				Treppio	89
				Val di Bisenzio	72
9 communes		16 communes		19 communes	
3752 mouths		2368 mouths		2099 mouths	

Totals for countryside: 44 communes, 8219 mouths. (Survey gives the incorrect total of 8211 mouths.)

7. The *Taxa boccarum* of 30 June 1404. ASP, Provv. Tomus 43, 169r.

Plain		*Middle Hills*		*Mountains*	
Agliana	596	Brandeglio	155	Calamecca	82
Burgianico and Val di Brana	74	Castellina	58	Casore del Monte	49
Canapale	114	Castra	70	Crespole	53
Casalguidi	478	Cecina	79	Cutigliano	269
Chiazzano	94	Conio	39	Gavinana	79
Masiano	142	Lamporecchio	616	Lanciole	36
Montale	419	Larciano	35	Lizzano	164
Montemagno	439	Marliana	79	Luicciano	100
Piuvica	537	Montagnana	26	Mammiano	19
Quarrata and Buriano	283	Piazza (S. Felice)	5	Momigno	26
Santomato	106	Piteccio	45	Piteglio	12
Tizzana	588	S. Quirico	71	Popiglio	106
Vignole	269	Sarripoli	8	Sammomme	20
		Saturnana	60	S. Marcello	169
		Serravalle	241	Serra	29
		Valdibura	255	Treppio	60
		Vinacciano	70	Val di Bisenzio	44
13 communes		17 communes		17 communes	
4139 mouths		1912 mouths		1317 mouths	

Totals for countryside: 47 communes, 7368 mouths

8. Pistoia's rural population according to the Florentine Catasto of 1427, ASF, Catasto, Vols. 262, 263, 264 and 265. The following list shows the number of households (H) and mouths (M) for Pistoia's rural communes arranged according to region. The "mouth" as used here is equivalent to a person. See above, pp. 66–67.

Plain

	H	*M*
Agliana	137	760
Bargi	6	26
Bonelle	16	97
Canapale	29	167
Casa al Vescovo	15	80
Casalguidi	92	400
Chiazzano	20	107
Cilegiole	16	69
Fontana	4	14
Gabbiano	5	18
Gello	10	38
Gora	27	130
Masiano	36	159
Montale	119	571
Montebuono	6	25
Montemagno	110	539
Pacciana	17	100
Piuvica:		
S. Bastiano	32	150
S. Agnolo	44	180
S. Maria a Canagnano	20	116
Quarrata	73	323
Ramini	19	93
Sala	3	17
S. Agostino	17	78
S. Pantaleo	12	68
Santomato	31	139
Sarlocco	10	43
Solaio	5	30
Spazzavento	4	23
Tizzana	142	639
Vicofaro	14	59
Vignole	64	370
Vincio	15	72

Middle Hills

	H	*M*
Brandeglio	53	204
Castellina	16	63
Castra and Conio	48	226
Cecina	31	130
Lamporecchio	204	881
Larciano	86	309
Marliana	24	80
Montagnana	9	30
Piteccio	19	113
S. Bigiano	12	46
S. Quirico	20	99
S. Romano	5	26
Saturnana	20	81
Serravalle	73	289
Uzzo	13	53
Valdibura	78	312
Vinacciano	21	67

Mountains

	H	*M*
Calamecca	23	98
Casore del Monte	15	65
Crespole	20	102
Cutigliano	118	688
Fossato	5	33
Gavinana	39	172
Lanciole	17	60
Lizzano	110	545
Luicciana	29	114
Mammiano	17	78
Migliana	22	108
Momigno	12	43
Piteglio	8	36
Popiglio	64	271
Sambuca	10	48
Sammomme	7	27
S. Marcello	66	314
Serra	10	50
Treppio	13	76

(*table continued on page 282*)

Plain	*Middle Hills*	*Mountains*
33 communes	17 communes	19 communes
1170 households	732 households	605 households
5700 mouths	3009 mouths	2928 mouths

Totals for the countryside: 69 communes, 2507 households, 11,637 mouths

Appendix II

The Life Table of Pistoia's Population, 1427

1. The following table is based on the age distribution of persons in both the city and countryside of Pistoia, as recorded in ASF, Catasto, Vols. 260 to 265. See above, pp. 79–83, for additional comment.

Age	Numbers reported	Assumed mortality rate between age x and x+5	Numbers in population at age x and over	Assumed years of life remaining	Expectation of life at age x
		$_5q_x$	L_x	T_x	e°_x
0	646	(21.0)	15,775	457,120	29.0
1	726	17.7*	15,129	441,345	29.1
2	700		14,403	426,216	29.5
3	735		13,703	411,813	30.0
4	483		12,968	398,110	30.7
5	356	10.5	12,485	385,142	30.9
6	289		12,129	372,657	30.7
7	227		11,840	360,528	30.5
8	260		11,613	348,688	29.7
9	205		11,353	337,075	29.7
10	317	11.2	11,148	325,722	29.2
11	195		10,831	314,574	29.0
12	286		10,636	303,743	28.8
13	206		10,350	293,107	28.3
14	237		10,144	282,757	27.8
15	238	10.3	9907	272,613	27.5
16	231		9669	262,706	27.2
17	146		9438	253,037	26.7
18	311		9292	243,599	26.3
19	110		8981	234,307	26.1
20	390	12.9	8871	225,326	25.4
21	74		8481	216,455	25.6
22	302		8407	207,974	24.7
23	112		8105	199,567	24.6

Age	Numbers reported	Assumed mortality rate between age x and x+5 $_5q_x$	Numbers in population at age x and over L_x	Assumed years of life remaining T_x	Expectation of life at age x e_x^o
24	270		7993	191,462	23.9
25	306	13.0	7723	183,469	23.7
26	218		7417	175,746	23.6
27	111		7199	168,329	23.4
28	263		7088	161,130	22.8
29	44		6825	154,042	22.6
30	473	13.5	6781	147,217	21.8
31	34		6308	140,436	22.3
32	181		6274	134,128	21.4
33	69		6093	127,854	21.2
34	155		6024	121,761	20.2
35	235	14.0	5869	115,737	19.7
36	295		5634	109,868	19.5
37	65		5339	104,234	19.3
38	197		5274	98,895	18.7
39	26		5077	93,621	18.5
40	616	18.3 (16.4)†	5051	88,544	17.5
41	10		4435	83,493	18.8
42	129		4425	79,058	17.8
43	47		4296	74,633	17.3
44	115		4249	70,337	16.6
45	346	15.2 (17.9)†	4134	66,088	16.0
46	112		3788	61,954	16.3
47	32		3676	58,166	15.8
48	128		3644	54,490	15.0
49	15		3516	50,846	14.5
50	630	24.7 (21.2)†	3501	47,330	13.5
51	14		2871	43,829	15.3
52	98		2857	40,958	14.3
53	40		2759	38,101	14.0
54	88		2719	35,342	13.0
55	217	16.5 (23.3)†	2631	32,623	12.4
56	105		2414	29,992	12.4
57	29		2309	27,578	11.9
58	72		2280	25,269	11.1
59	14		2208	22,989	10.4
60	602	36.0 (29.5)†	2194	20,781	9.5
61	11		1592	18,587	11.7
62	59		1581	16,995	10.7

Age	Numbers reported	Assumed mortality rate between age x and x+5	Numbers in population at age x and over	Assumed years of life remaining	Expectation of life at age x
		$_5q_x$	L_x	T_x	$\mathring{e}_x$
63	31		1522	15,414	10.1
64	89		1491	13,892	9.3
65	217	24.3 (33.0)†	1402	12,401	8.7
66	55		1185	10,999	9.3
67	25		1130	9814	8.7
68	37		1105	8684	7.9
69	8		1068	7579	7.1
70	441	51.1 (42.7)†	1060	6511	6.1
71	11		619	5451	8.8
72	37		608	4832	7.9
73	20		571	4224	7.4
74	32		551	3653	6.6
75	106	33.1 (47.8)†	519	3102	6.0
76	40		413	2583	6.3
77	16		373	2170	5.8
78	15		357	1797	5.0
79	4		342	1440	4.2
80	225	77.0 (59.2)†	338	1098	3.2
81	3		113	760	6.7
82	12		110	647	5.9
83	7		98	537	5.5
84	13		91	439	4.8
85	27	50.0 (59.6)†	78	348	4.5
86	7		51	270	5.3
87	3		44	219	5.0
88	2		41	175	4.3
89			39	134	3.4
90	31	84.6	39	95	2.4
91	2		8	56	7
92			6	48	8
93			6	42	7
94			6	36	6
95	2	33.3	6	30	5
96			4	24	6
97			4	20	5
98			4	16	4
99			4	12	3
100	3		4	8	2
101			1	4	4

Age	Numbers reported	Assumed mortality rate between age x and x+5 $_5q_x$	Numbers in population at age x and over L_x	Assumed years of life remaining T_x	Expectation of life at age x e_x°
102			1	3	3
103			1	2	2
104	1		1	1	

* for interval age 1–4

† smoothed

† smoothed

2. Abbreviated life tables, men and women, 1427.

Age	Men: Assumed mortality rate between age x and x+5 $_5q_x$	Men: Numbers in population at age x and over L_x	Men: Expectation of life at age x e°_x	Women: Assumed mortality rate between age x and x+5 $_5q_x$	Women: Numbers in population at age x and over L_x	Women: Expectation of life at age x e°_x
0	21.0	8306	28.4	20.8	7469	29.8
5	12.5	6561	30.0	9.3	5924	31.8
10	12.8	5789	28.6	9.3	5359	29.8
15	11.0	5041	27.4	10.0	4866	27.5
20	13.4	4489	25.5	12.4	4382	25.4
25	12.7	3882	24.0	11.8	3841	23.5
30	11.8	3395	22.1	13.0	3386	21.3
35	14.5	2925	20.2	14.7	2944	19.1
40	17.4	2534	18.5	18.6	2517	17.0
45	15.0	2093	16.5	15.4	2041	15.5
50	23.6	1775	14.0	27.1	1726	13.0
55	15.1	1357	12.7	18.0	1274	12.1
60	34.0	1150	9.6	38.4	1044	9.3
65	26.8	759	8.6	21.5	643	9.2
70	51.5	555	6.0	50.5	505	6.3
75	37.1	269	5.8	32.4	250	6.2
80	78.1	169	3.1	75.8	169	3.4
85	51.3	37	3.9	48.8	41	5.0
90	100	18	1.1	71.5	21	3.6
95				33.3	6	5.0
100				100.0	4	2.0

3. Abbreviated life tables, city and countryside, 1427.

	City			Countryside		
Age	*Assumed mortality rate between age* x *and* x+5	*Numbers in population at age* x *and over*	*Expectation of life at age* x	*Assumed mortality rate between age* x *and* x+5	*Numbers in population at age* x *and over*	*Expectation of life at age* x
	$_5q_x$	L_x	e°_x	$_5q_x$	L_x	e°_x
0	19.7	4319	30.9	21.3	11,456	28.5
5	10.3	3471	31.8	11.0	9014	30.5
10	11.0	3118	30.1	11.2	8030	28.8
15	9.7	2769	28.5	10.6	7138	27.1
20	12.4	2498	26.4	13.2	6373	25.0
25	11.8	2193	24.6	12.7	5530	23.4
30	12.3	1953	22.3	13.8	4828	21.4
35	13.4	1713	20.0	14.2	4156	19.5
40	16.8	1482	17.8	18.8	3569	17.4
45	15.4	1234	16.0	15.4	2900	15.9
50	23.8	1044	13.5	25.1	2457	13.5
55	10.2	795	12.2	15.8	1836	11.8
60	35.8	650	9.6	36.4	1544	9.4
65	24.0	418	8.9	24.4	984	8.8
70	50.3	318	6.2	51.4	742	6.1
75	43.8	158	5.8	31.0	361	6.1
80	73.0	89	3.8	78.4	249	3.0
85	41.7	24	5.0	53.7	54	4.2
90	88.6	14	2.7	84.0	25	2.3
95		2	8.0	50.0	4	3.5
100	100.0	2	3.0	100.0	2	1.0

Appendix III

The Wedding Expenses of Lotto Di Gualfredi Cancellieri

From ASP, Provvisione e Statuti, Tomus 699, Estimario della Città (1415), 158v.

Spesa ch' io Lotto di Gualfredi o fatta dal dì presi la donna per in fino al dì ch' io la menai. E questo scrivo perchè chiaro veggiate che de' fatti della donna non ch' io n'abbia avanzato ma io o speso del mio proprio. O speso per lei quando v'andai io a fare il compromesso cioè la giurra che fumo cavalli otto e per più altre volte vi tornai cioè a far fare il forzerino e altre cose speci in tucto fl. dieciotto cioè:

fl. xviii.

Item spesi per uno forzerino d'avorio entrovi tre cintole belle cioè una a falchoni una a razzi e una smaltata. Item due ghirlande una piena di smalti parigini e un' altra più feriale. Item una cathena d'ariento inorata et uno coltellino smaltato in tucto fl. novantauno cioè:

fl. lxxxxi.

Item spesi per una cioppa dipicciolato in grana col fornimento d'essa. Item un'altra di rosato richamata di bottocini con le maniche larghe. Item un' altra d'azzurino fine fornita d'ariento. Item un' altra d'azzurino fine asettata. Item una gunnella una gamurla abotonata d'ariento. Item uno fodero. Item uno capuccio dipicciolato. In tucto fl. cento settantacinque.

fl. clxxv

Item spesi in anella cioè diamante zaffrio e perla e una vergha fl. trentacinque.

fl.xxxv.

Item spesi in massarize di casa o comperate cioè una lettiera nuova intarsiata con casse da pie caviglaio et lettuccio. Item uno paio di forzieri belli. Item un paio di lenzuola belle. Item un paio di più feriali. Item due copertoi. Item par guanciali. Item pannolino. Item tovagluole da mano. Item una caldaia. Item par sachoni e più e più altre massarize per case in tucto fl. ottanta. Di tucta la scritta massarizia avea gran bisogno imperciò che la mia si perde al tempo della guerra della Sanbucha che metiereno i soldati in casa fl. lxxx.

fl.lxxx.

Item spesi in una cioppa rosata colle maniche larghe foderata di drappo di grana nuova. Item per un' altra rosata fodrata di vaio. Item in uno farsettino di rosato e una cintola fiornita d'ariento in tucto fl. ottanta.

fl. lxxx.

Item spesi nelle nozze quando la menai che feci nozze di mie spesi tra mandare per lei et per la via et per camiere et per cavalli in tucto spesi fl. sessantacinque.

fl. lxv.

Item per cose comperai cioè cintole due e altro le quali dono la donna mia a' suoi parenti in tucto per gabella di contracta in tucto fl. trenta.

fl. xxx.

Summa in tucto fl. 574 d'oro.

Index

LaVergne, TN USA
21 January 2011
213401LV00004B/92/A
9 781597 404792